RIVERSIDE COMMUNITY COLLEGE
1916

P9-AFI-549

TODAY'S CHILDREN

David A. Hamburg, M.D.

RANDOM HOUSE

TODAY'S CHILDREN

Creating a Future for a Generation in Crisis

 Published in the United States by Times Books, a division of Random House, Inc., New York, and simultaneously in Canada by Random House of Canada Limited, Toronto.

Library of Congress Cataloging-in-Publication Data

Hamburg, David A.
Today's children : creating a future for a generation in crisis / David A. Hamburg—1st ed.
p. cm.
Includes bibliographical references and index.
ISBN 0-8129-1914-9
1. Family—United States. 2. Children—United States. 3. Child development—United States. 4. Child rearing—United States. I. Title.
HQ536.H318 1992
305.23′0973—dc20 91-50188

We express our appreciation to the Carnegie Council on Adolescent Development's Task Force on Education of Young Adolescents, which prepared *Turning Points*, for identifying and describing several educational innovations that are included in this book.

Manufactured in the United States of America
9 8 7 6 5 4 3 2

For Betty,

whose vision, insight, wisdom, and dedication made this book possible—and much more besides

Contents

TODAY'S CHILDREN

Introduction

My grandfather came to the United States in the great wave of immigration at the beginning of the twentieth century. Like so many others, he was fleeing persecution and poverty in Eastern Europe, seeking a fresh start in the legendary land of opportunity. A young man of intellect, ingenuity, and courage, he was eager to enter a fascinating new world—with no money, no formal education, and no facility in the English language. He started out as a pushcart peddler and earned enough money to bring his immediate family—including my father, then a small child—to America. He devoted the rest of his life to his family, putting a large part of his energy and income into bringing as many relatives as possible out of danger in the old country to unimaginable opportunities in the new. My childhood memories of his vision, courage, and devotion to family are still vivid.

Many of those memories have to do with "Second Street," the house my grandparents bought in Evansville, Indiana, the city where my grandfather settled soon after his arrival. This house became the family headquarters. My grandparents raised their seven children there, and in time, the house became a kind of community center—not just for their seven children and their many grandchildren, of whom I was the first, but also the regular gathering place for other relatives, neighbors, and friends.

The door at Second Street was always open. When I was a child, my parents and I would drop in several times a week to visit. We never knew which relatives and friends we would find, but we could always count on lively conversation, warmth, and support. Everyone shared ideas and information freely, alerted others to new opportunities, and offered help to whoever needed it.

My own family was relatively small. An only child, I lived with my parents and my mother's mother. But my second family lived just around the corner on Iowa Street—Aunt Winnie, Uncle Alex, and three cousins who were more like sisters to me. I was constantly in and out of their home and felt a total sense of belonging throughout my childhood and adolescence.

I was very lucky. My parents and grandmother were profoundly supportive and encouraging, giving me all the stimulation and guidance that anyone possibly could, and I also had the love and affection of my extended family at Second Street and Iowa Street. There was another branch of the family in Chicago that was also a constructive influence. All in all, I benefited from an unusually supportive family network that was the quintessence of respect, encouragement, and mutual aid—an experience that has had a lifelong influence on me that is reflected in this book.

I don't mean to suggest that I lived an idyllic childhood or had a picture-book family. We had our share of problems, tensions, disappointments, resentments, and fears. To some extent, these reflected the deep stresses of the Great Depression: the strains of adjustment to a new culture, including intergenerational tensions; the persecution of Jews in Europe that culminated in the Holocaust and World War II. And of course, each family member had his own idiosyncrasies and foibles. We were, in short, fully human.

The values of education and health were highly prized at Second Street. Our family believed that the prime opportunity of the new land was the ability to pursue education—partly for its own sake, in keeping with Jewish tradition, and also as the main pathway to economic opportunity and social respect. A vital part of our family's education—formal and informal—centered on learning how we could best take care of ourselves given what was known then about health. Although terms such as disease prevention and health promotion were little known in the Evansville of the first half of the twentieth century, those notions were certainly alive in my family.

No profession was more respected than medicine, and the children were strongly encouraged to pursue higher education and good health throughout our lives—for ourselves and for others.

But neither education nor health was possible without an utterly dependable family whose support and love made it possible to survive the deprivations and difficulties. My life would simply not have unfolded in the way it has without the secure foundation of my family. This kind of support seems to me to have broad social implications—implications I will explore in this book.

Another enduring influence from my childhood was the heterogeneity and openness of my hometown. My parents, and the other immigrants who had come to Evansville in the decades preceding my birth, spoke a variety of languages, prayed to diverse gods, valued different customs—and shared a common faith in democracy. Despite wariness, sometimes suspicion, occasionally even downright hostility toward their neighbors, they nevertheless learned to live with one another, maintaining civility and earning one another's respect. Even in the post–World War I isolationist Midwest, tolerance for others' differences prevailed. Here was a microcosm of the nation: large, heterogeneous, rough at the edges, susceptible to prejudice, full of human shortcomings—yet fundamentally open and willing to live and let live. This is most vivid for me in the memory of wonderful friendships with high school friends from many different backgrounds.

The world in which my wife and I started our own family was very different from that of my grandparents. We grew up against the backdrop of the Great Depression, World War II, and the Holocaust. Our children entered school on the wave of the famous post–World War II baby boom—a wave predicated on hope for a much better world. My generation, bred in war and hardship, was eager to promote peace, prosperity, higher education, and a whole range of new possibilities emerging from science and technology. Internationally, we sought to heal global wounds—hence the Marshall Plan to rebuild Europe, the rapprochement with Germany and Japan. At home we witnessed the stirrings of a civil rights movement and the quest for expanded economic opportunity for all. Many American families prospered and moved to the suburbs. Everything seemed possible. (I will have more to say about this in the first chapter.)

Our children—and most American children growing up in the 1950s and 1960s—had high expectations, many doors open to them, lots of choices, windows on the whole world—indeed, for many, a bewildering array of possibilities. Yet others, left behind in the inner city and remote rural areas, were deeply mired in poverty and despair.

Our children were born in the 1950s, part of the baby-boom era. They had no Second Street. The large extended family of my youth was gone, dispersed across the country. We tried to keep in touch but were never as close as in the old days. Instead, my wife and I made new friends and created new circles of support for ourselves and our children as well as we could. These were not weak or undependable relationships, but they had to be painstakingly invented, not taken for granted.

With fewer relatives nearby to lend a hand or give advice, more responsibility fell on my wife, Betty, and me—mostly, I regret to say, on Betty. In this we were like most Americans. I knew that somehow both parents should participate in child-rearing and duties at home. However, I, like most men, made only modest adjustments. In part, my career gave me little scope to do more. In part, society did not really expect men like me to do much. So my wife, like most women, had to bear the disproportionate burden of juggling her own job and the responsibility of raising the family.

Betty and I met at Yale when we were doing our post–medical school specialty training together. We were married right after she completed her training in child psychiatry and pediatrics. Soon thereafter, she took time out to raise our children, Eric and Peggy. In their early years, Betty was at home full-time while keeping her hand in professional activities such as consultations, journal articles, and book reviews. After the children entered school, Betty gradually increased her time in academic psychiatry, which eventually became full-time. Throughout the children's growing years, Betty devoted an impressive amount of time, energy, and attention to them. Betty's professional interest in children has been profound; and so, too, are her understanding of and devotion to supporting children's issues. She has helped me to learn a great deal about the development of children and adolescents, and, as a result, I have been endlessly fascinated by their world, with all its individuality, love of discovery, shared pleasure, and ability to cope with the inevitable vicissitudes of growing up. Moreover, I learned about the necessity of renegotiating relationships as spouse and parent while our family grew and developed. I came to appreciate better the complexity of women's lives as they strive to balance their work and home lives. I also learned a great deal about the critical importance of schooling in children's lives.

When our children were in their earliest years, we were almost totally absorbed with them. Out of inexperience, we had to build our competence as parents. We shared the joy of each infant's discoveries, each new level of capability. We tried to balance our desire to foster our children's needs to explore their worlds with the necessity of protecting them from danger.

One of the most difficult transitions our children faced—albeit a predictable one—was that from elementary to junior high school. The intimately familiar and generally supportive environment of Peggy and Eric's small neighborhood school suddenly became the remote, impersonal, strange environment of the massive junior high school. This stressful transition drew my attention to the need for reform of middle-grade education—a major theme of this book.

When we decided to move across the country from the National Institutes of Health to Stanford University in California, we worried about the trauma of uprooting, losing the familiar, entering into a world of strangers. Our children depended on us to support them in forming new friendships. In a society so characterized by mobility, this experience made us more sensitive to the disruptions as well as the opportunities of coping with major transitions.

The rapidity of social change and the upheavals in the course of our children's growth and development were vividly illustrated during our fourteen years on the medical faculty at Stanford University. Eric and Peggy mainly grew up in our home on the Stanford campus. It would be difficult to imagine a more attractive setting for children in the 1950s and 1960s: natural beauty, wonderful climate, lots of space, good friends, intellectual stimulation, humane values, and a thoroughly peaceful environment. Then came the Vietnam War. This was a difficult time for our family, friends, and colleagues—distant though all of us were from the tragic realities of the Asian battlefields.

The Vietnam War brought an upsurge of bitter alienation, drugs, even a "war" on campus. If any demonstration were needed of the power of the social environment to affect adolescent development, this era provided it for millions of Americans. At the same time, another equally devastating example of the destructive power of society on children came with the deterioration of the inner cities—something we as a family were painfully aware of even though we were lucky enough to live in far better circumstances. So this book addresses the impact of the social environment on young people, for better and worse—and seeks ways to shift the balance toward better.

As I reflect on Betty's and my experience raising our children, I am impressed with the immense, unending, deeply gratifying investment we have made in them—and they in us. It is hard to grasp how much we have learned from each other and helped each other—partly by jointly coping with life's difficult vicissitudes. For me, this precious experience highlights the profound challenge of supporting families and creating circumstances favorable for each child's healthy development, personal fulfillment, and social contribution in a world so complex, so rapidly changing, so full of novelty and surprise. In large measure, that is what this book is about.

Most parents are deeply concerned about finding ways to raise children successfully in this hyper-modern world. What does it take now for them to grow up healthy and vigorous, inquiring and problem-solving, decent and constructive?

As we struggle with these issues as individuals, we tend to turn to science for answers. Ongoing research in the fields of child and adolescent development is helping us reassess the conditions that influence our children's development, and learn how they can best cope with the changes within themselves and those of the world swirling around them. Although I didn't originally intend to pursue child and adolescent development, my own personal experiences, which have meshed with my scientific and professional work over the last forty years, have drawn me into that field.

During a quarter-century of research at the Walter Reed Army Institute of Research, the Michael Reese Medical Center in Chicago, the Center for Advanced Study in the Behavioral Sciences, the National Institutes of Health, Stanford University, the Institute of Medicine (National Academy of Sciences), and Harvard University, I have had the privilege of working with outstanding colleagues in tackling problems of stress and coping, conflict and its resolution, health and behavior—from many biological and behavioral perspectives. Time and again over those years, evidence highlighted the importance of a developmental perspective on issues, such as when children are most sensitive to crucial aspects of their environment and the significance of prior experience for determining a child's later behavior, health, and well-being. Even as we identified the means by which society can build a solid foundation for children's healthy development, the evidence grew that we very often miss these opportunities, with tragic consequences.

When I became president of Carnegie Corporation of New York in 1983, I had the great privilege of leading a concerted effort to tackle crucial problems of children and youth. Carnegie was the earliest general-purpose foundation and from the beginning has been dedicated to fostering opportunities for a decent start in life. This reflects Andrew Carnegie's passion for education—witness, for instance, the nearly three thousand Carnegie libraries. The foundation has been fruitfully involved with virtually every aspect of education for more than three-quarters of a century. During the past decade, this engagement has become deeper than ever, spanning childhood and adolescence, dealing with factors that influence learning and development in and out of school.

What is the problem? Why should we spend roughly half the foundation's resources on children and youth in the United States? There are after all, many urgent needs in this country and abroad. Isn't this one of the most affluent countries ever? Don't children usually grow up healthy and fine? Don't they usually emerge intact from their early "growing pains"? Yes and no. While it is certainly true that many turn out well, with or without great difficulty in mid-passage, it is also true that far too many are experiencing the formidable but preventable burdens of ignorance, illness, suffering, failure, humiliation, and lost opportunities. For instance, the evidence indicates that about one adolescent in four is in really serious trouble, such as pregnancy, drug use, dropping out of school, depression and suicide. We lag well behind the other advanced democracies in preventing infant mortality; during the eighties, twenty nations did better. Measures of educational achievement—in reading, math, science—reveal that our children badly fail to meet the standards of other technically advanced nations. In short, a variety of indices indicate that we are suffering heavy casualties during the years of growth and development, and these casualties not only are tragic for the individuals but also bear heavy costs for American society.

During the several years I have worked on this book, my concerns about the fate of our children have deepened. The more I probed into the problems of children and youth in contemporary society, the more worried I became by their magnitude. The situation is even worse than I had imagined; true, I learned more about it as my work on the book intensified, but also the situation itself became even more dire as we entered the nineties. My concerns focus not only on poor children but on society as a whole.

New research into the lives of inner-city children starkly documents the disastrous nature of growing up there. Not only are many more children growing up in poverty than was the case a decade or two ago, but many more are mired in persistent, intractable poverty with no realistic hope of escape. They are profoundly lacking in constructively oriented social-support networks to promote their education and health. They have very few models of competence. They are bereft of visible economic opportunity. The fate of these young people is not merely a tragedy for them, but for the entire nation: A growing fraction of our potential work force consists of seriously disadvantaged people who will have little if any prospect of acquiring the necessary competence to revitalize the economy. If we cannot bring ourselves to feel compassion for these young people on a personal level, we must at least recognize that our economy and our society will suffer along with them. Their loss is our loss.

Distressing as this bad news is, there is much more. Reports of domestic violence and child abuse are on the rise. Over the past several decades, the largely unrecognized tragedy of moderately severe child neglect has been added to more visible, flagrant child neglect. This is most obvious in the large number of adolescents—even preteens—having babies and then walking away from them. But insidious problems have arisen in a much wider portion of society.

When we think about the requirements for healthy child development, we usually consider an intact nuclear family to be the model setting in which children can fulfill their potential. We assume that two parents who respect each other and their children and are both intelligent and well educated will be able to provide the best opportunities for their children. But even in these favorable circumstances, parents face major obstacles in translating their good intentions into action. Most likely, both parents are working out of the home full-time. Their families are small and other relatives are not available to help with the children, who will not have regular, dependable contact with their grandparents or other close relatives, although they do keep in touch by telephone, often long-distance. When the parents do have time for the children in the evening, all too often they are tired, sometimes irritable—and the notion of "quality time" with their children goes out the window. The parents are more successful when measured by the yardstick of material benefits for their children, but often have great difficulty in fulfilling their traditional functions. As women have opened up unprecedented new opportunities for themselves and are making an enormous contribution to the well-being of the economy and the society, they have less time for their children. By and large, fathers and grandparents simply are not compensating for this historical shift.

So families are living in a time of flux. It is a time of magnificent opportunities and of insidious stress. Just as the economic functions of the family moved out of the home early in the Industrial Revolution, so child-care functions, too, are now moving outside the home to a large extent. The child's development is less and less under parents' and grandparents' direct supervision and increasingly placed in the hands of strangers and near-strangers. In the main, this transformation was unforeseen and unplanned, and it is still poorly understood.

As child-rearing moves beyond the home, the quality of outside care becomes crucial. Responsible parents are eager to ensure that the care their children get will facilitate their healthy development. Just as they want a competent doctor to foster their children's health, so they want a capable caregiver, too. Yet, the more I have probed into the issue, the more I have become impressed with how difficult it is to meet this need. There is little precedent for outside-the-home care on such a vast scale as is now emerging in the United States. The crucial factor in quality of care is the nature and behavior of the caregiver. As the demand for child-care givers has surged, those trying to provide child care have frantically sought workers. But even with the best of intentions, this field has been characterized by low pay, low respect, minimal training, minimal supervision, and extremely variable quality. Although most child-care workers try very hard to do a decent job, the plain fact is that many of them do not stay very long and this in itself puts a child's development in jeopardy. Especially for young children, for whom long-term caretaking relationships are crucial, a revolving door is all too common.

The world transformation driven largely by unprecedented advances in science and technology has brought about exceedingly rapid, far-reaching changes in the modern economy. The side effects of these powerful changes, largely unforeseen, involve rapid social dislocations of many different kinds—some of which are inimical to family functioning. Some of this dislocation is literal; many families with young children move very often. For the more fortunate, this involves going where they perceive opportunity, but all too many others move because of desperation, trying to escape poverty or oppression or both. I am speaking not only of the immigrants who have come to the United States, but of the many American families who are tearing up their roots, running large risks, and bringing their children into situations that are highly uncertain, often frightening, and certainly stressful. One consequence of this mobility is that children have fewer opportunities to grow up near their grandparents. Both affluent and poor parents move away from grandparents; among affluent families, grandparents often move away from their children in search of better places to retire.

The erosion of the family has taken many forms in recent decades. There are fewer people around to help as families grow smaller and more mobile. Moreover, society puts a greater emphasis on options, freedom, new horizons—an accentuation of the longstanding American emphasis on individuality. This basic value has many evident virtues, yet its side effects clearly contribute to the problems outlined in this book, including the sharp increase in the rate of divorce, which turns out to have more adverse consequences for child development than most of us had expected. The conventional wisdom on this issue, which I once shared, was that if the parents handled the situation well, with sensitivity to their children, the effects of divorce on the children would be minimal. And this certainly can be the case. But practically speaking, divorcing couples find it exceedingly difficult to handle such situations well enough, over a long enough period, to protect their children from the harsh psychological and economic fallout of divorce.

Another factor contributing to the erosion of the family is sexual activity without a strong sense of responsibility. This is clearest in the case of "babies having babies." The family is also threatened by most couples' lack of preparation for parenthood. Since they did not grow up in a relatively large family and thereby did not acquire much practical experience in caring for young children, a large proportion of those coming to parenthood today are simply not ready. They have neither the knowledge, the skills, nor the confidence to master the complex and enduring tasks of competent parenthood.

In 1991, the Census Bureau reported that more people are now living alone in the United States than ever before. The average American household has diminished to its smallest size ever. One-quarter of the nation's households consist of people living alone. This is twenty-three million individuals. The change has come rapidly. The number of people living alone more than doubled between 1970 and 1990—yet another indication of the dramatic transformation of American families taking place in recent decades. While this finding has positive as well as negative implications, it certainly highlights a major challenge to the adequacy of social supports under the transforming conditions of contemporary life.

The eighties saw a great deal of social reinforcement for self-centered beliefs and attitudes. From presidential rhetoric to public policy to mass-media messages to business practices to private excesses, there was a great deal of explicit and implicit emphasis on getting all you could and living for the moment, devil take the hindmost. This attitude is completely inconsistent with the self-giving dedication and nurturing that parenting demands.

The generation that came to maturity in the eighties was the first ever to grow up on a heavy diet of television. This is a large and complex subject, beyond the scope of this book. And yet it must be noted that this medium is far from fulfilling its potential for education or constructive problem solving. In any event, TV as babysitter is not a substitute for intimate personal contact between parent and child. Television's graphic portrayal of violence as a means of dealing with life's problems has extensive repercussions. Although violence has long been an integral part of human history and of child development, no generation in history has ever grown up with so much exposure to vivid, immediate, and wanton violence divorced from moral as well as physical consequences.

During the past three decades, as all these remarkable changes increasingly jeopardized healthy child development, the nation took little notice. One arcane but important manifestation of this neglect was the low research priority and inadequate science policy for this field. As a result, the nature of this new generation of problems was poorly understood; emerging trends were insufficiently recognized; and authority tended to substitute for evidence, and ideology for analysis. Until the past few years, political, business, and professional leaders had very little to say about the problems of children and youth. Presidents have tended to pass the responsibility to the states and the private sector. State leaders often passed the responsibility back to the federal government on the one hand or over to the cities on the other. And so it goes. This book is one small effort to make us face the nature and scope of the problems and their growing severity, and to take responsibility in a shared, cooperative way throughout the society.

Consider how children grow. From the moment of conception until emergence into full maturity, a series of predictable phases of growth and development occurs, each with its distinctive attributes and needs. Healthy growth depends on appropriate biological, social, and environmental nurturance. Each phase builds on earlier ones; if at any stage requirements for healthy development are not met, later ones are put in jeopardy without some remedial steps. For each phase, it is possible, therefore, to determine a set of needs and opportunities, and to construct conditions that will dependably foster healthy physical development, as well as a vigorous promotion of learning and of social development. At Carnegie we have tried to chart these developmental processes for each phase of a child's development. In doing so, we have given special attention to two crucial periods in the formative years of life: early childhood and early adolescence. These two phases of development—the prenatal period through the first few years of life, and early adolescence, ages ten through fifteen—involve the most rapid change and growth. Both are times of inordinate vulnerability but also of great malleability and responsiveness to environmental challenge, so they provide exceptional opportunity to prevent casualties by intervening in ways that have lifelong impact. I have organized this book to reflect those two unique phases in a child's life.

Early childhood is clearly one of the most crucial periods of development. It is characterized by rapid growth, specific environmental needs, maximal dependence on caretakers, great vulnerability, and long-term consequences of failures in development. It is a dramatic period, with great changes and striking contrasts. First, the nine months of pregnancy—from a single cell to a very complex organism. Next, the critical transition from living inside the mother's body to living in the world outside. Then, the period of forming the initial human attachments that shape so powerfully the possibilities for human relationships and social skills—and the infant's beginnings of discovery, the building blocks of learning skills. So this initial phase has a strong bearing on a child's entire life. Especially in poor communities, the risks of permanent—and largely preventable—damage are formidable.

Early adolescence, ages ten through fifteen, is another critical period of biological and psychological change for the individual. Puberty constitutes a far-reaching biological upheaval in a youngster's life span. For many who must make the transition from elementary to secondary school, it involves drastic changes in the social environment as well. These years are highly formative for attitudes and behaviors regarding education and health that have lifelong significance. Some of them involve high-risk behavior including school alienation; using tobacco, alcohol, and other drugs; careless driving of automobiles and motorcycles; eating junk food; not getting enough exercise; and engaging in patterns of sexuality that lead to high-risk pregnancy and sexually transmitted disease. In early adolescence, before damaging patterns are firmly established, there is a crucial opportunity for preventive intervention.

The general outlook of my work can be expressed in a few sentences. What people experience early in life provides the basis for all the rest. The early years can build the foundation for a long, healthy life characterized by sociability and learning. Health and education are closely linked in the development of vigorous, skillful, adaptable young people. Investments in health and education can be guided by research in biomedical and behavioral sciences in ways likely to prevent much of the damage now being done to children and adolescents—and thereby contribute substantially to a dynamic economy and flourishing democratic society in the next century. This book is urgently devoted to giving all our children a decent start.

SECTION I

A LONG VIEW OF TODAY'S CHILDREN

1

Families in Crisis, Children in Jeopardy

Today's children are in crisis because today's families are in crisis. Before we can begin to address the problems children today face, however, we need a better understanding of how society in general and the family in particular—the most elemental crucible for child development—have evolved, with a special focus on the drastic changes in the past several decades.

GROWING UP HUMAN: OUR ANCIENT LEGACY

Ninety-eight percent of our genes are identical with those of chimpanzees. Modern science, using techniques of molecular biology, has demonstrated the close affinity of humans with the great apes. Our biological inheritance is reflected in our brains and in some behavioral tendencies that have been built into us because they worked so well in survival for such a very long time. So we bring to contemporary circumstances an ancient heritage of genes, brains, and customs that must now be related to the contemporary world. The years of infancy through adolescence have always been crucial in human adaptation. They provide the fundamental opportunity for learning the basic elements of what we need to know—about ourselves, about each other, about the world around us, about ways to cope and to solve the problems of living. In this complicated quest for adaptation in modern circumstances, we cannot afford to waste the critical years of growth and development, let alone use them destructively.

Human societies evolved slowly from prehuman ancestors over more than a million years of time with continuing selection for structures and functions that foster healthy, adaptive development during childhood and adolescence—the essence of survival. For most of human history, small, stable communities provided enduring, intimate relationships from birth, with many opportunities for children to acquire traditional adult life skills and roles gradually through observation, imitation, and practice as well as exploration and discovery.

Primates—monkeys, apes, and humans—more than other mammals, undergo a long period of dependence and development before they reach reproductive maturity. Much of what we've learned about the functions of this extended period of immaturity derives from research on the nonhuman primates—monkeys and apes. The primary significance of the extended period of development centers on the opportunity to learn about the environment in its unique physical and social features. Overwhelmingly, this time is spent in social relations with other primates of the same species, who offer attachment, protection, modeling, feedback, stimulation, and guidance. Such survival skills as obtaining food and avoiding predators are acquired in a social context, largely through observation, imitation, and practice. A critical aspect of this early learning depends on the development of mother-infant attachment. But after infancy, primates typically enjoy growing social interaction with other relatives, peers, and some unrelated adult members of the social group. So, survival-relevant adaptive learning is largely social learning.

Secure early attachments are essential for primate and human development. Experimental research has demonstrated that development goes drastically awry when infants are deprived of the opportunity to develop an attachment to a caregiver early in life. Monkeys raised in total social isolation during infancy develop extremely abnormal behavior patterns that last over their lifetime. These include drastic withdrawal, peculiar postures, and self-punitive behavior such as repetitively biting one's own body. These findings are mirrored in a grotesque way in observations of children who have been reared under conditions of extreme deprivation or isolation during their early years.

On the other hand, rearing by a caring adult leads to a strong attachment and provides a secure base from which the infant can explore the larger social and physical world. In the natural habitat, monkeys and apes cling reflexively to their mothers from birth. Mother-infant bodily contact is virtually constant for many months until the infant can walk, climb, and keep up with the mother on its own. Safely in contact with the mother, the infant first begins social learning and later explores the wider world. These explorations, in turn, facilitate cognitive development and friendly relations with peers. The infants and juvenile primates learn a lot in play, mostly with peers and also with older relatives. Indeed, most of their waking time during the years of growth and development is spent in play. Play is highly functional. During play, juveniles learn dominance relationships, communication skills, the regulation of aggressive behavior, and a variety of social skills—adult behaviors they can practice without penalties or serious consequences. In play, they acquire the repertoire of skills that are the precursors of almost everything they will need to know or do as adults. So there is much continuity over the generations resulting from gradual, incremental cultural learning in childhood with acquisition of practical knowledge and social skills necessary for survival and reproduction throughout the life span. This developmental theme foreshadows important adaptive features of later human evolution.

In significant ways, nonhuman primate societies anticipate features of human societies. Although human societies have become far more complex than those of our ancient ancestors, human societies are also fundamentally adaptive mechanisms. Thus, through the long evolution of our species, societies have been built on the basic evolutionary requirements of survival and reproduction—and successful individuals have had to learn rules of the game compatible with these requirements. There are many types of cooperative activities that must be learned for survival: reproduction, care of the young, obtaining food and water, defending against predators and other dangers. These patterns of interaction must be learned over a considerable period of time.

Our ancestors lived for many millennia in hunting and gathering societies—long after they had acquired fully human biological characteristics. These early hunting and gathering societies are characterized by the small size of their communities—typically between twenty and fifty people. Children growing up in these societies show many characteristics similar to those of close nonhuman primates such as chimpanzees.

Early human children learned a great deal through play and especially through observing and imitating adults. In these simple societies, the occupations of their parents were clearly visible throughout childhood. At an early age, boys joined the men in their regular activities and girls joined the women. Thus, both sexes prepared very directly for the tasks of adulthood. A great deal of attention to the child from parents and older siblings was the rule, much of it in shaping the attitudes and skills essential for everyday life. In this way, children and adolescents participated extensively in their small society as age and circumstances permitted, and in doing so, they learned the skills necessary to sustain life.

Thus, human biology and learned traditions evolved over many millennia in a world of small, mainly stable, face-to-face groups within which people were linked by ties of kinship and lifelong familiarity. Although small-scale, traditional societies around the world have adapted in many ways to different ecological settings, their societies share certain essential features. Traditional societies typically possess clear guidelines for behavior. These guidelines had probably proven useful in their past for coping with adaptive tasks under circumstances that were largely predictable and changed only slowly over the course of human history until the world transformation of the past couple of centuries. These guidelines cover basic categories of experience: human relationships; relations between people and their environment; ways to cope with problems and take advantage of opportunities bearing directly on survival and reproduction. They are primarily learned early in life, shaped by powerful rewards and punishments, invested with strong emotions, and supported by shared and highly valued social norms.

Such early learning of norms in small-scale societies tends to induce lifelong commitments to traditional ways of life. These commitments are reinforced by the continuing experience that self-respect and close human relationships are intimately linked with behaviors conforming to social norms. A sense of personal worth is predicated on having a meaningful role and belonging to a valued group; a sense of belonging, in turn, depends on the ability to undertake the traditional tasks of that society with skill, to engage in social interactions in ways that are mutually supportive, and on the personally meaningful experience of participation in group rituals marking shared experiences of deep emotional significance. All of these traditional activities are experienced within the context of a small, intimate group that provides the security of familiarity, support in times of stress, and enduring attachments through the life cycle. These are powerful attributes in the light of human vulnerability to environmental vicissitudes—disease, attack, extremes of climate, or other jeopardy in the habitat. The enduring group offers guidance, protection, satisfaction, life itself.

RECENT PAST AND PRESENT

In the past two hundred years, a large proportion of humanity has experienced a very different sort of life. Technological advances have rapidly opened new opportunities, changed lifestyles, and disrupted traditional patterns. Disruptive factors involve increased geographical mobility, including massive migrations; crowding of lonely strangers in vast urban societies; conflicts of values; emergence of very complex, largely unprecedented living circumstances; and the immense novelty and heterogeneity of the modern world. These factors disrupt long-term bonds, force individuals to compete with strangers for scarce and valuable resources, and confront people with all sorts of unfamiliar outlooks and behaviors that often are very difficult to reconcile with their own traditions. At best, these circumstances are very stimulating and creative, but they can also be impersonal and even harsh. When small, familiar groups are replaced by shifting collections of relative strangers, then suspicion, fear, and hostility are likely to ensue. Cooperation and a sense of mutual responsibility tend to be replaced by the pursuit of self-protection.

Social support networks have been fundamental in human life for millennia. They still bear directly upon basic human needs. But they are jeopardized in many different ways by the formidable pressures and disruptions associated with modern transformation. They can no longer be taken for granted. Under contemporary circumstances, we have to improvise a great deal to protect, strengthen, and create the social support networks that are vital to meet basic human needs.

To some extent, this book is about the implications of a dramatic contrast: growing up *now*—on the verge of the twenty-first century—and growing up *then*—hundreds, thousands, even millions of years ago. How can modern societies reconcile the fundamental ontinuity of the ancient human organism with profound ogical and social change?

FAMILIES: AN OLD STORY

Over many millennia, in the simple societies of human origins, the basic integrative force has been the family. The kin group served many functions: political, economic, educational, religious, and psychological. As societies grew in size and complexity, changes were inevitable. New opportunities called for new tasks, new roles, new organizations, new institutions. Gradually, century by century, such changes emerged as a part of human adaptation. Nevertheless, family ties continued to provide the fundamental basis of life throughout millions of years of the hunting and gathering era, and after it during the thousands of years of the agricultural era.

In the agricultural era, the nuclear family, consisting of a mother, a father, and their children, continued to be the central organizing principle of society. The family was a fundamental unit for almost all activity. The household was the main site of production of necessities as well as of the upbringing of children, their acquisition of economically useful skills, their more formal education (to the extent it existed), and the care of all family members, old and young alike. Boys learned mostly from their fathers, and girls from their mothers. Children learned through direct observation, and as they grew and developed were able to participate more fully in adult activities, with increasing responsibility as they matured. Typically, members of the extended family were nearby, able to help in monitoring and guiding the young as well as to respond supportively in times of stress.

If you had looked into the home of one of the early American colonists in the seventeenth century, you would have witnessed this typical nuclear-family arrangement, yet forces were already at work that would soon change it. Carl Degler, a professor of history at Stanford University, has researched the historical forces that have shaped American families. He reports that in the early seventeenth century, when the United States was emerging as a nation, the economy was mostly agricultural, and living conditions were exceedingly demanding. All members of the family had to work together to the maximum extent possible. Men and older boys performed the most physically taxing labors, while women and girls did a great deal in and near the home. Besides caring for the children and preparing the food, women planted gardens and looked after the preparation of soap, candles, clothing, and medicines. Division of labor by gender continued even after towns emerged from the early forests. This basic American family pattern persisted through most of the eighteenth century, but events in Europe would have impacts in the nineteenth century, and beyond, that have caused drastic changes in the family.

FAMILIES AFTER THE INDUSTRIAL REVOLUTION

Toward the end of the agrarian era, the rate of innovation in Western Europe took off. By the end of the eighteenth century, the Industrial Revolution had clearly come to England—the first industrial society—and later to America. Societies were now able to obtain most of their income from productive work using machines powered by inanimate energy sources. Among the most notable technological advances were the steam engine, the rapid growth of the railroad industry, the replacement of sailing ships with steamships, the mass production of steel, and the use of the new technology in agriculture. After its first century, the Industrial Revolution gained new momentum with the rise of the automobile, the telephone, and the electrical and petroleum industries. In the middle of the twentieth century, World War II accelerated developments in such fields as aviation, electronics, plastics, and computers, making worldwide, instantaneous communication a possibility for the first time. This profound transformation had economic, political, social, and psychological ramifications that continue to the present time.

New technology brought about the creation of the factory system, which required a concentrated supply of labor away from the home. This in turn prompted a mass migration to cities on a scale beyond all precedents. The migrants were not prepared for their new way of life. Their family relationships, sanitary practices, and other aspects of their prior rural lifestyle were ill suited to the rapidly growing, crowded, urban landscape. Particularly serious among the many social dislocations was the disruption of kinship and friendship. The social supports provided by local customs and traditional institutions were suddenly ripped away from the transplanted rural villagers, and proved to be very hard to replace.

So progress was a mixed blessing, offering the hope and stimulation of new opportunity and new mixtures of people, but also uprooting and vulnerability in a mass of strangers. Poverty, disease, and such related social problems as alcoholism became widespread. The factory system itself was severe, with laborers working very long, demanding hours, often in dangerous ways and confined spaces. Rapid industrialization was highly stressful for large numbers of people, but it nevertheless continued at a relentless pace.

Gender differentiation in work was largely maintained in the face of these changing conditions. However, it turned out that women were highly restricted in the range of new work options allotted to them. There was more latitude on the farm. In the city, women were mainly confined to the house: rearing children, preparing meals, and generally doing the household chores. In the city, men's work was typically done at a distance from home. Fathers left home in the early-morning hours to do unseen, remote work that their children often did not understand. Boys no longer apprenticed themselves by watching their fathers work; fathers were no longer the direct role models they had been a generation earlier. For both men and women, work was much less related to land and nature than it had been before. The change from the family-as-producing-unit to the family-as-consuming-unit emerged in this transition from rural to urban life.

One of the striking changes in the nuclear family during the nineteenth century was the shift toward marriage based on affection and personal choice rather than on an economic or culturally based determination by parents. Considerations of family, money, and status were far less determining than they had been historically. The emphasis on young people's romantic choice was more prominent in the United States than elsewhere. Although there were precursors as far back as medieval times, the romantic perspective on marriage was very weak in the eighteenth century. But by the end of the nineteenth century it was powerful. Particularly striking is the fact that this gave young women a larger freedom of choice than they had ever had before. The wife and mother in this new kind of family enjoyed a freshly elevated status. The home became the woman's sphere, and her role was enlarged beyond household chores: She was the moral and spiritual bulwark of the family.

Concurrent with these changes, a new image of children began to emerge. Given our view of children today, it is difficult to imagine how children were thought of in the seventeenth century. The child of that era was viewed essentially as a small adult, to be trained as quickly as physical development enabled him to earn his way and undertake the tasks of adulthood. By the end of the eighteenth century, however, childhood was coming to be viewed as a distinct period, a time of innocence and intense joy without much responsibility. Birthdays began to be celebrated during the eighteenth century, and toy stores appeared. Early in the nineteenth century, books written especially for children were published for the first time. Other books were oriented toward parents to give them guidance about child-rearing—one of the early signs of the professionalization of this function. Degler noted one interesting index of the changing view of children. Before 1750 portraits of boys of seven always showed them dressed like men; but this declined to about half of the portraits between 1750 and 1770; and then to less than a quarter after 1770. As children came increasingly to be seen as very special and important, their mothers, and women in general, gained prestige in their crucial role as caretakers and moral developers of children. Yet by the same token, the mother was increasingly confined to her own household. Child-rearing and household maintenance were perhaps a more full-time job than ever before.

Historians describe the restriction of the wife's role to the household as a source of discontent but also as an opportunity to redefine the roles of wife and mother. But many adult women of the nineteenth century chose to avoid marriage and childbearing altogether. As economic activity expanded and diversified, opportunities increased for these unmarried "spinsters" to support themselves in the work force. By the middle of the nineteenth century, when the Industrial Revolution was in full swing, American marriage was in a state of flux. Even as relationships were more romantic and compassionate, women were still largely confined to a narrow range of tasks at home. At the same time, education was beginning to open up wider horizons. As public schools sprang up throughout the country, girls were admitted along with boys, and even higher education became an option for some women after the Civil War. Still, it was generally understood that a married woman would not work in the paid labor force even if she was highly educated.

These tensions—the tedium of the home, the rising level of aspirations, the openness and diversity of society, and the rapidity of social change—all contributed to a rising divorce rate. At the time of the Civil War, the American divorce rate, though low in comparison with the present, was higher than in any country in Europe, and it rose steadily. Although in the nineteenth century this reflected the choice of some women to leave the household, that was not the majority position. Most women were pressing for greater recognition within the home. Nonetheless, at the onset of the twentieth century most divorces were obtained on the initiative of women. The relatively high divorce rates were distributed widely across social classes. But even in the presence of such high divorce rates, the most common disruption of marriage was not by divorce but by death, as it always had been. Although there are major differences between the two kinds of disruption, there are some attributes in common: children are left, at least for a while, with only one parent, and later the surviving spouse is likely to remarry and reconstitute the family.

Families in colonial America, like those in Europe, were large. During the seventeenth and eighteenth centuries, women typically had seven or eight children spread over twenty or more years of childbearing. By the end of the nineteenth century, the typical American family had three or four children. A drop of 50 percent in the size of the average family in a relatively short time is an extraordinary change. The decline occurred in rural as well as urban families. The main methods of birth control were reduction in the frequency of sexual intercourse within marriage, and withdrawal prior to ejaculation. Thus, it was not so much new contraceptive techniques but new attitudes that brought about the declining family size. The literature of the time indicates that parents' desire to have more control over their own lives was an important factor in reducing family size, as was the growing feminist movement.

At the onset of the twentieth century, children were staying at home for a longer time, even after completing their formal education. Most children were by then completing grammar school at age fourteen. Some went on to high school, but very few attended college. Girls typically lived at home until they were married, and so, too, did many unmarried boys, even after they had full-time employment. Getting married clearly implied the establishment of one's own household. Another common assumption was that the young woman would drop out of the paid labor force when she married; the expectation was that the young husband would first establish himself in a job with sufficient pay to support a wife who was a full-time homemaker and the mother of several children. By and large, this was the prevailing pattern during the nineteenth century and the first half of the twentieth century.

FAMILIES UNDER SPECIAL STRESS

Most of the historical records have dealt with the white middle class. But recent scholarship has clarified a great deal about poor families in America, particularly enslaved and immigrant families. Even under the harsh conditions of severe poverty or of enslavement, the support and resourcefulness of the family have proven to be adaptable and valuable for its members.

From the colonial period to the Civil War, most Americans of African origin were slaves. Slave women were the primary caretakers of children. In the agrarian society of the time, these slave women also had to work in the fields along with the men, so the demands on them were very heavy indeed. Although it has long been supposed that slavery shattered the black family, recent research has documented the widespread existence of intact slave families, of the value slaves attached to the family, of the importance given to maintaining family ties even in the face of forced separation, of the support the family provided under great stress, and of the resiliency of black families in the face of adversity.

The initiative for family formation came from the slaves themselves, who arrived as strangers to each other, ripped out of their families of origin and flung together in a melting pot of languages and cultures. By the time the last slaves were brought over from Africa early in the nineteenth century, the great majority of slaves were living in families. Contemporary documents attest to the ways in which the slaves cherished their family relations. Tragically, at least 10 percent of those families were disrupted by slave masters. Most runaway slaves were attempting escape to reunite with their families. Still, the largest source of family disruption, among slaves as among free people, was death.

Most immigrants to America were also very poor, but they were not subject to the overwhelming distortions of the slavery experience. Still, they were entering a strange land, often alone at first, unable to speak the language and subject to great hardship in a period of raw growth of industry and urbanization with many harsh edges. The historical evidence shows that immigrants' nuclear families were quickly reconstituted and that extended-family members were often nearby, though not so frequently living in the same household as had earlier been supposed. In the period of peak emigration at the turn of the twentieth century, about a quarter of all immigrant households included some relatives. Many others were nearby in the neighborhood. Together, the nuclear and extended families created a powerful support system that enabled the immigrants to cope with adversity.

AMERICAN FAMILIES IN THE TWENTIETH CENTURY

At the outset of the twentieth century, wives typically did not work outside the home—with the notable exception of wives in families of African origin, where 40 percent were in the paid labor force in 1900. In general, it was assumed that it was a sign of a husband's weakness if he could not support his wife; in 1900, only about 6 percent of all married women worked for wages.

World War II changed all that. As millions of men entered the armed forces, women responded to the call for help in war production and services. The federal government's bountiful incentives, including some day-care centers, and the appeal of patriotism were so powerful that when the war ended in 1945, well over half of all employed workers were women. Although it had been generally anticipated that women would return to the home at war's end, many instead elected to continue work outside the home, having found work to be interesting, satisfying, and feasible. Moreover, employers had an economic incentive to keep these relatively lower-paid employees in the work force.

In the immediate aftermath of World War II, in the late 1940s and early 1950s, there was a surge in marriage and parenthood across America—the dawn of the baby-boom era. A great many young families moved to the suburbs, seeing them as an ideal setting for child-rearing: space for play, a safe and attractive environment, good schools, a feeling of intimacy with other like-minded people that might offset the anonymity of big cities and large, bureaucratic work organizations. The typical suburbanite married young, was between the ages of twenty-five and thirty-five, and had several young children.

The national mood was expansive, and since the United States was the world's leading power economically, militarily, and politically, jobs were plentiful and remunerative. Rates of divorce and numbers of births out of wedlock and of single-parent families were at about half of present levels. This family-centered culture rested on the concept that a woman's place was primarily in the home, where she could devote her attention to her children and to the community to enhance the family's well-being. Although many older women stayed in the work force after the war, young mothers were overwhelmingly devoting their full time to the family.

Despite the rosy cast of this era, evidence reveals a dark side to the suburban experience. For example, there was a rapid turnover in the suburbs. Families uprooted themselves frequently, moving from one area to another as corporate and professional opportunities arose. Friendships were easily made but just as easily disrupted. Moreover, most men worked in large organizations, often far from home. The pressure to achieve, to succeed, was great. The net effect was that many of the husbands and fathers were home very little, and tired much of the time when they were home; thus was born the stereotype of the office toiler, the anonymous commuter who took the early train in and the late train back home to the wife, with barely a moment to see his children. Survey research indicates that about one-fifth of these young married people were unhappy in marriage. Another fifth were dissatisfied with the quality of their lives.

In the late fifties, sixties, and seventies, once the postwar baby boom peaked, women poured into the labor force again at a rapid rate. The contrast between 1950 and 1975 was dramatic. In 1950, the husband was the sole earner in well over half of all families. In 1975, this was the case in only a third of American families. Public-opinion polls made during the seventies showed very broad support for these changes. In the younger age groups, the approval of this pattern was overwhelming, representing a drastic change from public-opinion findings in the period at the end of World War II.

The single-parent household headed by the mother was a small, newly emerging phenomenon in the fifties and sixties. The extent and importance of this rising trend was then only a cloud on the horizon.

THE THREE-DECADE DIVIDE

It is apparent that there have been dramatic changes in the structure and function of American families in just a few decades. Some of these changes represent new opportunities and tangible benefits. Others represent serious jeopardy to the well-being of children—on a large enough scale to pose a major problem for the entire society.

The extent of the transformation of American family life is highlighted by comparing 1960 with 1990—only three decades apart. At the University of Houston, Steven Mintz and Susan Kellogg studied this era. Their research indicates that until about 1960 the vast majority of Americans shared a common set of beliefs about family life.

1. A family consists of a husband and wife living together with their children.
2. The father is the head of the family and should earn the family's income and give his name to his wife and children.
3. The mother's main tasks are to support and facilitate the work of her husband, guide her children's development, look after the home, and set a moral tone for the family.
4. Marriage is an enduring obligation for better and worse; the husband and wife have the joint task of coping with stresses, including those of the child's development; and sexual activity, especially by women, should be kept within the marriage.
5. Parents have an overriding responsibility for the well-being of their children during their early years; until they enter school, the parents have almost sole responsibility, and even later must be the primary guardians of their children's education and discipline.

Of course, even in 1960, families recognized the difficulty of converting these ideals into reality. Still, they devoted an immense amount of effort to approximating them in practice. Over the past three decades, however, these ideals have been drastically modified across all social classes.

The dramatically increased movement of women into the labor force in the sixties exemplified the pervasive feeling of restlessness many women experienced staying at home. Many of them had been well educated and had every reason to believe that they were generally as capable as their husbands. The technical revolution of television ushered in a social revolution. The television screen showed wider horizons, different ways of life, and new opportunities. While the women's movement would not become fully fledged for a decade or so, in its embryonic state it had a great impact on women, stimulating them to create new balances between career and family.

In 1960 only about one-quarter of married women living with

their husbands worked outside the home. But by 1990 about two-thirds did so. Perhaps the most striking change from the perspective of child and adolescent development is the rapid entry of mothers of young children into the work force. By 1990, more than half of all mothers of young children, preschool as well as school-age, held jobs outside the home.

Between 1960 and 1990, birthrates fell precipitously and divorce rates surged upward, as did the number of single-parent families. Patterns of sexual behavior changed markedly. Acceptance of premarital sexuality, especially for women, increased dramatically, as did attitudes toward living together outside marriage.

American families in 1990 are far more likely than earlier families to postpone marriage or to reject it altogether, to live with children in single-parent families—typically with the mother present but with no adult male and very often no other adult person. Voluntary marital disruption was a rare event at the beginning of the century—commoner in America than in Europe, but still unusual; today at least half of all marriages end in divorce. The great majority of adults no longer believe that couples should stay married because divorce might harm their children.

It is startling to realize that today most American children spend part of their childhood in a single-parent family. By age sixteen, close to half the children of married parents will see their parents divorce. Usually the child remains with the mother. For nearly half of these children, it will be five years or more before their mothers remarry. Close to half of all white children whose parents remarry will see the second marriage dissolve during their adolescence. Black women not only marry less often and experience more marital disruption, but also remarry more slowly and less often than white women. America exhibits a revolving-door pattern in marriage that is certainly stressful for developing children and adolescents.

Remarriage brings a complex set of relationships. Many different family configurations have emerged. About two-thirds of the children in stepfamilies will have full siblings plus either half siblings or stepsiblings. Many children have multiple sets of grandparents. On the other hand, children of single mothers or mothers who do not remarry have fewer active family relationships than children with two parents.

While the proportion of single-parent families is on the rise for whites, blacks, and Hispanics, the majority of single-parent families are black. Female-headed families with children are much more poor than are married-couple families with children, of race. By conservative estimates, one-fifth of young ...can children are raised in poverty, many by their mothers ...one. Black families with children are more likely to be poor than are white families with children, regardless of family type.

Current overall birthrates are lower than zero population growth, which would be about 2.5 children. Survey research shows a great decrease in the proportion of women favoring large families, an upsurge in assertiveness about the personal needs of women, and the balancing of these needs with those of their children and the men in their lives. A clear and increasing majority of women believe that both husband and wife should be able to work, should have roughly similar opportunities, should share household responsibilities and the tasks of child-rearing. There is a growing minority of young married women, often highly educated and career-oriented, who are choosing not to have any children and have little interest in children's issues. Altogether, it is hard to imagine a more rapid and clear-cut social tidal wave than reflected in these changing circumstances and views.

WHAT'S HAPPENING TO OUR CHILDREN?

With all the radical shifts in family life, it is not surprising that surveys of public opinion indicate that American parents are much more troubled about raising their children. Parents' concerns mirror the widespread belief that our society is falling prey to increasingly serious problems: educational failure; delinquency; suicide; adolescent pregnancy at increasingly early ages; fatal accidents and homicides; sexually transmitted diseases. At the same time, there is much concern in general about a broad trend toward the decreasing commitment of parents to their children. Two-thirds of parents now report that they are less willing to make sacrifices for their children than their own parents would have been.

Children today differ in many ways from those of earlier times. They are more likely to survive childbirth and the first year of life; they live in smaller families; they are more likely to lose a parent through divorce but less likely to lose a parent through death; are more likely to live with just one parent; are more likely to be in school instead of working; are more likely to live in an urban or suburban than in a rural area; are less likely to see their parents at work, and are less likely to have daily contact wi extended family.

Between 1960 and 1990, the change in regu tact between children and their adult relatives i only are their mothers home much less but th evidence that fathers spend more time at home to co the mothers' absence. Moreover, only about 5 percent of A children see a grandparent regularly, a much lower level than in past. Children spend a huge chunk of time during their years of most rapid growth and development gazing at the mixture of reality and fantasy presented by the television—in addition to a variety of out-of-home day-care settings and "self-care" (i.e., taking care of oneself; often meaning no care at all). Adolescents increasingly become involved in the separate "teen culture," which often lacks adult leadership, mentorship, and support, and at its worst can manifest itself in violence-prone gangs.

Today's growing children and young adolescents have less and less opportunity for meaningful participation in the adult world. It is less clear to them how to be useful and earn respect. Adolescence, the time between childhood and adulthood, has emerged as a distinctive status in its own right. The requirements, risks, and opportunities of this period are now highly ambiguous for many adolescents. They are held in a lengthy limbo—no longer children, yet not quite adults, either—at a time when they have the physical attributes of adults and much pressure to engage in such adult activities as smoking, drinking, and sex.

HOW ARE TODAY'S PARENTS COPING?

By and large, young people moving toward parenthood have less experience caring for children than any of their predecessors had. Moreover, they face more rapidly changing circumstances and a wider spectrum of life choices. But choices and decisions and transitions can be burdens, even as they offer attractive opportunities and privileges. A young couple today almost certainly agonizes over decisions taken for granted even a generation ago. Should they get married? If yes, should they wait until one or both has a steady job, until after college, or graduate school, or postgraduate work? Where should they live? What about the fateful decision to have children?

Once married, since it is very likely that both husband and wife in the paid labor force, they will have to renegotiate their relationship with the advent of the baby. How will they divide the baby-care chores? What sort of parental leave, if any, will each take? What kind of flexibility can they build into their schedules? How will they handle the housework? How can they balance work and family life? If the mother takes off from work for a while, when is it sensible to go back, and how can she best make the transition? Can they afford quality child care? At what point is it safe to bring the baby to a day-care center? How will they recognize high-quality child care when they find it? When the child is ready for preschool education, should it be geared toward play or be strongly academic? When the time comes for school, should it be public or private?

Studies on parents' efforts to balance their various interests and responsibilities in new ways show that they have scarcely begun to address this complicated issue. While the government has provided little encouragement or incentive for employers to take constructive steps in helping parents balance family and work, there is an upsurge of community organizations seeking to provide child care, support, and guidance for young parents and their children. Meanwhile, the debate is growing among policy makers as to which measures can strengthen today's families: family leave for new fathers, job sharing, part-time work and flexible schedules, and so on. University of California sociologist Arlie Hochschild, coauthor of *The Second Shift: Working Parents and the Revolution at Home,* conducted a personal experiment, which she describes as preindustrial, when she reintegrated the family into the workplace by bringing her young baby to the office with her on a regular basis. She was fortunate that this was permitted and feasible. Although it is an unlikely solution for most parents, it certainly does highlight the problem.

Hochschild has conducted systematic research that illuminates the tension between work and family. She describes the tremendous cost women pay whether they choose to concentrate on working at home or on having a paid career. The housewife pays the cost of remaining outside what is today the mainstream of society. The career woman pays the cost of the drain of time and energy from family commitments. Many creative efforts to synthesize these roles are now being explored.

The research evidence clearly indicates that husbands share very little of the burden of raising their children and caring for their homes. Hence, as Hochschild describes it, many women are coming home from a paid job and working a "second shift." Most men devote long hours to their work. Even if they want to be helpful at home, their institutional settings usually do not make it easy for them to do so. How is it possible to create flexible work schedules and a supportive community for joint parenting? How can we achieve better balance among those on the second shift?

Currently, great numbers of both husbands and wives work full-time on a year-round basis. There is no reason to believe that this phenomenon of the two-parent working family is a transient one. Indeed, a variety of economic and psychological factors reinforce the persistence of the pattern as a financial necessity. For a great many families, dual careers are a necessity to maintain their accustomed standard of living. The actual and proportionate costs of raising children today are much higher than in the 1950s and 1960s. The industries that have declined in the United States in relation to foreign competition, such as the automobile and steel industries, are precisely the ones that historically provided relatively high-earning positions for men, especially working-class men who did not go on to higher education. On the other hand, economic growth in recent decades has been mainly in the service sectors that are historically major employers of women. Thus, employment opportunities for women are going up faster than those for men, although, as I mentioned earlier, women traditionally are paid less than men for comparable work and have other employment constraints. Still, the trend is toward growing opportunities over the next few decades.

This overview of the past three decades should make it clear why concern about healthy child development is by no means limited to high-risk populations such as those in impoverished areas. Rather, such worries are shared across the spectrum of America's parents.

In the face of the world transformation of the twentieth century and its profound effects on families, one of the basic issues of human survival becomes how to meet the crucial requirements for healthy child development and adolescent development under new circumstances—how to cope with modern imminent dangers, how to make a living, how to live harmoniously with other people, how to meet one's personal needs and integrate them with those of a valued group, how to participate in the society in ways that ensure the well-being of oneself and one's family. The task was relatively simple in earlier, small, stable societies. Although modern developments have provided immense opportunities, they have also made learning and social tasks more complex, development more prolonged, and long-term outcomes more problematic. Today there is less continuity between the behavior learned in childhood and youth on the one hand, and tasks of adulthood on the other hand, than there ever was before.

In the space of just three decades—a single generation—consider the tremendous upheaval within the traditional family unit. We may no longer assume that most children will grow up with the benefit of two attentive parents, one of whom—typically the mother—will stay at home to devote her time primarily to child-rearing. Today's children are very often children of divorce, children of single-parent families, children whose parents both work full-time outside the home, children whose care outside the home is highly variable and weak in sustained personal attention by caring and responsible adults.

Despite these dramatic demographic shifts, our society has barely mobilized to respond to the needs these new family situations create. We have only begun to examine issues of parental job leave, health-care coverage, day care, preschool education, corporate policies to facilitate care of young children by both parents, government-funded allowances for children, and more. We have only begun to cope with the economic and psychological toll that separation, divorce, and remarriage take on our children. We are learning how to create high-quality child care and other family-equivalent functions outside the home. We have begun to consider the new challenges—and the new threats—today's adolescents face so that we can find ways to help them make the transition to adulthood safely and creatively.

Centuries of tradition in parenthood and millions of years have made the baby's genes the way they are; yet we have had hardly any time at all to adapt to the new social setting in which today's young people find themselves as parents. We are all now struggling as never before to manage the once-in-a-lifetime experience of raising a child. We have unprecedented opportunities to explore the world we have invented and to see how it can work for children and thereby for the future of humanity; but today's families are also facing unprecedented stresses, and today's children are being raised in a time of crisis as the world undergoes an accelerating transformation.

2

Infants and Children at Risk: Society's Toll

Yes, most children in affluent countries survive the perils of birth and the first year of life, grow up healthy, and appear reasonably happy. The progress of science and technology has paid off handsomely in improved health and material well-being. Much of that progress has direct and fundamental benefits in the early years of growth and development. Yet gross casualties to children of all ages are apparent in every sector of every society for those who care to look. In early death, disease, and disability, in ignorance and prejudice, in failure and humiliation, in hatred and violence, alienation and drugs, suicide and depression, the casualties are abundant. This tragic waste of human resources and this pointless suffering are more common in poor communities than in affluent ones, more obvious in developing countries than in developed ones. But they are everywhere.

In the previous chapter, I discussed the evolution of the modern family and how its rapid transformation has left us unprepared for the challenges of raising children today. Families play a crucial role in the health, education, and general well-being of children. But families do not function in isolation. They need an appropriate social environment to be successful. Every child needs a supportive social network, the family's ability to earn a living, a firm sense of community and belonging. Yet just as the family unit has evolved, creating both more opportunity and risk for a child, so have societal trends created new barriers to healthy development. Before we can turn to solutions, we need to understand some of the main social risk factors that make modern children vulnerable to becoming casualties of the newly evolving world.

POVERTY

Bureau of the Census figures indicate that in 1988, about one-fifth of children under eighteen lived below the poverty line. These thirteen million children represent two-fifths of all poor people in the United States. They and the adults in their households made up more than two-thirds of the poor. It is a sad fact that the poor in America are largely women and children, and the situation is worsening. The poverty rate among preschool children was higher at the end of the eighties than it had been for a quarter-century. In the United States there is a widening gap between rich and poor. The ranks of the poor are growing and the middle class is shrinking.

When social class is comparable, there are no differences between blacks and whites in divorce rates, proportion of births to unmarried mothers, proportions of children living in female-headed families, and proportions of women working outside the home. However, since poverty rates are far higher for blacks than for whites,[1] among blacks there are far higher percentages of such family problems. As a result, marital and family experiences for whites and blacks have sharply diverged over the past thirty years, and today major differences exist between the two groups.

In later chapters I will examine how these new realities of economic and family factors translate into risks for children, especially during the first few years of life. Fred Hechinger, the distinguished education writer of *The New York Times*, gives a cogent summary of some of the important issues.

[1] In 1986, the poverty rate for blacks was 31 percent; for whites, 11 percent. The poverty of black children is even more severe. In 1985, 44 percent of black children lived in poor households, as compared to 16 percent of white children. These figures include all family-assistance benefits and other government transfers. In 1985, 75 percent of black children living in poverty were in female-headed households, while 42 percent of white children living in poverty were in such households.

Mother, in increasing numbers of families, is not at home during much of the day; she is out and at work. In 1984, 48 percent of women with infants under one year old were in the labor force, and there were over twenty million children under 13 years of age with working mothers, including nine million under age six. It therefore is no longer a question whether it is better for children in their early years to be tended by their mothers; it is simply a fact that about half of all mothers with small children work. In the years ahead, that number will grow. Modern economics makes this inevitable, not only for single mothers but for old-fashioned families as well.

These simple facts illustrate the need for new arrangements to care for children in their early years. This includes simple child care and what has come to be known as early childhood education.

What has put the spotlight on those new needs is the plight of poor children. Their neglect has long been sending them to school with serious deficits in cognitive skills and in social behavior. They have grown up in a generally nonverbal and often illiterate environment. Their homes are devoid of books, of art, of adults who speak to them, encourage them to ask questions, and answer when questions are asked. While those deficits are most devastating for children of the poor, they are of increasing concern also for children of affluent families. Frequently, the television set becomes the baby-sitter, leaving youngsters inactive and exposed to an unmonitored impact of a medium that, with rare exceptions, presents intellectual fare that is unsuitable for children, and often downright harmful.

The labor market does not provide an adequate supply of literate substitutes for mothers: children are often left to the care of only marginally literate women who may speak little English. In many day-care centers, similarly inadequate persons are hired. This amounts at best to safe storage; it is hardly an adequate substitute for old-fashioned home care.

RISKS FOR EDUCATIONAL UNDERACHIEVEMENT AND FAILURE IN SCHOOL

Today, high standards of literacy and numeracy are necessary for most jobs. They are also essential to authentic citizenship in a modern, complex, democratic society. Moreover, the standards of literacy, quantitative skills, and scientific thinking required for the most desirable jobs will rise further in the foreseeable future. Yet low-income and minority students are disproportionately unlikely to achieve even the minimal standards of education necessary today, let alone the higher standards of skills and knowledge essential to attain mainstream opportunities in the next century.

We have made considerable progress in the past twenty years both in giving minority children greater access to education and in raising their achievement as reflected by standardized tests. Black students now attend desegregated schools throughout the American South and in many northern communities. They now graduate from high school at almost the same rate as whites, far above the negligible black graduation rate in 1944, when Gunnar Myrdal's *An American Dilemma* was published. Significant gains were made from 1960 to 1980: Young black people were attending college in proportions not greatly below those of whites and they entered a wider range of colleges than they did in the past. Nevertheless, these gains are fragile. Entry of blacks into higher education has steadily diminished with the severe student-aid cutbacks of the eighties. Blacks' college-graduation rates continue to be far below those of whites. Despite much progress, we have a long way to go before the educational potential of black Americans is fully realized. The picture is similar for other disadvantaged minorities.

There are deep concerns about the education of non-English-speaking students, the majority of whom are Hispanic. It is only within the past few years that data sources have begun to report information separately for Hispanics. Since doing so, they have alerted us to the fact that the high-school dropout rate for Hispanic students seems to be the highest among all the minority groups.

Fourteen percent of all seventeen-year-olds in the United States can be considered functionally illiterate, and functional-illiteracy rates among minority students are well above that level. Such illiteracy means that individuals cannot read and understand material of practical significance in everyday life. This virtually rules out any but the most unskilled jobs in a modern economy. Literacy is equally important for young women and for young men today, since increasing numbers of families are supported by women only. Children who fail to learn to read or compute, or who are far behind in reading level, are at high risk not only of dropping out of school but also of falling victim to a whole range of serious adolescent problems.

Each year about 700,000 students drop out of school. About 25 percent of all American eighteen- and nineteen-year-olds have not graduated from high school. Blacks, Hispanics, and Native Americans are twice as likely as whites to fail to graduate from high school.

For some inner-city schools, dropout rates have been estimated to be from 30 to 50 percent. The costs of dropping out of school amount to many billions per year in lost tax revenues, welfare, unemployment compensation, and crime-related matters. Students at high risk of dropping out generally have low self-esteem, stressful home situations, harsh economic realities, a fatalistic outlook, and very little hope for their future. A number of these youngsters drift into the illegal economy. A very high percentage of incarcerated youth are illiterate or seriously educationally handicapped.

Major studies and commission reports during the eighties have documented significant problems in the underpinnings of education. These problems begin in children's earliest years. Teachers often report that children from very poor and socially depreciated communities are unprepared for the demands of school even in kindergarten and first grade. The attention spans of such children are relatively short, their verbal fluency is not well developed, and they lack basic skills. They frequently also lack social skills, are emotionally troubled, and may be listless, hyperactive, or aggressive. Very early on, they are likely to be labeled slow learners and/or behavior problems. Each year of school, they lose ground. They become predisposed to various kinds of failure in school. By the third grade, many of them are unprepared for the science education that could equip them for even moderately skilled technical occupations later in life.

There is disturbing evidence that most American children are not, in fact, receiving an adequate math and science education. The great majority of secondary-school students stop science and mathematics early, learn less, and do worse on their exams than their predecessors did and worse than do students in other industrial countries. There is general agreement that both the number and the quality of mathematics and science teachers have declined. Serious questions are being raised about the adequacy of the present curricula in mathematics and science at all levels. Girls and minorities are often discouraged from pursuing these subjects, victims of myths that they will not be interested in or cannot learn science. Many inner-city secondary schools do not even offer courses in higher math and hard sciences.

RISKS AND PROBLEMS IN HEALTH AND DEVELOPMENT

When we compare our record in health with those of other highly developed nations, we simply do not measure up. Our record is worst in health measures for infants, adolescents, and the disadvantaged. In terms of our own potential, there are glaring inequities in the availability of health care and in health outcomes for differing sectors of our population. The parallels between health and education are not surprising, because these realms are deeply intertwined. Good health is an important underpinning of cognitive development and ability to learn. Educational level has been shown to have a strong and independent effect on the health of individuals and, when they become parents, on the health of their children. Significant gains in either health or education cannot be made without concern for the other.

Today, the most prevalent health problems can be traced to family, environmental, and behavioral roots. This current burden of illness has been termed "the new morbidity" by Dr. Robert Haggerty, president of the W. T. Grant Foundation. In infancy, these problems include infant mortality, low birthweight, neonatal AIDS, fetal alcohol syndrome, and neurological problems of babies born to drug-addicted mothers. In childhood, the leading cause of death is accidents and other injuries. These poisonings, falls, fires, and other traumas are mainly the toll from living with unsafe conditions such as unrepaired buildings, faulty household wiring, defective appliances, lack of window guards, and dangerous litter on sidewalks and yards. Infants also bear the burden of preventable illness. They fall prey to the effects of malnutrition, lead toxicity, respiratory illness such as asthma, frequent ear infections, learning disorders, and conquerable childhood diseases against which they have not been immunized. Among adolescents, the leading causes of death are suicide, homicide, and accidents. Adolescents also face the heavy burden of illness due to nonfatal injury, substance abuse, teenage pregnancy, sexually transmitted diseases, AIDS, mental disorders (especially depression), and the consequences of violence (chiefly stabbings and gunshot wounds).

At all ages, there has been a sharp increase in childhood chronic disease that often represents a paradox of success. We now have the technology to save extremely low-birthweight babies—some less than 1,000 grams. However, many will emerge from their stint in the neonatal intensive-care nurseries with blindness, lung damage, or brain pathology. Another paradox of success is represented by children whose organs have been transplanted but who must be maintained on powerful immunosuppressive drugs that often can stunt their growth and are likely to damage liver or kidneys.

Most American children grow up enjoying vigorous, healthy growth and development. These are the children who have the benefits of quality health care during their mother's pregnancy and throughout their childhood. For a great many other children there is no ready access to quality care. About 35 million Americans have no public or private health insurance or any kind for themselves or for their children. These uninsured are usually the working poor. They work in part-time or low-level jobs that do not provide health coverage.

Many of the nation's poorest children are insured by Medicaid. This insurance has improved health and made a difference since it was instituted in the mid-sixties. However, it has serious flaws. The physician's reimbursement rates are so low that many doctors refuse to take Medicaid patients. For example, today it is virtually impossible for many pregnant women on Medicaid to find an obstetrician willing to take care of them. Medicaid patients receive their care chiefly in the emergency rooms and in clinics of public and voluntary hospitals. There is no continuity of care as there would be with a private physician. Because of problems of access, many patients delay seeking care for themselves or their children until their disorders have reached an advanced stage, when treatment is more difficult and outcomes are less favorable.

Poor children are at higher risk of death, disease, disability, and injury than are economically advantaged children. They have more frequent and more serious health problems. Children living in poverty-concentration areas are born and raised in families with formidable vulnerabilities that increase the risk of health problems for these children even before they are born. These are the children at highest risk for low birthweight, neonatal damage (becoming apparent right after birth), malnutrition, untreated childhood illness, uncorrected early problems of hearing and vision, accidents, and physical abuse. Moreover, these children are exposed to an extraordinarily high degree of stress and violence in their social environment on a continuing, long-term basis. They grow up in disorganized and very poor neighborhoods, often with socially isolated, very young, and very poor mothers—all too often without fathers and with minimal support from other family members or friends. Many of their very early developmental or health problems go unrecognized at home.

For all these reasons, poverty is a profound and pervasive exacerbator of illness and disability. For example, children who are not poor are likely to receive early and effective treatment and recover completely from the middle-ear infections that affect almost all children. Poor children are likely to suffer a great many more of these infections, to receive incomplete treatment or no treatment at all for them, and as a result to suffer hearing loss that can cause major problems at home and in school. Similarly, poor children with vision problems are less likely to receive proper corrective eyeglasses and therefore more likely to have learning problems at school.

Lead in the environment provides another clear example of a health risk that burdens the poor disproportionately. All children are exposed to some lead in the environment, but the urban poor have an even greater exposure, for several reasons. They live in buildings with old and peeling paint, have lead in their drinking water because of old, faulty plumbing, and are more likely to live near highways or industrial plants where the air and soil are contaminated with lead from auto exhaust and industrial pollution. Four percent of all children have unacceptable levels of lead in their blood, but among American blacks, mainly the urban poor, the figure is 12 percent. Frank poisoning with very high doses of lead is extraordinarily damaging, but even modest elevations of lead in the body tend to affect the brain and cause hyperactivity, attention problems, and poor learning. New research shows that early exposure to such lead levels produces continuing long-term effects on behavior, including measured intelligence. Research evidence confirms that when children develop learning problems as a result of lead exposure, treatment of the lead poisoning improves their school performance. Preventive measures include lead screening to detect individuals in need of treatment, followed up by environmental controls, particularly of paints and air pollution.

CHILD ABUSE

Research documents that children who grow up in disturbed family environments where substance abuse as well as serious and continuing conflicts are rampant, where one or both parents are frequently absentees, or where the parents suffer from psychiatric disorders, are very likely to have difficulty with interpersonal relations and other social behavior. Even though as a group these children suffer from only slightly impaired measured intelligence, their actual difficulties in education are much greater than their intellectual capacity would suggest. Michael Rutter, a professor of child psychiatry at the University of London, has studied family influences in relation to children's mental health. He found that family discord and disturbance, even in the absence of overt child abuse, adversely affect children's school performance. This is primarily due to impacts on children's social, emotional, and behavioral functioning rather than to poor cognitive development or impaired learning ability.

Each year in the United States more than a million children are seriously abused by their parents and others; several thousand die as a result of their injuries. Violence against children is not a new phenomenon, but until recently it was not identified as a major problem. And it has worsened in recent decades. The signs of physical injury from abuse are distinctive: blows to the head or body, bite marks, and scalding or cigarette burns. There is characteristic X-ray evidence of new healing and old bone fractures that does not occur in any other condition. The term "child abuse" is often used in a broader sense to refer to virulent emotional abuse that does not necessarily include a physical component. Sometimes the term may include serious neglect as well.

Although child abuse is by no means limited to children growing up in poor and disintegrated communities, it does tend to be heavily concentrated and to be more readily observed and reported there. Physical abuse is likely to happen to children living in severe poverty and social deprivation, when caretakers lack ties to others, have weak or absent religious norms, or are very immature and inexperienced parents who are easily and seriously frustrated. Well-documented risk factors include living in very crowded and disorganized urban communities; the presence of four or more very young children in the household; a highly authoritarian parent; the presence of only one parent in the household; frequent changes in the place of residence; a violent environment; and a history, in one or both parents, of having been similarly abused during childhood. Parents who use drugs are at risk of becoming abusers; alcoholics appear to be the worst offenders. Parents who have continuing, multiple stresses or who suffer severe rejection or loss of self-esteem

—e.g., after losing a job—also are susceptible to abusing their children. The absence of a lifeline into a supportive group during the crisis is an important factor.

Consequences of abuse are observable in the first few years of life. Research on toddlers between one and three years old in day-care centers specifically designed for abused children demonstrates that these children were less likely to approach adult caregivers, more likely to be aggressive to adults, and more likely to respond in wary, suspicious ways to friendly approaches made by either peers or adults. The child who has been abused early in life lacks the underpinnings for positive expectations about relationships with other people and will behave in a way that tends to discourage new, positive ties to adults and to constrict opportunities. In contrast, the child who has a secure attachment very early in life is more likely to make constructive social and physical contact with the widening world.

In summary, almost every form of childhood damage is far more prevalent among the poor—from increased infant mortality, gross malnutrition, recurrent and untreated health problems, and child abuse in the early years, to educational disability, low achievement, delinquency, early pregnancy, alcohol and drug abuse, and failure to become economically self-sufficient. Still, adequate income and high social status provide no guarantee of healthy development. Alcohol and drug abuse, accidents, child neglect, and a host of health problems as well as educational difficulties are plentiful in middle-class and highly privileged populations. The problems addressed here truly affect all our children everywhere. Growing up in the very modern world is in some ways easier but in other ways much harder than it was in the past.

In health, education, and the social environment, we humans have been doing a lot of damage to our children—inadvertently for the most part, and with great regret—but serious damage nonetheless. Yet there is good reason for hope. This book calls attention to what we can do in the near future to prevent much of the damage now being done, and to promising lines of inquiry and innovation that could diminish the casualties still further in decades ahead.

SECTION II

PREVENTING DAMAGE IN THE FIRST FEW YEARS OF LIFE

3

Stopping the Damage Before It Starts: Better Prenatal Care

PRENATAL CARE MEANS HEALTHIER BABIES

The infant mortality rate is widely recognized as an indicator of how advanced and humane a society is. As I've stated earlier, in recent years the United States has ranked no better than twentieth in the world, well behind comparable industrialized nations such as Japan and the Western European democracies. Within the United States, the burden of this excessive infant mortality is not evenly spread. Some may take comfort in the fact that in affluent American communities, infant mortality rates are among the world's lowest. But this is more than offset by tragically high rates of infant death and disease in our poor communities, which affect poor white, African-American, Hispanic, and Native American populations disproportionately. In some areas, the infant mortality rate begins to approach those of poor developing countries in Asia, Africa, and Latin America. Infant mortality rates are, in any event, the tip of the iceberg. What lies just beneath the surface is a huge continuum of casualties in early life, many with lifelong consequences: disease, disability, behavioral disturbance, and educational failure.

Good prenatal care dramatically improves the chances of a

woman bearing a healthy baby; mothers who do not have access to it suffer higher rates of infant mortality or give birth to premature, low-birthweight babies. Black American women, who generally receive far less prenatal care than white women, experience almost 20 infant deaths per 1,000 births—double the rate for whites.

Eleven percent of American schoolchildren are classified as handicapped. A recent study estimates that one-third of these children would have a lesser handicap or none at all if their mothers had had early and adequate prenatal care. Many other examples make it clear that prenatal care is a prime opportunity for action to protect against a wide range of serious disorders, including some genetic diseases.

The report of the National Commission to Prevent Infant Mortality, *Death Before Life: The Tragedy of Infant Mortality*, makes a central and crucial recommendation: Women need universal access to prenatal and infant care. Every pregnant woman should be presumed to be eligible for and promptly receive health care. Since prenatal care is especially critical in the first few weeks after conception, it should not be withheld until the mother's qualification for the program is established; everyone must be presumed qualified, with payment to be arranged later. The report also recommends removing other barriers to care, especially bureaucratic obstacles. Moreover, it recommends aggressive outreach to bring in women who would otherwise be likely to miss this important opportunity.

Reports from the congressional Office of Technology Assessment and the National Academy of Sciences provide overwhelming evidence that preventing low birthweight can markedly reduce infant mortality. Full-term infants weighing 5.5 pounds or less (the cutoff point for low birthweight) are almost forty times more likely to die in the first four weeks of life than infants of normal birthweight (about seven pounds). In addition, low-birthweight babies are at increased risk for health problems ranging from neurological handicaps to breathing problems. Full-term, low-birthweight babies and premature babies face equally high potential for central nervous system damage and dysfunction, including cerebral palsy and seizures.

As continuing data are collected on surviving children who were born at very low weight (below 2.2 lbs)—who can increasingly be kept alive by highly intensive, sophisticated medical management—there are signs that such children manifest more subtle central nervous system damage in terms of cognitive deficits, learning problems, and other behavioral disorders, even among babies with otherwise good outcomes. Moreover, low birthweight is a predictor of school failure, especially for babies small for their gestational age. Thus, being born at term and of sufficient weight are foundations for healthy, normal development; and high-quality prenatal care is an effective measure to prevent babies from being born too soon or too small.

Yet, in spite of the fact that the total cost of good prenatal care is much less than $1,000 per pregnant woman and that intensive care for a premature or small-for-age baby costs at least $1,000 a day for many days or weeks (often a total cost of $100,000), huge numbers of women never receive adequate prenatal care.

HOW PRENATAL CARE COUNTERACTS RISKS OF PREGNANCY

A recent National Institutes of Health (NIH) report on prenatal care, prepared for the Public Health Service, goes far beyond the traditional medical concerns of preventing the sickness and death of mother and baby, to include the promotion of healthy child development, positive family relationships, and family planning. The report identifies four major components of adequate prenatal care:

1. Early and continuing risk assessment
2. Health education and promotion
3. Medical and psychosocial support
4. Follow-up

Risk assessment includes a complete medical history on the expectant mother; a physical examination; laboratory tests; and assessment of the fetus's growth and well-being. It is essential that this risk assessment continue throughout the woman's pregnancy, because her risk status may change. The specific content and timing of prenatal care should depend on the risk status of the woman and her fetus. Health education and promotion includes information about family planning, counseling to support healthy behaviors, and general information about pregnancy and parenting. Interventions include treating the woman's illness, steering her behavior in healthy directions, providing her with opportunities for essential social and financial resources, and referring her to specialists as needed.

Risk Assessment

The NIH report defines risk to include both psychosocial and medical risks. Much of the data collection standard in prenatal care is designed to identify only medical risk factors, e.g., components of blood and urine, weight gain, and so on. A pregnant woman's psychosocial risk factors are equally important. They include social factors, psychological factors, and unhealthy behaviors. Social risk factors include inadequate housing, low income, low education, working in a physically strenuous or chemically toxic environment, being single, having inadequate nutritional resources, and being under age eighteen or over thirty-five. Psychological risk factors include inadequate personal support systems and coping mechanisms, excessive ambivalence about pregnancy, high stress and anxiety, living in an abusive situation, and behavioral or mental disorders. Unhealthy behaviors include smoking, use of drugs and alcohol, poor nutrition, and excessive or inadequate exercise. Some risks are population-specific. For example, the risk of sexually transmitted diseases is associated with being young and unmarried and living in a high-prevalence area. In every high-risk situation, the NIH panel recommends that the expectant mother receive more frequent screening.

Generally, a risk-responsive approach means the expectant mother needs to make more visits early in her pregnancy to identify her needs and take the necessary preventive steps. Prenatal-care providers who regularly serve women at psychosocial risk should have a core set of services available within their practices. These services should help women at risk receive early prenatal care, build positive relationships with their health-care providers, and use outreach visitor programs if necessary to motivate the mother and to facilitate assessment of the family's home environment. The provider's schedule should meet the high-risk woman's needs, offering evening or weekend hours if necessary.

In addition to providing traditional medical care, a team serving women at psychosocial risk should have basic expertise in social work, public-health nursing, nutrition, and psychological and health-education skills. Core services in a psychosocial risk program should include home visits, which have been shown to be effective in promoting many of the objectives of prenatal care; case management; and services to facilitate access to care, including assistance in financing, transportation, and child care. Later in the chapter, I'll discuss programs that implement these services.

Health Education and Promotion

Early detection of pregnancy—a simple, inexpensive procedure—is the first step in prenatal care. Most of a fetus's organ development takes place in the first eight weeks after conception. This is a time when drugs or other toxic substances can cause irreversible damage to the development of the central nervous and musculoskeletal systems and that of the reproductive tract. It is also a time when many women, particularly very young mothers, may not know they are pregnant. If they suffer discomfort, nausea, or vomiting, as is often the case early in pregnancy, they may respond inappropriately—perhaps by taking medicine to control the symptoms—especially if they are unaware of the pregnancy. If they know they are pregnant and are informed about risks to the fetus, they are more likely to avoid alcohol and other drugs and to eat properly and drink enough water.

Recent studies show that 30 percent of blacks and 15 percent of whites in America are malnourished in a variety of ways. This problem has many ramifications. Dietary habits of many poor women, migrants, and refugees cause iron-deficiency anemia, with resulting adverse effects on both mother and child. Malnutrition caused by insufficient protein and calorie intake also poses a serious threat to the unborn child. We can prevent both deficiencies by educating expectant mothers and providing them with nutritional supplementation and primary health care. This integrated approach has been demonstrated to work for millions of people who participated in the Special Supplemental Food Program for Women, Infants, and Children (WIC) and in school-based meal programs.

The damaging effects on the developing baby of smoking cigarettes, drinking alcohol, and taking many drugs (illicit or over-the-counter) have been amply documented. Women with little formal education tend to be the heaviest smokers. Carefully designed studies have demonstrated that when an expectant mother cuts back or stops smoking during pregnancy, she improves the birthweight of her infant and its chances for survival. Therefore all prenatal programs need to help expectant mothers stop smoking (and other substance abuse) by providing them with information, support, practical guidance, and behavioral strategies. In one study, the mothers who received such help delivered over 25 percent fewer low-birthweight babies than smokers did. In view of the rising number of women smokers and the efficacy of newer programs to stop smoking, efforts are under way to enlist medical practitioners in antismoking activities as an important part of routine obstetrical care.

About one-quarter of pregnant women are smoking at the time of their first prenatal visit; evidence is good that efforts during pregnancy to encourage women to stop smoking can be highly effective. Health-care providers can also tackle the problems of alcohol and drug use by identifying women at increased risk of substance use and counseling them to avoid drugs and the risk of AIDS. When expectant women face occupational and environmental risks, the prenatal-care provider should define the problem and counsel them accordingly.

The NIH panel does not recommend changing the basic pattern of services between a woman and her prenatal-care provider, although some providers will have to be more flexible in the scheduling of their hours and the content of their programs to accommodate risk assessment and to incorporate a strong emphasis on preconception care—including family planning. The panel's recommendations are within the capability of many existing practices and clinics.

While many pregnant women have scant knowledge about their own health, they are highly motivated to understand aspects of physiology, nutrition, exercise, and stress in relation to their own health and that of the developing fetus. Prospective parents should also be made aware of serious hazards in the home, work, and environment that can affect the pregnancy. Pregnancy may well provide the best opportunity of a lifetime for women to learn about their own health in order to protect it.

A commitment to care before conception means a commitment to the health of all women in their reproductive years who might at any time become pregnant. In particular, this means we have to target more education to early adolescents, who are often sexually active and become pregnant, so often without anything remotely resembling adequate preparation. Adolescents can be taught parenting, as well as pregnancy prevention, well before pregnancy makes becoming a parent inevitable. Parenting education in high schools, or even junior high and middle schools, might well be beneficial for many adolescents. Later, we will see how the middle-grade schools can provide a useful vehicle for this and other health-related purposes: life sciences, life skills, social supports.

Ideally, the educational component of prenatal care can embrace issues beyond the birth of a healthy baby. For women at highest risk—those who are poor, uneducated, or very young—the birth of a baby may provide the impetus for other life changes. Most parents feel a strong desire to do well for their children. That inclination can lead to job training, formal schooling, or other education likely to improve the prospects of the mother and her new family. In the long run, these improvements can benefit later children and perhaps even grandchildren.

Psychosocial Support

For many women, particularly those at high risk for socioeconomic reasons, medical care and education are not enough. Women who are poor, who are victims of domestic violence or psychiatric illness, who are overstressed and anxious, or who are not prepared for parenthood may require social support—a network of personal contacts through which they can receive emotional support, material aid and services, information, and new contacts. It is pointless to teach a woman about nutrition if she does not have any money or access to food.

Social intervention is crucial in the inner cities, where pregnant women may be poor, homeless, unemployed, hungry, drug-dependent, or victims of violence. These women, who are inherently at high risk for delivering unhealthy babies, often require much social support in order to have a healthy baby who grows into a healthy child. Any form of health education can be undermined without the social support necessary to sustain a mother's hope and help her acquire relevant skills.

Any prenatal program must have as one goal the development of the expectant mother's self-esteem. High self-esteem can make all the difference in the young parent's inclination and ability to take full advantage of other aspects of prenatal care. If we can teach the expectant mother that pregnancy can be a positive turning point, we can help her build a sense of self-esteem through earned respect that can sustain two generations: parent and child.

PRENATAL CARE IS USEFUL ONLY TO THOSE WHO GET IT

Study after study in recent years has piled up disturbing evidence about the extent to which American women miss the opportunity that excellent prenatal care can provide. Two major studies, the Alan Guttmacher Institute (AGI) report published in 1989 and the Institute of Medicine (IoM) report, *Prenatal Care: Reaching Mothers, Reaching Infants*, published in 1988, reveal some alarming facts about the numbers of pregnant women who don't receive adequate prenatal care:

- Blacks and Hispanics are much more likely than whites to obtain late or no care. In the eighties, approximately 40 percent of black women and 20 percent of white women received no prenatal care in the first trimester. Twenty-seven percent of all black mothers and 30 percent of all Hispanic mothers obtain inadequate care.
- Young mothers, especially those under fifteen, are likely to obtain late or no care. Fifty percent of black women under age twenty received no early prenatal care and 15 percent received care only in the last trimester—if at all.
- In 1985, 88 percent of mothers with at least some college education began care early, compared with only 58 percent of mothers who had not completed high school. So here as elsewhere, education matters.
- Unmarried mothers are almost four times as likely as married mothers to obtain late or no care.
- Low income, residence in an inner city, and residence in an isolated rural area are all associated with less adequate care.

The IoM report identifies several primary barriers to obtaining adequate prenatal care: financial barriers; inadequate system capacity; problems in the organization, practice, or atmosphere of services; and cultural and personal factors. Let us consider these in turn.

Pregnant women and obstetricians cite financial barriers as the most important obstacle to adequate care. Many areas have few obstetricians. Moreover, because of low Medicaid reimbursement rates and fears about malpractice suits, many physicians accept only patients with private insurance. Thus, excess capacity for affluent women can exist in the same area where there is inadequate capacity for low-income women and where clinics are overcrowded.

For women who are not privately insured, individual payment becomes a government policy issue. It is poor women who are at highest risk and most in need of early prenatal care. In the United States, many insurance companies do not pay for any aspects of prenatal care that are not deemed medically necessary by a narrow definition or that are not provided by an obstetrician. For many women, then, there are meager resources to cover the essential nonmedical aspects of prenatal care, particularly the educational components, which are beneficial for women at any risk level. Adequate funding is critical both to implementing the expanded components of care and to ensuring access to care for all women.

The federal and state Medicaid program, which provides health services for poor people, poses additional problems beyond payment for specific services. The bureaucratic process required for Medicaid eligibility is an important barrier to prenatal care for many poor women. It often takes weeks and repeated trips to the Medicaid office to be declared eligible and receive a card. Some states have tried to overcome this obstacle. In Massachusetts, for example, a program of presumptive eligibility has been established; women automatically receive care regardless of their means of payment, and the state is the payer of last resort. Nonetheless, the problem remains of finding a physician who will accept Medicaid patients. One way to encourage physicians to accept Medicaid patients would be to increase reimbursement to the level paid by private insurance companies.

Solving the funding problem would help with the related issues of personnel and necessary facilities. To do so, policymakers must understand that improving access to enriched prenatal care is cost-effective in terms of the long-term medical and socioeconomic costs of unhealthy babies who do not develop their full potential as adults.

The IoM report cites a plethora of problems in the delivery of services. These include poor links among institutions such as health-department clinics, private physicians, and welfare, housing, and social services; bureaucratic procedures in Medicaid enrollment; transportation and child-care problems; long waits and inconvenient hours at clinics; communication problems between providers and clients, which can be aggravated by language and cultural barriers; unpleasant surroundings; and lack of easily accessible information about where to go to obtain care.

Women's attitudes and beliefs shape their use of prenatal care. Women who plan and feel positive about their pregnancies are more likely to obtain adequate care, as are women who believe prenatal care is important. Fear of medical providers, fear of others' reactions to the pregnancy, and fear of the discovery of one's illegal residence in this country can all keep women from seeking prenatal care. In addition, some women avoid prenatal care because they fear disapproval for their smoking or drug use.

The 1988 IoM study examined programs to promote *early entry* and *continued participation* in prenatal care. It found that most programs have no funds earmarked to evaluate their effectiveness and that services take priority over evaluation when unrestricted funds are allocated. The evaluations that are made rarely take into account the differences between women who choose to participate in a program and women who do not.

Nevertheless, there is sufficient evidence and experience to conclude that various kinds of programs can succeed in bringing women into prenatal care early and maintaining their participation. Success is often modest, however, because good programs that work are a rarity in a complicated, fragmented nonsystem of maternity services crippled by pervasive financial and institutional obstacles to care.

Programs That Work

The IoM study categorized programs to improve the use of prenatal care into five types corresponding roughly to how the programs attacked existing barriers:

1. Programs that reduce financial obstacles for poor women
2. Programs that increase the capacity of the prenatal-care system relied upon by poor women
3. Programs that improve institutional practices to make services more accessible
4. Programs that emphasize finding and identifying women in need of prenatal care
5. Programs that provide social support to encourage women to continue in prenatal care, increasing their chances for a healthy pregnancy and a smooth transition to parenthood

Let us consider some of the more successful programs here.

Programs to Remove Financial Barriers

Although financial barriers are a major reason why women do not seek prenatal care early or complete the recommended number of visits, the IoM committee found few programs that address financial barriers directly. Federal action had been very limited until the expansion of Medicaid in the late eighties.

The Healthy Start program in Massachusetts, initiated in December 1985, illustrates an innovation in the field. This statewide program offers financing for a full range of maternity services for uninsured pregnant women not on Medicaid who have incomes below 185 percent of the poverty line. (This limit was later raised to 200 percent of the poverty line.) Because the staff believes it is important that participants can choose their own provider, the program emphasizes expanding the number of providers, including ones in private practice, from whom low-income pregnant women can receive services. The staff makes referrals upon request, and the registration process for providers and participants is simple. Women can complete an application at home and mail it in, so they never have to visit a public agency. Physicians and community health centers are reimbursed at the Medicaid rate, hospitals at the non-Medicaid public-assistance rate.

A preliminary evaluation found success in enrolling both providers and participants. As of February 1988, all of Massachusetts' two thousand hospital-based physicians and nurse-midwives, including 476 obstetricians, some of them not Medicaid-certified, had enrolled. About 85 percent of eligible women had enrolled. Participation was particularly high among minorities, teenagers, unmarried women, and those with less than a high-school education. A comparison between Healthy Start participants and women insured under other programs or not insured at all suggested that the program was more successful in maintaining participation than in encouraging early entry into care. Program participants generally had good pregnancies and delivered healthy babies. The evaluators attributed the success of the program to its emphasis on continuity and content of care, links with other health services and social services, and the reduction of stress on the mother from financial worries. It remains to be seen whether the state will sustain adequate support for this program on an enduring basis.

Programs to Increase Capacity and Improve Practices

We can increase the capacity of the system for pregnant women by expanding clinic facilities, opening new facilities, or paying private providers to care for uninsured women. Because it is not always possible to enlist the full cooperation and assistance of the private sector, most capacity expansion is accomplished through publicly financed facilities staffed by nurse-practitioners and certified nurse-midwives, who work well with low-income, high-risk clients and are less expensive than physicians. (It is difficult to find physicians to work with low-income women, partly because there is considerable fear of malpractice liability.)

We can make it easier for pregnant women to use these facilities, once they find them, by expediting registration procedures, providing interpreters, shortening waiting time, offering child care and transportation, and monitoring staff courtesy. For example, expediting the method of determining Medicaid eligibility at Columbia Presbyterian Medical Center in New York was very effective in overcoming bureaucratic obstacles. Unfortunately, most programs do not take this self-examination to heart.

Casefinding to Increase Participation in Prenatal Care

Casefinding, the process of identifying potential program participants, encompasses a range of activities. The most labor-intensive approach puts outreach workers on the streets and in housing projects, schools, and welfare offices to seek out pregnant women to enroll in prenatal-care programs. The next most labor-intensive approach is the telephone hot line, whereby workers dispense information and help pregnant women to obtain prenatal-care appointments. The less labor-intensive approaches include soliciting referrals from other agencies; incentive programs, such as public baby showers or cash or gifts for keeping appointments; and public-information efforts. It is difficult to make such initiatives effective given the inhospitable and bureaucratic health-care system we have today, but they are crucial if we are to reduce casualties among very young, poor, socially marginal women and their children.

Several outreach programs have been especially successful. The Better Babies Project, attempting to reduce the rate of low birthweight in an area of Washington, D.C., began in 1986 and ran for several years. It used several methods to locate and enroll pregnant women: radio announcements, stopping people on the street, knocking on doors, visiting local businesses, recruiting in the waiting rooms of public and private clinics, and soliciting referrals from local social-service agencies. (Telephone canvassing was found to be unproductive.) Once enrolled, pregnant women were linked to prenatal-care services, their risks were assessed, and they received individual treatment plans. Most enrollees were in monthly or weekly contact with the program; they received $10 per month if they kept all their appointments.

The Pregnancy Healthline in New York City is an ongoing project of the city's health department. The Healthline is staffed during weekday office hours; at other times callers can leave a number at which their call can be returned. The Healthline's staff are all female, with education ranging from a high school degree through master's training. All the staff are trained in women's health issues. During the call, Healthline staff can schedule prenatal-care appointments. Over seventy facilities provide blocks of time for Healthline referrals. Staff contact these facilities weekly to transfer appointment information and to check on appointments. They try to contact women who miss appointments and help them overcome obstacles. The Healthline is advertised through a variety of techniques, including mass media advertisements, subway posters, and mailings with welfare checks. Sociodemographically, callers are at high risk for inadequate prenatal care: 16 percent were under eighteen, and 76 percent were uninsured. In the most recent nine months for which data have been analyzed, the Healthline received twenty thousand calls.

The Special Supplemental Food Program for Women, Infants, and Children requires local agencies to check whether pregnant participants are receiving medical care and refer them if they are not. Several studies have found that women who participated in WIC were more likely to get adequate prenatal care than those who did not.

Programs That Add Social Support and Education to Medical Care

There are numerous examples of programs offering enriched prenatal services, although we know that many low-income women do not receive even adequate traditional medical care during pregnancy. Most of the enriched programs depend on specialized and often short-term funds. Routine, reliable funding for such care is very limited. Many programs appear to work around, rather than with, the medical system. Yet some exemplify effective cooperation of medical and other components. Helping women overcome obstacles to obtaining medical services is one major task for these programs. It is entirely appropriate for people other than doctors to provide services such as parenting education or nutrition education, but greater appreciation on the part of physicians for the importance of such services, and better coordination among medical and nonmedical service providers, would surely be beneficial. The Perinatal Positive Parenting program at Michigan State University (described later) is a rare example of this kind of cooperation.

Programs that provide social support typically use workers who communicate empathically with pregnant women and their partners; educate them about prenatal care, labor, delivery, and parenthood; provide referrals and follow-up; and act as advocates. These functions may be called social support, case management, patient counseling, case coordination, or home visiting. The workers may be trained social workers, public-health nurses, neighborhood residents, or volunteers. Women may receive services in their home, in a prenatal-care or social-service facility, in school, or by telephone. These programs tend to improve pregnancy outcomes by promoting adequate prenatal care, partly by helping women adhere to health instructions and form constructive habits, as well as by reducing their stress. The women at greatest risk for inadequate prenatal care, such as young teenagers and low-income minority women, often require significant social support, and evidence indicates that such programs can indeed encourage pregnant women to make more prenatal visits to their doctors.

The Resource Mothers program, which began operating in 1981 in three counties in South Carolina, is a good example. It serves teenagers under eighteen who are pregnant with their first child. The teens are counseled by "resource mothers" who are all experienced mothers, high school graduates, and residents of the area. The counselors are selected for personal warmth, their success as parents, and knowledge of community resources. They participate in a six-week training course and receive ongoing training and supervision. Each resource mother counsels about thirty-five pregnant teens, who are referred to the service by schools, health departments, doctors, social-service agencies, civic and church groups, and peers.

The resource mothers visit the teenagers during their pregnancy, in the hospital at the time of delivery, and during the first year of a child's life. Resource mothers are encouraged to get to know each young woman and her family well. They make sure the participants keep all doctors' appointments, provide transportation if necessary, and encourage the women to follow medical recommendations. A comparison with similar teenage mothers in other counties suggests that the program participants received better prenatal care than those without resource mothers.

The resource mothers' approach has now been put to use in several other areas. Typically, the counselors are women living in the same neighborhood as the adolescent mother who have raised their own children successfully and can show these young mothers the ropes. These mentors each counsel a small group of young women, in some areas only ten or twelve. The mentors take a serious interest in the adolescent mothers, try to understand them, help them with their programs, and in general provide them with sympathetic, sustained attention as well as gateways to community resources. They also provide the teen mothers with information about infant development and parenting skills, and help them obtain emotional support, health care, social services, and other resources.

The IoM study underscored the particular problems pregnant adolescents face. For example, adolescents often have difficulties using health services designed for older women: Office hours may conflict with school; the facilities may be inaccessible by public transportation; the providers' attitudes may be judgmental and the services unable to educate adolescents adequately. The best services for pregnant teens address these issues by holding separate clinic sessions for adolescents, emphasizing the importance of continuing to see the same provider, holding special group education sessions, providing transportation, or arranging services in schools or at home. Often, these services assign each adolescent participant an individual case manager, relying heavily on referrals from current and former clients. Schools and pregnancy-testing sites are additional sources of referrals.

The Prenatal and Infancy Home Visiting Program in Elmira, New York, which operated from 1978 to the early eighties, was a particularly effective program for adolescents. The program recruited first-time pregnant women under nineteen who were single and of low socioeconomic status. Four hundred enrolled in the program and were assigned randomly to four groups. Counselors visited one group to assess the health of their infants but provided no other services. Counselors visited the second group to monitor the infants and to give the mothers transportation to and from their health-care providers if necessary. Counselors visited the third group during the teens' pregnancies, monitored the infant's health, and provided transportation assistance. The fourth group received all the above services in addition to home visits during the first two years of the child's life. During these home visits, nurses saw the women once every two weeks for one hour or more, with three basic objectives: educating the prospective parents, especially on health and child care; building up the women's informal support networks; and linking them with community systems. The nurses involved the teens' friends and relatives in the visits to create a supportive atmosphere for learning and rearing children.

Women in each of the four groups made the same number of prenatal-care visits, perhaps because prenatal care was readily available in the area. But the women who received visits from nurses were more aware of community services, attended more childbirth classes, received more WIC vouchers, and talked more with service providers and members of their informal network about the stresses of pregnancy and family life. The nurse-visited mothers also reported greater interest by their babies' fathers in the pregnancy, and the men accompanied the women more frequently during labor. More of the women also stopped smoking. Several longer-term measures also indicated that the nurse-visited mothers fared better. Despite the success of this program, it was terminated after funding ran out.

Home-visitor programs tend to be more useful with families whose members are at greater than average risk of developmental and educational problems. Research on home-visitor programs shows that they can increase the use of preventive services; decrease child abuse and neglect, injuries, and hospitalizations for neonatal intensive care; improve the developmental status of children; and improve parents' health habits and parenting skills. Evaluating home-visitor programs is difficult, however, because so many variables are involved, including the quality of program leadership, the adequacy of funding, and the lengthy time frame to determine effectiveness. Still, the research to date is encouraging and I will pursue it in the next chapter.

WHICH PRENATAL PROGRAMS WORK BEST?

The IoM study found that the most successful programs had clearly defined, reasonable goals that could be translated into quantitative measures. Program activities were carefully monitored. There was an adequate planning phase before the program began operating, and community residents and care providers were involved in its design. The news media were used to generate support and to communicate the existence of the effort and its goals. Staff recognized the multiple burdens facing their clients, maintained ties with other social services, and were responsible to needs in their clients' lives that competed with prenatal care. Volunteers were carefully recruited, trained, supervised, and supported.

The Community Infant Program of Colorado, the Parents Too Soon program of Illinois, and the Parents as Teachers program of Missouri are three of the success stories. The Community Infant Program is designed to prevent or modify parents' poor habits during the prenatal period and the first few years of the baby's life. The program encourages mothers to participate as early as the third trimester of pregnancy. Services are provided primarily through home visits by nurses, parent-infant therapists, and trained community volunteers. These home visitors provide instruction in infant care and information on child development and available community resources. The Parents Too Soon program serves pregnant and parenting adolescents and is sponsored by the Ounce of Prevention Fund and the state of Illinois. It uses home visitors to train parents in child care, makes high-quality day care and medical services available to them, and funds pregnancy-prevention programs. The Parents as Teachers program also provides parent education during pregnancy. This program is unusual in that it is open to families at all income levels.

PUBLIC EDUCATION TO SUPPORT PRENATAL CARE

Only a few broad efforts have been mounted to educate the public —adults as well as youngsters—on reproductive health, with special attention to prenatal care. One example is the Mississippi Perinatal Awareness Project.

In 1983, the Mississippi Department of Health initiated a publicity campaign to inform the public about the importance of prenatal care by distributing posters, buttons, and brochures. The program also implemented a statewide toll-free telephone line for information and referrals for maternal-health and child-care needs. Although the original grant has ended, some components of this program are still operating. The focus has shifted, however, from pregnant women to sick infants—a shift that probably reflects the availability of funding. This is one of many exasperating examples of missed opportunities in prevention, partly a function of the perverse incentives throughout our health-care system. We continue to pay for expensive treatment after the damage is done, but fail to fund the preventive interventions that could avoid much of the damage in the first place.

LESSONS FROM THE EUROPEAN EXPERIENCES

For the 1988 IoM study, Professor Arden Miller of the University of North Carolina analyzed prenatal-care outreach programs in several countries abroad. He compared prenatal-care systems in the United States with systems in ten Western European countries whose infant mortality rates are below that of the United States: Belgium, Denmark, France, the former Federal Republic of Germany, Ireland, the Netherlands, Norway, Spain, Switzerland, and the United Kingdom. All of these countries, except the United Kingdom, have lower rates of low birthweight than the United States. Several even have rates of low birthweight below that for United States whites only.

Attracting women to enter care early is not a problem in Europe because many perinatal benefits are contingent on confirming pregnancy and registering with the appropriate official agencies, a procedure that takes place at the first prenatal-care visit. The focus in improving care, therefore, is on women who do not return after their first visit.

The rate of adolescent childbearing is much higher in the United States than in European countries. It appears that the onset of sexual activity does not vary greatly among these countries, but access to contraception and family-planning services, including counseling, is much more readily available in Europe than in the United States. Proportionately more children participate in organized programs of sex education in Europe than in the United States.

The average household income is higher in the United States than in six of the nations studied that have better records of infant survival. Three of these countries—France, Denmark, and Spain—also have income distributions nearly as disparate as those in the United States. These facts suggest that specific, direct approaches to improve pregnancy outcomes are feasible within the United States' present income structure. The recent success of programs in Ireland and Spain also provides compelling evidence on this point.

The United States spends a higher proportion of its GNP on overall health care than do any of the ten European countries. The bulk of health-care spending in the United States, however, is for hospital care and high-technology procedures; only a small fraction is spent for prevention. The predominant health-care provider systems and their means of financing vary greatly among the European countries, but they have all been consistent in pursuing policies to reduce hospitalization except for childbirth. They have also emphasized organized community services with decentralized administration and uniform national standards for preventive measures. Even when private intermediaries participate extensively, the government has removed all barriers to obtaining maternity care. The full range of services around the baby's birth is provided, usually with no or low fees, to women at all socioeconomic levels.

All of the European countries have public-education programs and use the media to inform women about the desirability and availability of prenatal care. These programs are often under the auspices of volunteer organizations. The European countries conduct highly organized programs of education about sexuality and human reproduction in schools.

Midwives are extensively involved in European maternity care. They are usually confined to hospitals and clinics, except in the Netherlands, where they are independent, office-based practitioners, and obstetricians are involved only in complicated pregnancies. In Denmark, midwives are public employees who work out of public offices or clinics. In most of the countries studied, midwives attend uncomplicated deliveries for women who have received routine prenatal care from office-based general practitioners. In Norway, each municipality is required to maintain at least one public multidisciplinary health center. Other countries provide public clinics in selected areas for hard-to-reach populations.

The officially required or recommended number of prenatal visits for an uncomplicated pregnancy varies from four to twelve among these countries. The average number of actual visits closely approximates the guidelines or exceeds them. Instructional classes for pregnant women are offered by volunteer organizations, agencies, and clinics. They are well used but are not standard for prenatal care.

Studies of statistical indicators, policies, and practices in Denmark, Finland, Norway, and Sweden are of special interest because of the excellent results obtained in these nations. Women there have two to three physician visits and ten to twelve nurse or midwife visits during their pregnancy. The attendance rate for prenatal care is practically 100 percent in all these countries, where indices of infant mortality and morbidity are among the lowest in the world.

Home visiting is a feature of nearly every country's maternity care, more often after delivery than before. Visitors are sometimes midwives, more often nurses. Only the Netherlands uses health aides or neighborhood workers and provides extensive postnatal homemaking services. Every woman is visited at home by a midwife or general practitioner. A maternity home helper stays with the new mother for up to eight hours per day until ten days after the birth. In all of the countries studied, postnatal home visiting is seen as a means to counsel about infant care, follow up on the mother's health, offer advice about family planning, perform neonatal screening, and set up additional appointments for the infant and mother.

Each of these ten countries provides paid maternity leave, ranging from nine to twenty-nine weeks, and regulates the working circumstances of pregnant women, generally transferring them to nonstrenuous jobs. Several countries require that pregnant women be paid wages during absences for prenatal visits or classes. Maternity leave can often be extended on an unpaid basis without loss of job or benefits. For example, in France and the former Federal Republic of Germany, maternity leave can be extended for one to three years. Payment during nursing breaks is usually assured, ranging from two half-hour breaks to two one-hour breaks. In all these countries except Denmark, maternity grants or bonuses are paid at the time of birth, regardless of the family's income, and ongoing family allowances are paid for each child.

Miller concludes that early and continuous participation in prenatal care could be achieved in the United States by establishing easily understood and readily available provider systems, removing all barriers to services, and linking prenatal care to substantial medical and social benefits. While most of the ten European countries in the study have impressive programs of outreach, women appear to be especially attracted to prenatal care by the medical and social benefits that attach to pregnancy and childbearing. The European experience demonstrates that a variety of coherent, systematic arrangements can lead to better prenatal care and better pregnancy outcomes than those that prevail in the United States.

TAKING THE FIRST STEPS TOWARD PRENATAL CARE FOR ALL

If our goal is for all women to be healthy, have healthy babies, and be able to keep themselves and their families healthy, we must expand the essential components of prenatal care to include educational and psychosocial aspects of care. The same is true if we expand these goals to include the welfare of the parents and child beyond the pregnancy itself. We need a new *vision* of prenatal care, with broader goals and expanded means of reaching them. The reports I have cited are helping to build this vision. Once it is well understood and widely accepted—and that in itself is an enormous undertaking—our critical task will be to provide access to prenatal care for all pregnant women, particularly for low-income women in inner cities and isolated rural areas.

Educating the public broadly on the value of prenatal care and ways to make effective use of the opportunity is one of the critical missing pieces in health education today. We need to bring the full strength of communication research and media expertise to bear on increasing public awareness of this urgent issue.

One of the main reasons women miss the opportunity to receive prenatal care is that most pregnant women do not fully grasp the importance of prenatal care. Some women believe that they need pregnancy care only if they are ill. Low-income, unemployed, and poorly educated women are often unaware that prenatal care is available and important for delivering a healthy baby. Certainly the media are underutilized for the purpose of heightening such awareness—television and radio being the most obvious vehicles. One neglected way to reach most women with information about prenatal care is through magazines. Surveys show that women read a variety of magazines, particularly women's magazines, and get much of their information about health from them. Similarly, physicians and other health-care professionals have given little attention to enriched prenatal care—its medical, educational, and social-support components. Their professional organizations can make a major contribution here.

We need to do more research to determine what women perceive about prenatal care, where they get their information, and how they make their health-care decisions. We also need to know what women think of the care they do receive and the people who administer it. For instance, many women are afraid of doctor's offices or of any health-care professional. The more we understand about such matters, the more effectively we can intervene.

It is also vitally important that national, state, and local policymakers understand that prenatal care is much less expensive to society in the long run than medical care for low-birthweight or otherwise unhealthy babies, particularly those born to poor women. They have already been influenced by the findings of the various recent reports on child health and prenatal care, but broad public understanding can bring constructive pressure on and strengthen the resolve of policymakers. They must come to see that prenatal care, and maternal and child health in general, are a crucial, high-yielding investment.

While far too few women understand the need for prenatal care, there are many others who badly want care but do not have access to it. They have no way to pay for care, have no clinics and health professionals to provide it, or find the clinics are too hard to use. Who will provide enriched care and where? The issues of manpower and infrastructure are most critical in inner-city and rural areas where neither is available enough. What system will work best?

The lack of enough clinics to provide care to underserved women is largely one of money and qualified people. However, we must ask ourselves: Must *all* the components of care be provided in the setting of a doctor's office? Several model programs have shown that home visiting of mothers by nurses, paraprofessionals, or community volunteers can be effective in providing the educational and psychosocial components of prenatal care. These programs, however, require more personnel than traditional care of limited scope, and that means higher costs. Even when programs, such as Resource Mothers, use volunteers, the volunteers themselves require professional guidance, and that training costs money. Even if more nurses and nurse-midwives do become available to provide valuable educational and social services, where should these activities take place —in clinics, physicians' offices, community centers, or at home? In inner-city areas, clinic space is very limited; therefore, the need for space for educational activities that is convenient, accessible, and user-friendly is a very real problem.

Can we expect obstetricians to provide all aspects of care in the time of an ordinary office visit? Do they wish to do so? Should nurse-midwives or certified midwives provide some components, with obstetricians reserved only for medical problems and emergencies?

How extensively can volunteers be used—for example, in mother-to-mother programs? Who will administer the new educational and social-support programs? If it is unreasonable to expect one person, such as an obstetrician, to provide all the components of care, it may be equally unreasonable to expect any one pregnant woman, of any income or educational level, to be receptive to countless different providers. The time has come to devote concerted attention to these questions. Some conflict is inevitable, especially over professional turf. But with so much constructive concern and goodwill, these are surely not problems beyond human ingenuity.

It is time to say emphatically that we need a national commitment now to universal, early, high-quality prenatal and infant care. If we provide every single pregnant woman in the country with this care, we can no doubt save many thousands of babies every year. But save them for what? To accelerate them into a brick wall later? We now have compelling evidence that the actions we take in a child's first few years can shape that person's life in a healthy, learning, constructive way. I am talking about early pediatric care with emphasis on disease prevention and health promotion; education to strengthen parents' competence and build close parent-child relationships; and social-support networks in which parents give mutual aid to foster health and education for their children and themselves.

Many thousands of babies die unnecessarily each year—and hundreds of thousands are seriously impaired in terms of health, education, and accomplishment. It is time to hold ourselves accountable.

4

Health from the Start: Preventive Health Care in the First Few Years

It is almost axiomatic: Whatever our aspirations and dreams for our children—fine education, solid job opportunities, decent human relationships, the ability to contribute to society—we must begin by giving them the foundation of good health. Every other consideration we have for our children's future radiates from the fulfillment of that most basic need. Yet providing our children, especially those in urban areas, with even the most basic health services, particularly preventive health care, continues to be a formidable task.

In 1989, a distinguished national group of health leaders surveyed the prospects for child health in the city of New York—a prototype of urban health problems across the land. The report of the Mayor's Commission on the Future of Child Health in New York City described the nature and scope of the health problems, suggested which programs provide the best solutions to more problems, and outlined the steps we need to take in the nineties to give every single newborn the best chance for a healthy start.

Several key findings emerged. One, the health status of New York City children is poor and has been worsened by socioeconomic problems facing New York City's families. Two, comprehensive health services provided by a team of health professionals can be valuable in reducing the burdens of poor children. Three, a wide array of public and private institutions, including a variety of public and private facilities, offer health care to children. Despite these resources, the present system does not have the organization and functions required to provide the essential services for child health. Four, substantial sums are spent on child health services by public and private sources, yet an excessively large share of this spending goes to inpatient hospital care. Too small a proportion goes to services that could prevent much of this hospitalization in the first place, and poor children remain highly vulnerable.

The commission asked whether models exist for high-quality health services that could solve these problems. These services would have to have five characteristics:

Comprehensiveness. Services should include not only sound medical care but also health-education and psychosocial services to help prevent disease in early life. There should be convenient access through primary care to community resources such as mental-health services, day care, parenting education, family planning, and substance-abuse programs.

Continuity. Each child should have a durable relationship with one health-care provider that amounts to a "medical home." That provider should be familiar with the child, with his or her family, and with the family's background.

Coordination. Health care should be connected with school, preschool, and social services as needed. Moreover, children should have ready access to specialized care for complicated medical problems, including hospitalization if necessary. Programs should link pregnant women with high-quality prenatal care and register the child with a physician, preferably before birth.

Accessibility. Many of the children most in need of preventive care are not getting it now. Therefore, outreach is essential. Services must have hours and locations that accommodate hard-to-reach families; they must be prepared to deal with language and cultural barriers.

Accountability. Every program needs systematic quality control so it can meet the best standards of pediatric care, including prevention.

Do such services actually exist? Yes, they do. The commission gives one such example that has been of national significance over several decades: Community Health Centers, originally known as Neighborhood Health Centers, spread throughout the nation with federal support in the sixties and seventies. Some still flourish despite inadequate funding. These centers offer a range of medical and support services in the community and have proven their accessibility to low-income populations. Some of them have been carefully evaluated, but even though they have proven valuable, decreases in funding have reduced the number nationwide. Similarly, New York City has had for some years Maternity Infant Care Projects, which offer free and comprehensive services to pregnant women and their young children. Studies have shown that these projects provide prenatal care effectively and so reduce the number of low-birthweight babies among high-risk women. They also bridge the transition from maternity care to infant care. As another example, the commission notes that prenatal and postpartum home-visiting programs have proven successful for high-risk pregnant women, especially young adolescent mothers. These results include less prematurity, more normal birthweights, and fewer emergency-room visits, accidents in early childhood, and cases of child abuse and neglect.

The commission concluded that effective child health systems of this sort are not widespread in America today. But it emphasized that these systems do exist and they do work, so clearly it is feasible to provide excellent services that improve children's health, relieve their suffering, reduce their need for expensive hospitalization, and have lifelong benefits.

This New York City commission addressed the problems and opportunities characteristic of urban life today. The kind of care they recommend would be good for children and families at all income levels, but would be especially helpful in diminishing the heavy toll of casualties among the poor. Other cities are addressing these same issues. For example, the Ounce of Prevention Fund in Chicago is vigorously tackling the hardest problems of the inner city. Pediatrician Billie Wright Adams, who works for the fund, has focused her efforts on very poor children, but her emphasis on preventing disease and encouraging good health reflects the best pediatric practice across the entire spectrum of families.

Indeed, this "well-baby care" is the mark of the future. In addition to providing immunizations during infancy, pediatricians who support well-baby care also monitor children's growth carefully to detect nutritional problems and treat infectious diseases. Usually, pediatricians should go beyond these medical interventions to provide well-informed guidance and emotional support to direct families toward healthy lifestyles. They should not only answer parents' questions but also anticipate their concerns about their children's growth and development.

Ideally, pediatric preventive medicine should begin before birth so the doctor can help the pregnant woman understand not only the risks to the fetus of using alcohol, tobacco, and other drugs, but also the benefits the infant derives from breast-feeding. Moreover, establishing this medical relationship can help ease the transition from pregnancy to the first few weeks of the newborn's life.

Immediately after delivery, the pediatrician should assess the newborn's health and discuss the baby's status with the parents. He or she should not only give the child the proper immunizations, but also pay careful attention to any injuries the child may have, since they are the leading cause of death and disability. This is also the time When the pediatrician can foster attachment between parent and child and prepare the parents to cope with the predictably difficult phases of the baby's growth.

As the infant becomes a toddler, the pediatrician should teach parents how to provide play areas safe for their children's exploration, and should also discuss normal child development; e.g., that the difficult behavior so characteristic of toddlers—the infamous "terrible twos"—is not a sign of belligerence but, rather, an indication that the child is acquiring important skills and is developing normally. The pediatrician can also help parents ease the transition to out-of-home care and preschool education.

Since pediatricians are often in short supply, particularly in poor city neighborhoods and remote rural areas, it is essential to extend their reach. We need to enlist the aid of pediatric nurse-practitioners, home visitors, parent-support-group workers, and primary-prevention-program directors. We already have a handful of programs such as Chicago's Ounce of Prevention Fund that are doing just that; if we can build on their promise, we can give the lifelong benefit of preventively oriented health care in the earliest years to all children.

In 1990, the Head Start Bureau of the Administration for Children, Youth and Families announced its nationwide Comprehensive Child Development Program, which will develop a modest number of projects for intensive, comprehensive, integrated, and continuous supportive services for infants, toddlers, and preschoolers from low-income families. The plan is to enhance the children's intellectual, social, emotional, and physical development, and also to provide support to their parents and other household members. This program is one indication of awakening national interest in the importance of protecting and enhancing the first few years of life—and a good sign that policymakers are taking a broader view of what children need for healthy development. It also illustrates the intimate link between health and education in preventing damage to children in the early years of life. These projects will be evaluated periodically; if they prove successful, they could pave the way for a greater number of comprehensive programs nationwide.

Although it is heartening to see that more and more policymakers are seeing the wisdom of preventive care for infants and toddlers, more progress has to be made on the most critical fronts: immunization, low birthweight, and health education involving the fundamentals of constructive child care.

IMMUNIZATION: A VITAL STEP IN PREVENTION

The most effective preventive medicine we can give our infants is immunization against the common infections of childhood. The biomedical advances and dedicated efforts of this century have made great progress on this front. Paralytic poliomyelitis, which once struck over fifty thousand children each year in the United States, has all but disappeared in this country. Those who remember the advent of Jonas Salk's vaccine in the fifties are still inspired by it. Measles, only a few decades ago a very common disease with serious complications, declined to a low of just under 1,500 cases in 1983, several years after the introduction of an effective vaccine. Then federal support for immunization declined in the eighties. As a result, measles has reemerged as a problem in the United States, with almost 3,400 cases reported for 1988, nearly seven times the 1990 objective set by the Public Health Service. Unimmunized children under age four are the primary victims, but epidemics are turning up in teenagers and young adults who were immunized too early or not at all. For this age group, measles is a fairly serious disease. Now a mass reimmunization campaign for teenagers is under way. Clearly, the best course to pursue is comprehensive immunization at appropriate times in the child's earliest years.

The last major epidemic of German measles, which can cause serious handicaps in infants whose mothers contract the illness during pregnancy, occurred almost twenty years ago. Immunization has all but eliminated the illness. Diphtheria, whooping cough, and tetanus are also under control, thanks to effective immunization. In just the past decade, smallpox has been eradicated worldwide, so vaccinations are no longer needed. The conquest of this ancient scourge of humanity is a moving story of international cooperation for health. An improved whooping-cough vaccine is likely in a few years. Most recently, there has been encouraging evidence of an effective chicken-pox vaccine. Chicken pox is the last nonpreventable infection that attacks most children in this country. Though usually not a severe disease, chicken pox can cause serious complications, such as pneumonia, in a small percentage of children.

Most school-age American children are fully immunized, largely because immunization is mandatory for school entry. Yet many preschool children are far from fully vaccinated. Indeed, less than half of poor and minority children under age four are fully vaccinated against the preventable infections of childhood.

If we can devise ways to reach all children with the available vaccines, we can prevent untold avoidable damage. Moreover, the powerful surge of current scientific advance in immunology and molecular and cellular biology—including genetic engineering—will make additional vaccines available in the foreseeable future. We must use a combination of public education, medical care, and judicious regulation to make these advances very widely available to children and their families.

LOW-BIRTHWEIGHT INFANTS: PREVENTING DAMAGE AFTER BIRTH, AND IMPLICATIONS FOR OTHER HIGH-RISK BABIES

In the last chapter, I discussed the steps we need to take to minimize the number of low-birthweight babies. True, technically advanced care of low-birthweight infants has advanced brilliantly in the United States in recent years. However, the increasing survival rate for these infants has raised questions about their subsequent health and development; and, the lower the birthweight, the more survivors have permanent mental and/or physical disabilities. A number of studies have found that low-birthweight infants are also at increased risk for developmental delay and more subtle problems that may be detected only months to years after birth. Low-birthweight babies often grow up into children who have more difficulties in behavioral adjustment, more learning problems, lower test scores on intellectual functions, and poorer academic achievement than children born at normal weight, even when their IQs are normal.

Therefore, the Robert Wood Johnson Foundation initiated a ground-breaking research effort called the Infant Health and Development Program. It was a multi-site randomized clinical trial—the most rigorous experimental design—to evaluate the efficacy of combining early childhood development and family-support services with pediatric follow-up to reduce developmental, behavioral, and other problems among low-birthweight premature infants. The study released its report in 1990 and found that medical and social support can have profound effects on the cognitive and behavioral development of these children born at risk.

Eight medical institutions participated in the study, led by a team based at Stanford University. It included 985 children born in 1984 and 1985, who were born at 2,500 grams (5.5 pounds) or less and at thirty-seven weeks' gestational age or less (a full term is forty weeks). Two-thirds of each group received only pediatric follow-up, whereas one-third received full services, consisting of pediatric follow-up, home visits, developmental day care, and parent-group meetings, beginning from the moment mother and child left the hospital nursery and continuing until the child was three years old. For the first year, the parents receiving full services got weekly home visits from health-care providers who gave them health and developmental information and family support. After the first year, the visits were biweekly. The home visitors taught the parents games and activities they could play with their children to enhance their cognitive, linguistic, and social development. They also helped the parents manage any problems they brought up. The full-service group was provided with day care five days a week for children from age one to three years. Group meetings were held monthly during the first year to give parents information on child-rearing, health, safety, other parenting concerns, and some social support. These parent-group meetings were bimonthly after the first year.

The initial research set out to answer three main questions. At three years of age, how did the children who received full services differ from the comparison group in (1) cognitive development; (2) behavioral competence; and (3) health status?

The results clearly indicate that this comprehensive program makes a difference for low-birthweight and premature infants. Compared with the control group, children in the group receiving full services had significantly higher IQs and fewer behavioral problems. Even though they spent a good deal of time in day-care centers, where children often spread illness to one another, they experienced no epidemic or serious illnesses.

This study shows that such comprehensive programs are feasible in a variety of communities. The results could not be more timely; there is an urgent need for day care and early intervention. Enhancing the development of children at risk because of low birthweight may improve their performance in school and also reduce the money we would need to spend on their developmental disabilities. If we cannot prevent low birthweight completely, it is encouraging to know that we can prevent further damage to those who are born particularly vulnerable. Furthermore, we may be able to apply these same principles of intervention to a wider range of children at risk in poor communities.

CHILD ABUSE

Child neglect and abuse can be physical, sexual, or psychological. Although statistics on death from maltreatment cannot be precise, between 1,200 and 5,000 children die from abuse each year. Six to ten times as many children survive abuse with serious injuries. In addition, abused children tend to suffer severe psychological problems later in life, and they all too commonly perpetuate this violent behavior toward their own children. Although reports of child abuse and neglect have increased almost 200 percent in the past ten years, these problems have not received high priority from the scientific, educational, or health communities. The health-care system has the primary responsibility for dealing with the results of this epidemic and in the nineties is coming to recognize this as a major public health problem. An effective response requires conjunction of the medical–public health system with education and social services. I will pursue this joint approach in a later chapter.

Although abuse is most vividly pictured in images of bruises, fractures, and malnutrition, the long-term damage must also be seen in social and emotional terms. Maltreated infants and young children, when compared to normal children of the same social group, have less secure attachments to their primary caregiver, are less cognitively mature, tend to be fearful about developing relationships with new adults, and are less likely than others to explore and master their environment.

The solution to the crisis of child abuse begins with prevention. Prevention efforts must include: parent education about child development and parenting behavior; counseling; parent self-help support groups; crisis centers and protective day care; home visitor programs; and attempts to promote stronger early attachment between mother and infant among mothers at high risk of abuse, such as young adolescents. Research indicates that some kinds of home-visitor activities and parent-education programs can help families prone to abuse—and help with other difficulties as well.

HOME VISITING AS PREVENTIVE INTERVENTION

I have already touched on home visiting as an effective way to prevent casualties in early life. It has proven helpful for all the problems discussed so far in this and the previous chapter: prenatal and follow-up care; health care utilization; immunizations; low-birthweight babies; and child abuse. The widespread use of home visits now deserves attention in its own right. Fortunately, two substantial reports were released in 1990 analyzing the uses of home visiting for health-related purposes.

The National Center for Children in Poverty, a resource institution created by the Ford Foundation and the Carnegie Corporation of New York to provide reliable information on these hard problems, notes in a 1991 report that health and social-service workers have visited disadvantaged or isolated families in their homes for many years. Home visiting can be a relatively efficient and effective way of addressing the many needs of poor families with young children. Home visitors can engage family members in solving problems of housing, food, health, child-rearing, child development, and family relationships. Researchers and policymakers have also become interested in home visiting as a preventive technique for child abuse and neglect, prematurity, and school failure.

Workers can use home visits to instruct and motivate mothers, listen to them, observe them interacting with their children and other family members, give them constructive feedback, discuss service needs, and connect the family with community resources. Typically, a particular program uses home visits to tackle more than one problem.

Home visits can be an effective way to teach parenting skills to high-risk families who suffer from multiple stresses and even clinical depression. Such families are the least likely to come to health clinics for prenatal care of well-baby checkups, to participate in parent education classes, to attend parent support groups, or to seek quality preschool programs for their children. They are at relatively higher risk than other parents of abusing or neglecting their children.

The United States General Accounting Office (GAO), an agency of the Congress, published a comprehensive study of home visiting in 1990. Its main focus was on families that face barriers to getting the health-care or social-support services they need. Is home visiting effective in delivering or improving access to early intervention services—prenatal counseling, parenting instruction for young mothers, and preschool education? What are the characteristics of programs that use home visiting? Where successful, are there opportunities to expand the use of home visiting?

This report concluded that home visiting can be an effective form of early intervention for at-risk families with young children. Such programs may have various goals (improving parenting skills, enhancing child development, improving health outcomes), may provide various services (information, referrals, emotional support, health care), and may use different types of providers (nurses, paraprofessionals, teachers, social workers).

Home visits may also be an effective way to provide services on a temporary basis—during a family crisis or particularly stressful period: for example, during the pregnancy of a low-income mother with medical complications; the arrival at home of a frail premature baby; or the imminent possibility of foster-care placement.

One type of home visiting is directed toward keeping families in crisis together after an acute episode of child abuse. The Homebuilders program of Tacoma, Washington did ground-breaking work on this approach of family preservation during the seventies and eighties. The success of family preservation services ultimately depends on whether they can really keep families together that would otherwise disintegrate. The evidence suggests that they can. For example, in the work of Homebuilders, more than 80 percent of the highly vulnerable families are intact one year after they have received the services. Independent assessments suggest that most of these families would have been separated without this intervention. Comparable evidence has shown that a similar project in Hennepin

County, Minnesota, has also helped keep families with at-risk adolescents together.

Thus, research evaluations of home visiting programs show that they can have positive effects on health and well-being, especially for adolescent mothers and their families, low-income families, and rural families. Families that have had the benefit of home visiting have lower rates of small-for-gestational-age and low-birthweight babies; the babies are healthier at birth, have fewer accidents in the first year of life, are immunized more often, experience less child abuse and neglect, and demonstrate improved cognitive performance. Several studies indicate that these benefits can endure over many years. The available data suggest that home visiting of high quality is probably a good deal less costly in the long run than paying for the problems of seriously neglected children, especially very poor children who get no care.

EDUCATION FOR HEALTH

A recurrent theme in these pages is the close relationship of education and health. Children in poor health have difficulty in learning. Common experience makes that intuitively clear. Somehow, however, we have neglected the other side of the coin—fostering good health through education. In health care worldwide, the responsibility of education to promote health is at last being recognized.

The perinatal Positive Parenting Program, based at Michigan State University, is an interesting example of a relatively long-term program involving parent education and social support for health. The original program provides support for the first-time parents of healthy infants during the prenatal and early postnatal period. A more recent variant of the program serves parents with newborns hospitalized in intensive-care units. The work is being extended to serve high-risk pregnant women and their families.

Both versions of the program train experienced parents to offer support to new parents in three phases. First, the volunteer parent visits the new parents in the hospital shortly after the birth. At this point the volunteer may show the new parents one of several videotapes on child care, postpartum blues, and related topics. He or she offers printed materials on parenting and tries to establish a relationship of trust. Next, the volunteer meets with the new mother in her home when the baby is one to four weeks old. The volunteer visits the new mother at least three times in the first three months after birth. Third, the volunteer arranges for the parents to attend support groups, which eventually take the place of the one-to-one relationship between the volunteer and the parent. These groups begin when the babies are four to eight weeks old.

The program design is based on several considerations. First, many new parents are unaware of what to expect in raising an infant. But knowledge alone is not sufficient. Their feelings of inadequacy can be exacerbated by lack of outside resources for advice, support, and help. Therefore, a support system can give them encouragement, realistic expectations, and useful information. While preparation for parenting is a lifelong process, the period surrounding the birth of the first child is uniquely important because parents are motivated to learn and because it is an ideal time to reinforce positive relationships and foster the desire to nurture one's child. The experienced parent volunteers to help the new parents learn and gain confidence. Hospital volunteers provide another useful source of support.

In an evaluation of the program for parents of healthy infants, forty-eight new mothers were randomly assigned to two groups. One group received counseling from experienced parents; the other did not. After fifteen months, the families receiving counseling showed better mother-infant interactions and had created more nurturing environments. The impact of the service was greater for younger mothers (under twenty-four) than for older mothers (over twenty-seven). An evaluation of the program for parents of hospitalized infants showed similar results. In addition, mothers who received counseling showed less anxiety, fatigue, confusion, and depression than those who did not.

By looking at developing nations, we can see most vividly how education fosters health. Moreover, the problems of poor communities have much in common throughout the world. Building education for health into the schools, the media, and primary health care can make a large difference in the well-being of people everywhere. Primary health care as defined by the World Health Organization includes education about the prevention and control of health problems; building an adequate food supply and proper nutrition; adequate safe water; basic sanitation; maternal and child health care, including family planning; immunization against the major infectious diseases; prevention and control of locally prevalent diseases and injuries; promotion of mental health; and provision of essential drugs. Primary health care is at the heart of the global strategy for health improvement in this century, especially because of its potential significance for developing countries.

No matter how comprehensive and widespread health services may be, they will not be effective if people are not educated for health. Mothers are uniquely motivated to learn the principles of good health. Further, we can use health services as the thin edge of the wedge of the general education of girls and women, including basic literacy. The most effective approach is to promote health and prevent disease by teaching individuals, families, and communities to become active agents in promoting their own health—even, and perhaps especially, in poor communities.

The link of health to education is illustrated in the United States by the high rate of low-birthweight babies born to women with less than a high-school education. In developing countries, infant mortality is clearly related to the mother's education. Twenty-four separate studies in fifteen nations have established that the level of the mother's education—even within the same broad socioeconomic class—is a key determinant of her children's health. Infant-mortality rates are consistently high in countries with a low literacy rate and better in equally poor nations with a high literacy rate.

UNICEF's valuable reports make clear that it is usually the mother's level of education and access to information that determine whether or not she goes for a tetanus shot; whether a trained person will be present at the birth; whether she knows about the advantages of breast-feeding; whether she will wean her child at the right time; whether she will cook the best available foods in the best possible way; whether she will boil water and wash her hands; whether she will treat her child's bouts of diarrhea by giving him or her food and fluids; whether she will have her child weighed and vaccinated; and whether she will leave an adequate interval between births.

Empowering women by education—even as little as four years of education—can have a remarkable impact. It is very encouraging that since 1960 the proportion of six- to eleven-year-old girls who are enrolled in school in the poorest half of the world has jumped from 34 percent to 80 percent. If this breakthrough can be sustained, it would make a substantial difference for these nations.

Community-based efforts to educate people for health are eliciting worldwide interest, and efforts are being made to build a scientific basis for enhancing their effectiveness. A strong impetus for pursuing this approach has come from the success that research and public-health education have had in getting people to change the lifestyle habits that cause heart disease and strokes—especially cigarette smoking, high fat intake, and sedentary habits. I will discuss this further in the chapter on adolescent substance abuse.

How do we get people to change their behavior voluntarily to promote good health? We must first determine the specific knowledge deficits in each community with respect to health, taking cultural factors into account. Then we must teach the skills necessary to maintain health-promoting behavior, using constructive motivations—for example, those of pregnant women to provide the best protection and care for their babies. We must find the channels through which community members may understand and take seriously information pertinent to their own health. These community-based initiatives to promote lifestyle changes are difficult to achieve, and we need to do more research to clarify what it takes to make these changes happen. Here are the crucial steps:

- Getting accurate biomedical and behavioral information about risk factors in a community
- Clarifying the psychosocial obstacles to health-promoting behavior change in order to cope with them
- Using modern behavioral and social sciences, including communications research, to create opportunities for promoting health that the community can fully understand

We can apply these lessons to our children's health in the earliest years of life. It all starts with fostering a healthy lifestyle. Preventing illness and promoting health give our children the best chance to grow and develop. Yet it is only in the past few decades that we have laid the necessary scientific and operational foundations that will allow families throughout the world to plan for their future with confidence.

5

The Family Crucible: Opportunities for and Obstacles to Healthy Child Development

The first few years of a child's life are a critical period of his or her development physically, emotionally, and psychologically. It is a time when the family's capacity to nurture—or its failure to do so—has the most profound effect on the child's growth. Beyond the provision of food, clothing, and shelter, what else must families do to enable a child to flourish? What developmental needs must be met? And what stands in the way of meeting those needs?

The field of child development has been the focus of considerable research over the last few decades, and scientists have now identified the distinct phases of development in a child's life and the conditions families must create to meet the child's needs in each of those phases. In this chapter I will summarize what science has revealed about a child's developmental needs and consider how disruptions within the family may threaten the fulfillment of those needs.

ATTACHMENT

One of the most dynamic subjects in child-development research is attachment, the process by which the infant and the caretaker—

usually the mother—bond with each other in the first critical months of life.

The basic attachment of infant to mother has long been a biological mechanism for survival. Recent research evidence strongly affirms that from early infancy until about the age of two years, a child's normal development is crucially nurtured by such a core attachment. It provides a sense of personal worth and a foundation on which to build solid human relationships for the future. Children who do not have a strong attachment to their mother or other caregiver become frustrated when confronted with problems, tend to give up easily, and suffer other long-term effects. Although good later experiences can, to a large extent, overcome poor early experience, children who are severely deprived of early attachment may be irreversibly damaged.

Research findings strongly support the centrality of a loving, dependable relationship for a good start in life. This does not mean that only one person matters in a child's life, or that the biological mother must be that person. In intact, cohesive families, it is very likely that the child will develop a secure attachment with the father as well during the first year of life. And certainly a baby can form secure attachments with other caregivers and with siblings. Nevertheless, the research evidence indicates the great importance of one central caregiver who creates a sustaining, loving relationship with the infant.

What is it about the mother-infant relationship that fosters secure attachment, with all its later opportunities and benefits? At the heart of the matter is a dependable relationship with one person reinforced by regular interactions throughout the first year of life. Attachment develops from a loving relationship in which affection is manifested in many different ways: cuddling, tender contact, frequent smiling, laughing in play, and general enjoyment between infant and caretaker. It is a relationship of sustained emotional involvement, caring, and sensitivity.

Sensitivity in communication is an important part of attachment, and emotional expression in infancy is an important form of communication. An infant communicates pleasure by smiling, and frowns or grimaces to indicate displeasure. Emotional displays, such as crying, in the first years of life are one of the earliest means by which the infant can gain a measure of control over its environment. Sensitive mothers are responsive to these cues.

Attachment grows through a series of events in the first half-year of the infant's life. At first, the infant is attracted to humans in preference to inanimate objects. Then the infant learns to discriminate between familiar and unfamiliar humans. Finally, a special relationship develops with one, two, or perhaps a few specific individuals. Such distinctions between familiar and unfamiliar people begin very shortly after birth. Experiments have shown that in the first weeks and months of life, infants can distinguish between their mothers' voices and those of other women. They can also distinguish familiar and unfamiliar smells. At the same time, parents are becoming attached to the special individual who is their baby. It is especially important for caretakers to learn how to read the baby's signals, how to evoke smiles and laughter, how to relieve its distress, how to find shared pleasure.

Even in the first month of life, spontaneous or reflex smiling may be elicited by stroking the baby's cheek or lips. In the second month of life, infants smile in response to social stimulation, especially that provided by certain expressions on a parent's face, or better yet the combination of a high-pitched voice with a moving face. This is one of many instances in which a parent can affect an infant's behavior. When she returns the smile, coos, or hugs or kisses her baby when he smiles, she is not only shaping his social behavior in constructive ways, but she is providing a very special, distinctive, and deeply appreciated form of positive reinforcement. For instance, even by three months of age, infants smile much more when they see positive reinforcement from the smiles and vocalizations of their mothers than when reinforced by similarly behaving female strangers.

By four months of age, infants are not only smiling but also laughing. This behavior naturally tends to deepen and enhance the mother-infant relationship. In the second half of the first year, infants respond increasingly to social games such as peekaboo. Experimental studies show that stimulation from adults, particularly familiar caregivers, not only elicits smiles and laughter from babies, but also can make children smile and laugh more often if the adult responds immediately with the appropriate reinforcement. Such smiling and laughter are part of the biological heritage of our species. They are important in strengthening the attachment between the primary caregiver and the infant.

The fact that the three-month-old infant already smiles more at its mother than at a stranger indicates that it is well on the way toward forming an attachment to her. This attachment in turn increases the parent's leverage during the child's later development.

Early in the second half of the first year of life, the baby shows evidence of particular attachments. The infant actively tries to be near specific people, typically first the mothering person, and protests when these people go away. This behavior shows the interaction between cognitive and social development. The baby must attain a certain level of cognitive development before it can make specific attachments. The infant must be aware that a person exists even when out of sight. Moreover, the sheer distinction between familiar and unfamiliar implies a certain amount of cognitive skill. Having made such distinctions, the infant is then likely to protest when placed in an unfamiliar situation, when put with strange people even in a familiar context, or when faced unexpectedly with something of great novelty or high intensity. Even in the first year of life, the infant is capable of making impressive distinctions. Children protest less when the mother leaves them in a familiar home setting than when she leaves them in an unfamiliar laboratory setting. As the child grows, and especially as it develops secure attachment, its reactions to separations become less severe; the child learns that indeed the mother will come back. Such dependability is an inherent component of a secure attachment and of human relations later in life.

The biological mother, or another adult in the consistent caregiving role, has formidable responsibilities and therefore needs appreciation, encouragement, and opportunities for learning how to deal with a young child. It is not surprising that overstressed, very young, poorly educated mothers in poverty have serious difficulty in accepting and caring for a child, and particularly in making enduring attachments. But effective parenting techniques, including those that foster attachment, can be taught to expectant and new mothers. Parents and other guardians need strong support systems—often lacking in very poor communities—and encouragement in seeking help to become effective parents.

Since attachment has such formidable consequences in later life —or put another way, since it builds such a solid foundation for the social, emotional, and cognitive growth of the child—it is important to focus on the aspects of parental behavior that contribute most to the development of secure attachment. Research shows that infants become securely attached to adults who respond promptly to their cries and other evidence of their distress, and who also spontaneously initiate friendly interactions with them. This applies to both parents.

Recent research has expanded the evidence supporting the

concept that parental sensitivity is crucial in the formation of secure attachment. In the early years of life, it is especially important that children interact with caregivers who are sensitive to their cues, responsive to their behavior in consistent ways, stimulating in a friendly but not overwhelming way, and protective but not highly restrictive. Such caregivers permit the infant to play an active role in shaping their relationship. For instance, they are responsive to the infant's cues in determining when and how much to feed them. In turn, the infant learns that he or she can depend on the caregiver.

Such sensitivity and responsiveness may be expressed in many different ways. But they are reliably detectable by observers, and evidently by the infant as well. In effect, during the first few months of the baby's life the adults are learning to interpret the infant's signals and to take the signals into account in their own behavior. These are the building blocks of attachment; they may foster or hinder the formation of secure attachments, depending in large part on what the adults do. It is interesting to note that much of this behavior is generally playful in character. Here as at other times in the first few years of life, play is significant in the development of skills that bear upon children's long-term adaptability.

Since attachment is fundamentally important in human development and adaptive behavior, we turn next to a closer look at its implications for preventing casualties in early life.

THE SIGNIFICANCE OF EARLY ATTACHMENT AND PROSOCIAL BEHAVIOR

Careful, systematic studies have characterized various patterns of early attachment during the first year of life. Indeed, a great deal of experimental and longitudinal research has been stimulated in the past decade by John Bowlby's ground-breaking work on human attachment. His synthesis of research on animal behavior, child development, and clinical problems led to a comprehensive formulation of the origins of human attachment and the consequences of its disruption.

Child-development experts have devised experiments to distinguish securely and insecurely attached one-year-old infants. The securely attached infant seeks and maintains either direct physical contact or close proximity to the mother. This is particularly true when the infant and mother are reunited after a brief absence. The baby shows clear indications of preference for the mother over a stranger, and greets the mother with a smile or a cry after a brief separation. But some babies do not form solid attachments; they appear insecure in various ways. One kind of insecurely attached baby appears detached or avoidant; such babies avoid or ignore their mothers at reunion after brief separation and show little tendency to seek contact with the mother at any time. They do not hold on if picked up. They respond to a stranger in approximately the same way as they do to the mother. Another kind of insecurely attached baby appears resistant or ambivalent. Such an infant seems to be experiencing mixed feelings, evidently wanting contact and yet resisting it when offered; it tends to be highly distressed when separated from the mother.

There is growing evidence that first attachments have long-term effects on children's later behavior. Infants who are rated as securely attached when observed in a "strange situation" test at one year or eighteen months, are later observed to be more sociable and skillful with peers. They also appear to teachers to be more mature in their initial school experiences. They explore new spaces more independently and thoroughly than do children who are rated as insecurely attached at one year of age. Thus, several years after the initial establishment of secure or insecure attachment, independent observations show that children who have had the benefit of a secure attachment in the first year of life are more curious, exploratory, and effective in relation to both social and physical aspects of their later environments. A friendly and trusting curiosity seems to guide their behavior and in turn gives them the basis for developing cognitive and social skills in later years.

This does not mean that attachment in the first year of life is the only crucial underpinning for later development. Another one occurs in the second year of life when the child's language begins a burst of development. At that time, lively interactions with the mother and other caretakers are of great importance: talking and reading to the child, playing games, experimenting with varied and interesting toys, encouraging ever-widening yet safe explorations—all these contribute much in the second year and beyond to the development of the child's cognitive and social skills.

Children raised in very poor, disorganized, and socially disrupted circumstances are likely to miss out on some of these vital interactions in the first and second years of life. Although there is abundant evidence that children with poor early relationships can recover later if their environment improves, these early experiences tend to put children on different developmental pathways. The paths are not totally separate, nor do they go in altogether different directions, but they tend on the average to be associated with different outcomes. The quality of human relationships in the first two or three years of life has a substantial bearing on later development. While we are far from knowing the exact nature of the various developmental trajectories, it is clear that a secure early attachment, along with consistently friendly stimulation and guidance during these first few years, can make a constructive long-term difference. Similarly, the nature and adequacy of cognitive and verbal stimulation provided for the child in the family or in surrogate-family situations during the first several years of the child's life seems to be important for the course of the child's cognitive development.

Studies of preschool children show clearly that those with secure attachments do better in human relations than do those with insecure attachments. Even two-year-old toddlers tend to differ in this regard: Those with secure early attachment behave more positively toward peers, show more interest in engaging them in play, and are rated by observers as more sociable not only with peers but with their mothers. Thus, the securely attached infant quickly develops social skills upon which to build in subsequent years—skills that are important for accomplishment in school and beyond.

Attachment is a relationship requiring two participants. It can go wrong because either of them lacks the necessary signals, skills, or motivation to enter into the process. Sometimes the infant lacks such skills, as in the case of blind, deaf, or otherwise handicapped babies. Because they do not respond in the expected ways during the first few months of life, parents may withdraw with feelings of helplessness or think that these infants are rejecting them. Attachment then is jeopardized. But the parents can be helped to overcome these difficulties—for example, by learning to "read" the child's hand and body movements instead of waiting for the infant to smile or to make eye contact. Such training has been shown to help the parents of blind babies strengthen their attachment to the infants. Similar work has been done with parents of children who have other physical handicaps. An interesting observation is that this parent training works best when some activity can be found that the child and parent can do together, bringing pleasure to both. When both parent and child enjoy being together, the parent can more readily be helped to become highly attentive and responsive to the child's individual signals.

More commonly, it is the parent who lacks the essential skill to form a secure attachment. This can happen if the parent lacked such an attachment in his or her own early development. Another hindrance is sheer immaturity, and lack of knowledge and experience, as in the case of very young adolescent mothers and fathers isolated from the extended family. A mother under chronic stress, who has recurrent anxiety and low self-esteem, is also unlikely to foster a child's secure attachment. Unfortunately, all these conditions tend to occur jointly in high-poverty areas. In all such circumstances, there is a palpable need for parent education and social support in some readily available form. This need has stimulated a growing social movement to provide parent education and social-support systems, or a combination of the two—as well as other interventions intended to prevent serious damage to children early in life. I will examine such interventions later. Before doing so, we need to consider some additional factors that bear upon healthy child development.

When children enjoy secure attachment and valued adult role models—when children are provided with at least a modicum of warmth and trust by either a cohesive family or a more extended social-support network—they establish certain social norms early in life. These are (1) taking turns; (2) sharing with others; (3) cooperating, especially in learning and problem solving; (4) helping others, especially in times of stress. These norms, which are established in only a rudimentary way in the first few years of life, open the way to much more complex and beneficial human relationships that have significance throughout the child's life. They tend to earn respect, provide gratification, and amplify the effectiveness of anything the individual could do alone. For this reason, early-intervention programs need to take account of the factors that influence the development of attachment and so-called prosocial behavior.

Marian Radke-Yarrow and Carolyn Zahn-Waxler of the National Institute of Mental Health, in a valuable review of research on this topic, define prosocial behavior as helping rather than hurting or neglecting, respecting as opposed to denigrating, and being psychologically supportive and protective rather than dominating or exploitative. Empathy appears to exist even in newborns, who make distress cries in response to cries of other infants. Children in their second and third years show emotional distress and try to help when they see others in distress.

How important is the family in promoting or retarding these tendencies? Unfortunately, less research attention has been devoted to the development of prosocial than to that of antisocial behaviors. In addition, research that does deal with prosocial behaviors has rarely taken a developmental approach. Nevertheless, useful information is available.

There is evidence that settings in which children are required and expected to behave prosocially do in fact foster such behavior. For example, children who are responsible for tasks helpful to family maintenance, especially caring for younger siblings, are generally more altruistic. Parents' warmth and affection alone does seem to foster children's altruism. However, when combined with responsiveness, high expectations, and firmness, parents' warmth and caring foster a sense of social responsibility in children—and behavior to match.

Both direct observations of families and experimental studies have examined the effects of role models on later prosocial or antisocial behavior. In typical experimental studies, an adult (presumably someone much like a parent) demonstrates a prosocial act such as sharing toys, coins, or candies that have been won in a game. The adult explains to the child that he or she is sharing with someone else who is said to be in need, though not present in the experimental situation. The adult then leaves the child to play. Similar designs are used in studies of honesty.

The results of such experiments clearly show that children exposed to such models, when compared to similar children in control groups, tend to imitate the adult's behavior, be it honesty, generosity, helpfulness, or rescue. There is also evidence that toddlers imitate their mother's ways of comforting and helping spontaneously when trying to help others. Indeed, the imitations often involve exact reproductions of the mother's behavior. Given the child's constant exposure to the parents, the potential for learning through observation is very great.

Many laboratory and clinical studies of social learning indicate that certain factors enhance the impact of an adult's behavior on the child. These are the adult's power, perceived competence, and long-term nurturance of the child. Securely attached children are in a strong position to adopt salient patterns of behavior through observing and imitating their parents and other family members. The combination of early attachment plus abundant modeling over the years of growth and development can firmly establish prosocial behavior, which in turn can open up new opportunities for the growing child, strengthen relationships with others, and contribute to the building of self-esteem.

During the eighties, several longitudinal studies reinforced the prior, path-breaking research, showing that the quality of early parent-infant attachment has a major effect on a child's later prosocial behavior, self-control, and conduct. A longitudinal study in Germany has reported similar results to those in the United States and the United Kingdom.

Although most research has involved stable, middle-class families, there has been recent work on poor families and the results are much the same. Early attachment is connected to later social competence in disadvantaged families as well as advantaged ones. The infants securely attached at one year get on better with their preschool teachers at age four and a half, for example. Similarly, securely attached preschoolers from high-risk families have stronger self-control than do insecurely attached peers. Thus, early secure attachment, regardless of social class, tends to set the child on a path toward positive experience and valued accomplishments.

On the negative side, recent research in both disadvantaged and relatively affluent families has shown that insecure attachment in infancy is predictive of later behavior problems in early and middle childhood. These behaviors include the violent use of toys, physical aggression, and verbal threats—behavior patterns that tend to interfere with the child's subsequent relationships and put his educational accomplishment at risk. Also, insecurely attached children in preschool are more likely than securely attached children to be emotionally upset, to cry, and to run out of the classroom precipitously. They are also more likely than securely attached children to develop behavior problems in school. They tend to be less capable of independent action, less empathic, less socially competent, and more emotionally troubled, and to have lower self-esteem than children who have been securely attached in infancy. They tend to be described by preschool teachers as hostile and socially isolated from their peers.

Altogether, research on attachment has progressed to a point at which a variety of reliable measures can predict links between the security of infant-parent attachment and later social competence, emotional distress, functioning in school, and prosocial behavior. In essence, a secure attachment in the first year of life is predictive of enhanced skill and competence between the ages of two and five years.

We can use this body of research to design early interventions that bear upon the relationship of caretakers and young children in the home, in school, and in child care. Since we now understand the conditions that favor secure early attachment, we can design ways to foster it deliberately and shape a child's prosocial behavior. By doing so, we open doors of opportunity in the years ahead.

It may be relatively simple to explain how parents should ideally behave to foster their child's secure attachment in the first few years of life, but this is more complicated in day-to-day application. In my view, parents need to have five basic qualities:

1. The ability to *nurture,* providing their child with adequate food, shelter, and protection
2. The capacity to *love,* cherishing the life of the child and making a patient investment in the child's future
3. The readiness to *enjoy,* finding opportunities to interact with their child to provide mutual satisfaction
4. A passion for *teaching* and enough understanding of child development to interact constructively with the child, to become skillful as mentors, and to sharpen the child's skills gradually as the individual capacities evolve
5. The ability to *cope,* actively seeking ways to develop their child's skill in handling the inevitable vicissitudes of life

The scientific community has something useful to say about all of these matters. But the daily application of the basic principles draws in practical ways upon the individual strengths and social supports of particular parents. We need to find ways to connect the relevant knowledge generated by the scientific community with the social-support system of particular parents. Then we can put that knowledge to use in ways that reduce human suffering and disability, even tragedy.

GROWING UP IN DISRUPTED FAMILIES

It is a sad fact that all too many children are not raised in an environment that encourages attachment. Families can be disrupted in a variety of ways—through poverty, social disadvantage, divorce, widowhood, domestic violence, mental illness, homelessness—that can in turn challenge a child's natural development. Is the damage permanent? Can children raised in disadvantaged families escape the toll? Why do some children fare better than others? Many studies offer fascinating insights into how children weather the fateful first years in the family crucible.

DEVELOPMENTAL RESEARCH ON COPING WITH ADVERSITY

An important source of insight into children's ability to cope and adapt comes from longitudinal research. Some scientists have been able to carry out long-term studies in which they followed infants from birth through adulthood, periodically making detailed observations about the lifestyles, attitudes, and behavior of both child and caretakers. In recent years, there have also been well-documented reports from several short-term longitudinal studies (spanning a few years); and also some new analyses of long-term longitudinal studies (spanning up to two decades).

One of the most valuable of the latter is the report of Professor Emmy Werner's longitudinal study of all the babies born during 1955 on the island of Kauai, Hawaii. Werner, of the University of California–Davis, examined seven hundred children from different ethnic backgrounds, looking at data from the prenatal period to young adulthood. Werner studied everything from the pregnant mother's health and environment to the quality of care for the infant as well as the vulnerability and resiliency of these children in the face of a formidable range of biological and psychosocial risk factors. Her observations provide exceptional insight into the capacity of children to cope with perinatal stress, poverty, and family instability. They also identify factors in the child's personality and in the caregiving environment that protect the child from these risks.

The study included measurements and interviews during the mother's pregnancy, during the postpartum period, and when the children were at ages one year, twenty months, ten years, and eighteen years. Records of community agencies provided information on social, medical, and mental-health services, police and court contacts, and special-education placements. Pediatricians rated birth outcomes and birth-related stress based on clinical judgment and an assessment of some sixty complications occurring during the prenatal, labor, delivery, and neonatal periods.

The study was conducted on a small island on which many families lived in chronic poverty or in a persistently disorganized family environment. The living conditions clearly affected the perinatal and psychosocial risk factors, many of which could be detected even before the child's birth. The island also had many assets, however. Kauai's medical, public-health, education, and mental-health services compared favorably with those in most communities of similar size throughout the United States. Given this mix of conditions, it is striking to observe the scope of the casualties during the first two decades of these children's lives. About one of every three children in the group Werner studied had a significant learning or behavior problem before age ten. About one of every five young teenagers had serious mental-health problems or was delinquent. The majority of these troubled adolescents had multiple problems.

Werner found numerous predictors of mental retardation, learning disabilities, serious mental-health problems, delinquency, and other adverse outcomes. These risk factors include perinatal stress, congenital defects, low birthweight, and physical handicap, and environmental factors such as the mother's lack of education; a low standard of living, especially at birth; and family instability between the child's birth and second birthday.

Some of the most stimulating observations from this long-term study are those of highly resilient children in chronic poverty. There were seventy-two children in this category, each of whom had four or more risk factors before age two. Nonetheless, when last studied at age eighteen, none of these highly resilient individuals had experienced any serious learning or behavior disorders or had required any mental-health services despite the formidable risks of their earliest years. Werner studied the children's early caregiving environment to see if it could explain how children in poverty cope with adversity.

Werner learned that all of these children had grown up in relatively small families, with no more than four children. The spacing between each two children was more than two years—presumably adequate time to give considerable individual attention to each infant. Additional responsible caretakers—e.g., the child's father or grandparents or much older siblings—were available within the household. The primary caretakers devoted a substantial amount of attention to the child in infancy. Siblings were available either as able caretakers or as confidants. Also, an informal multigenerational network of relatives, friends, and other interested people—neighbors, teachers, clergymen—surrounded the child and family. In time of stress, these people were supportive and available. All in all, these children enjoyed two types of protection in the early caregiving environment: *individual attention in the early years* and *a readily available social-support system*.

Even the few children who had grown up with psychotic parents fared well if they received this individual attention and had an accessible support system. The resilient children of psychotic parents had not been separated from their primary caretaker for extended intervals during infancy. Home observers recorded that despite her mental illness, the mother's way of relating to the child of one year was mainly appropriate and positive. When these babies underwent a developmental examination at twenty months of age, independent observers noted their positive orientation to other people and evidence of age-appropriate self-help skills. Like the resilient children in chronic poverty, these children, as they grew older, drew upon the emotional support of alternative caretakers in the household, such as a grandparent, aunt or uncle, or older sibling, as well as peers and parents of friends, to give stability to their lives and to cope with the stresses in their turbulent families.

This major longitudinal study shows that in the face of disadvantage, many children can cope effectively with their adverse socioenvironmental conditions. Moreover, most of those who had learning and behavior problems in childhood had made considerable progress by the time they reached young adulthood. Although most of the children and adolescents with serious and persistent learning and behavior problems were poor, poverty alone did not inevitably stunt their development.

The serious, persistent learning and behavior problems of both middle-class and poor children in the study arose mainly from the joint impact of perinatal risk factors (prematurity, low birthweight, obstetrical problems) and family instability during early life. Although such conditions occur more readily under circumstances of poverty and social disadvantage, they do occur to a considerable degree in every social class. Werner emphasizes that, across socioeconomic strata, infants with difficult temperaments who interacted with distressed caretakers in turbulent families had a greater chance of developing serious problems than did infants who were experienced as rewarding by their caretakers and who grew up in consistently supportive homes.

This study documented the pervasive effect on social relations in early childhood of the quality of mother-child interaction in infancy and emphasized once again that children fare better when there is more than one caretaking adult in their immediate household. The family that is embedded in a strong network of social support is buffered against stressful experiences.

The investigators in this study also were impressed by the strong positive effects of children's competence in reading and writing their primary language—in this case, English. Success in school was an important contributor to children's resiliency, especially in the face of poverty or serious family disruptions. On the other hand, children who lacked such skills had cumulative difficulty in cognitive and interpersonal matters during middle childhood and adolescence.

In other research, Professor Craig Ramey and colleagues at the University of North Carolina studied how children with severely disadvantaged mothers develop. These mothers shared three qualities: an extreme sense that they had little capacity to shape their destinies; low self-esteem; and a pessimistic perception of opportunity. These mothers' caretaking was likely to be inadequate, unresponsive, and not conducive to healthy child development. Children reared in such circumstances are most at risk for retarded intellectual development and adaptive behavior. They are also likely to develop educational handicaps during their public-school years.

These children may, indeed, learn behaviors specifically disapproved by the larger society, particularly in the school system—e.g., strongly aggressive behavior. As a result, they often are stereotyped in ways that, sharply deprecatory, restrict their opportunities for learning and adaptation. A vicious cycle is perpetuated: These children see themselves as having limited life options, a perception that only confirms their alienation from the mainstream.

Within poor and socially disadvantaged settings, there are distinctive patterns of parent-child interaction that tend to be associated with differing patterns of intellectual development, social responsibility, and motivation for later education. Professor Michael Rutter of the University of London has found that children who grow up amid marital discord and family disturbance often emerge with learning difficulties. These affect academic performance more by influencing the child's social and emotional development than by impairing his or her cognition.

Ramey, in an excellent review that synthesizes research from diverse disciplines, underscores the critical importance of parents' behavior—especially continuing, active encouragement of infant's responsiveness to appropriate stimulation; engagement in systematic, often playful, activities with the child; and provision of a variety of stimulating intellectual experiences for the child. He recommends that intervention programs teach parents to be teachers; to help them convey to the child the strong value they put on learning and intellectual achievement and give them the skills to guide the learning. The focus of this analysis is on parents and their children in seriously disadvantaged communities.

Another aspect of healthy child development is illuminated by research on the organization of a child's physical environment. Excessive stimulation, for example, may increase a child's distractibility and irritability and cause stress. Various studies have shown that continual loud noise, crowded living conditions, a great deal of unstructured experience, and massive exposure to television in the early years all tend to be detrimental. At the other extreme, it is clear from animal experimentation and from human clinical observations that an environment of severe sensory deprivation or one that restricts active exploration is also harmful to a child's cognitive development. Parents need to understand that there is an optimal range for the intensity and variety of stimulation for a child's healthy development, and early-intervention programs should reflect this fact in their design.

It is compelling that time and time again, research confirms that family climate predicts cognitive development. The commitment, support, encouragement, and practical help of a cohesive, resourceful family are fundamental to a healthy child's development. The great challenge is to move in this direction from a starting point of weak family ties and relative social isolation, to devise family-centered interventions that will help children develop the resilience they need to overcome such adversity and strengthen their families' cohesion.

LEARNING TO COPE

Even under very adverse circumstances, some children develop stable, healthy personalities. These children are resilient; they can recover from and adjust competently to misfortune and sustained stress. How do these children manage? How can we help others become less vulnerable to life's adversities?

Werner has identified clues about the sources of resiliency from her own longitudinal studies; from studies of minority children who succeed in school despite chronic poverty and discrimination; from studying the resilient offspring of psychotic parents; from studying children of divorce; from observing strength and kindness among the uprooted children of contemporary wars and among child survivors of the Holocaust. The personal competencies of these children, and support from their caregivers, either compensated for, challenged, or protected them against the adverse effects of a stressful life.

Werner concludes that resilient children have four central characteristics in common:

- An active, vigorous approach to solving life's problems
- A tendency to perceive their experiences constructively, even if they involved pain or suffering
- The ability, from infancy on, to gain other people's positive attention
- A strong ability to maintain a positive vision of a meaningful life

From birth onward, these children also have temperamental characteristics that make them very appealing to family, as well as to strangers. As babies, they are active, affectionate, cuddly, good-natured, and easy to manage. They elicit some positive responses even in a depriving environment. As children they display both a pronounced self-sufficiency and a strong sociability. They play vigorously, seek out novel experiences, lack excessive fear, and are self-reliant; but they are able to ask for help from both adults and peers. They often find refuge and a source of self-esteem in hobbies and creative interests. In middle childhood and adolescence, resilient children are often engaged in helpful activities such as caring for younger siblings or working part-time to help support their families. Some studies have found that these temperamentally "easy" traits characterize about 65 percent of all children. About 10 percent of children have difficult temperaments; they tend to have negative moods and intense emotions, and are difficult to soothe. These children tend to elicit negative responses even in nondeprived situations.

Adaptability may vary with age and sex. Most studies in the United States and Europe have shown that boys are more vulnerable in childhood to chronic and intense family discord, while girls are more vulnerable in adolescence.

The family crucible can also foster resiliency. Most resilient children have had the opportunity to establish a close bond with at least one caregiver from whom they received much attention in the first year of life. They have had enough good nurturing to establish a basic sense of trust. A mother who is gainfully and steadily employed seems to be an especially powerful model for resilient girls reared in poverty. The fact that these girls need to help out by caring for their siblings while their mothers work contributes to their autonomy and sense of responsibility.

Structure, rules, and assigned chores in the household also support resilient children and enable them to cope well. Resilient children seem to have been imbued by their families with a sense of coherence, a belief that life makes sense, that events are fairly predictable, and that they have some control over their fate.

Resilient children also find much emotional support outside the family. They tend to be well-liked by classmates and to have at least one and usually several close confidants. They rely on informal networks of neighbors, peers, and elders for counsel in times of transition, even crisis. They are apt to like and do well in school, not only in academics but also in sports, drama, or music. Extracurricular activities can be a very important source of support. Resilient children often make school a home away from home.

For these children, schools are most helpful if they set appropriately high standards; if teachers provide effective feedback with ample praise when deserved and serve as good models of behavior; and if students have positions of responsibility.

Resilient children seem to be especially adept at recruiting surrogate parents. Siblings, grandparents, aunts and uncles, foster parents, and baby-sitters may serve as role models and sources of emotional support. Outside the family, the most commonly mentioned role models in studies of resilient children are favorite teachers, good neighbors, and members of the clergy.

Focusing on children's resiliency, their self-righting tendencies, gives us a hopeful perspective. For some children, moderate stress seems to have a strengthening effect. Werner suggests that we can help tilt the balance from vulnerability to resiliency if we:

- Accept children's temperamental idiosyncrasies and offer them some experiences that challenge but do not overwhelm their coping abilities
- Convey to children a sense of responsibility and caring, and in turn reward them for helpfulness and cooperation

- Encourage children to develop a distinctive interest that can serve as a source of gratification and self-esteem
- Model a conviction that life makes sense despite the inevitable adversities that each of us encounters
- Encourage children to reach out beyond the nuclear family to a sympathetic relative or friend

We need to strengthen informal support for children and families that lack—temporarily or permanently—the close relationships that buffer stress: Those in need of such support include working mothers of young children without stable child care; single, divorced, or teenage parents; migrant or refugee children; and hospitalized or handicapped children who are separated from their parents for extended periods.

The research on resilient children suggests that requiring children to be helpful in the family, neighborhood, or community may lead to enduring and positive changes in them. Finally, we can help put children on the path to healthy development if we can sustain their faith that obstacles can be surmounted even under adverse circumstances and that they can find dependable and caring relationships.

So while being raised in a disrupted family can be a formidable challenge to a child's healthy development, the good news is that children can and do survive adverse experiences intact. Some have the good fortune to be born naturally resilient; many are able to build beyond their family limits to meet their needs. And research has uncovered many ways both to strengthen family ties and help children find strength beyond their families. The lessons learned from resilient children and their growth-promoting circumstances can be helpful in preventing damage to many other children. In the subsequent chapters, we will pursue this line of inquiry and innovation.

6

Who's Minding the Children? Confronting the Child-Care Crisis

We are in the midst of a child-care crisis. The dramatic shifts in the roles and responsibilities within the family and the changes in the fundamental composition of the family itself have forced the issue of child care to national prominence. Despite the urgency of the problem, however, parents are far from clear on what constitutes good child care and how they can find it.

It is especially important to understand what constitutes high-quality care and how it can be put into practice on a wide scale. The current surge of demand for child care outside the home is relatively new and is occurring on an unprecedented scale; we have only begun to assess the effectiveness of various ways of responding to this demand. Ideally, child care should enhance the child's development as well as relieve the strain on the parents from competing demands to earn a living. Does that ideal exist in practice?

In this chapter I will discuss the present ferment in finding ways to create child care adequate to the tasks of the new world we have created. We can learn some lessons from other nations that have addressed this problem seriously. We also need to clarify ways in which the policies of powerful institutions might help to fulfill the potential of this extraordinary effort. While there is an emerging professional consensus on what we can achieve, the nation has yet to find an effective response to this great challenge.

Mothers of children under three years of age are the fastest-growing segment of the labor market in the United States, so child-care arrangements at the preschool level are of enormous practical significance. For single parents—those who are divorced, widowed, or never married—the difficulties of handling work and home responsibilities are exacerbated. Parents who have never been married are probably under the greatest strain; they have total responsibility as head of household and the least help available. About two-thirds of single mothers with preschool children are employed, most of them full-time. No matter how poor they may be, they must find some kind of arrangement for care of their very young children.

Working mothers face a daunting task: Research shows that after they put in forty hours or more a week on the job, they work an additional thirty-six hours or more with their children. For all practical purposes, they have two full-time jobs with heavy demands. This is an inherently stressful situation, and many women report feeling chronically fatigued, often harassed, and concerned about the adequacy of their performance in the many roles they play. Too-great pressures can have a strong effect on mothers' relationships with their children. Not surprisingly, studies find that dissatisfied women tend to be less involved, playful, stimulating, affectionate, and effective with their children than women who feel generally satisfied. In order to feel reasonably satisfied and competent in dealing with the many complex demands on their time, working mothers—rich and poor—put a premium on finding suitable child care, especially for their very young children.

Child care is now provided by an array of professionals in diverse settings, including child-care centers, family day-care and group homes, public and private nursery schools, prekindergartens and kindergartens, Head Start programs, before- and after-school programs, and informal arrangements such as care by relatives, in-home baby-sitting, and nanny care. The professional service community encompasses two separate traditions. The social-welfare tradition views child care as a custodial and protective service for poor and dependent children whose parents are unable to provide adequate care because they are working or for other reasons. In contrast, the early-childhood education tradition is more child-centered, viewing child care as an opportunity to give social and cognitive enrichment for children of middle-class families. There has been a lack of detailed information about costs, benefits, and feasibility of alternative policies. This lack is due in part to the insufficiency of federal support for research on child care in the eighties.

Let us take a closer look at the three major forms of child care: home, family, and center-based.

A common arrangement is to keep the baby in the parents' home and bring in others to help while the mother is at work. However, this arrangement has been the subject of very little research, so it is difficult to assess. Home care is convenient, flexible, and comforting in its familiar setting. In principle, it is very appealing; yet much depends on the quality and reliable long-term presence of the people who provide the care. In practice, at-home care tends to be unstable and uneven in quality. It usually requires a great deal of improvising by individual families, who often have no reliable support system. It is also likely to be the most expensive form of care.

The second common form of child care, at this writing perhaps the most popular for children younger than age three, is family child care in a private home. This, too, has the advantage of relative familiarity since the homes are typically in the neighborhood and the caregivers are often people known to the parents from the outset. Private-home care replicates the home environment; it often provides a small group size; children enjoy continuity of care; and the cost is only one-half to three-fourths that of center-based care. Many parents use family child care for infants and then place their children in a preschool environment between the ages of two and a half and three and a half. Since two very influential determinants of the parents' choice of what kind of day care to select are cost and proximity to home, family child care is popular. A good many flexible arrangements are possible. But family child care is regulated poorly or not at all, and there is enormous variability in the quality and continuity of the caregivers. An important issue is to find ways of making family child care of high quality, consistent, and accountable. The task is very difficult.

The fastest-growing type of child care today is for infants and toddlers. We are witnessing a new social form in the United States —caretakers taking care of a child for as long as eight to ten hours a day, five days a week, from the first days of life to age five or six. For the very youngest children, parents clearly prefer family child care to center care.

About 2 million women care for two or more unrelated children in their own homes. Providers earn, on the whole, low wages, often less than the minimum wage. Black women earn significantly less than white providers. An increasing number of women, many of whom have raised their own children and helped with others, are seeking to enter family child care on a professional basis. In order to make a worthwhile income, a provider usually has to take in six to eight children. There are substantial costs in starting up family child care—equipment; educational curriculum; meeting fire, health, and safety standards. For many, the temptation is to increase the number of children so much that individual attention declines and quality of care suffers.

Centers provide the third major form of child care and are the most visible and clearly accountable kind. They make possible a degree of professionalism that is hard to come by elsewhere. Yet they tend to be relatively expensive and at a distance from the familiar setting of the child's home; and they differ a good deal among themselves. They have been the object of much more formal research than the other settings of child care in recent times. Child-care centers include proprietary and commercial ones, community or church-based centers, company centers at or near the location of a large employer, cooperative centers, public-service centers, and special research centers. They have been growing rapidly in recent years. We will see their advantages when we consider research on quality of care. The crucial challenge is to create widely accepted standards of care based largely on research evidence for all child-care settings.

According to a landmark report published by the National Research Council in 1990, most children under one with working mothers are cared for by fathers as well as mothers, other relatives, or nonrelatives in their own or the caregiver's home. In 1985 only 14 percent were cared for in an organized child-care facility. The proportion is higher now and rising each year. The use of organized child-care facilities has also risen among preschoolers. In 1985, 25 percent of working mothers with children under five used a child-care facility as their primary form of care, compared with 13 percent in 1977.

Child-care arrangements are often quite complex. About one-quarter of preschoolers in cities are cared for in more than one arrangement. Mothers are expressing an increased preference for center-based care as a way to enhance children's learning experiences.

Parents' most urgent needs are for organized programs of high quality for infants and toddlers, before- and after-school programs for the nation's estimated 2.1 million "latchkey" children, child-care and preschool programs for children with disabilities, and comprehensive child-development programs for economically disadvantaged children. Mere custodial care is no longer an acceptable option; our children need and deserve more.

We also must provide adequate child care to enable adolescent mothers to complete their education and to provide relief to parents under intense stress who might otherwise abuse their children.

THE EFFECTS OF CHILD CARE

The first question on most parents' minds is: Am I harming my child by turning him or her care over to someone else? Working mothers often shoulder a large burden of guilt when they return to their jobs and delegate the care of their children to another. Are we damaging our children by putting them in day care? Research efforts have done a lot to clarify the issue.

The first wave of research into this issue compared the effects of child care in general with parental care. This research showed that participation in child care is not per se a form of maternal deprivation. Children can and do form attachments to multiple caregivers, if the number of caregivers is limited, if relationships are enduring, and if caregivers are responsive.

Indeed, this research showed that children can benefit from child care. There is no evidence that child care has negative effects on the cognitive development of middle-class children; and high-quality cognitive-enrichment programs can enhance cognitive development among low-income children at risk for declining IQ scores. Overall, children with child-care experience have greater social competence. Compared with children cared for by their parents, they show a pattern of peer interaction that is richer and more complex, but also includes more conflict.

In this entire field, the greatest doubt centers on how out-of-home care affects the child's first year of life. The findings so far are mixed. Some show that out-of-home care can disrupt the process of forming a secure attachment with the parents during the first year, especially if such arrangements are unstable, as they tend to be. Children beginning full-time child care in the first year of life and children cared for by their parents alone have different patterns of attachment to their mothers (though this is not true for children beginning in part-time day care). These differences are often open to a range of interpretations that further research should resolve.

Studies have found that it is certainly possible for infant development to proceed in a healthy way with high-quality child care. However, some recent studies of less than excellent child care, often in unstable or patchwork arrangements, indicate that there is a tendency for infants involved in such care during the first year of life to show insecure attachments. Some scholars in this field are concerned that, given current day-care options, it is very difficult to provide adequate conditions for attachment outside the home during the first year of life. Yet infants can benefit from such early day care if the conditions are favorable. For example, infants with prior child-care experience adapt more quickly and explore more fully in an unfamiliar environment. They tend to be more ready to play with peers and appear more confident in social situations, less fearful of unfamiliar adults. Against a background of neglect at home, early experience in quality child care may be valuable. All this suggests a great need for more differentiated assessment of child-care practices, including quality, timing, and relation to home environments, and kind and amount of parent participation.

At present, most professionals recommend that parents defer day care beyond infancy if possible. But as a practical matter, in the absence of policies for paid maternity leave, the trend seems to be increasing toward day care for infants. Therefore many clinicians and researchers are working to develop effective modes and standards of dependable day care that will promote the normal, vigorous child development that research and practice have shown to be possible. They are also mindful of the importance of a continuing, unbroken relationship with at least one caregiver through infancy and into the childhood years, whatever the infant-care arrangements may be.

The psychological development of children in day care is fostered by secure attachments to parents as well as to caregivers. Children who have problems cooperating with peers and adults may be getting poor-quality care, or care focusing exclusively on cognitive development rather than mastering social skills.

Language development in child care is fostered by frequent talk between children and caregivers. Other aspects of cognitive development are supported by some, but not excessive, organized learning that allows children to initiate and pace their own activities. For disadvantaged children, intensive exposure to well-planned child care can enhance their intellectual development as well as how they adapt later to school and social life, especially if child-care activities involve both child and family.

Unfortunately, there have been few studies of how children fare in after-school care, although there is some evidence that "latchkey children," who must care for themselves after school, tend to have problems. Limited data suggest that children can benefit from high-quality after-school programs that involve communication between teachers and caregivers, and activities that complement the regular school curriculum.

An interesting study directed by Alison Clarke-Stewart, then professor of psychology at the University of Chicago, systematically compared different types of child-care provided in the Chicago community for two- to four-year-olds from differing backgrounds. The centers included nursery school, child-care centers, or a combined arrangement of a center and a baby-sitter. These programs were generally regarded as responsible but were not chosen as examples of extraordinary or outstanding day-care operations. The children were tested on measures of intellectual and social competence. Clarke-Stewart's remarkable and somewhat surprising finding is that on a variety of measures of intellectual competence, there was a consistent difference in favor of the children who received care in a center. In all cases, the children's growth in intellectual competence was greater than the growth of those who were in home care, no matter what that home-care arrangement was. This finding cut across different family backgrounds and covered both sexes—and was most striking for poor families. Evidently, there is something particularly stimulating for intellectual development in the pooling of resources that the center makes possible.

But this is not all. Clarke-Stewart's findings with respect to social competence are similar. At least in the age range from two to four (we know much less about day care in infancy), the effects are generally favorable. While children sustain strong attachments to their parents, they nevertheless learn to relate well to peers in their center experience and tend to be more advanced in this respect than children who do not have day-care-center experience. Day-care children are somewhat more independent on the average, but not unfriendly. In social situations, they tend to be more outgoing, less apprehensive, and more cooperative with other children than those who are being cared for entirely at home. However, they also tend to be characterized as boisterous and vigorously assertive with their peers. Though this latter characteristic may be troublesome, it may also be a part of their social competence. These children are relatively self-confident and assertive in unfamiliar situations, which appears to help them in transitions to higher levels of education.

Indeed, the effects appear to be remarkably persistent. The longer the child is in a child-care center of some kind, the more enduring the effects on his or her intellectual and social competence. To some extent, children retain this advantage into the first few years of elementary school.

One of the most important findings of this research is that the children who benefited most from child-care centers were those who came from relatively poor families. Perhaps the contrast of the rich experience at the center with the relatively impoverished setting at home provided special opportunities they would otherwise have missed.

Children raised at home or in day care do not differ in the kinds of diseases or injuries they experience. Children in child care have a mildly to moderately increased risk of contracting several common infectious diseases, but generally with no long-term consequences. Viral respiratory diseases are more common among children in child care in the first three years, but may be less common in later years. The one possible long-term consequence of the increased rate of common infections is lasting effects on hearing and language development if the more common middle-ear infections are not treated promptly.

Group care increases the risk of a few rare but more serious infectious diseases, notably hepatitis A and meningitis. There is no evidence of increased risk of infection with HIV, the virus that causes AIDS. There is no evidence so far that child care influences children's risk of physical injury, sexual abuse, physical abuse, or neglect.

Scientific evidence and professional experience from pediatrics and public health indicate that child-care facilities need safeguards to ensure the health and safety of children. These include limitations on group size, separation of groups by age, hand-washing, regular cleaning of diaper-changing surfaces and communal objects, exclusion of children with certain infectious diseases, and appropriate immunization.

The quality of care a child receives is crucially dependent on his or her relationship with caregivers, which should be enduring, dependable, and limited to a few central people. Unfortunately, these attributes are not widespread in American child care.

Research shows that within fairly broad limits, the ratio of children to caregivers is not as important as the behavior of the caregiver over time. The main criteria are active involvement of the teacher with the children, the provision of interesting materials, sensitivity in responding to the children's initiatives and interests, and encouragement for constructive behavior along with concrete suggestions tailored to the individual child. Professionalism, including staff training, explicit standards, and participation in a network of staff activities for mutual aid and support, also appears to be important. As research on these issues continues, it will increasingly be possible to sharpen the criteria for high-quality child care and to find ways of meeting these criteria in all kinds of child care.

Disturbingly, much of what we know about what constitutes high-quality care is not put into practice. State regulations and parents' decision-making often do not take into account the quality standards recognized by researchers and professionals.

The second wave of research on the effects of child care examined links between variations in child-care quality and children's development. This research demonstrates that child-care quality is vitally important to children's cognitive and socioemotional development. Low-quality care has high costs in children's comparatively poor social, emotional, and cognitive development, behavioral difficulties, and health problems in the short run, as well as poor skills, high-school dropout rates, reduced earnings, antisocial behavior, and economic dependency in the long run.

An emerging third wave of research is investigating links between family and child-care environments. This research suggests that the quality of care a child receives depends in part on the family's socioeconomic and psychological conditions. In general, children who grow up in less favorable family environments receive lower-quality care. For example, families with fewer economic and social-support resources, and families characterized as restrictive and stressed, are more likely than other families to have children in poor-quality care. As research progresses, we will better understand how children's home and child-care environments influence each other. For example, one study found that children who participated in high-quality infant day care experienced positive changes in their interaction with their parents, apparently modeled after the child-care staff's behavior.

Research findings of the beneficial effects of day care during the immediate preschool years, and carrying over into the early elementary-school years, naturally stir curiosity about what it is that constitutes high-quality care. Can we extract the essential ingredients and heighten the efficiency with which they are made available? Such information would be exceedingly useful to parents who must choose as well as they can, on the basis of limited information, among the variety of possibilities available. If the parents are seeking competent supervision, stimulating play, and preparation for elementary school, they are likely to choose a day-care *center* of some kind, provided they can afford it. On the other hand, research shows that home-based care tends to provide more authoritative discipline, strict training, and one-to-one adult-child relationships, in addition to the aura of familiarity—all of which count heavily with many parents.

Overall, the best results in intellectual and social development in child care appear to draw upon a balance of academic and playful activities. The best results are also associated with environments that are not crowded but do contain a variety of play materials, providing many different learning opportunities. The best group composition seems to be a small group of children of both sexes and an age range from youngest to oldest of about two years. Such settings offer many opportunities for cooperation, sharing, and individual relationships with other children as well as with the caregiver.

The National Research Council panel reached seven general conclusions. First—and most striking—existing child-care services in the United States are inadequate to meet the current and likely future needs of children, parents, and society as a whole. Second, a large number of children are now cared for in settings that neither protect their health and safety nor offer them appropriate developmental stimulation. Third, child care has become a necessity for the majority of American families irrespective of family income. Fourth, arranging quality child care can be difficult, stressful, and time-consuming, especially for low-income families. Therefore, public policies should give priority to the economically disadvantaged. Fifth, the diversity of existing child-care services is both a strength and a challenge to the development of a more coherent child-care system. Sixth, there is no single policy or program that can address the child-care needs of all families and children. We need a comprehensive array of coordinated policies and programs. Seventh, responsibility for meeting the nation's child-care needs should be widely shared among individuals, families, voluntary organizations, employers, communities, and all levels of government. Child-care policies should affirm and support the role and responsibilities of families in child-rearing.

The panel identified three overarching goals of a child-care system: to achieve quality; to improve accessibility for all families; and to enhance affordability for low- and moderate-income families. All three goals are critical to the development of an improved child-care system.

Child care is no longer simply a protective or remedial service for poor children or those from troubled families. It is an everyday arrangement for the majority of children in the United States. Child care has become a large and diverse enterprise of public and private, for-profit and not-for-profit services.

There are some useful steps we must take to improve family child care. First, we must guarantee providers a decent income to encourage capable people to participate. Second, we must institute standardized training, both before day-care providers begin to work and while they are on the job; this will promote acceptance of and adherence to high standards of care. Third, we must construct local and regional mutual-aid networks so providers have access to other resources for help, encouragement, and inspiration. Fourth, we must find emblems of recognition and status for providers of quality care, including licensure on the basis of reasonable, explicit criteria. Finally, we must inform parents about what constitutes quality care and how they can select and monitor high-standard providers.

Improving quality by raising staff–child ratios and staff salaries will increase the cost of child care. It is unlikely that low- and moderate-income families will be able to afford high-quality child care without more assistance from government or employers. So this will have to be an area of policy innovation in the nineties. We can look outside this country for inspiration.

CHILD CARE IN INTERNATIONAL PERSPECTIVE

Many other Western industrialized countries have also experienced a rising influx of women into the labor force. These countries have invested more public resources in child care than has the United States. Most have parental-leave policies, and most make early-childhood education available for children aged three to five, regardless of mothers' work status.

We can learn a lot about improving the quality and accessibility of child care from the experience of other nations. Indeed, Europe is deeply committed to the child-care enterprise, and several countries have already instituted programs that address eight issues deserving serious consideration in the United States.

1. Extend the length of day in existing nursery-school arrangements to accommodate full-day working mothers.
2. Extend the age of admission in day-care centers to include infants, and establish special infant and toddler facilities.
3. Encourage an explicit, developmentally appropriate, curricular component in day care.
4. Select caregivers on the basis of aptitude and give them systematic training.
5. Integrate day care into a larger system of child-care supports.
6. Have more systematic supervision of care facilities.
7. Include the various kinds of care, whether center-based or home-based, in a mutual-aid network of cooperating facilities.
8. Use centers as sites for health improvement and supportive parent education.

Let us examine how these potentially valuable practices are reflected in the experiences of various European countries.

Scandinavia

In 1990, Fred and Grace Hechinger, noted education writers, reported on child care in Scandinavia based on visits to institutions and interviews with experts in Denmark, Norway, and Sweden. They emphasized that, in all these countries, child care has support from the entire political spectrum. One reason for this wide support is that Scandinavian child-care policies are not narrowly targeted to the poor or disadvantaged. Another is the relative homogeneity of values, compared with the United States. Scandinavia's child-care policies are far more generous and comprehensive than those of the United States, although they too have problems. These nations began with virtually universal prenatal care, including home visits before and after birth. Their policies include guaranteed, paid one-year maternity leave.

In Sweden, parents pay 10 percent of the cost of child care. In Denmark they pay 35 percent. Child-care centers are abundantly staffed. Two or three adults care for ten to twelve preschool children, or for twenty to thirty kindergarten children. Child-care professionals have three years of college training with a concentration in child care. As in the United States, however, they have lower pay and status than elementary-school teachers. As a matter of policy, children in preschools are not formally taught. (In Denmark this prohibition is a matter of law. In Sweden there is an active controversy about this topic.) In general, Scandinavian child-care centers are bright, cheerful places, with children engaged in creative group activities indoors and out.

When places are limited, top priorities go to immigrants, handicapped children, and poor children. Since there are insufficient places at child-care centers, home care is also used in Sweden. Home-care providers are screened and their operations inspected. They are paid on a level below that of the professional child-care workers. They are encouraged to take advantage of special regional centers where children can participate in larger groups. "Libraries" of toys are also available.

The expansion of high-quality child care has been associated with reduction in serious childhood accidents. Good child-care facilities evidently provide safer environments than other settings.

In Sweden, a law provides for readily available parental education, viewed as a very important component of child health care. Parents attend daytime parental-education classes without loss of income. The goal of the education is mainly to increase the parents' knowledge of children—their development and rearing—and to encourage contact and solidarity among families.

France

Child care also has support across the political spectrum in France. Services are intended for all social strata, not just for poor or at-risk children, and are largely tax-financed, with parents paying 20 percent of the costs. The system is a blend of child care, education, and health services based on free full-day preschool, subsidized day care, and licensed care in private homes.

The noncompulsory preschools serve 90 percent of French children aged three to five, offering language arts, exercise, crafts, and play. Parents may purchase additional care before and after school and during vacations for about $210 per year. Family day care is widespread, and about 75 percent is licensed, compared with about

10 percent in the United States. The government offers incentives for family day-care providers to become licensed, including retirement benefits, disability insurance, and a minimum wage. In addition, parents receive a tax deduction for using licensed rather than unlicensed care.

Staff quality is generally high. Preschool teachers are required to have the equivalent of a master's degree in early-childhood education. There are staff-child ratios of one teacher to every twenty-two preschoolers, eight toddlers, or five infants—ratios that are far from optimal. Other problems include heavy central government control and lack of parental involvement. A shortage of infant-toddler care is an additional problem, but the government is providing funds for more centers and family day care for this age group.

Great Britain

Jerome Bruner, one of the pioneers of modern developmental psychology, studied child care for children under age five in Great Britain. His study highlights the strengths and limitations of different arrangements for child care and clarifies important ingredients of care that foster healthy child development. It also reflects the considerable difficulty Great Britain has in meeting the need for out-of-home child care.

The major forms of child care in Britain include child-minders, day nurseries, nursery schools, and voluntary play groups. I will confine my attention to the first two of these, child-minders and day nurseries, which are the two forms of full-day care.

A child-minder typically looks after her own as well as others' children in an arrangement similar to family child care in the United States. She typically does her housework while minding her charges. She may or may not be registered with the local authorities. If she registers, she must have her premises approved as suitable and as meeting safety and space standards. There is no particular incentive for registering, and there are no sanctions for not registering. There is wide variation in what children do at the child-minder's. The study finds that child-minding creates problems for between one-third and one-half of the children—for example, a significant number of children in these situations become mildly depressed. The heart of the problem is the discontinuity for the child between his or her parents' home and that of the minder, and the lack of adequate communication between the minder and the mother. With neither social services nor health services readily available, the minder has nowhere to turn when she is concerned about a child. Most minders do not see their jobs as involving professional skills. A good part of the task of improving child-minding will be making minders see such skills as necessary and attainable. Although there are differences between child-minding in Britain and family day care in the United States, there are enough similarities that we should take seriously the implications of Bruner's analysis. If family day care is to continue as a major component of American child care, we will have to pay much more attention to creating programs with consistent quality.

Full-day nurseries, similar to American day-care centers, almost always include conventional nursery-school or play-group activities. There are fully state-maintained day nurseries, as well as nurseries run by charitable or community organizations and by commercial organizations. Priority in state nurseries is usually given to children at risk and to children of single parents.

Bruner recommends against expanding child-minding until it has been extensively reexamined and reorganized. He suggests parents use child-minders chiefly to supplement organized care after hours or during school vacations. Some children can thrive at the child-minder's, but children who do not should be placed in a day nursery instead. Bruner also recommends that children with troubles at home not be placed at a minder's.

In summary, France and the Scandinavian countries are much more generous and comprehensive in their child-care arrangements than is the United States. These countries are characterized by broad political support for child care, high-quality and widely used services, and extensive use of taxes more than parent fees to fund child care.

The United Kingdom, on the other hand, shares several problems with the United States. Child care is not available for many parents who want it, and quality is highly variable. Bruner's study expresses particular concern about the adequacy of care provided by child-minders, the British rough equivalent of family day-care providers, and recommends some form of institutional support for these providers. Alfred Kahn and Sheila Kamerman of Columbia University, in an international analysis, make a similar recommendation for family day-care providers in the United States. They further point out that family day care is largely used by families who cannot afford more expensive, higher-quality forms of care, thus creating a two-tier system of care.

SEARCHING FOR ADEQUATE CHILD-CARE POLICIES

How can we draw on the lessons from other nations as well as create innovations of our own to reform American child care?

In a 1988 review and analysis, Professors Alfred Kahn and Sheila Kamerman of Columbia University outlined three main differences between social policies concerning children in the United States and in the Northern and Western European countries. Kahn and Kamerman focused primarily on financial policies, although they dealt with the nature of services to a lesser extent. The first striking difference is that almost all European countries provide child benefits through income transfers to all children. The few that do not have universal coverage provide benefits to all poor children. In contrast, the United States provides benefits only to some poor children. Second, social-insurance benefits for children in Europe are far more generous and more extensive than in the United States. Third, European countries have used income transfers as a supplement to family earnings, whereas the United States has largely provided income transfers only when families have no earned income.

To explain why these differences exist, Kahn and Kamerman point out that the United States began to develop its national income-transfer programs much later than the European countries did; that our complex pluralism has constrained the development of national policy on children or families. To the extent that social equity has been a goal of American policy, the issue of race has received priority over class or income.

All of the industrialized countries including the United States provide free compulsory education from the age of five, six, or seven up to age fifteen or sixteen. However, almost all the Continental European countries finance free or low-fee optional preschool or child care for children from age three or younger up to school age. Government support for preschool and child care is quite restricted in the United States.

All of the European countries mentioned above, and many others, provide universal health insurance or health services for children and their families. All have fairly comparable systems of social insurance for the elderly, surviving family, the disabled, and the unemployed. The United States employment-insurance system is lower in both the level of payments and their duration. All of the European countries provide short-term disability or sickness benefits through the social-insurance system, and provide paid maternity or parental leave. There is nothing comparable in the United States.

In pensions, health-care, disability, and sickness insurance as fringe benefits, the private sector in the United States compensates somewhat for the very limited role of government compared with the European countries. But there is no such private-sector provision of family benefits, with the exception of a tiny proportion of United States employers who provide family-support services such as child care.

In contrast with the United States, almost all other industrial countries provide a public, universal child or family allowance based on the number of children in the family. Typically, these allowances for each child are equal to about 5 to 10 percent of the parents' average gross wages. A growing trend among the European countries is provision of a guaranteed minimum child-support payment for single mothers in cases where the father will not or cannot pay an adequate amount. These programs, in combination with means-tested income assistance, can make a large difference to the income of, for example, a single mother who has two children yet is earning half the average wage. Such a policy is absent in the United States, where more than one in five of our children younger than six lives in poverty.

In the United States, the supply of child care has expanded since the first half of the eighties, in spite of reduced direct federal funding and little federal leadership, encouragement, or aid. However, a gap remains between demand and supply. Access to many programs is limited to those who can afford to pay market rates. Infant-toddler care and school-age care are especially scarce at any price.

How can child care become universally available, readily accessible, and high in quality while remaining voluntary and responding to communities' cultural, ethnic, and demographic needs? We do not yet have a clear-cut path to a solution.

Among the priorities delineated by Kahn and Kamerman are adequate federal and state financial support for child care for low-income families; state action to improve regulation of quality; federal or state actions to ensure a paid, job-protected disability; and parenting leaves. They predict a major role for the public schools in providing preschool services. (I will consider this in the chapter on implementation.)

Kahn and Kamerman also highlight the need to develop information and referral programs to help parents find appropriate child care; family day-care systems integrated with broader programs that foster quality; education of parents as child-care consumers; and integration of education, social-welfare, and child-development functions.

The government can subsidize child-care centers and parents' fees, provide services, organize the delivery system, and help consumers find their way in the child-care system. Until recently, the only formal public commitment was to provide services, as is the case with kindergarten and Head Start. This situation began to change when the federal child-care tax credit was created—a demand subsidy rather than direct provision. Tax incentives for employers provide a supply subsidy. Demand subsidies assume that consumers are sophisticated enough to use them, and that there are reliable information and referral systems and professional or governmental monitoring of quality and of unmet need. We now have the technology, knowledge, and practical competence to develop such systems, but they are not yet widespread.

Much of the encouragement to business must come from the federal level, since tax benefits in return for day-care provision are the major public leverage. Leading scholars believe that work-site child care will probably be only a small part of the future response to need. Only major employers, or employers with special circumstances, are likely to undertake significant child-care activities. Incentives for most employers are few, and concerns are widespread. Some firms, however, have found that they can attract employees by providing related services such as information and referral, education about child care and parenting, and including child care in a fringe-benefit menu.

Even though a highly decentralized system is likely to expand in the United States, the federal government will be needed to subsidize low-income parents; set minimum standards for facilities to receive federal subsidies or tax incentives; invest in research and demonstration programs, and disseminate findings; provide start-up funds for low-income regions; provide scholarship or training funds to prepare the work force; and lend technical assistance.

The child-care dilemma is upon us now. Solutions have yet to emerge. The ferment of curiosity, concern, and innovation in child care will help us find ways to foster our children's development in the earliest years of precious life. But how many children will get lost in the cracks while our society struggles to adapt to a transforming world?

7

Protecting Our Children in Their First Few Years

PREVENTING DAMAGE TO YOUNG CHILDREN AT RISK

Too many infants are at risk for developmental impairment—those who show insecure attachment in the first year of life, and many at risk by virtue of growing up in very poor or socially disorganized circumstances. What early intervention can we take to prevent serious damage to these children? Numerous studies confirm that a difficult situation in early life does not doom the child to destruction. One of the recurring themes of research and carefully examined clinical experience is that social support can help young parents, whether they're coping with irritable or temperamental infants or with other pressures in their lives. Advice on child care, help with practical arrangements, social companionship, and parent education all can make a crucial difference between competent and inadequate parenting. Research into difficult family circumstances such as those involved in divorce, loss of a job, or change of residence demonstrates that it is not unusual for infants to shift from a secure to an anxious attachment, but then to shift back toward a secure attachment when the family situation has improved. In other words, attachment relationships can change when children are very young. Positive, supportive interventions can shift a child's attachment in the direction of security and dependability.

Even within severely disadvantaged families—although more commonly in relatively advantaged families—mother and child can be taught to interact in ways that tend to foster healthy child development. Numerous studies confirm that the mother's responsiveness strengthens the child's learning and sense of self-sufficiency and thereby opens doors to development that would otherwise be closed. For instance, several experiments indicate that a mother's interactive response to her infant's signals and behavior during the first year of life enhances the child's later language development and general learning capabilities. Dispirited, depreciated, isolated, or immature mothers ignore signals from their infants and are generally unresponsive to the infants' needs; those infants lose their spontaneity in generating social behavior and exploring their environment.

Fortunately, we can apply what we have learned from the research on child development to offset some of the worst effects of poverty and social depreciation. Research within poor communities, as well as across social classes, has clarified some of the key factors that determine whether children can develop successfully and fulfill their potential for educational achievement and constructive human relationships. Such research, summarized in prior chapters, has paved the way for valuable interventions. These have been carried out with entrepeneurial ingenuity in a variety of settings and have addressed very tough problems in a courageous way.

Such interventions have taken many forms:

(1) *Home visiting services.* Often indigenous to the community, these engage the child and the mother in organized activities appropriate to the child's phase of development.

(2) *Parent-child centers.* Located in poor communities, these bring in disadvantaged infants and their parents, undertaking parent education and infant stimulation; the main thrust is to teach young mothers how to become effective teachers of their own children and to develop mutually beneficial mother-child relationships.

(3) *Child and family resource programs.* These aim to provide families with children from infancy to school age with a broad range of services in health, education, and counseling. Services are provided both at home and at centers, depending on the specific problem.

These various programs strive to meet families' basic needs in ways that fit their particular circumstances: by providing information on child development; by promoting activities to foster stimulating and mutually gratifying parent-child interaction; by giving parents opportunities to explore their concerns, get help with the problems of living, and build coping skills; and by connecting the parents with community resources that can open up opportunities and meeting families' needs for health, food, shelter, clothing, training, and employment.

Interventions so complex and sensitive as these are difficult to evaluate. Research in this field has neither been adequately supported nor sufficiently rewarded to become fully adequate to its crucial tasks. But careful assessments provide substantial evidence that these programs are making a difference in children's lives.

Is there a research basis for believing that we can affect the long-term course of a child's development by improving his or her environment in the early years? The weight of the evidence says we can—even after the child has gotten off to a bad start. In fact, a landmark study published in the 1940s reveals that children born to mothers of below-average measured intelligence, when adopted into homes of people with higher measured intelligence, showed considerable gains not only in measured intelligence but in educational accomplishment.

More recent studies in a similar vein have yielded similar results. One of these involved children of unskilled workers who were abandoned at birth and adopted by families of strong professional achievement and high socioeconomic status. The adopted children were later compared systematically with their biological half siblings who had been reared by the biological parents, with the children of unskilled workers in the general population, and with children of comparable age from upper-middle-class families. The results clearly showed that children from a socially disadvantaged background made gains in measured intelligence after they were adopted into a more favorable social environment.

A major project in Milwaukee is another instructive example. It focused on socially disadvantaged children whose mothers had an IQ of 75 or less. The children were divided into an intervention group and an untreated comparison group and were followed from infancy to the fourth grade of elementary school. The mothers in the experimental group were given home-management and job training as well as remedial education. However, there was little direct effort to improve their parenting skills. Their children participated in a structured educational program from infancy until six years of age. These activities centered on the development of skills in language and problem solving. The children in the intervention group showed greater measured intelligence and educational accomplishment than those in the untreated comparison group. In essence, the results indicate that a sustained and extensive intervention during the preschool years can improve children's cognitive skills and probably their interpersonal skills as well. It is interesting to note that, when the children were between ages six and ten and the intervention was over, the benefits of their enrichment diminished though they did not disappear. This raises the important question of the conditions under which children may receive cumulative beneficial effects. Several lines of inquiry suggest that continuing "boosters" or reinforcement programs can be very useful.

A similar program, the Abecedarian Project in North Carolina, has recently been designated by the American Psychological Association as an outstanding example of preventive intervention. The children were randomly assigned to intervention and comparison groups and were followed from infancy to five years of age. Their parents were seriously socially disadvantaged and mostly black, and most children came from female-headed households. The children started in the program as infants and received year-round daily care during their preschool years, with an emphasis on the development of language and adaptive social behavior. The program was well organized and systematic in its educational activities. However, parental involvement was minimal. Beginning when the children were about eighteen months of age, differences in their measured intelligence emerged, favoring the intervention group. These children also adapted better to new situations, used language more adeptly, and performed tasks more effectively than those in the comparison group. Remarkably, despite limited parental involvement, there were signs of benefit for the mothers of the intervention group. At follow-up they were better educated and had lower levels of unemployment than the comparison mothers. Altogether, the children showed substantial benefits in cognitive and social functions.

Such research is inherently time-limited. The inquiry puts a question to nature and seeks an answer. Then what? Can the findings be useful for children at risk? Research evidence of this kind suggests that it may be possible to nip in the bud a variety of potential harms to children by enhancing the competence of their parents and the support available in their social environments.

The Yale Child Welfare Research Program is further illustrative of valuable efforts in this field. It squarely focused on seriously disadvantaged families. Through home visitors, regular medical care, and an optional day-care program as well as regular developmental assessments, it provided services to children from birth to thirty months of age, and then a follow-up evaluation when the children were seven or eight years old. These interventions in infancy had a long-term impact on the children's intellectual and academic development. Those in the intervention program not only had higher measured intelligence but also more consistent school attendance and higher school achievement. Particularly striking was the effect on their families. At the time of the follow-up, they were doing better in educational status, economic self-sufficiency, housing, and general quality of life. Taken together, the research and experience in this field indicate that many useful interventions can be made in the first few years of life.

FOSTERING PARENTAL COMPETENCE AND CHILD DEVELOPMENT

It has become apparent that many young parents feel the need to educate themselves to develop their competence. Presumably the growth in the demand for parent education has been influenced by the erosion of the traditional extended family and the lack of guidance from experienced parents. Experts in this field indicate that the widening scope of parent education has been stimulated by rising divorce rates, the spread of single-parent families, the surge of births to unmarried adolescents, and the broad movement of women into the paid labor market. In addition, the growing respect for child-development professionals and a widespread acceptance of the contributions of modern science have added to the belief that young people should draw upon a body of knowledge for guidance in becoming adequate parents.

To some degree, this field has moved beyond its relatively affluent origins to include a broader range of parents, especially young ones. The growing demand has been reflected by widespread interest in parent-education materials—e.g., the Systematic Training for Effective Parenting curriculum and the guidebook designed for supervisors of the parent-to-parent program of the High/Scope group, which I'll discuss later in this chapter.

Although middle-class parents can pay for such services and

relate them to the higher education they have already achieved, it is more difficult to reach low-income families, whose needs are greater. But the national interest in early-childhood interventions, stimulated especially by Head Start, has proved strong enough to encourage parent-education activities broadly. In particular, family-support or family-resource interventions have been linked with parent education. Such combined efforts take many forms and occur in a variety of settings—e.g., schools, day-care centers, hospitals, health centers, and churches. They are conducted by people with diverse professional and paraprofessional backgrounds. They cover a considerable range of target populations. Their most common frequency of contact with participants is once a week. The most commonly provided services are educating parents to become more competent and foster child development; building social-support networks among parents; and providing information about and referral to community resources.

PARENT-EDUCATION AND FAMILY-SUPPORT INTERVENTIONS

Whereas parent-education efforts have historically focused on the child, family-support efforts view the entire family as one unit. The goals of community-based early intervention programs are: (1) augmenting parents' knowledge of and skill in child-rearing; (2) enhancing their skill in coping with the child and other family matters; (3) helping families gain access to services and community resources; (4) facilitating the development of informal support networks among parents; (5) organizing to counteract dangerous trends in the community, such as the spread of drugs. Although there is much overlap in practice between family support and parent education, they are conceptually distinct from each other. One can occur without the other. But the interesting development in recent years has been their conjunction in community-based early-intervention programs.

These programs are implemented by agencies located in or near the neighborhood of the families targeted for service; they employ paraprofessionals, usually members of the community being served, who often work with professionals; and they devote attention to the family and the extrafamilial environment. Overall, they focus on the parents' ability to care constructively for young children; they work with families in which developmental risk to the infant is believed to spring mainly from his or her social environment.

Such interventions may involve arrangements for home visiting by laypersons, or for visits to a parent-child center. The centers typically have both parent-support and education activities as well as other forms of child care and community access.

Among the most prominent programs that have concentrated their effort on the *parents* more than on their children were the nationwide Parent-Child Development Centers (PCDC). These centers, stimulated in part by Head Start, included preschool education for the children and an extensive curriculum for mothers of low-income families, involving information on child-rearing and home management as well as family support. The family was involved from the child's birth until age three. Families were randomly assigned to intervention and comparison groups, and results were carefully evaluated using multiple methods of measurement. Since each Parent-Child Development Center had considerable latitude in the design of its intervention, it is not surprising that the results varied from one center to another. Nevertheless, reasonable evidence of benefits emerged from all centers for families who were in the intervention groups.

Mothers in the intervention groups communicated more effectively with their children, were more sensitive and emotionally responsive to them, encouraged them more often, and gave them more information when talking with them. For their part, the children in the intervention group scored higher on intelligence tests and showed more advanced social behavior and more positive interactions with their mothers. A net assessment of the various centers across the country in PCDC indicates that children received beneficial effects in their first few years of life from this program. Unfortunately, a shortage of federal funding consigned PCDC to oblivion prematurely. Nevertheless, the program's influence continues to be felt throughout the country in the developments that have occurred since then.

A number of interesting features of the PCDC effort may well prove to be stimulating and useful for renewed efforts in the foreseeable future. For one thing, there was a deliberate effort to involve different kinds of low-income families: white, Hispanic, and black. For another, the experiment was carefully conceived and given a long time frame for its work. The intervention was from birth to three years of age, thus in effect filling the gap from prenatal care to Head Start. Each site was given latitude to reflect the distinctive characteristics of its location. Although the funds were ultimately withdrawn, there was a plan to replicate the initial results and then to disseminate them on a wide scale, with careful consideration of evaluation and adaptation at the appropriate stages. The programs were designed to take a comprehensive view of the problems of poor families, including education, health, nutrition, employment, and social environment. The intervention was managed by university-based scientists and scholars in each community who worked closely with community members. Each center had a parent advisory council. Altogether, the PCDC project was an intensive intervention that addressed serious problems in a deliberate, thoughtful, and sustained way. If the nation had been ready to provide funding to follow through on the initial plans, we would probably be in a much better position today than we are now. Still, valuable experience has been gained and useful lessons have been learned.

Very likely, the most important finding of the PCDC studies was the effect on interaction between mother and child. Despite local variations, it is clear that the mothers' behavior became more positive toward their children; they showed more affection, gave more praise, showed appropriate restraint, and encouraged their children's language development. There is ample reason from this experience to believe that even poor and seriously disadvantaged mothers can initiate behavior to improve mother-child interactions when they get a modicum of parent education and social support.

The most interesting follow-up study in the PCDC group occurred in the Houston, Texas, area. One round of follow-up occurred when the children were five and a half and another when they were between the ages of eight and eleven. In both rounds, there was evidence of direct effects on mother-child interaction. The gist of these findings is that the mothers and children became more effective collaborators; they learned to work together and to be sensitive to each other's needs.

As we look back over the whole sweep of such programs, it is reasonably clear that their strongest effects occurred in whatever arena they committed their major concentration of effort. In some programs, this was in parents' child-rearing skills. In other programs, it was in the personal development of the parents. Another general point of practical significance: More beneficial effects occurred, both with respect to parenting skill and child development, with the more intensive interventions that included professional as well as paraprofessional involvement. Thus, even though funding dwindled—and other difficulties were inevitably formidable in such a complex, ground-breaking enterprise—much of value was learned that can now be adapted to current circumstances and enriched by subsequent research.

RESULTS OF RESEARCH ON RECENT COMMUNITY-BASED EARLY INTERVENTIONS

Most of the recent community-based early-intervention programs throughout the nation represent innovative attempts to respond to urgent needs. They have been straightforward service programs with little or no attempt at evaluation. However, a few programs have conducted systematic assessment with comparisons between participating and nonparticipating families from similar backgrounds. Even though it is true that judicious reflection on the rich experience of unevaluated programs can also be useful, programs that have undergone careful evaluation are the most helpful in allowing us to set future standards.

One of the most interesting community-based early interventions is the Parent-Infant Project in Denver, Colorado. Started in 1977 as an experimental home-visiting program for low-income families, it involved weekly home visits by laypersons, beginning in the mother's mid-pregnancy and continuing until the child was one year old. Its main emphasis was on emotional support and practical help with immediate concerns. The program was intended to strengthen both the self-esteem and the interpersonal relations of family members as well as to facilitate their use of community resources. It was based in three local health-department clinics. The lay home visitors, from the community served, functioned as health-department aides; their training and supervision were provided by clinic nurses.

Participants in the Parent-Infant Project were randomly assigned to intervention and comparison groups, and results were evaluated at entry, postpartum, and when the child was one month, four months, and twelve months old. The evaluation included psychological measures involving the mother and infant, medical assessments, observations of maternal teaching and feeding, maternal-infant attachment measures, and assessments of the home environment. Unfortunately, participation in parent groups was very low. Altogether, serious operational difficulties interfered with the adequacy of the intervention. Nevertheless, one interesting point emerged: Mothers in the families at higher risk in terms of their socioeconomic status as well as in maternal history of abuse or neglect grew warmer toward their children and learned more appropriate parenting skills. Against an impoverished background, such interventions can fill gaps not present in more fortunate settings.

In the chapter on prenatal care, I touched on the promising intervention of the prenatal and early-infancy program of Elmira, New York. Started in 1978 to help low-income families during their first pregnancy, the program undertook home visits in mid-pregnancy, continuing twice a month during pregnancy, weekly during the first month after birth, and then with decreasing frequency throughout the first two years of the child's life. Beneficial effects on adolescent-pregnancy outcomes were noted.

The focus of the home visiting was on parent education, on strengthening the informal support system of the family, and on connecting the family with community resources. As it turned out, the main emphasis of the program was on parent education, starting with a serious effort to develop a trusting personal relationship between mother and nurse-visitor. The nurse-visitors used a detailed curriculum, which they applied flexibly in accordance with individual circumstances. Their immediate postnatal visits focused on the temperament of the baby, why it was crying, and other factors relevant to understanding its development during infancy.

When the postnatal efforts were evaluated, the nurse visits seemed to diminish the number of accidents children had in the second year of life; this was presumably due to better care by their mothers. There was also less abuse and neglect if the nurse visits occurred during both pregnancy and infancy. Similarly, the impoverished adolescent mothers in the intervention group punished their children less and gave them more play materials than did the mothers in the comparison group. In general, the program seemed to foster infant development. A replication is now under way in a very needy community in Memphis, Tennessee.

Another current innovation is the Family Support Project of Cambridge, Massachusetts. This involves home visiting for multiple-risk mothers and infants. All the mothers are in a psychiatrically vulnerable condition—indeed, 60 percent have had major depressive episodes. Problems of incipient abuse or neglect are common.

This project compares the relative effectiveness of a lay home-visiting program with home visiting by mental-health professionals that is supplemented by parent groups. Both are oriented toward depressed mothers and their capacity to give adequate care to their infants. The lay visits are operated by a community agency and the professional visits by the Cambridge Hospital Departments of Pediatrics and Psychiatry. Families are referred to the programs by local pediatricians and social-service agencies when infants are anywhere from newborn to nine months of age. The visits are on a weekly basis for one and a half years.

The lay home visiting involves both mother and baby. The home visitors bring toys, demonstrate parent-child activities, explore safety questions, give attention to the mother's concerns, seek to model joint problem solving, help families get needed services, and arrange for transportation. They sometimes leave written instructions after a visit. The home visitors also act as group leaders for the weekly parent meetings. This program is conducted by master's level psychologists who focus on the mother's emotional experiences—e.g., her own experience as a child and her relatively close personal relationships. The parent groups focus on sharing of feelings about family, friends, and important problems in human relationships.

Both of the comparison groups showed a substantial increase over time in the percentage of infants classified as securely attached. Also, mothers in both groups showed considerably more warmth and affection the longer they were in treatment. The most striking effects on maternal-infant attachment and on infant development occurred with those mothers who reported depressive symptoms at the time the program began. Evidently, the treatment mitigated the effects of their depression on their infants.

One interesting difference between the professional and lay home-visiting approach is that the lay visitors were more available after hours and between visits. They were also more oriented toward practical matters, providing respite and material assistance, and more inclined to share their own experience as parents and to focus on coping skills.

In general, this project indicates that home visiting can be useful in establishing a caring relationship with depressed, high-risk mothers, and at least stabilizing their parental behavior at the mother's best level of capability. Both direct home visiting by professionals and lay home visitors supervised by professionals can be helpful, albeit in somewhat different ways.

Another highly innovative approach is the AVANCE program in San Antonio. AVANCE is a center-based parent-support and education program serving low-income Mexican-American families. It has been functioning since 1973, and anyone who has visited it can hardly fail to be impressed. It now has two centers, one in a federal housing project and another in a low-income residential neighborhood. It has been directed from the start by Gloria Rodriguez, a highly skillful, dedicated, and charismatic leader. It is staffed largely by former program participants, trained by core professional staff. Parents enroll when their children are anywhere from newborn to three years of age and all families in the community are welcome. In addition, the staff does systematic, door-to-door recruitment.

A community survey conducted by AVANCE in 1980 revealed how badly needed knowledge was in the community: Parents were ignorant of children's developmental needs, how to acquire job skills, how to sustain hope in the face of long-term adversity, how to build a sense of control over one's life, and how to overcome social isolation. Indeed, a high incidence of abuse and neglect of children among young parents was detected in this survey. The staff used the survey to focus its program more sharply, emphasizing parents' own development, especially a basis for self-esteem and perception of opportunity, improved decision-making skills, and specific knowledge of child development. In the latter respect, the staff provided direct demonstration and modeling, encouraging play, seeking points of mutual pleasure between mother and child, and giving feedback in constructive ways.

The core component of AVANCE is a nine-month parent-education program consisting of monthly two-and-a-half-hour sessions —one hour devoted to toy making, one hour to child-development instruction, and a half hour to a community-resource speaker. The parents are taught that they themselves can be educators, and they are shown concretely how to facilitate their own children's development. While the classes are going on, the young children of the participants get good care in the same building. Participating mothers take part in child care once a month, where they can observe a child-care specialist at work while interacting with the children. They also get monthly home visits during which the home visitor videotapes mother-infant interaction. These tapes are used in subsequent classes.

The AVANCE experience has pointed to the importance of

ancillary services: transportation to the center; home visits for the new parents as a transition to participating in the activities of the center; day care; pleasurable outings—e.g., to the circus; graduation ceremonies as a focus for solidarity and reward for accomplishment; employment training; family planning; learning how to use community resources; driver education. In other words, AVANCE tries to offer one-stop support; many needs can be met in one place. The approach has grown increasingly comprehensive over the years. In a variety of ways, parents are taught basic social skills as an integral part of the program. Staff training and supervision are an ongoing, vital part of the activity.

AVANCE already has some evidence that the program fosters parents' knowledge of child development, increases their hopefulness about the future, enhances prospects in this poor community, decreases punitive approaches to child discipline, and generally improves the climate of mother-child interaction. The results of the ongoing systematic assessment will be of great interest.

In reviewing parent-education and family-support programs, it is clear that innovation and service far outrun research; there is nevertheless a sufficient convergence of evidence to make the case that both kinds of programs are effective. Even without a conjunction of parent education and family support—a conjunction that holds much promise—many investigations support the value of parent-education programs alone when they are done at a high level of quality. The same is true for the best family-support interventions. But we need to learn so much more about what programs are effective for different populations. It is clear that we cannot focus on cognitive measures alone; we must teach our children social skills as well. One crucial element in future innovation will be a close working relationship between practitioners and researchers. Several interesting statewide efforts have recently been mounted in this field—most notably in Missouri, Minnesota, Kentucky, Maryland, and Connecticut.

Altogether, the evidence to date indicates that community-based early intervention can benefit the personal development of young parents, their ability to use available community resources, their attitudes and behavior toward their children, and the healthy development of the children. While the effects are not massive, they are constructive and fairly consistent. The strongest effects on parenting skills and knowledge—with at least moderately beneficial effects on child development—seem to come from programs that emphasize parenting skills in a deliberate and systematic way, drawing effectively on what we know of child development and using practical demonstrations for the parents and constructive feedback to them. Professionals are usually involved with these programs, even though much of the operations may rely on paraprofessionals. Vague and diffuse supportive interventions, however well intentioned, have proven less effective. Once again, research confirms the difficulty of reaching out to very poor young people in socially depreciated circumstances, yet it appears that this can be done. To do so through mutual-aid interventions probably requires a mixture of relatively competent and effective people along with the highly vulnerable ones—and access to professional help. In smashed communities, the peer group alone is not enough.

PRESCHOOL EDUCATION

When Head Start began more than two decades ago in the United States, its long-term impact was obviously unknown. As this ambitious public program was being launched, however, a number of research projects were initiated to test the basic thrusts of the program. Does early education make a difference in the lives of children, the family, and the community? If so, how long do such effects last? What areas of growth do they affect? Today, these carefully conducted research projects have provided valuable empirical evidence to guide us in decisions on education and public policy. In essence, research on early-childhood education such as Head Start has clarified three core elements whose value is now clear: developmentally appropriate, enriching stimulation; medical care, especially in disease prevention; and active, informed participation of parents.

In 1976 the Consortium for Longitudinal Studies, a group of twelve independent investigators, pooled the data from their individual research and collaborated in conducting follow-up studies. This work provided strong evidence from many sources that early-childhood programs can make a positive difference.

A variety of cognitive-intervention studies have been carried out in poverty concentration areas. Some are preventive in nature; others are remedial. Some emphasize the teaching of specific skills; others focus on general problem-solving strategy or the improvement of communication. A great variety of approaches have been able to produce at least short-term improvement in the school achievement of young children and in their performance on academic tests. But long-term gains are more difficult to achieve. Nevertheless, much has been learned that is encouraging.

It has increasingly been recognized that early education is not only a matter of cognitive stimulation and improvement but also of emotional and social development. A young child who does well in school also builds self-esteem on the basis of earned respect and the reinforcement provided by teachers and parents. There appears to be inherent gratification and self-esteem for the child in accomplishment and a sense of mastery. On the other hand, there is abundant evidence of the widely damaging effects of a child's low self-esteem and feelings of failure, which can derive from depreciation in school or from teachers' very low expectations, even in the preschool years. So intervention programs have increasingly come to recognize that emotional factors need to be considered along with cognitive ones —i.e., we need efforts to build children's motivation for academic performance, ways of earning respect and hence strengthening self-esteem, as well as cognitive stimulation and improved learning strategies. Such interventions aim to change not only children's skills but also their attitudes toward themselves and toward learning opportunities, and to give them a sense of control over their own destiny, particularly in learning situations, and to teach them strategies that can be used over and over again in a variety of circumstances.

Such programs must also attempt to strengthen children's social relations with parents, teachers, siblings, and peers. Increasingly, these interventions start early and include the parents in some way as educators of their own children or at least as supporters of their education. The programs strive to strengthen the existing support system of the family or to provide an alternative support system if necessary. Such supports are intended not only to tide children over times of stress but also to provide long-term encouragement for education and for promoting good health.

Impoverished parents can be involved actively in the education of their children—whether as participants in a governance committee of the school, as teaching aides in preschool centers, or as collaborators with their children in educational activities. The latter may include reading to their children (with the parents themselves learning to read if necessary), demonstrating educational toys, entering into lively play with young children, and various other interesting parent-child interactions. What seems to be essential is shaping the parent-child interaction in ways that are positive, mutually gratifying, and encouraging for the future. This enhances the capacity of parents, even very low-income parents, to be adequate teachers of their own children and to learn how to use resources available in their community.

The Beethoven Project

In Chicago, a courageous project is tackling one of the hardest of all problems—how to provide a decent start for children born into the harshest environment of urban poverty. The project is stimulated and supported by a Chicago businessman, Irving Harris, who is an authentic pioneer of philanthropy for children and youth. The task is so difficult that only a modest gain can be anticipated. Yet it has the great virtue of focusing attention on a badly neglected and very important problem.

The Beethoven Project is set in a run-down housing project, the Robert Taylor Homes. This is one of the nation's largest and poorest housing projects. Nearby is the Beethoven Elementary School, which has given the project its name. The average age of a new mother at Robert Taylor is sixteen. More than 90 percent of the residents get public assistance.

The project undertakes to reach children before birth, to help the pregnant adolescents and then the children in ways that will prepare them for good health and for starting school as active learners full of curiosity and hope.

The outreach activities aim to contact the mother in the first trimester of pregnancy for prenatal care and extend to the baby right after birth for preventive health care. The developmental sequence of interventions continues with parent education oriented to child development, then school for the children when they become toddlers, and after that a Head Start program. On completion of this preschool sequence, these children will enter kindergarten at age five reasonably prepared to make the most of their educational opportunities.

Difficult as this task is, the prospects are that these children will reach school in better shape than their counterparts do now. Teachers at this school have reported for years that entering stu-

continued on next page

continued from preceding page

dents in kindergarten class have a very short attention span; many have very limited speech and minimal familiarity with the simplest concepts, and are easily distracted and upset. The teachers believe that most of the children are potentially capable but almost totally unprepared for school. So the teachers begin with basic self-care and constructive human relationships. But the gap is so great that even with valiant efforts by dedicated teachers only a small fraction are fully ready for the first grade at the end of their kindergarten year. They are on a slippery slope leading to educational failure.

The setting at Robert Taylor is one of despair and distrust. Although many mothers show concern for their babies, they are also suspicious, preoccupied, and hard to reach. To overcome these and other obstacles, the Beethoven Project relies heavily on family advocates. These women, operating as a team, are residents of Robert Taylor or a nearby community. They too were adolescent mothers and have managed to cope with the same kinds of problems now experienced by the younger women. They systematically scour the Robert Taylor homes for pregnant women and those who have recently had babies. They explain to the mothers what is possible in the way of care and education and tap into their positive motivations for their children. They suggest practical, concrete steps and revive the young mothers' hope for a better life. Thus, the opportunity exists for a two-generation intervention, facilitating the development of both the adolescent mother and her infant. Careful assessment of this and similar projects can in due course show the way toward coping with the most difficult problems of child and adolescent development—and toward a real opportunity for health from the start.

Carefully designed research has shown that high-quality day care plus parent education can strengthen children's cognitive development during infancy and early childhood. The effect is particularly striking in high-risk populations. Sustained contact with such children and their mothers has turned out to be particularly valuable; these are two-generation benefits. Often the *adolescent* mothers involved in these intervention efforts derive personal benefit, going on to higher levels of education. There is also evidence of a beneficial effect on younger siblings. Although the main focus of such studies has been on poor, high-risk populations, there is also evidence of benefit from similar interventions with middle-class parents, and this may be important in the general acceptance of such efforts.

Early-intervention studies have given a good deal of attention to children's ability to master language, since it is so important for success in school. In addition, it is now generally accepted that schools need to have an adult-to-child ratio that permits sustained individual attention, group size small enough to be manageable, and consistent parental involvement. Experience has shown that interventions must take into account the specific emerging capacities and limitations of children in each phase of development.

Much of the focus in early-intervention programs has been on training the caregivers: the mother; sometimes the father; often day-care providers; sometimes the caregiver and infant. Well-designed early intervention can prevent much of the serious damage now being done.

An interesting example of work on the long-term effects of preschool education comes from one member of the Consortium for Longitudinal Studies, the High/Scope Educational Research Foundation of Ypsilanti, Michigan. This group followed children who were from poor and black families; many were presumably destined for school failure and a bleak future. Of the families in the study, 50 percent received welfare assistance; 47 percent were headed by single parents; only 21 percent of the mothers and 11 percent of the fathers had graduated from high school.

Of the 123 children in the study, about half were randomly selected to serve as an experimental group and attend preschool in the Head Start mode. The other half did not get preschool education. These 123 young people have participated in the follow-up study for two decades. The study has found that high-quality early-childhood education does permanently and positively alter the life course of the participating children in a number of major areas consistent with other research and demonstration projects of similar nature.

Moving beyond this specific study, there is additional evidence indicating that preschool education provides the setting for early intervention needed to ensure good health throughout childhood and into adulthood. For example, many programs offer children medical screening and inoculations against several infectious diseases. Poor children who would otherwise miss the opportunity can receive the powerful effects of early immunization and related measures of preventive medicine. Early education can foster lifelong health.

The Brookline Early Education Project

One of the stimulating projects in this field was carried out in Brookline, Massachusetts, over many years by a highly interdisciplinary team. The Brookline Early Education Project (BEEP) provided services to 285 preschool children and their families. Assumptions underlying the program design were that parents are the most influential teachers of their children; that communication between parents and teachers is critical; and that early childhood is a time of great potential for learning.

Program staff used outreach to minimize the self-selection process that might result in an excess of education-oriented parents. The group that enrolled included substantial numbers of ethnic minorities, children whose mothers had obtained less than a college education, children from homes where English was not the first language, and children from single-parent families.

The BEEP Center, a former college dormitory, included a lending library of books and toys, meeting rooms, and indoor and outdoor play areas. It provided a convenient place for families to drop in informally. As the children turned three, space became available in several elementary schools for pre-kindergarten classes.

The program consisted of three interrelated components:

1) *Parent education and support.* Families were randomly assigned to receive different levels of parent support. Some parents received frequent home visits and meetings. Some received no outreach, but information and support were available at the BEEP Center or by phone if parents took the initiative. Transportation to the Center, the lending library of books and toys, and the BEEP newsletter were available to all families.

2) *Diagnostic monitoring.* Children received frequent health and developmental examinations, and results were shared with parents.

3) *Education programs for the children.* Beginning at age two, children participated in weekly playgroups of six to eight children. The routines of these groups were geared to the develop-

continued

mental level of the children. Parents were expected to observe the sessions frequently and discuss mutual insights with the teaching staff. At ages three and four, the children could be enrolled in a daily morning pre-kindergarten program. Classes typically consisted of fifteen to twenty children and three adults. Curriculum emphasis, influenced by the High/Scope program, was on giving each child the opportunity to develop a sense of effectiveness, explore concepts, develop mastery and social skills essential for school. Individual children's goals were determined mutually by teachers and parents. Extended day care was available each afternoon in the same setting. Parents paid on a sliding scale.

The program's impacts on parents and children were assessed at several points—thirty months, kindergarten entry, and the spring term of second grade. At kindergarten entry the participants had significant advantages in several areas of social behavior and other kindergarten skills. In the spring of second grade, three years after the end of the BEEP program, BEEP children were compared with other children selected randomly from their classrooms. The rate of difficulties with classroom learning behaviors was significantly lower among the BEEP children, regardless of their background characteristics. These findings are illustrative of the many ways in which early-childhood education had beneficial effects.

A recent follow-up study of intervention during the first five years of life found that effective programs can lower adolescent delinquency. Children of the low-income families who participated in the Family Development Research Program in Syracuse, New York, had a 6 percent rate of juvenile delinquency, compared to a 22 percent rate for children in a comparison group. Not only was the comparison-group delinquency rate almost four times greater, but the juveniles' offenses were considerably more severe. Thus, another piece of evidence was added to the growing account of long-term benefits from carefully crafted early interventions in circumstances of formidable disadvantage.

Overall, individuals who have been in early-education programs have shown better achievement scores in elementary school, are less likely to be classified as needing special education, have higher rates of high-school completion and college attendance, and have lower pregnancy and crime rates than comparable students who were not in preschool programs. The confluence of evidence from a number of studies—High/Scope, Brookline, the most recent Head Start evaluations, and the consortium of longitudinal projects—strongly supports the value of preschool education.

The issue is how to make such education more widely available. This can be done in a variety of ways: through expansion of the Head Start program; through inclusion of educational curricula in child-care settings; through school systems making preschool education available; or through parent-support programs. All are currently being pursued with vigor.

Communication of the research findings and dissemination of information about model programs to leaders in many arenas have been dynamic in recent years. This spread of information has increased contributions to preschool education from different sectors: pediatricians; state and federal legislators; senior school and city officials; business and church leaders; the media; and those who train teachers, social workers, and other professionals who work with children. At the 1989 educational summit meeting of governors, Cabinet members, and President Bush, there was strong agreement on both federal and state responsibility for widening the availability of preschool education.

Early education can help mitigate a variety of social problems. The lessons of Head Start have wide applicability. The kind of early stimulation, encouragement, and instruction provided in quality preschool programs, which can also be incorporated into a variety of child-care settings, can help reduce school failure and other casualties. High-quality preschool-education programs can become an important avenue for education about child health as well as a place where disadvantaged youngsters can develop language ability and quantitative skills. But they should not be mini-universities with intensive instructional curricula. We need to blend our knowledge of child development and education to create early-education programs that are developmentally appropriate and that integrate a great deal of learning into playful activities in the early years of life.

In short, there is compelling evidence that quality preschool education helps prevent the waste of human potential. Significant benefits to society at large include not only great long-term educational accomplishment but also reduced crime and delinquency, improved productivity of the labor force, reduced welfare dependency, and better health. The lessons of early education are ripe for adaptation to a variety of settings that can influence healthy child development.

8

Saving Lives in the Early Years: Putting Knowledge to Widespread Use

The path we have traveled together in these pages so far has shown us a world in process of rapid transformation—a drastic departure from the world of our ancestors, recent and ancient. This new world we are making has many advantages and novel opportunities, but also has disrupted family relationships in ways that jeopardize child development in the earliest years of life. The fundamental requirements of young people that have been built into us by virtue of our very long evolutionary history are in some ways easier to meet now because of scientific and economic advances; but in some ways they are much harder to meet because of family and community disruption. We are in process of adapting to these unprecedented sociotechnical conditions; but our child-rearing practices have not caught up and the casualties of early life are heavy, as we have seen.

Yet there is reason for hope. We have also seen a variety of research studies, demonstration projects, and practice innovations that offer a solid basis for meeting the essential requirements for healthy child development under the radically changed circumstances of contemporary life. Many of these have been encouraged and supported by foundations like the Carnegie Corporation.

Foundations try hard to get the facts straight by supporting specific research studies as well as syntheses of research, the big-picture studies. Based on such work, objective analyses of plausible policy options are often undertaken. This may lead to working models or demonstration projects in communities on ways to deal with serious educational and health problems. When the results are in, they are likely to be disseminated actively so that the public can be well informed about its problems, opportunities, and choices.

What if the results are good? We come to a paradox of success. As we have seen, there are a variety of well-established or highly promising ways to prevent serious damage to children. But foundations and other philanthropic activities can only manage to demonstrate what is possible in a modest number of settings. The resources are far too limited to go beyond this point. So we know many useful things to do but must find ways to do them widely—the problem of scale-up to meet national (or international) needs. How can this be done?

In a society so large, heterogeneous, and complex as that in the United States, this necessarily involves many sectors: government at all levels, business, professions, labor, churches, public movements of various kinds. Moreover, there are patterns of organization that make a difference; and ways of interacting among public and private sectors that make a difference. In this chapter, we examine some of the ways in which vital opportunities for healthy child development may be realized; how useful experiences and services may be made truly available as needed to create a decent future for our children.

A CONTINUUM OF EDUCATION

The deep commitment to children is a fundamental attribute of being human. But more and more, we are failing to meet the basic developmental needs of young children. We may even be on the verge of an epidemic of inadvertent child neglect that could put the future of our society in jeopardy.

In one way or another, all families need help, and disadvantaged families need it desperately. Can we find informed, dependable ways to meet this profound challenge?

In my judgment, there is no one right way to do this vital job. Many European countries—and some American communities—are meeting the need by a variety of means. No single pattern of organization, no unique institution is likely to provide the solution to our children's needs. But social neglect is not the answer to the crisis our families face.

The United States is a very large, highly heterogeneous, and strongly individualistic country. These are all potent assets, but they also engender the distrust and impersonality that have complicated reaching widely acceptable decisions about social policy.

So we are struggling to reach consensus about coping with the problems of today's children. Our first and crucial task is to reach broad agreement on the nature and scope of the problems and then on the specific steps we need to take to address them.

Within the scientific and professional communities, a remarkable degree of consensus on the core facts has been emerging in recent years; I have tried to reflect it in these pages. Sadly enough, this consensus is not widely understood by the general public or by policymakers in public and private sectors. So it is crucial now to have a well-informed, wide-ranging public consideration and to link experts with open-minded policymakers in an ongoing process of formulating constructive policy options.

How can we save our children? How can we build a decent future for them? As a practical matter we need to think in terms of a continuum for education, from prenatal care through adult life. No single program is a panacea. We need many to span the main years of growth and development during early childhood—from enriched prenatal care, preventive pediatric care in infancy, and high-quality day care, to parent education, social supports, and preschool education.

We must address a number of issues in implementing or expanding such interventions. How can we translate scholarly research into practice? Do we need a new institution for young children, or can we expand services for them by building on existing institutions such as schools, the health-care system, and community agencies? How can we better coordinate services that are now fragmented among different bureaucracies? How can professionals with different training and cultures learn to cooperate to serve families? Research and practice provide insights into these questions.

It should be possible in the foreseeable future to design interventions that go beyond what has been possible up to now. How can we be so optimistic? First, we can use our experience from the programs so far undertaken. Second, we can draw out the implications of research on child development, health, and education to ascertain which programs are the most effective, which need the most attention, and how we can construct informed models for future interventions; this book has highlighted some of the most innovative solutions we can identify. With so much at stake—terrible suffering, grievous loss of talent and life—we can surely find ways to make these interventions feasible.

In 1975, Urie Bronfenbrenner of Cornell University, a leader in this field, reviewed the effects of early child-care interventions in light of the knowledge and experience that then existed. He reached several interesting conclusions:

1. Center-based programs that combined structured learning with play were more beneficial to children than programs relying largely on play.
2. Programs that included parents benefited not only the children in the classroom but their younger siblings as well, and had positive effects on the parents themselves.
3. Families subjected to the greatest economic and psychological stress, and who therefore need help the most, are the least likely to become involved in any program. This has important implications for the outreach necessary to involve such families.

In general, these observations suggest that a combination of approaches may be most effective in helping our children.

Most of the research referred to in this book has been published since Bronfenbrenner's synthesis and strengthens his conclusions. It is now possible to build on the earlier experience and go beyond it. We now know that early-education programs have a number of unforeseen beneficial effects, including parent involvement and satisfaction, improved health benefits, a lower dropout rate in high school, and less delinquency. Research indicates that some of the effects of early intervention need to be reinforced with follow-up activities or "boosters" to ensure that the early gains will not be lost.

BUILDING PARENTAL COMPETENCE

One of the most important and recurring themes in the research on early intervention is the potential value of teaching young parents to deal with their own children constructively. Yet the task is a difficult one, particularly in poor and disadvantaged communities, and tensions inevitably arise in view of the novelty and complexity of the questions. The parent-education movement has been struggling with problems of hierarchy, democracy, and the extent to which research evidence matters. For this movement to become more effective, it will be essential to avoid two extremes. One is a rigid hierarchical structure espousing dogmatic beliefs, which would be insensitive to or even depreciating of poor and minority parents. At the other extreme is a touchy-feely, vague, wishful, uninformative approach—no doubt well-meaning, but nevertheless ineffective. We need to combine the strength of informal and inclusive social-support networks with organized intellectual discipline in the service of our children's development and health.

It is clearly impractical for each parent group to make its own decisions about what the scientific community has to offer. Parents should not be left at the mercy of hucksters who distort, even with good intentions, what the available expertise is supposed to be. We have to look to the scientific and scholarly community to devise a standard of reference for prospective and actual parents to use. Indeed, some responsible efforts along this line have been made already. But can we devise a long-term process that could improve on existing standards and that could be continually updated as our knowledge increases over the years?

We need to start with a process of careful, systematic assessment of knowledge regarding the first few years of life. I have sketched with broad brushstrokes the research to date, but we need an ongoing report of what the scientific and scholarly community has to say about early-childhood development. The stature of the participants and the quality of the process would have to be such that a continuing series of reports would have authentic credibility. The reports would constitute a reliable synthesis of existing knowledge scattered throughout a variety of disciplines and nations. Updates would take into account ongoing social change as well as new research on child development, health, and education.

A high-quality synthesis of this sort—indeed, a series conducted over the years in a rolling reassessment—would have to be presented in a way that is intelligible and accessible. I envision several steps in this process:

1. Translation of the scholarly work into clear, cogent, nontechnical language
2. Adaptation for particular groups—e.g., early adolescents, urban blacks, rural poor—to be sure of clarity and relevance to their concerns

3. Availability of information in attractive printed form, with graphics
4. Availability in videocassettes and other convenient, interesting formats
5. Distribution of information through whatever institutions could make good use of the material: e.g., schools, churches, community organizations, clinics, libraries, doctors' offices, and agencies concerned with children and youth

FAMILY CHANGES AND SOCIAL SUPPORTS

An important area for innovation is the strengthening or construction of social-support networks, such as self-help and mutual-aid groups, when families lack the natural support of extended family and friends. How can other institutions compensate in part for the family's vulnerabilities? We can start by looking at the cooperative efforts among relatively strong institutions such as churches, schools, and community organizations. Indeed, a variety of institutions can focus intensively on health and education programs—for example, by helping young people to master the tasks of parental responsibility as they become heads of families. These problems are most formidable among high-risk youth in poverty-concentration areas, but are also problematic throughout all modern society.

When I say "social support," I do not mean another kind of dole, giving out financial support to people who may or may not deserve it. That is a very different matter. The thrust of this effort is to mobilize caring, dependable human relationships where they are now weak so as to promote healthy child development. For this purpose, we need a fusion of the best available science-based knowledge and mutual aid through groups, networks, or organizations. Perhaps some other term such as "coping network" or "parent skill network" would convey more adequately the active, constructive, high-initiative orientation of these efforts by which people help each other.

These interventions are intended to supplement or replace functions served in smaller, simpler, less rapidly changing societies by the nuclear family, the extended family, and nearby friends. This implies that the people involved in such interventions need to develop special relationships with these parents. But what should the depth of the relationship be with young parents or with their infants? How long should each relationship last? For at least some of the people taking on the responsibility to intervene, the relationships they form have to be more than superficial; they have to make more than transient contact; and we need to avoid a revolving-door situation in which a bewildering array of strangers comes in and out of the lives of young parents or their young children. We need to clarify carefully the functions of different people in the intervening system and to identify programs that require the greatest depth, duration, and continuity. Many of the programs described in these pages exemplify such characteristics.

Building the Talent Pool

If we are serious about strengthening or constructing social-support systems that draw upon the best available knowledge from child-development and child-health research and that function systematically to promote health and education in young families, where will we find the people to staff them? One potentially important talent pool consists of older people, mostly retirees with available time, many of whom have been parents, grandparents, aunts, or uncles. Their real-life experience with a variety of growing children has prepared them to tackle the difficult tasks of dealing with socially disadvantaged young parents and children. Some of these older people will serve as volunteers. Others will have paid employment—usually at a modest level. They can derive considerable satisfaction from making a clear social contribution. Thus, these are interventions of two-generational benefit.

We should also consider the potential contribution of young people. College students and even high-school students can serve as volunteers or in part-time paid jobs; these workers will preferably be those who have had extensive contact with younger children in their own families, in baby-sitting activities, or in organized community service.

This potentially large pool of older and younger people would supplement the core of full-time, deeply committed staff in each program. They might be drawn from a variety of sources: churches, schools, and civic and community organizations, including minority organizations. But we will need some orderly, systematic mechanism to recruit, evaluate, train, and supervise them.

Across the United States, there are many promising examples of programs in which older people serve effectively in caring roles for young children. We need to involve them more fully in innovative programs of prenatal care to reach out to poor communities, to use pregnancy as a meaningful way to prepare for future life. These efforts need to help not only the socioeconomically disadvantaged, but also the middle-class working mothers who are moving up in their careers and at the same time deeply concerned about adequate care for their children. Indeed, such connections can become a unifying influence in our very diverse society.

To be effective, these systems need to have readily available, accurate, relevant information. A mixture of professional and paraprofessional talent can help them grasp the best available information and translate it into useful form. Moreover, both professionals and paraprofessionals have vital functions in amplifying this knowledge and its practical application throughout the community in which the work is done, as well as fostering its diffusion much more widely.

In community-based social services it is often paraprofessionals, rather than professional staff, who develop the personal relationships with participants so crucial to the community-based approach. Paraprofessionals have been widely used since the sixties, when the rapid growth in human services led to a shortage of trained workers. They continue to be used because their salaries are lower than those of professionals and they are assumed to have a greater understanding of their clients because they share their background. The paraprofessionals themselves enjoy the benefits of employment and personal growth.

We must widen the use of paraprofessionals in social services, and at the same time address the common problems that arise from their employment. Programs often fail to provide specific training and job descriptions, leaving paraprofessionals unclear in their role. Moreover, they are often placed in the uncomfortable position of balancing the conflicting demands of the community and the agency. They may overidentify with the clients or impose their own values. Finally, tension between professionals and paraprofessionals may result from their contrasting cultural styles, education, goals, and values.

We can overcome these drawbacks by selecting paraprofessionals on the basis of their empathy and genuine warmth, providing them with an appropriate program of training and ongoing supervision, clarifying their relationship with appropriate professionals, and fostering mutual respect.

The composition of the group receiving social support is as important as that of the people servicing it. Groups can benefit greatly from a mutual-aid ethic among peers. Yet there are limits to the capacities of peers. If an entire mutual-aid group consists of people who have virtually no resources to solve the problems at hand, little can be achieved. On the other hand, if they are so diverse that communication is very difficult, then they are not likely to develop mutual aid, either. Such mutual-aid groups—e.g., of young parents—work best if members share a commitment to a common concern. There should also be sufficient overlap in the social backgrounds of the members so that they feel comfortable with one another, if not at the very beginning then within a reasonably short period of time. The members should have sufficient diversity to bring a range of experience to bear on their joint problems, thus pooling a variety of coping strategies and tactics so that sharing can lead to mutual benefit. Finally, they need an acceptable, accessible, convenient, and attractive link to sources of solid information about the problems they face, mediated by a mix of professional and paraprofessional collaborators.

DO WE NEED A NEW INSTITUTION? CAN WE STRENGTHEN OLD ONES?

What institution can serve children from birth to age five as schools serve them from age six onward? Should there be a child-development center in every community? Or if not a new institution, how can we build on the capabilities of existing institutions in facilitating early-childhood development?

Most research on child development and child health makes very little reference to institutional questions—e.g., how to use relatively strong existing institutions such as the health-care system, the school system, or the churches for these purposes. There has been a lot of ingenious improvisation to make use of existing institutions but little systematic consideration of the ways in which these institutions could build their capacity for contributing to healthy development in the early years of life.

There is no clearinghouse, in most communities, for information about the well-being of young children. In principle, it is attractive to conceive of a children's institution in every town, community, or neighborhood—one place where the largest possible quantity of information about child development and child health is available. This would mean information about pathways to health, education, child care, and other community resources—the entire range of opportunities bearing on the fateful choices that shape human life in the early years. Such an institution should be easily accessible, visible, well known, respected; it should have clout in the community and yet not be intimidating to parents. Could such an institution be best built on a medical or public-health base? On a church base? On a school base? Or would it really be most effective if it were freestanding, created solely and specifically for the purpose of fostering healthy development in the early years? If government at whatever level were to play a role, as it would probably have to in the long run, should it operate such centers directly, or contract with nongovernment entities to develop these functions?

Private foundations can construct models to test different ways of approaching this problem. For example, community clearinghouses with up-to-date information and referral services can be constructed. It may not be feasible to have "one-stop shopping"—all services available in one setting—but it should be feasible to have a place where all relevant knowledge about early-childhood development is available and from which all gates can be opened.

In principle, the starting point for interventions that could be helpful in the crucially formative first few years of life would be early prenatal care involving both parents. Ideally, this would comprise not only obstetrical measures designed to protect mother and infant throughout pregnancy, labor, and delivery, but also some basic preparation for both mother and father regarding their tasks as parents and their own life course; in the case of low-income parents at least, this would include connection with opportunities to develop occupational skills.

Health institutions could have an important role to play, not only in direct care but also in organizing community-wide activities in the framework of public health, or at least as an organized gatekeeper for access to other opportunities in parent-child development. However, it seems very unlikely that health institutions alone can evolve to fully meet the needs we are addressing here. It is not difficult to conceive—at least in a better world—how the schools, media, churches, businesses, community organizations, government at various levels, and organizations of the scientific community might cooperate in addressing these problems. In a later chapter, when I discuss education in early adolescence, I'll examine a model of this sort for the transformed middle-grade school.

THE SCHOOLS AND EARLY-CHILDHOOD DEVELOPMENT

Edward Zigler, a professor of psychology at Yale University and a major contributor in this field, formulates several principles and criteria that must be met before a satisfactory child-care system can emerge:

1. The child-care system must be reliable and stable. It must be tied to a major institution that is well known throughout American society.
2. Every child should have equal access to child care, and all ethnic and socioeconomic groups should be integrated as fully as possible.
3. The primary goal of the system is the optimal development of the children using it. High-quality care is essential.
4. Child care of high quality should be readily accessible from early in pregnancy through the first twelve years of life.
5. Such programs should address the entire range of human development, from cognitive and personality development to physical and mental health.
6. The child-care system should involve true partnership between parents and the children's caretakers.
7. We should do everything we can to train, upgrade the pay, and increase the status of those who care for the nation's children.

Zigler believes it is feasible to develop a second system within already existing elementary-school buildings. This system would operate on-site child care for children ages three to twelve, going beyond traditional formulations of day care. It would offer three services: a family support system for first-time parents; support for family day-care homes within the neighborhood; and information and referral services. Such a system need not be owned and operated by the schools; it might have a contractual relation with them.

Various scholars predict that schools are likely to play an important role in future expansions of child care. For example, Alfred Kahn and Sheila Kamerman have examined the advantages and disadvantages of school-based child care. They point out that schools already provide most child care for children over age five, although it is not labeled or thought of as such. It is reasonable to cooperate closely with schools in making child-care arrangements for the periods before and after school.

Many European countries already have public or publicly funded nursery schools for ages three to five, based in the educational system. These nursery schools are usually free, universally available, and widely used. So we know a school-based system can work.

It is increasingly understood that day-care centers do not offer only custodial care, and that preschools are not interested only in children's cognitive development. Group services in various settings for children age three to four are now guided by the knowledge and aspirations of the field of early-childhood education.

Many public officials and parents want to start children's education earlier. School systems have an established funding base that, despite problems, is more reliable than the variety of sources that fund child care. Many parents view schools as trustworthy institutions. They are easy to locate in every community. Elementary schools are usually near children's homes. A broad early-childhood program in the schools could provide a universal, integrating experience, in contrast with the current two-tier system of marginal day care for the poor and private nurseries for the affluent. School-building space is available in some areas, and school-based preschools could use existing school transportation systems. Many successful Head Start programs have been school-based.

There are also arguments *against* expanding preschool programs in the schools. Educators have not shown much interest in developing full-day programs. Some day-care advocates argue that, since many inner-city schools have done badly at educating minority children of school age, it would be foolish to hand over preschool children to their care. They assert that the insensitivity of traditional teachers, lack of adequate resources, resistance to parental involvement, and lack of minority teachers that characterize these failures would doom expanded programs to even more failure. On the other hand, Evelyn Moore, the head of the Black Child Development Institute, maintains that blacks should support the public schools in this function, since the public schools are where their children are. However, she recommends a diverse system, rather than one dominated by the schools.

Kahn and Kamerman conclude that the schools will have to play a large part if the United States is to have adequate child care. They envision the day-care field concentrating on infants and toddlers, children with special needs, and possibly before- and after-school care. However, they recommend against making a full and final choice or giving the schools a monopoly. They recommend an experimental approach with diverse models, including such options as:

- Publicly operated, public-school-controlled preschools
- Publicly contracted preschools using the nonprofit day-care system
- Community child-care agencies using school buildings
- Proprietary agencies providing publicly subsidized or purchased services, operating in schools or in the community

School-based programs must have special standards, or general child-care standards must cover these programs. Experimentation will be necessary with different patterns of planning, administration, leadership, and monitoring, as well as with transportation and food programs, parent involvement, and parent education.

In 1988, the Bank Street College of Education in New York published a study called *Early Childhood Programs and the Public Schools—Between Promise and Practice.* It clarifies the assets and limitations of this approach, examining the actual experience in this field so far. The study finds several advantages of the public schools as providers of early-childhood programs. They traditionally fund services entirely from taxes, without fees from parents; they exist in every community; and public-school teachers have higher education and status than early-childhood educators.

The study notes also several disadvantages. Public funds for education are not secure; overcrowding is more common than extra space; public-school teachers' training is not in early childhood or child development, nor is their experience appropriate for working with younger children. There are concerns that the increasingly academic nature of kindergarten is a movement toward an unbalanced program.

Public-school early-childhood programs serve a wide variety of purposes and use a wide variety of funding sources. They are becoming more widespread, but still comprise only a small part of the early-childhood system. About one-fifth of United States public-school districts now offer some program for children before kindergarten, but these are only about 5 percent of all prekindergarten programs. In the eighties, there was rapid growth in state-funded prekindergarten programs. These programs are usually part-day, school-year programs for at-risk four-year-olds. School regulations, developed for older children, are often inappropriate and inadequate for public-school early-childhood programs. There is much variability in the adequacy of teachers' preparation. About half the programs surveyed required staff to have early-childhood certification.

The quality of the environment and the materials in public-school early-childhood programs is also highly varied. Most programs surveyed had some elements of an early-childhood environment, such as child-sized tables and chairs and play equipment, but there was a striking lack of appropriate equipment beyond the basics. Nearly one-quarter of programs surveyed used inappropriate materials. Equipment for and attention to children's physical development was rare.

Few public-school administrators appeared to be aware of the need for continuity in the transition to kindergarten, or indeed during the preschool day. Except for child-care and Head Start programs, most public-school early-childhood programs had limited parent involvement. Most state-funded programs did not provide comprehensive services.

Above all, we must keep in mind the great importance of *what actually goes on* in child-care settings. From infancy through kindergarten, decent, humane care is essential but not sufficient to foster the development of children who are vigorous and healthy, inquiring and problem-solving, prosocial and constructive individuals. The most promising approaches are those that effectively integrate knowledge of child development and child health with knowledge of learning principles and techniques. Naturally, the quality of the caregivers, resting in substantial part on the adequacy of their training, is crucial.

A school-based approach to early-childhood care would require that the schools connect strongly with the health system—and more besides. As a practical matter, it will probably be necessary to achieve cooperation among several institutions in a particular community—and the mix might well differ from one to another. Schools, universities, clinics, media, churches, business, community organizations, government at various levels, and professional organizations—all of these could play a highly constructive role. To do so, they will need attention, stimulation, and incentives beyond those present in most communities.

Whatever combination or permutation of institutions might evolve to meet these needs, it is reasonably clear that they will have certain key functions:

1. Clarifying the nature of child-care problems
2. Stimulating interest and hope in the possibility of useful interventions
3. Facilitating the delivery of appropriate services
4. Providing resources: not only money but people, organization, and technical skills. Participating institutions would need to have a steady flow of the most reliable and up-to-date information about what works for whom in fostering healthy child development during the earliest years.

COORDINATING SERVICES TO MAKE THEM TRULY USEFUL

In the early seventies, Elliot Richardson, then Secretary of the Department of Health, Education, and Welfare, pointed out that the human-service system was not a system at all, but rather a collection of independent, political, highly specialized public agencies whose number and magnitude were expanding beyond anyone's ability to understand or manage. The department contracted for a study of necessary collaboration among diverse services required to help handicapped children. This study documented the disorganization, complexity, and fragmentation of the service-delivery system. It identified five major problems: inequity; gaps in service by state, age, type of handicap, and locality; insufficient information for planning; inadequate control; and insufficient resources. Other studies on the ability of the health-care system to coordinate services drew similar conclusions.

Service coordination remains an important problem and has recently become a focus of attention, mainly because constrained fiscal resources favor more efficient operations and less duplication of services. Second, there has been an increase in public awareness of the problems posed by ineffective bureaucracies. Public agencies have not lived up to expectations. Third, both providers and consumers of services for children have found the system so complex and disorganized as to be inaccessible. Many parents, especially in the baby-boom generation, are demanding more choices from the service-delivery system. Fourth, there is a growing awareness of the impact, for better or worse, of service providers on the family system. In analyzing these problems, Gloria Harbin and Brian McNulty identify several important dimensions, including political climate, availability of resources, and leadership.

Political climate depends on the attitudes of key decision makers, direct service providers, and the public. The value placed by each of these groups on children and on collaboration affects the success of interagency coordination. One reason for lack of support is that agency administrators, elected officials, or the electorate may view the problems of young children as relatively insignificant. If key decision makers compete for control and resources, protect turf, and resist cooperation, then the competitive climate will affect everyone. The best that can be accomplished under such circumstances is an occasional local success at coordination.

Important resources for coordination include money, people, and facilities. An interagency-coordinating group requires time and effort to find ways of marshaling resources appropriate to the task. Too often, staff are assigned to such a group without any relief from their other responsibilities. It is not surprising when the results are poor.

A skilled leader is critical to the success of interagency coordination. Someone has to take charge of communication, planning, and resolving conflicts. Once an interagency group develops a plan, the leader needs to get the plan adopted by the administration and the legislature. The individuals directly involved in planning a coordinated service system often suffer from turf pride, believing that their own perspective or their agency's methods are the only right ones. They usually lack experience in interagency work, competence in dealing constructively with interpersonal problems, and conflict-resolution skills.

The development of effective coordinated services requires a systems approach. Again, overarching leadership is crucial: from the legislature, among agency administrators, in interagency-coordinating bodies, among direct-service providers, and among parents. These leaders must provide structures that value diverse perspectives, yet lead to consensus. Agencies must develop policy jointly, to focus on identifying and achieving common goals.

If we can use such interagency coordination to bring the services that make sense to people who most need them in *one accessible site*, fine. If not, then bring all relevant, practical *information* about children's services and opportunities into one visible, attractive site.

In either case, young children and their parents will need guidance in mapping the territory—figuring out how to get the help they need. Case managers are one solution to this problem, a way that parents can cope with the all too often bewildering array of locations, procedures, forms, strange terms, and not-so-friendly people. This is especially important in the provision of early-intervention services.

Case management is a system of service delivery in which workers take responsibility for individual persons, rather than for discrete tasks. Such an approach has a number of advantages. The most obvious is that children or families who have a case manager are likely to receive the services they actually need. The case manager may also assume some of the costs, in frustration and time, of obtaining services. In addition, simply having a case manager available may constitute an important social support for families. These benefits are particularly important for families that lack the skills to negotiate service bureaucracies on their own, or for families burdened by severe problems. The more fragmented or complex is the system of available services, the greater the need for case managers. The case manager must be aware of all available services and resources and must actively coordinate across agencies and disciplines. The responsibility for problem solving and the broad approach of case management promote creativity in service organizations—and a flow of useful information for managers about problems in service delivery.

Training in the human services must support interagency coordination and prepare service providers to involve parents. Most current training programs in health, education, and social services do not prepare professionals to work as part of a multidisciplinary team or an interagency planning group. It should become an integral part of professional standards to work effectively across turf boundaries to accomplish whatever is necessary for the well-being of children.

EXPANDING CHILDREN'S SERVICES

How do we create an expanded system of services for young children? Once again, a case-management approach is potentially valuable. But to make it work we must ensure that caseloads are small enough to allow workers to have an impact while avoiding the excessive stress of a crushing workload. Even more important, since case management entails a high degree of worker discretion and its quality is not easily monitored, we must ensure that case managers are relatively well educated, with strong professional standards. Case managers must also have the respect of other service providers if they are to coordinate services effectively. Second, a significant degree of service decentralization seems essential to promote local creativity, to allow responsiveness to local conditions, and to allow involvement of the local community in the governance of service agencies. Finally, an expanded system of services for young children must have some means of reaching families who are not likely to seek out services on their own—e.g., the employment of indigenous paraprofessionals who can deal sensitively with people in difficult circumstances.

Although, for the reasons considered earlier, the schools are tempting targets for service expansions, one major disadvantage is the school's current narrow focus on traditional education with relatively little attention paid to broader services for children and families or to parent involvement. Schools would have to broaden their mission considerably in order to take on a case-management role. However, New Jersey's recent experience in implementing school-based health and social services for adolescents suggests that schools will respond when offered funding to expand their services in unaccustomed directions. Although the program has been operating for only a few years, its administrators report that tying funding to certain critical requirements (such as coordination with community agencies), while allowing schools the independence to design the details of their own programs, appears to be an effective strategy. In any event, if schools are to take on such valuable functions, they will need technical and financial help from other sectors.

One major advantage of tying service expansion to the health-care system is that the latter reaches virtually all children at birth. No other service has a comparably universal point of contact until children begin school at age five or six. Since we already know a fair amount about a child's risk of later problems based on the family's characteristics at birth, hospitals could screen children and refer families to services such as the perinatal support programs at Michigan State University considered earlier. Another advantage is the high level of training of doctors and nurses, and their prestige. On the other hand, doctors and nurses are more highly educated and more specialized than necessary to serve as case managers. In addition, doctors and nurses traditionally occupy a role of great authority and are accustomed to directing patients' behavior more than helping individuals learn to help themselves. Furthermore, with the exception of public-health activities such as health education, community health centers, or visiting nurses, the health-care system has traditionally emphasized treatment of disease rather than preventive approaches.

The public-health system, however, represents an important structure within the overall health system that could offer an excellent starting point for an expanded system of children's services. In addition, it may be possible to design a system that would take advantage of the health-care system's access to nearly all children at birth, without perpetuating some of the disadvantages in the current organization of health-care delivery. The perinatal support programs in Michigan represent an example of a structure that uses the hospitals to identify and reach at-risk families in order to provide social services that are linked with health care.

On the basis of an extensive national survey in the eighties, Lisbeth Schorr identified the major common attributes of programs that could change the lives of seriously disadvantaged children. Her book, *Within Our Reach*, is an important contribution to improvement of services for children. She defines successful programs as comprehensive and intensive; they overcome fragmentation through staff versatility and by active collaboration across bureaucratic and professional boundaries. Staff have time, training, skills, and support to build relationships of trust and respect with children and families. They deal with children as parts of families, and with families as parts of neighborhoods and communities. Programs that are successful with the most disadvantaged populations design their services to respond to the distinctive needs of those at greatest risk. They persevere in their efforts to reach the hard-to-reach. They continue to evolve over time in order to maintain their responsiveness to changing local needs.

Schorr concluded that the attributes of successful programs are fundamentally at odds with the dominant ways that large institutions and systems are funded as well as the ways they are expected to ensure accountability, quality, and equity. More specifically, she noted that comprehensiveness is at odds with categorical funding that sharply restricts flexibility of needed services; front-line worker versatility and discretion are often at odds with rigid ways of running agencies; intensiveness and individualization are at odds with pressures to reach large numbers of people in spite of inadequate resources; and efforts to design services to meet the distinctive needs of the truly disadvantaged are at odds with concerns about the political hazards of targeted, nonuniversal programs.

Finally, Schorr investigated strategies to overcome the barriers to implementation and expanded services for children. In general, policymakers, funders, and program managers must find ways of changing systems to accommodate the attributes of successful programs rather than vice versa. We could use several strategies to do this:

First, use federal and state mechanisms to provide funding to local communities in ways that encourage the provision of coherent, comprehensive services. State and federal funding should provide incentives to encourage collaboration and should be adaptable to local circumstances.

Second, provide training programs to equip professional staff and managers with the necessary skills. Such programs would include training for collaboration among professionals in health, mental health, education, and social services, and would instill a respectful, sensitive attitude toward working with clients, patients, parents, and students from different backgrounds.

Three, use widespread evaluation to determine what intervention is useful for whom, how funds are being spent, and whether the services are altogether useful.

LEADERSHIP IS CRUCIAL

Given the history and prevalent values of the nation, it seems likely that our ways of improving the chances for our children will be pluralistic. We cannot look to a single pattern of organization to solve our problems. Yet chaos will not work better than neglect. We must find ways to fit the pieces together, to bring about articulation of the moving parts—without any centralized domination. Americans are not partial to overconcentration of political, economic, or social power. Yet high-level accountability—which we do not now have—is also important. The buck must stop somewhere. If we kill and maim thousands of babies every year unnecessarily, however inadvertently, is no one responsible?

There has never been a clearer need for high-level leadership in government—for stimulation and coordination, more by persuasion than by command. Governors and mayors should see this as a vital responsibility. Large cities need a deputy mayor for children and youth—or a deputy mayor for health, education, and human services—to give these critical needs the coherent approach they deserve. By the same token, any President of the United States in the nineties and beyond must provide clear, decent, informed, determined leadership to obtain strong public support and a broad bipartisan consensus in the Congress and among the state governors. This is the single transforming factor that could greatly accelerate the process of saving our children for the benefit of the entire nation in the next century.

In the late eighties, we began to see evidence that powerful sectors are becoming interested in the problems of children and youth: governors, senators, members of Congress, leaders in science, business, clergy, even the President of the United States. Interestingly, this convergence is not limited to higher education or even kindergarten through high-school education, but specifically includes preschool education such as Head Start. Such a process is usually slow, fitful, and uneven. It will be crucial for the leaders in each sector to persist, not to lose interest in the absence of a quick fix.

One vital element is the role of the media as an educational system. For better and worse, the media are that now. Much of our information and even more of our attention is shaped by media coverage. So the implementation of rational, constructive interventions for healthy child development and education will depend on the extent to which the media can play a responsible, informative role. Just as the policy community needs the input of experts to get the facts straight, so, too, the media should have systematic linkage with the relevant scientific and professional communities.

More than ever before in American history, the powerful business community is showing signs of life with respect to children and youth. If this interest can grow and be sustained, it could make a great difference to the outcome. The business community can contribute in several ways: money and talent used in direct efforts to help the schools, as well as for preschool child care and education; community leadership in mobilizing intersectoral cooperation for young people; political clout at local, state, and federal levels to get governments to meet their responsibilities.

In 1987, an in-depth report was published by a group of eminent business leaders under the auspices of the Committee for Economic Development. Called *Children in Need: Investment Strategies for the Educationally Disadvantaged*, it set forth a well-documented rationale and agenda for tackling the problems of early-childhood development and effective education for all. "Quality education for all children is not an expense," the report said, "it is an investment. Failure to educate is the true expense. In addition to improving our schools, investing in the careful nurturing of children from before birth through age five will deliver handsome profit to society and to the individuals and families who have so much to gain. . . . Every $1 spent on early prevention and intervention can save $4.75 in the costs of remedial education, welfare, and crime further down the road."

The report concluded that most of the children at risk of educational failure can be rescued if their schooling is improved and society reaches out to them and their families in their earliest years: "It is clearly a superior investment for both society and individuals to prevent later failure by working with at-risk parents and their children from prenatal care through age five. We call for early and sustained intervention into the lives of at-risk children as the only way to ensure that they embark and stay on the road to successful learning. We also urge that community support systems be mobilized on behalf of disadvantaged families and children."

If a broad public consensus emerges on the facts, if leadership from many sectors continues to grow, and if constructive policy options are fully considered, we could see a real transformation. As a nation, we may well face up to this crisis, find ways to save our children's lives, and put them on a path to healthy development.

SECTION III

PREVENTING DAMAGE IN EARLY ADOLESCENCE

9

The Transition to Elementary School and Development in Middle Childhood

MASTERING THE TRANSITION TO ELEMENTARY SCHOOL

I have focused on children in the first few years of life and in early adolescence because those are the ages during which their lives are the most turbulent. These years are crucial for healthy child development and offer neglected opportunities to prevent serious damage. But we cannot ignore "middle" children, those between ages six and eleven, who enjoy the relative calm before the storminess of adolescence. Their intermediate years in elementary school are important, partly because school is a crucible and a defining experience for them that will heavily influence their adolescence and beyond. The importance of success in school cannot be overestimated. A child's fundamental sense of self-worth depends substantially on his or her ability to achieve in school. A child who fails in school sets in motion the self-defeating attitudes that can dim prospects for an entire life span.

During most of the twentieth century, the entry into elementary school represented a very big change for the child because it signaled the first time he or she would spend virtually the whole day away from home. In the seventies and eighties, as more women joined the work force and more children were enrolled in preschools, many children made this transition at earlier and earlier ages—a formidable challenge for the very young. Today's children still have a lot to cope with as they move into the elementary school —a new setting, new teachers, new peers, and new intellectual challenges. Yet elementary schools have strong inherent advantages. Typically, they are smaller and more intimate than middle and high schools, so each student can receive sustained individual attention from a teacher. Moreover, these schools are often moderately familiar—not far from home, in recognizable neighborhoods, and attended by friends or acquaintances. The student stays with the same group of peers and the same teacher all day long—or most of it. If parents and teachers cooperate in the early days of a child's entrance into elementary school—and this is a crucial point—then the child should weather the transition fairly well. Indeed, the very process of mastering his or her initial apprehensions about school can build a child's confidence and skill, especially in the vital experiences of relating to other people. Entry into school, like other major transitions, widens a child's experience. Children undertake new and more varied tasks and their work is assessed by peers and teachers. Their social contacts expand beyond the family neighborhood.

Research has demonstrated that a family's socioeconomic status has a great effect on a child's cognitive achievement during the transition to full-time schooling, particularly during the first year of school. Children profit more from the first phase of elementary school if they have previously developed some ability to postpone gratification, to be socially responsive in appropriate ways, to maintain control over their emotions, and to take an optimistic outlook. Ideally, family members and other caregivers will have instilled these qualities in children before they enter school. But if they have not, then school provides one more crucial opportunity to foster them. This is one of the reasons that James Comer's New Haven project has been so successful. (I will take a close look at this program in the chapter on education for disadvantaged minority students). His approach reaches out to involve poor parents constructively in their child's school experience; and it helps teachers to understand what the child needs to make the transition from home to school, especially when there is a chasm between the two worlds. Parents' attitudes and expectations strongly influence a child's school achievements, particularly in reading and mathematics.

UPGRADING THE EARLIEST YEARS OF ELEMENTARY EDUCATION

As we have seen, research confirms that preschool education programs such as Head Start provide valuable preparation for young children entering kindergarten and first grade, especially those from disadvantaged backgrounds. Such programs get preschoolers ready for more formal education, provide health services, involve many of their parents in their education, and open doors to community resources. So far, so good. But there is a long way to go.

Next comes the transition to elementary school. As in other major transitions, children need special attention to cross the threshold successfully. Fortunately, research efforts directed at these early years have given us some valuable guidance. A good example is provided by Success for All, which was started in 1986 when representatives of the Baltimore city schools asked researchers at Johns Hopkins University to develop an elementary-school experience that would help all children, including the disadvantaged, learn more effectively. The representatives wanted a program that would help prevent the inevitable downward spiral through the course of elementary and middle-grade schools that occurs when children do not master the crucial skills of reading: the student who cannot read well falls further and further behind as the school years go by.

The Success for All program makes intensive, sustained, systematic efforts toward an attractive ideal: By the end of third grade, all children should be performing on grade level in the basic skills of reading, language, and mathematics. In so doing, they acquire the basic skills necessary for success in later grades and indeed the years beyond formal schooling.

To fulfill this dream, the Success for All program incorporates several exceptional elements. It emphasizes prevention of learning problems by involving parents in their children's success in school and by using high-quality classroom instruction. It relies on intensive and immediate interventions to correct children's learning problems before they get out of hand. The program includes preschool education, kindergarten, a family-support team, a reading program that offers the help of tutors, individual academic plans based on frequent assessments, a program facilitator, training and support for teachers, and a school advisory committee that includes parents.

Success for All programs consider the whole child, taking into account the factors that influence learning in and out of school. Two social workers and one parent liaison work full-time in the school to educate parents and engage them in fostering their children's efforts in school. The team also helps children who are not receiving adequate sleep or nutrition, who need glasses, who are not attending school regularly, or who have behavior problems that interfere with school.

Schools participating in Success for All provide a full-day kindergarten, since research has found that full-day kindergartens are more effective than half-day ones in teaching disadvantaged children. The curriculum emphasizes the development and use of language, balancing academic readiness with music, art, and movement. The kindergarten activities are built upon knowledge of child development and so are able to engage children effectively.

Midway through kindergarten, Success for All students move from discussing stories to actually reading special minibooks designed to be interesting and educational. Part of the narrative is written for teachers or parents to read aloud to the students. The children's narrative is made up of simple, phonetically regular words, so they need only know a few letters to begin reading and enjoying books at a very early age.

The reading program is based on the best available research. Its goal is to make every child literate, beginning with his or her development of language and comprehension skills in preschool and kindergarten. Students often work in pairs, reading to and learning to help each other. They are given books of keen interest to them and asked to read them in school and at home.

Success for All includes a system of intensive tutoring to develop children's reading skills. Six tutors help the three hundred students in grades K–3. The tutors, who are professional teachers, work intensively with individual children who are having difficulty in their regular reading groups. Each tutor works one-on-one with a total of eleven students per day. The tutoring is conducted in twenty-minute sessions. This time is extracted from an hour-long social studies period and so does not make extraordinary time demands. The tutors also serve as additional regular reading teachers. First-graders receive priority for tutoring, getting them off to a good start so that they can enjoy reading, become proficient, and keep up as schoolwork progresses.

A full evaluation of the Success for All program in seven schools demonstrates that students benefit substantially from this academic boost. The earlier students start the program, the more benefits they derive. Not only is their academic accomplishment higher than that of children who receive traditional instruction, but they have fewer behavior problems and better attendance, and their parents are more likely to become involved in their studies. In fact, a substantial body of research confirms that students benefit greatly from specific one-to-one tutoring activities—not only in Success for All but in other similar programs such as Reading Recovery, which originated in Australia and is spreading in the United States. The Success for All program has already been put to use in a variety of Baltimore-area schools. In the near future, we may well be able to tap trained paraprofessionals to serve as tutors in such one-on-one programs now that the basic groundwork has been laid. This would enlarge the pool of available tutors and keep costs down.

There is another language to be learned in elementary school —one that is increasingly important to function effectively in a modern, technical economy. I'm referring to mathematics, the language of the sciences—perhaps even the mother tongue for business, computer use, and the daily transactions of the twenty-first century. The same basic aptitudes that give young children great facility in learning ordinary languages also make it entirely feasible for them to grasp the essential concepts of mathematics. Responding to this growing need, the mathematics community made a major effort in the late eighties to upgrade the teaching of mathematics, starting in elementary school.

In 1989, the National Research Council of the National Academy of Sciences addressed this issue with a landmark report entitled *Everybody Counts*. The report formulates mathematics education as a coherent system, from kindergarten through graduate school, examining all its major components, including curricula, teaching, assessment, human resources, and national needs. It charts a course through which teachers, state and local authorities, and other sectors concerned with mathematics education can work together effectively. This inclusive approach is reflected in the broad composition of the group that prepared the report: classroom teachers; college and university faculty and administrators; research mathematicians and statisticians; scientists and engineers; mathematics supervisors; school principals and superintendents; chief state school officers; school-board members; officials of state and local governments; leaders of parent groups; and representatives of the business sector.

This report stimulated another from the National Research Council in 1990, *On the Shoulders of Giants: New Approaches to Numeracy*. It conveys the richness of mathematics in five essays that illustrate the fundamental themes in school mathematics. These essays—on dimension, quantity, uncertainty, shape, and change—illuminate the idea of mathematics as the language of patterns. They suggest imaginative ways in which mathematical concepts can be expressed in clear and interesting visions, often making use of everyday experience. These reports are now being taken seriously into account in schools throughout the country. There is growing optimism that mathematics can be taught in lively, engaging ways that overcome traditional barriers.

Here as elsewhere, parents can be of real help in making sure their children are numerate as well as literate—providing they are not themselves intimidated by math. Their children will need encouragement to pursue this vital subject, so often viewed as hopelessly remote and difficult. Parents can play a critical role by showing interest and assisting their children in studying math in elementary school. For young girls, blacks, and Hispanics, this parental role is especially important because these groups have traditionally been taught by implication that math is beyond their ability to grasp. Parents can make use of after-school and at-home projects to help their children. For example, Family Math is a program designed by educators at the Lawrence Hall of Science, University of California, to bring students and parents together to learn math jointly. It emphasizes hands-on activities that are interesting and practical and provides useful training for parents as well as numerous games and other activities to help students succeed.

Parent-Teacher Associations and other community organizations can strengthen the hand of parents in helping their children. Moreover, they can support the work of their own schools in upgrading the teaching and learning of math, thus laying the foundations for learning science and for critical thinking skills.

During middle childhood, children acquire a variety of skills: basic literacy, computation, and conceptual thinking. Equally important, they tend to crystallize enduring attitudes about school, learning, and their own capacities. Much research over decades has shown that parents' behavior—and most of the evidence involves mothers' roles—has a great bearing on their children's educational accomplishment. Reading to children, providing opportunities for their verbal expression, and encouraging their achievement helps children develop early reading skills. There is strong evidence that parents' involvement can help children adapt to school initially and spur their achievement later on. Intervention programs that actively involve parents in various ways, ranging from providing home education to serving as teacher aides or members of school governance committees, can be very successful, as we have seen in Success for All.

DEVELOPMENT IN MIDDLE CHILDHOOD

Historically, middle childhood, the period roughly between the beginning of regular school and puberty, was associated with family responsibilities and work roles. The tasks assigned to children were usually within their capabilities; they generally enjoyed the experience of success, appreciation for being helpful, and a sense of contributing to family well-being. This is very different from schooling today, when so many are poised for failure. It is only since the Industrial Revolution that children of this age have been removed from extensive participation in adult society. Existing research on this phase of the life span has been well reviewed by a National Research Council panel chaired by Professor W. A. Collins of the University of Minnesota.

Collins's panel notes that 60 percent of middle children's time is spent on compulsory activities such as sleeping, attending school, washing and dressing, and doing housework. Their remaining, discretionary time is dominated by two types of activities: watching television (often without adults) and spending time without adult supervision, either with peers or alone. These time-without-adults activities represent a substantial departure from historical patterns. Current estimates are that children aged six to twelve watch three to four hours of television daily, more than older or younger children. Viewing preferences during this period shift from special children's programs to general programing. Economically disadvantaged children are more likely to be heavy television viewers than are more affluent ones, though both groups watch a lot.

Over the years of middle childhood, children experience gradual changes that are significant for their long-range development. These changes are not as dramatic as those of the first few years or of early adolescence, but they are important. For example, children in these years typically develop greater complexity of intellectual problem-solving and greater capacity for close friendships. Similarly, they gradually develop more flexible abstract thinking, greater self-regulation, a more extensive repertoire of skills, and more effective techniques for social relationships. Some powerful predictors of later outcomes emerge in middle childhood. For example, school achievement at grade three predicts achievement at grade twelve much more reliably than does achievement at grade one.

Middle childhood encompasses several significant cognitive developments: a growing ability to deal systematically with abstractions; an increasing capacity for planned, organized behavior and for monitoring one's own activities; an increasing facility for acquiring information and using new knowledge. Informal learning about social systems also increases considerably in middle childhood, especially in school.

When children enter school, there is a marked decline in the amount of time they spend with their parents. The day-to-day challenges between child and parents also change. Major discipline challenges with preschoolers include bedtime routines, temper tantrums, fighting with siblings, attention seeking, and standards involving dressing and eating. Fighting and reactions to discipline carry over into the elementary-school years. New issues emerge: chores; encouraging children to entertain themselves; monitoring activities and relationships with peers; helping children with school matters.

Parent-child interaction during these years matters a great deal. It is not too late to overcome earlier difficulties (unless they were exceedingly severe), nor is it too early to anticipate and prepare for the great transition of adolescence. Studies suggest that uninvolved, self-centered parenting is associated with undercontrolled, impulsive behavior in children. The families of highly aggressive, predelinquent, and delinquent children are those who usually engage in mutually coercive behaviors. These families seem to lack the inclination or skill to terminate cycles of hostile interaction. Adolescent delinquents and young adult criminals usually showed evidence of this kind of difficulty in middle childhood, often as a consequence of serious family discord, inadequate parental supervision, family instability, or parents' mental illness or criminal behavior.

In this phase, children are beginning to develop a self-concept. Their self-esteem fares badly when their parents are harshly restrictive but is bolstered when their parents exert firm control, so long as that strictness is accompanied by emotional support, clear commitment to the child's well-being, and open exchange of ideas. By the same token, parents who show warmth and sustained interest in their children foster high self-esteem.

Parents who deliberately encourage their children to pay attention to the experiences of others—e.g., a victim's distress and his or her relief when helped—help foster their prosocial behavior. Such children are more likely than others to behave in helpful and emotionally supportive ways. Antisocial children tend not to be able to see other people's perspectives. Parenting techniques that foster such skills can help children to regulate their aggressive inclinations.

Although middle childhood is, on the average, less stressful than the years that immediately precede and follow it, some circumstances greatly increase the burden on the child. Children in the growing population of single-parent families, usually a mother with no other adults in the household, are particularly at risk. In general, single mothers suffer from task overload. They work full-time more often than married mothers, leaving less time for parenting. Their situation is often exacerbated by the turmoil of marital disruption.

Various studies of divorcing families reveal recurrent themes. Marital separation commonly involves major emotional distress for children and disruption in the parent-child relationship. Single parents, try as they will, are less able to parent effectively for several years after the breakup. Their parental skills improve gradually and are enhanced if the adults form close, dependable new relationships. Over the years, the noncustodial parent's involvement with the child tends to fade. The effects of marital disruption vary with the child's age. Children aged six to eight react with grief, fear, and intense longing for reconciliation. Children aged nine to twelve tend to be openly angry and are inclined to reject a stepparent. At both ages, the children's behavior often deteriorates at home or at school. Altogether, the tranquil passage through middle childhood is increasingly disrupted by drastic family changes.

Thus, the middle-childhood years, and especially the early grades of elementary school, offer children major opportunities for growth and development. But children still face plenty of stressful experiences during these years, and the opportunities to foster their health and education are all too often missed. These years, like the earlier and later ones, are strongly affected by the transforming world in which we live. The main institutions that shape development in middle childhood, families and schools, need urgent help to adapt to these changing circumstances.

10

The Nature and Scope of Adolescent Problems

THE EVOLUTION OF ADOLESCENCE

From time to time, we read about the death of an adolescent who was at the peak of youthful energy and promise, with the prospect of a long life in view. All these accounts are shocking, yet we become inured to them because they come along so frequently. The dramatic instances of adolescent suicide, homicide, drinking and driving, or drug overdose highlight the general predicament of adolescent development in a time of world transformation. How can a person with so much potential to build a rewarding and constructive life snuff it out so casually?

It is useful to view adolescence in a historical and even an evolutionary perspective. Adolescence is a time when our children experience drastic changes, both physical and behavioral. The timing of puberty is controlled by the brain, which stimulates the secretion of sex hormones, a development that evolved over millions of years. Our gradual understanding of this ancient biological system has made puberty one of the frontiers of neuroendocrine research—the interplay of brain and hormones. It is now also becoming a frontier of the behavioral sciences.

While the structure of our biological machinery has a genetic basis, its operation is linked to our environment. Drastic changes in the social and economic fabric of our lives since the Industrial Revolution have affected not only the timing of puberty but the whole nature of the adolescent experience. Today's adolescents undergo their transition from childhood to adulthood in circumstances that are unique in the long history of our species.

One important change—in fact, a distinctly human evolutionary novelty—is the lengthy period of adolescence. We now have two largely separate crucial periods in the transition from childhood to adulthood. At the beginning of adolescence, our children undergo a biological change; at the end of adolescence, a psychosocial change. For reasons not fully understood but including better nutrition and fewer serious infections, adolescence now starts earlier than it used to and ends later. The onset of menstruation, on average, occurs at twelve and a half years in the United States, whereas 150 years ago the average age at menarche was sixteen. In less-developed countries, the age of menarche is still high, but it is decreasing. Boys are also reaching reproductive maturity at an earlier age. Reproductively mature persons now spend years in childlike roles, or in any case in nonadult status, most of them for a decade or more—especially if they pursue higher education. The end of adolescence is ambiguous. When is a person considered fully adult in modern circumstances? How does the modern adolescent adapt to the lengthy transition?

By and large, it is not until roughly the end of the teen years that adolescents reach a fully adult state in brain development, let alone social maturity. The biological, cognitive, psychological, and social differences between the eleven-year-old and the nineteen-year-old are so great that it is barely meaningful to cover both under the label "adolescence." Yet most adolescents are ten to fifteen years old when they are exposed to sexuality, alcohol and other drugs, smoking, and the temptation to engage in a variety of health-damaging behaviors.

Complicating adolescence today is the easy availability of high-risk activities or substances that adolescents generally view as recreational, tension-relieving, and gratifying. Adolescents have ready access to deadly poison in the guise of casual experience: drugs, vehicles, weapons, and the many ways in which one's body may be used dangerously.

Exploratory behavior is central to early adolescence. But a large proportion of early adolescents are not well prepared to make informed decisions about the risks and opportunities they encounter. In many ways, they resemble a larger version of toddlers—having the newly acquired capacity to get into all sorts of novel and risky situations, but all too little judgment and information on which to base decisions about how to handle themselves. Historically, much of their information and worldview was shaped by the nuclear and extended family: parents, older siblings, older peers, and various other relatives. Today, adolescents' information comes largely from the media and unrelated peers, and much of it clashes with parental expectations.

A third historic change is the difficulty adolescents now have foreseeing the years ahead. In premodern times, children were regarded as small, inexperienced adults whose sole task was preparation for adult life. They had abundant opportunity to observe and imitate their parents and other adults performing the roles that they would one day occupy. Career options were limited. Strong social-support networks provided predictability, guidance, and strong coping resources in established, small societies. In today's highly technological and rapidly changing world, such direct modeling is much less widely available. Most societies are too large and their economies too complex to permit children and adolescents much direct observation of adult roles, especially occupational ones. Many jobs change so fast that skills needed today are obsolete fifteen years from now. Moreover, traditional social-support networks have been disrupted. Science and technology have liberated adolescents from the drudgery experienced by their predecessors but, as a paradox of success, have made it harder for them to view the future. What is the adult world, anyway? Is it really what you see on television?

Most early adolescents yearn to be adults without actually understanding what adults do and are. Thus, one of the most important things we can do for adolescents is give them a clearer view of constructive adult roles and what it means to be a respected adult.

One of the key tasks of later adolescence is to move toward a career that can earn respect and be compatible with one's sense of personal worth. We therefore need to ask what various institutions —particularly schools—can do to help adolescents build those careers.

Despite so much change in circumstances, the fundamental tasks of growing up endure—to find a place in a valued group that gives a sense of belonging; to identify and master tasks that are generally recognized as having value and therefore earn respect by acquiring the skill to cope with them; to acquire a sense of worth as a person; and to develop reliable and predictable relationships with other people, especially a few close friends and loved ones.

The growing adolescent has several specific developmental tasks:

1. Moving toward independence from parents, siblings, and childhood friends while retaining significant and enduring ties
2. Developing increasing autonomy in making personal decisions, assuming responsibility for oneself, and regulating one's own behavior
3. Establishing new friendships
4. Moving toward greater personal intimacy and adult sexuality
5. Dealing with more complex intellectual challenges

These are steps every adolescent must take on the road to adulthood, yet major indicators show that in contemporary society large numbers of adolescents cannot find avenues through which to accomplish them. The swiftness, in historical terms, of these drastic changes has outrun our understanding and institutional capacity to adapt. We urgently need to improve our capabilities to deal with the challenges of adolescent development. We may need to bring about a sea change in adolescents' preparation for adult life, taking into account the drastic world transformation that has recently occurred and is still rapidly under way.

THE BURDEN OF ILLNESS, IGNORANCE, AND WASTED POTENTIAL

Although most children grow up to be healthy and whole adults, substantial members encounter serious problems along the way that threaten their survival or leave their entire lives warped or unfulfilled. Some children are at great risk from the moment of birth, or even before; others are most vulnerable during early adolescence. The physical, social, and emotional changes of adolescence intersect with the new intellectual tasks and organizational structure in the middle-grade school. (This term covers both the junior-high schools and the middle schools. These overlap greatly and, taken together, they constitute the special institution we have created for education in early adolescence) For many students, the emerging sense of one's own future may be bleak, especially in areas of high joblessness, poverty, and disintegrated communities. During adolescence, a significant number of young people from many social groups drop out of school, commit violence or otherwise criminal acts, become pregnant, become mentally ill, abuse drugs or alcohol, attempt suicide, die, or are disabled from injuries.

In early adolescence, millions of American youths are at risk of reaching adulthood unable to sustain jobs, deep commitments in human relationships, or the responsibilities of participation in a democratic society. They often suffer from unrealized intellectual potential, indifference to good health, and cynicism about humane values.

These adolescents—like many others—are sorely tempted and often pressured to use alcohol, cigarettes, and illicit drugs. Far too many live in neighborhoods so dangerous that they fear walking to school. Many consider sexual experience at this age to be almost obligatory—a far cry from their parents' experience; they are prompted to some degree by incessant stimulation in movies, television, and music. Adolescents are similarly bombarded with messages about big money and conspicuous success as putative badges of real adulthood at the same time they are exposed to messages of concern for others, helping, even sacrifice for the common good. These conflicting messages are not easy to reconcile.

Stable, close-knit communities where people know each other well and maintain a strong ethic of mutual aid are less common than they were a generation or two ago. The nature of the economy has changed so rapidly that unskilled youth can find only low-paying work, often with little prospect of future improvement. Entire industries have virtually disappeared in recent years. Economic opportunities of adulthood are obscure to most adolescents. In this time of drastic change, young people need informed adult guidance from parents and others. Yet parents often mistake the stirring of independent thinking for the capacity to make informed, mature decisions. Adolescents do indeed have a growing desire for autonomy but also a continuing need for support, encouragement, and guidance. They need help making the developmental transition from dependency to interdependency with parents, friends, relatives, and other adults. Although they are renegotiating relationships with adults, and especially parents, in ways that are often tense and occasionally hostile, adolescents typically wish to maintain ties with and continue to receive help from the adults in their lives.

Let us now take a closer look at the common pitfalls today's adolescents face.

Substance Abuse

Experimentation with drugs, cigarettes, and alcohol is quite common during adolescence. The annual survey of the National Institute on Drug Abuse showed that most of the high-school class of 1987 (92 percent) had used alcohol at some time. Sixty-seven percent had smoked cigarettes, 50 percent had used marijuana, 22 percent had used stimulants, 15 percent had used cocaine, and 6 percent had used crack. Males had higher rates of use than females for most of these substances.

Far fewer adolescents use drugs, cigarettes, and alcohol habitually than have ever tried them. Among the high-school class of 1987, 5 percent had drunk alcohol daily during the month before they were surveyed, 19 percent had smoked cigarettes daily, and 3 percent had used marijuana daily. Binge drinking, on the other hand, is relatively common: 37 percent of high-school seniors (29 percent of females and 46 percent of males) reported having had five or more drinks in a row during the prior two weeks.

Smoking, drinking, and drug use frequently begin in early adolescence. For example, over half of those who smoke in the twelfth grade began daily cigarette smoking before tenth grade. Three out of five high-school seniors who have ever used alcohol, and about half of those who have ever used marijuana, first used it before tenth grade. Similar statistics apply to nearly all other drugs, except for cocaine, which was rarely used before high school for the class of 1987—though its use in early adolescence has increased since then.

Alcohol is frequently involved in motor-vehicle accidents. In approximately half the motor-vehicle fatalities involving an adolescent driver, the driver has an elevated blood alcohol level. Alcohol is also frequently implicated when adolescents die as pedestrians or while using recreational vehicles. Injuries resulting from accidents account for the largest number of hospital stays among twelve- to seventeen-year-olds. The combination of driving and drinking does not affect only those adolescents who are old enough to drive. Nearly one-third of eighth-grade students report having ridden in a car during the previous month with a driver under the influence of alcohol.

Alcohol use has become a more serious problem among ten- to fifteen-year-olds over the past two decades. Drinking patterns have changed remarkably. A greater proportion of early adolescents drink alcoholic beverages, have their first drinking experience earlier, and report more frequent intoxication. Although girls drink less than boys, the proportion who drink and who report intoxication has increased more rapidly for girls than for boys. There are similar patterns of increase in cigarette smoking among girls, and the gender gap in the use of illegal drugs has narrowed in the past ten years.

A striking increase in marijuana use began in the second half of the sixties, but has leveled off in recent years. Still, more than half of high-school seniors have had some experience with the drug, and the decline in marijuana use halted in 1985. Among dropouts, its use is at higher levels than among those in school. Between 1975 and 1980 there was a significant increase in first use of marijuana in early adolescence and that has been a common pattern ever since. Early use of marijuana has been shown to be associated with higher likelihood of using more dangerous drugs later.

Drugs that are manufactured or sold outside the law often are contaminated, of variable and unpredictable potency, or misrepresented—all factors associated with a higher incidence of medical emergencies. Moreover, the use of two or more illegal drugs—often along with alcohol—increases one's health risks considerably.

During the past decade, cocaine has emerged from the shadows as a major public-health threat. Epidemiologic surveys and public-health surveillance systems have documented remarkable increases in cocaine use not only in the general adult population but also among high-school students. As the use of cocaine has increased, particularly with the introduction of the inexpensive form of crack, so too have emergency-room visits, overdose deaths, and medical problems reflected by more and more adolescents entering treatment. The prevalence of "standard" cocaine use in the general population has leveled off since 1979, but the adverse consequences have continued to increase sharply. While there was some evidence that cocaine use reached a plateau in 1990, the problem is complicated by increased combination-drug use and by a shift to more dangerous ways of taking the drug.

Sexuality, Pregnancy, and Disease

The earlier onset of puberty is lengthening the period during which adolescents' physical maturity exceeds their emotional and cognitive maturity. Early initiation of sexual activity puts adolescents at risk of sexually transmitted diseases and unplanned parenthood. A recent survey found that by age fifteen, 13 percent of white males and 6 percent of white females had had sexual intercourse; 45 percent of black males and 10 percent of black females had had intercourse. By age seventeen, 44 percent of white males, 28 percent of white females, 82 percent of black males, and 45 percent of black females had had intercourse. Sexual activity is more common among adolescents who attend high schools with high dropout rates or who have poorly educated mothers.

Among sexually active girls aged fifteen to nineteen in 1982, about 15 percent had never used contraception. Over half had not used contraception when they first had intercourse. Black adolescents and younger adolescents generally were less likely than other adolescents to have used contraception.

Sexually active adolescents have much higher rates of gonorrhea, syphilis, and pelvic inflammatory disease than do older groups. An estimated one-quarter of sexually active adolescents are infected with a sexually transmitted disease before graduating from high school. In recent years, the AIDS epidemic has powerfully complicated this problem.

In 1986 there were about a million pregnancies among girls under twenty, of which about half resulted in births. Most of these pregnancies were unintended. Eighteen- to nineteen-year-olds accounted for nearly two-thirds of the births, but 180,000 births were to girls aged seventeen or younger and 10,000 were to girls aged fourteen and younger. Early motherhood is associated with dropping out of high school, low skills, and poverty.

While the overall rate of births to adolescents has fallen in the last few decades, the average age of initiation of sexual activity has decreased, the birthrate for those under fifteen has increased, and an increasing proportion of adolescent births are out of wedlock. During the past decade, research has clarified the medical, personal, social, and economic consequences of these early pregnancy and childbearing patterns. The consequences of pregnancy for an eighteen- or nineteen-year-old are very different from the consequences for someone still of school age, particularly if the girl is under fifteen years old. The consequences of school-age childbearing are almost all damaging—for the mother, the father, the child, and society. Therefore, a focus on early-adolescent pregnancy—as well as other *early*-adolescent problems—is crucial.

In the United States, the women at highest risk are very young, black, marginally nourished, and from a low socioeconomic status; they do not seek prenatal care. Research findings are strong on the damaging outcomes of early-adolescent pregnancy. Biologic risks to the mother include toxemia of pregnancy and complications during labor and delivery. Socioeconomic risks include interruption of the mother's education, which in turn fosters poor occupational prospects and an increased probability of a lifetime of poverty and less ability to provide a healthy environment for the baby. Infants of young adolescent mothers also are at health risk, especially if their mothers are regular smokers or users of alcohol or other drugs. They are likely to be born too soon or at low birthweight; this in turn predisposes them to a variety of developmental disorders carrying the risk of permanent disability.

Caretaking by very young mothers is also a problem. Adolescent mothers are often less responsive to the needs of the infant than older mothers are. They also tend to have more babies in rapid succession than do older mothers, placing their infants at greater biological and behavioral risk. Children of adolescent mothers tend to have more cognitive, emotional, behavioral, and health problems at all stages of development than do children of fully adult mothers.

The childbearing rate of American adolescents is among the highest in the technically advanced nations of the world. Adolescents account for two-thirds of all out-of-wedlock births. Although birthrates among both older adolescents and adults have declined since 1970, the birthrate among girls under fifteen has not. There are 1.3 million children now living with teenage mothers, about half of whom are married. An additional 6 million children under age five are living with mothers who were adolescents when they gave birth.

The majority of adolescent mothers drop out of school. Early childbearing is a route into poverty and a major obstacle to breaking out of intergenerational poverty. The outlook for the infant is often bleak. When the adolescent's extended family offers child-rearing support, the child's prospects improve. And if the adolescent girl has only one child, the outlook is more hopeful for both.

Social isolation and other socioeconomic stresses adversely affect very young fathers as well as mothers. The adolescent father is launched on a downward trajectory similar to that shown in studies of adolescent mothers—low educational accomplishment and employment opportunities, poverty, early divorce, and frequent changes of marital partner.

Throughout most of human history, adolescent childbearing—

within four years of menarche, while the mother was in her late teens—was common. But in those societies the community provided relatively stable employment and predictable networks of social support and cultural guidance for the young parents. For such adolescents to set up a household apart from either family was rare in preindustrial societies. Even more rare was the single-parent family, and rarest of all was a socially isolated, very young mother largely lacking an effective network of social support. Today these conditions are common.

Nutrition, Activity, and Fitness

The adolescent fondness for junk foods and fad diets contributes to their inadequate or poor nutrition. The National Health and Nutrition Examination Survey documented the tendency of adolescents both below and above the poverty level to take in less than the recommended daily allowance of calories and iron. On the other hand, about 10 percent of adolescents take in far too many calories and become obese. A common form of adolescent obesity is the consequence of chronic overeating because of depression, passivity, and low self-esteem. If this dietary pattern becomes firmly established, it can lead to cardiovascular disease, diabetes, and other health problems over the long term.

One in two hundred twelve- to eighteen-year-old females develop anorexia nervosa, a self-starvation through fanatical dieting. Somewhat more common is bulimia, a binge-and-purge pattern of behavior. Both bulimia and anorexia nervosa are associated with serious medical complications.

Physical inactivity is much more widespread among young people than it was a few decades ago. A sizable minority of ten- to seventeen-year-olds are weak or uncoordinated enough to be classified as physically underdeveloped by the standards of the President's Council on Physical Fitness and Sports. Here again, if the tentative patterns of adolescence become crystallized in a long-term pattern of behavior, these individuals put themselves at risk for cardiovascular disease, pulmonary difficulty, and lack of physical vigor in the adult years.

Depression and Suicide

Mood fluctuation and transient depression are common among adolescents. The hormonal and neuroendocrine changes of puberty, along with major changes in the social environment and stressful life transitions, all contribute to the problem. One national survey found mild depressive symptoms in 34 percent of males and 15 percent of female adolescents. In another sample, 6 percent had clinically significant depressive symptoms.

For some adolescents, depression is a precursor of suicide or attempted suicide. Suicide accounts for 6 percent of deaths among ten- to fourteen-year-olds, and 12 percent of deaths among fifteen- to nineteen-year-olds. It is more common among males than females, and more common among whites than blacks.

In addition to suffering depression, many adolescents feel driven to suicide by some combination of substance abuse, trouble with the law, intense anxiety in the face of social or academic challenges, feelings of personal worthlessness, impulsivity, guilt, and shame. Some suicide victims end their lives after a pattern of destructiveness to others, highlighting a link between suicide and violence.

Delinquency and Violence

Delinquency and antisocial behaviors are widespread, associated with but certainly not limited to conditions of poverty and educational failure. Delinquency is more frequent in adolescents from homes characterized by poor paternal supervision, extremes of discipline (absent or severe), minimal involvement by fathers in family activities, and little time spent at home. Intense family discord, both in childhood and in adolescence, is one of many factors that increase the likelihood of delinquency. But the most profound challenge lies in the "underclass." Growing up under conditions of extreme poverty, the absence of fathers, social disintegration, minimal perception of opportunity (except for the immediacy of the lucrative drug trade), and isolation from reliably nurturant human contacts puts an emerging adolescent on a very risky path indeed.

Fifty-two out of 1,000 twelve- to fifteen-year-olds annually were victims of robbery, rape, or assault during the early eighties. Among sixteen- to nineteen-year-olds, the rate of victimization was even higher, 67.8 per 1,000. These rates are about twice as high as the rate for people aged twenty and over. Victimization is more common among males than females, and among blacks than whites. This pattern is demonstrated by the rates of homicide among these four groups. In 1985, 8.6 fifteen- to nineteen-year-olds per 100,000 were murdered. The rate for white families was 2.7 per 100,000, for nonwhite females 9.4, for white males 7.3, and for nonwhite males a remarkable 39.9 per 100,000.

Many of the perpetrators of violent crimes are also adolescents and young adults. Risk factors for serious violence include a family history of violence, poor family bonding, weak ties to school and other conventional institutions, personal beliefs that justify crime and violence under a wide range of circumstances, and involvement in peer groups that encourage these behaviors. The presence of weapons intensifies the seriousness of violent incidents. One recent survey found that 23 percent of thirteen- to sixteen-year-old males reported taking a knife to school at least once during the prior year.

Television is a pervasive presence in the lives of most American adolescents. One responsible estimate is that the average seventeen- to eighteen-year-old has spent 15,000 hours watching television, compared with 11,000 hours spent in school. Television programs often present violence and sex in an attractive way. Contraception is rarely mentioned. In effect, television provides young people with guidance about how to be sexy, but not much about how to be sexually responsible. Explicit linkage of sex and violence has increased in recent years. The vast exposure to televised violence during the years of growth and development is well known. Some adolescents in turmoil are especially susceptible to this stimulation.

Adolescent Injury

Recent public-health research provides much information on the epidemiology and prevention of adolescent injury.

Injuries account for 57 percent of all deaths among ten- to fourteen-year-olds, and 79 percent among fifteen- to nineteen-year-olds. For every death from injury among youths aged thirteen to nineteen, there are an estimated 41 injury hospitalizations and 1,100 cases treated in emergency rooms. Death rates from injury are higher for males than females. Poverty is associated with greater risk of injury. Injury rates for Native Americans exceed those for blacks and whites by almost 100 percent, while Asians have the lowest rates. Homicide is more than five times as common among blacks than among whites. Suicide is more common among whites than among blacks or Native Americans.

Motor vehicles account for the largest proportion of deaths from injury among adolescents. Young drivers are especially vulnerable to crashes at night and are disproportionately responsible for the deaths of others. They are less likely than older drivers to use seat belts.

Homicide is the leading cause of death for black males between the ages of fourteen and forty-four. The majority of adolescent homicide victims are killed by guns. Forty percent of homicide victims aged fifteen to twenty-four have positive blood alcohol levels, and 25 percent are legally intoxicated (that is, their blood alcohol is over over .10 percent).

Suicide among adolescents has increased in recent decades; there has been a particularly dramatic increase in suicides among white males. It is the third leading cause of death for people between the ages of fifteen and twenty-four. About half of suicide victims aged eighteen to twenty-four have positive blood alcohol levels. Guns are used in the majority of suicide deaths among victims aged fifteen to nineteen. Intoxicated victims between the ages of fifteen and twenty-four are seven times as likely as sober victims to have used a gun.

Drowning accounts for over 1,200 deaths among ten- to nineteen-year-olds annually. Alcohol is involved in about 40 percent of drowning deaths.

Sports and recreational activities are leading sources of nonfatal injuries among adolescents. Football is one of the most hazardous athletic activities, with a rate of 28 injuries per 100 participants annually. Between 1973 and 1980, 260 high-school and college football players died.

Other recreational activities that contribute to adolescent injuries are bicycling and the use of all-terrain vehicles. Bicycling injuries among adolescents are most common at younger ages. Seventy percent of the 900 bicycling deaths and 550,000 bicycling injuries treated in emergency rooms each year are among riders under age fifteen. Bicycle crashes involving motor vehicles are more serious and tend to involve older youths. About 90 percent of bicycling fatalities involve motor vehicles, and largely result from head injuries. Only about 10 percent of recreational bicyclists use helmets. About two-thirds of the victims of bicycle-related brain injuries over age fourteen were intoxicated.

All-terrain vehicles can reach speeds as high as seventy miles per hour. They tend to be unstable, especially during turns. These vehicles were responsible for about 86,000 emergency-room admissions in 1985, and have caused twelve times more deaths than bicycles have. Adolescent males account for the majority of the cases; youths aged twelve to fifteen account for one-quarter of all injuries. Helmets are used by fewer than 20 percent of those injured, and head injuries are responsible for 70 percent of the deaths. Alcohol is involved in about one-third of the injuries affecting riders over age sixteen.

Altogether, adolescent injuries cause a surprising amount of suffering, impairment, even lifelong disability and death. Predisposing factors include poverty and low status; propensity for high-risk behavior; the search for new skills and adult status; the use of alcohol and other drugs; easy availability of dangerous objects, including weapons; and lack of information about actual risks and consequences. These risk factors apply to other adolescent casualties as well.

Living with Divorce, Single-Parent Families, and Stepfamilies

Divorce and births out of wedlock are increasingly common, so adolescents are more likely than ever to live with a single parent, to experience the breakup of their family, and to enter stepfamily relationships.

Among children aged between six and seventeen in 1985, 73 percent lived with two parents, 22 percent lived with their mother only, 3 percent lived with their father only, and 3 percent lived with neither parent. Among those who lived with their mother only, 10 percent lived with a divorced mother, 6 percent lived with mothers who were married but whose husbands were absent, 4 percent lived with mothers who had never married, and 2 percent lived with mothers who were widowed.

Single parenthood is especially common among blacks. In 1985, only 40 percent of black children aged from six to seventeen lived with 2 parents, and 50 percent lived with their mother only. Hispanic children's family arrangements fall between those of blacks and whites. In 1985, 66 percent of Hispanic children aged from six to seventeen lived with two parents, and 28 percent lived with their mother only.

Single-parent families are poor more often than two-parent families, for several reasons. One parent cannot earn as much as two; women, who head most single-parent families, do not earn as much as men on average; births to unmarried women are more common among women of low earning potential; and absent parents frequently fail to pay child support. One study of divorces that occurred during the seventies found that poverty rates for children rose from 12 percent before divorce to 27 percent after divorce. The 1987 poverty rate among female-headed families with children was 46 percent, compared with 8 percent among married-couple families.

In addition to having fewer financial resources, single parents may be less able to supervise their adolescent children. There is some evidence that both living in a single-parent family and having little parental supervision are associated with adolescent behaviors such as delinquency and substance abuse. Of course, some single parents do in fact maintain adequate supervision and overcome many difficulties, but on the average it tends to be a difficult situation for effective child-rearing, especially in poverty.

CLUSTERING OF RISKS AND PROBLEM BEHAVIORS

Since exploratory behavior is so characteristic of adolescents, and some of it is risky, we need to discuss the concept of risk here. The problem, of course, is that those behaviors that most adults recognize as threats to life and limb are not seen as risky by adolescents. In fact, adolescents do not generally have accurate perceptions of the probability, severity, and reversibility of the risks they take. To some degree, many adolescents find risk-taking behavior intrinsically pleasurable—a search for gratification through adventure and perhaps by beating the odds.

Adolescents put themselves in particular jeopardy because they often engage in several types of risky behavior simultaneously. Research done by Richard Jessor, director of the Institute for Behavioral Sciences at the University of Colorado, as well as epidemiolgical studies, indicate that problem drinkers are twice as likely as non–problem drinkers to have additional problem behaviors, a fact that obviously puts teens at risk.

A recent synthesis of research by Joy Dryfoos, a respected scholar in this field, documents the major extent to which adolescents tend to become involved in several problem behaviors at once. She identifies seven major common antecedents of delinquency, substance abuse, teenage pregnancy, and school failure:

- Early initiation of any behavior predicts heavier involvement in it later, and more negative consequences.
- Doing poorly in school or expecting to do poorly in school predicts all problem behaviors.
- Impulsive behavior, truancy, and antisocial behavior are related to all other problem behaviors.
- Low resistance to peer influences, and having friends who engage in problem behaviors, are common to all problem behaviors.
- All problem behaviors are associated with insufficient bonding to parents, inadequate supervision and communication from parents, and parents who are either too authoritarian or too permissive.
- Living in a poverty area or a high-density urban area is linked with all problem behaviors.
- Rare church attendance is associated with most problem behaviors.

Although no one study has been comprehensive enough to tell the whole story, numerous studies using different sources of data demonstrate that problem behaviors overlap. In general, adolescents engaged in any one are more likely to be engaged in the others. School failure begins at an early age, and once that failure occurs, other events begin to occur. As these high-risk children grow older, substance abuse and sexual activity enter the picture, followed by ever more serious consequences—early childbearing, heavy substance abuse, serious delinquency, and dropping out of school.

A variety of psychosocial factors contribute to problem behavior such as frequent drinking. Adolescents drink for several reasons beyond the desire to become intoxicated: to establish commonality with peers; to demonstrate independence; to express opposition to parents or society; to cope with stress; to achieve a new personal identity; to lubricate social interaction; and to mark the transition to a more mature status. They may use the effects of alcohol as a kind of self-medication for distress, or to facilitate their social performance, or to "act big" to signify their movement toward adult status.

In careful and systematic studies comparing non–problem drinkers and problem drinkers in adolescence, the problem drinkers place a lower value on academic achievement. They are less religious than their counterparts. They value independence and deviant behavior more than most of their peers do. They value personal independence more than they do academic achievement.

Also, as compared with non–problem drinkers among their peers, they report less compatibility between parents and friends, greater influence of friends on their decision making, and greater approval from their friends for problem behavior. More than their counterparts', their drinking is associated with delinquent behavior and marijuana use. They seem to relish being unconventional, perhaps as a reflection of a kind of pseudo-independence. Such characteristics are conducive to a variety of adolescent problems.

One longitudinal study indicates that about half of male adolescent problem drinkers and a quarter of females will become adult problem drinkers. Young adult problem drinkers also manifest a variety of other problems, such as heavy smoking and multiple arrests, as well as higher rates of divorce. The greatest differences in Jessor's longitudinal study are between the abstainers and the drinkers. Apparently, the decision to drink regularly is part of and contributes to a major difference in lifestyle. This is only one line of inquiry that highlights the linkage among adolescent problems. Such linkage deserves a high priority in research, so we can find out how to prevent adolescents from putting themselves at high risk.

Those who smoke and drink in early adolescence are also likely to try unprotected sex and to fail in school. In effect, they are trying out lifestyles that may be exploratory in this phase but all too readily can become entrenched as they move into later adolescence.

What proportion of young adolescents are clearly at risk of slipping into long-term patterns of unhealthy and unproductive lives? Recent estimates indicate that of the 28 million people between the ages of ten and seventeen in the United States, about 7 million are highly vulnerable to the negative consequences of multiple high-risk behaviors such as school failure, substance abuse, and early, unprotected sexual intercourse. So it is reasonable to say that one-quarter of American adolescents fall into a high-risk category. Another 7 million are at moderate risk by virtue of lesser involvement in such behavior patterns—e.g., occasional rather than regular substance abuse, protected rather than unprotected early sexuality, underachievement in school rather than flunking out.

A task force studying education in early adolescence under the auspices of the Carnegie Council on Adolescent Development assessed the cost of preventable problems. Their findings are sobering.

Dropping Out of School

- Each year's dropouts cost the nation about $260 billion in lost earnings and forgone taxes over their lifetime.
- A male high-school dropout earns $260,000 less than a high-school graduate and contributes $78,000 less in taxes over his lifetime. For a female dropout, the comparable figures are $200,000 and $60,000.
- Unemployment rates for dropouts are more than double those of high-school graduates.
- Each added year of secondary education reduces the probability of public welfare dependency in adulthood by 35 percent.

Adolescent Pregnancy

- More than $19 billion was spent in 1987 in payments for income maintenance, health care, and nutrition to support families begun by adolescents.
- Babies born to adolescent mothers are at high risk of low birthweight. Initial hospital care for low-birthweight infants averages $20,000. Total lifetime medical costs for low-birthweight infants average $400,000 per child.
- Of adolescents who give birth, 46 percent go on welfare within four years; of *unmarried* adolescents who give birth, 73 percent go on welfare within four years.

Alcohol and Drug Abuse

- In the eighties, alcohol and drug abuse in the United States cost about $150 billion per year in reduced productivity, treatment, crime, and related costs. If the toll of cigarette smoking is included, the costs are much higher.

TACKLING THE PROBLEMS OF ADOLESCENCE

The vulnerability of early adolescents to health and educational risks has only recently come into focus. It is essential to move these problems higher on the agenda of scientific research, public education, and institutional innovation. Promising leads exist. We need to identify the programs that are helping to foster responsible innovations. We must find ways to help families and communities foster healthy adolescent development. The present casualties are too high and much of the damage to our adolescents may well prove to be preventable.

There is not the slightest reason to believe that today's young people are less talented or resourceful than their predecessors, but their circumstances are considerably different, and so, too, their tasks and obstacles. To help them learn what they have to learn to survive and flourish and create, we have to understand these circumstances, tasks, and obstacles better than we now do. Then adults can help children and adolescents prepare adequately for adult life and perhaps shape a more humane and compassionate society together.

11

Education in Early Adolescence: Turning Points

THE TRANSITION FROM ELEMENTARY TO MIDDLE-GRADE SCHOOL

In modern societies, the process of growing up includes a landmark event in which the young person moves from a primary, small, intimate environment to a secondary, large, impersonal environment characteristic of the larger society. In the United States, children pass this landmark when they make the transition from elementary school to middle-grade school—i.e., junior high school or middle school. This usually means a change from a small neighborhood school where the student spends most of the day in one primary classroom with the same teacher and classmates to a larger, more impersonal institution, farther from home, with many different classes and teachers. This transition occurs at the same time when many adolescents are experiencing rapid physical, emotional, and cognitive change as well.

What are children's expectations about the transition and how do they perceive the experience? What are the effects of the transition on children? What characteristics of children and schools predict more or less difficult transitions? What are the consequences of the timing of the transition? The most extensive research is a longitudinal study of children in the Milwaukee schools, conducted by a University of Minnesota team led by Professors Roberta Simmons and Dale Blyth. The main findings can be briefly stated as follows.

- Children often view the transition with apprehension, but they find junior high or middle school somewhat better than their fearful anticipation.
- Children undergoing the transition to junior high school or middle school tend to view school in general less positively. They feel an increased sense of anonymity, participate less in extracurricular activities, tend to compare themselves unfavorably with others, and see themselves as targets for greater victimization. There is some inconsistency among studies regarding the effect of the transition on self-esteem, but the most thorough studies, using the longitudinal Milwaukee data, show a drop in self-esteem in girls making the transition.
- Sixth-graders who have positive self-images, positive peer relations, close friendships, and well-developed problem-solving skills are more likely than others to have successful transitions to junior high school.
- Smaller junior high schools appear to promote self-esteem for seventh-graders. This may well be because they tend to provide a niche for everyone, along with individual attention.
- Young adolescents appear to benefit from being grouped with younger more than older children. Evidently, they need some experience of being older, bigger, stronger, or wiser.

One study compared twelve-year-olds in elementary school (sixth grade) with twelve-year-olds who had entered junior high school (seventh grade) in the Baltimore school system. That is, the children were all the same age and otherwise very similar, but were in different school arrangements. The sample was over half black and contained more working-class children than the national average. The children who had entered junior high school, regardless of race, socioeconomic status, and gender, showed greater disturbance in self-image than those who had not: They had lower self-esteem, were more self-conscious, and had more unstable self-images. Since children of different ages in the same grade had similar self-images, the change appeared to be the result of the transition to junior high school rather than a consequence of being older or younger than classmates.

Another study found that the transition to junior high school damaged self-esteem in one specific respect but not in others. Students' social self-esteem—essentially their assessment of their ability to make friends—declined between the spring of sixth grade and the fall of seventh grade, and did not increase between the fall and spring of seventh grade. Related research looked at the effects of social-skills counseling in New Jersey elementary schools to help children adjust to middle school at the sixth-grade level. Middle-school students who had received problem-solving training in grades four and five differed from untrained students in the extent and severity of situations they considered problematic. Peer pressure, academic demands, coping with authority figures, smoking, and substance abuse were all considered more problematic by the untrained group. However, the differences faded somewhat during the sixth-grade year.

Evidently, social skills and problem-solving skills can be strengthened by deliberate efforts. They can build children's knowledge and confidence in a wide range of situations and buffer them against serious problem behaviors. But there is no lifelong immunity after such an intervention. Children and adolescents need continuing reinforcement, especially through social-support networks that facilitate education and health. I will discuss this in more detail later.

Altogether, the transition to junior high school appears to have a number of negative effects on adolescents. These changes do not affect all adolescents equally, however, and certain characteristics of adolescents can predict the difficulty of the transition. Gender, age, self-image, peer relations, quality of friendships, and problem-solving skills all have a bearing on the nature of the transition for individual adolescents. For instance, having sturdy friendships in a peer group oriented to education and health can be very helpful in coping with this transition.

SPECIAL FEATURES OF EDUCATION IN EARLY ADOLESCENCE

As I emphasized earlier, the world is being rapidly transformed by science and technology in ways that have profound significance for our economic well-being and for democratic society. One upshot is that work will require much more technical competence and a great deal of flexibility; each of us will need not just one set of skills for a lifetime, but an adaptability to an evolving body of knowledge and new opportunities calling for greatly modified skills in the years beyond formal schooling. The work force will have to be more skillful and adaptable than ever before—at every level from the factory floor to top management.

In the years immediately ahead, the number of young people in the United States will be smaller than in recent decades. Fewer college-age students will enter the work force. By the year 2000, about one-third of these young people will be black or Hispanic, the groups now at the bottom of the educational and economic ladder. Any modern nation needs to develop the talent of *all* its people if it is to be economically vigorous and socially cohesive in the next century.

To do so, it is essential to take advantage of the neglected opportunity provided by this fascinating period of early adolescence. This is a time when young people are not only inordinately vulnerable, but also highly responsive to environmental challenge. So it provides an exceptional chance for constructive interventions that can have lifelong influence.

There is a crucial need to help adolescents at this early age to acquire durable self-esteem, flexible and inquiring minds, reliable and relatively close human relationships, a sense of belonging in a valued group, and a sense of usefulness in some way beyond the self. They need to find constructive expression for their inherent curiosity and exploratory energy; and they need a basis for making informed, deliberate decisions—especially on matters that have large consequences, such as their educational futures and drug use.

The challenge for schools and related institutions is thus to help provide the building blocks of adolescent development and preparation for adult life. Yet most American junior high and middle schools do not meet the developmental needs of young adolescents. These institutions have the potential to make a powerful impact on the development of their students—for better or for worse—yet they were largely ignored in the push for educational reform in the eighties. As currently constituted, these middle-grade schools constitute an arena of casualties—damaging to both students and teachers.

There is a gradual deterioration, with age and advancing grade level, in students' general attitudes toward school. Young adolescents report less satisfaction with their teachers and more negative feelings toward specific academic subjects. Rates of absenteeism, dropping out, and general alienation from school, all begin to increase during this period, especially as students move into junior high school. During this same period, there is an upsurge in drug use: alcohol and cigarettes as well as illicit drugs.

In the drastic shift from elementary to junior high or middle school, students often find themselves in an environment that is initially bewildering and intimidating. For instance, they may have six or seven classes a day, each with a different teacher and largely different students. This makes it very difficult for them to establish stable peer groups, close relationships, and support from caring and reliable adults.

With each change of class comes a different teacher with his or her own expectations, teaching style, and way of relating to students. This sudden increase in the number of teachers and other school personnel comes at a time when young people are rethinking and renegotiating their relationships with their parents. While adolescents still look primarily to parents for guidance on fundamental, long-term values, their need for stable, caring relationships with other adults is increasing, not declining.

The emerging adolescent is caught in turbulence, a fascinated but perplexed observer of the biological, psychological, and social changes swirling all around. In groping for a solid path toward a worthwhile adult life, adolescents can grasp the middle-grade school as a handle, but only if it changes substantially to cope with the requirements of a new era. Middle-grade education should lead children through the initial physical, intellectual, and social transformations to adulthood and equip them with capacities for thought and action that will be fully compatible with a productive adult life.

A TRANSFORMED MIDDLE-GRADE SCHOOL: TURNING POINTS

The Carnegie Corporation of New York established the Carnegie Council on Adolescent Development in 1986 to place the compelling challenges of the adolescent years higher on the nation's agenda. In 1987, as its first major commitment, the council established the Task Force on Education of Young Adolescents under the chairmanship of David W. Hornbeck, former Maryland superintendent of schools and a nationally recognized leader in education. Members were drawn from education, research, government, health, and the nonprofit and philanthropic sectors. The task force commissioned papers, interviewed experts in relevant fields, and met with teachers, principals, health professionals, and leaders of youth-serving community organizations. It examined, firsthand, promising new approaches to fostering the education and healthy development of young adolescents.

The result was a ground-breaking report, *Turning Points: Preparing American Youth for the Twenty-first Century*, that fills a serious gap in reports on education reform in the eighties. It reinforces an emerging movement, still relatively unrecognized by policymakers, to build support for young adolescents and educate them through new relationships between schools, families, and community institutions, including those concerned with health.

Turning Points deals with more than educational reform. It deals with real people at a particular time of life, with a specific set of circumstances, in an extraordinary moment of history. These people are young adolescents just emerging from childhood and trying earnestly to steer toward the fog-enshrouded world of adulthood in the next century. Who really knows what that century will be like?

These young people are the victims of stereotypes—they are often described as cranky, rebellious, turbulent, self-indulgent, incapable of learning anything serious or civilized. These stereotypes are wrong.

In fact, adolescents are full of curiosity, energy, imagination, and emerging idealism. They also tend to be uncertain, groping, impressionable. They have lots of questions, some explicit and some vaguely formulated, about themselves and the world around them. Adolescents make choices that have fateful consequences both in the short term and for the rest of their lives, choices affecting their health, their education, and the persons they will become. The recommendations of *Turning Points* address this challenge in middle-grade schools, while recognizing that the schools cannot do what needs doing in the next century without a lot of cooperation from other institutions.

Let us look briefly at the report's main recommendations and then examine some of them in depth:

1. Large middle-grade schools should be divided into smaller communities for learning so each student will receive sustained individual attention.
2. Middle-grade schools should transmit a core of common, sub-

stantial knowledge to all students in ways that foster curiosity, problem solving, and critical thinking.

3. Middle-grade schools should be organized to ensure success for all students by utilizing cooperative learning and other techniques suitable for this age group.
4. Teachers and principals, not distant administrative or political bodies, should have the major responsibility and authority to transform middle-grade schools.
5. Schools should be environments for health promotion, with particular emphasis on the life sciences and their applications; the education and health of young adolescents must be inextricably linked.
6. Families should be allied with school staff through mutual respect and opportunities for joint effort.
7. Schools should be partners with various kinds of community organizations in educating young adolescents, including involving them in the experience of community service.
8. Teachers for the middle grades should be specifically prepared to teach young adolescents and be recognized for this accomplishment.

The recommendations in this report engage people in many sectors of society and all levels of government, and show how these groups, working together, can accomplish a fundamental upgrading of education and adolescent development.

A Closer Look

Let us take a closer look at the main recommendations to get a sense of how these aims can be pursued in and around today's schools.

1. Large middle schools should be divided into smaller communities for learning. Many middle-grade schools are large, impersonal institutions—indeed, some nearly have the character of warehouses. Schedules typically place students in six to seven different classes each day, each with a different set of classmates and a different teacher. The subject matter of one class typically has nothing to do with the next. Three steps can help transform middle schools into communities that really support and encourage education.

First, the impersonality of the enormous middle-grade school must be replaced by a more human scale. The student should, upon entering middle-grade school, join a small community that provides a sense of shared educational purpose and a distinctive place as a recognized individual.

Second, teachers' expectations and practices must be more consistent, subject matter must be integrated more fully from class to class, and peer groups must be made more stable so students can learn in a more coherent, predictable environment.

Third, every student needs at least one thoughtful adult who has the time and takes the trouble to talk with him or her about academic matters, personal problems, and the importance of performing well in school. This will build sustained and constructive individual attention into the structure of the school.

Middle-grade schools can develop these desirable qualities by feasible, straightforward measures that facilitate the work of teachers as well as students.

A. *The school should provide smaller learning environments.* A school-within-school, or house, is a group of students and teachers with a clearly named and marked area within the larger building designated for them. A house should contain two hundred to three hundred but certainly not more than five hundred students and should function as a self-contained, cohesive unit. Students should remain in the same house as long as they are enrolled in the school, providing them several years with familiar people in a well-known setting. The house creates the conditions for teams of teachers and students to come together, for the advisor and student to get to know each other, and for students to form close associations with their peers.

B. *Learning should take place in teams of teachers and students.* Most middle-grade schools are organized by academic department. This makes common planning by teachers of different subjects difficult. The result is a fragmented learning experience for students. In contrast, the team approach unites teachers of different subjects who teach the same students. This approach allows teachers to integrate curricula across subjects and to work together to meet students' needs. Teachers' morale often rises and classroom discipline problems often decrease with teaming—not least because of the mutual aid among teachers.

C. *There should be an adult advisor for every student.* Every student should be well known by at least one adult in the school. But guidance counselors in middle-grade schools are now responsible for as many as five hundred students apiece. Such caseloads spread their talents impossibly thin. Through small-group advisory units and homerooms, teachers and other professional staff can become mentors and advocates for students, as well as the primary contact for parents. Guidance counselors would retain vital functions—supervising teachers in their advisory role and counseling students with problems that go beyond the advisors' training.

Teaming for Higher Achievement

In some respects, Timilty Middle School is typical among Boston's schools: Its American flag has only 48 stars, several teachers lack desks, and the building, while clean, looks down-at-the-heels. Assigned by where they live, the five hundred students, 90 percent of whom are black or Hispanic, face the struggles of many urban adolescents: peer pressure, pregnancy, drugs, family crises, and poverty.

However, Timilty is part of an experimental program in team teaching called Project Promise, which has brought important changes to the school since the spring of 1985. The normal school day is extended from 1:40 to 3:10 Monday through Thursday. There is also a half-day Saturday program, increased pay for teachers selected by the building principal to participate in the program (twenty-one of twenty-seven were already Timilty teachers), and team teaching is a core organizational change.

The students and teachers at Timilty are divided into four teams. At the beginning of the school year, a team of seven to nine teachers are assigned 100 to 150 students, ensuring smaller class sizes than in non–Project Promise schools. Teachers on the teams make all academic and organizational decisions about who will teach which group of students when; how many periods of reading, mathematics, and other subjects there will be; and how long each period will last. The teachers adjust the daily schedule of classes frequently to accommodate instructional needs or special events.

The most important task of the team is to coordinate instruction. Timilty has adopted an interdisciplinary approach that emphasizes the development of communication skills. Each instructor teaches some reading, writing, and mathematics, regardless of his or her specialty. Students experience continuity in

continued

subject matter from class to class: When the social studies teacher is explaining the Bill of Rights, the English teacher has students read about Revolutionary War heroes and the mathematics teacher assigns problems related to the cost of the Constitutional Convention.

At Timilty, teachers have ample time for planning, an essential element in team teaching. Teams meet nearly every day for about forty-five minutes at 3:10 when students leave, and for two hours on Friday afternoon. At team meetings, the teachers agree on what skill to emphasize. If, for example, the emphasis is on topic sentences and supporting details, every teacher in every class will ask students to find topic sentences and the supporting details. Timilty students may cover fewer of Boston's required curriculum objectives in various subjects, but the teachers are convinced that their students learn more of the needed skills. Improving the quality of the learning experience, they claim, is more important than covering all of the curriculum superficially.

Taking charge of what students are taught as a team has given Timilty teachers more pleasure in their work than most of them have ever known. Along with the additional time for instruction and other elements of Project Promise, "teaming" has contributed to impressive gains in student achievement in its first year of implementation. In 1987, when standardized test scores across the city went up an average of 8 percentile points, Timilty's scores, although still low, went up 17 points in the sixth grade, 19 in the seventh and 7 in the eighth. Students wrote an average of sixty papers, in draft and then final form, an unheard-of number for middle and even high schools in Boston or almost anywhere else.

Teaming at Timilty is one of the keys to a school that works.

This account is based, in part, on a Boston Globe *article of September 27, 1987. It appears in* Turning Points.

Advisors and Students Build Relationships of Trust

A young person entering a middle-grade school for the first time needs to feel a sense of belonging, of being able to form bonds with teachers and classmates and to trust adults. Too often, the entering student feels alienated, alone, and suspicious of adults.

continued on next page

continued from preceding page

Thus, when planners and parents designed the Shoreham–Wading River Middle School on Long Island seventeen years ago, they created an advisory system that assigns an adult advisor-advocate to each student. The system has become the core organizing principle of the school.

The ratio of advisors to students is never lower than one adult for ten students. To maintain small advisory groups, virtually all school staff, including administrative, art, health, physical education, and library staff, and even the principal, serve as advisors.

Advisories start the day. The advisor meets with his or her group for ten minutes before classes begin to discuss school issues and students' activities. This session, similar to the familiar homeroom period, sends the students off to class from a secure and stable base. Students and their advisors meet later in the day for fifteen minutes to eat lunch together.

Advisors meet twice a month before classes begin with each student on a one-to-one basis or in small groups. Two bus runs each morning ensure that students scheduled for preclass sessions can get to school. The sessions offer a chance to discuss academics, projects, home or school problems, or anything that interests the student and advisor. When a student seems uneasy in the one-to-one setting, the advisor may suggest bringing a friend for support.

The advisor, assigned to the student for the entire year, observes the student both in classes and in after-school activities and discusses the student with other staff and faculty. The student gets to know this one adult well, and learns that there is at least one person at the school with the time to hear the student's side of things. If the student misbehaves, for example, the principal consults the advisor before deciding if punishment is called for, and the advisor may, after discussing the case with the student, suggest alternative treatment.

Advisors also meet with parents twice a year to discuss the student's grades and progress in school. Teachers send all grades and comments to the advisor, who collates the information, enters it on the report card, and discusses the student with the parents. Individual parents' meetings with advisors are attended by 98 percent of the parents.

The advisors, for their part, do not try to become amateur

continued

therapists. The guidance counselor and psychologist train and support all advisors and offer specific recommendations for handling particular problems.

The Shoreham–Wading River advisory system includes every student, not just those who demand attention or earn special recognition. The system makes it possible for a young person to develop a supportive relationship with an adult who is not a parent. The system ensures that each student has access to a trustworthy adult with whom the student can communicate and share ideas and concerns.

The effect of the advisory system appears to be to reduce alienation of students and to provide each young adolescent with the support of a caring adult who knows that student well. That bond can make the student's engagement and interest in learning a reality. For these reasons, *Turning Points* selected this school for special attention.

2. Middle-grade schools should transmit a core of knowledge to all students. To have a dynamic, adaptable democracy requires that everyone, not just a select elite, contribute to the common good. At present, many students leave the middle grades without the skills necessary to meet such obligations. Education in early adolescence often promotes students' competence in specific subjects but not their ability to think imaginatively about topics that cross categories. Middle-grade schools can ensure that every student knows how to think critically, how to lead a healthy life, how to behave ethically and lawfully, and how to meet the responsibilities of citizenship in a pluralistic society. An essential part of the core curriculum is community service to promote values for citizenship.

A. *Schools must teach young adolescents to think critically.* Students must learn to do much more than merely retain facts: They must learn to challenge the reliability of evidence; to recognize the viewpoint behind the words, pictures, or ideas presented; to see relationships between ideas; and to imagine consequences. Curricula and teaching methods should be designed to stimulate thinking, not merely to transmit information; and it is vital to stir students to participate actively. Teaching subjects grouped around integrated themes can help students to see systems rather than disconnected facts.

B. *Schools must teach young adolescents healthy lifestyles.* Early adolescence provides a unique opportunity to capitalize on the young person's natural curiosity about bodily changes and the transition to adulthood. Understanding human biology and behavior is crucial in developing the ability to make wise choices about cigarette, alcohol and drug use, diet, exercise, sexuality, and other aspects of health. Yet schools' prevailing approach treats health education as a fringe elective of minor importance. Instead, health should be an integral element of life-sciences education, and the life sciences should constitute one of the central organizing principles for education in early adolescence.

C. *Schools should teach young adolescents to be active citizens.* Every middle-grade school should include supervised community service in its core instructional program. Examples of service opportunities within the school include working as tutors, laboratory assistants, or student-court officers. Outside the school, youth can assist in child care, help the handicapped, or work with the elderly. Service can teach values for citizenship and for the workplace such as responsibility, developing empathy, respect for diversity, and cooperative problem solving.

3. Middle-grade schools should maximize opportunities for success for all students. Success of one kind or another is an attainable goal for all students in the transformed middle-grade school. Everyone can be good at something. There is an ecological niche for each student if we just take the time and individual attention to find it. There are many ways to earn respect and build self-esteem.

A. *Students should be grouped for learning.* Tracking by achievement level is a widespread practice intended to form relatively homogeneous groups of students in which teachers adjust instruction to a narrow range of students' knowledge and skills, thereby enhancing learning for students in each group. In practice, however, tracking is divisive and often damaging. Lower tracks tend to be dull and repetitive, and the students in them usually achieve only minimum competency. They are vulnerable to a weak curriculum and low expectations and have few opportunities to move out of the lower tracks, even if their performance improves. Socially disadvantaged adolescents are disproportionately placed in lower tracks, reinforcing their sense of depreciation. Two well-documented alternatives to tracking for teaching students of diverse experience and rates of learning are especially noteworthy. In carefully designed research as well as in school practice, both have shown beneficial effects on academic achievement and other capabilities. These benefits apply to students from all social backgrounds.

In cooperative learning, students from various backgrounds work together in small groups. They help each other in the process of joint problem solving. They get group recognition as well as individual grades. High achievers clarify their own thinking by explaining material to lower achievers, who gain from this instructional help of their peers, but also can find ways of contributing to the group. Cross-age tutoring among students provides similar benefits both for tutors and for their pupils. Slightly older students serving as tutors can sharpen their basic skills without embarrassment, while pupils receive individual instruction from positive role models. This technique has been shown to work provided there is adequate supervision, over a wide range of educational levels.

B. *Schools should provide flexible scheduling and expanded opportunities for learning.* A fixed class period of forty or fifty minutes may not allow enough time to learn material in depth. A day filled with short, unrelated classes may foster boredom rather than learning and excitement. Class schedules should be flexible to accommodate an integrated curriculum and joint planning by teachers. Teacher teams should control schedules to meet the needs of student and subject matter, rather than being locked into a rigid schedule.

C. *Expand opportunities for learning.* Some students need extra time, encouragement, or instruction to learn. The needs of a particular student vary from time to time. Middle-grade schools should take account of the diversity of student needs by extending the school day, providing summer school or Saturday programs, providing specialized daily instruction, and fostering greater involvement of the home in learning activities. In this way, the school can build on the distinctive strengths of each pupil and find opportunities for many different kinds of accomplishment.

4. Teachers in the middle grades should be specifically prepared to teach young adolescents. Teaching in a middle-grade school has not been a priority choice for most teachers. On the contrary, they are prepared for elementary and secondary education and often feel apprehensive about early adolescents. But the success of the transformed middle-grade school will depend on the desire of teachers to invest in the education of young adolescents and their competence in doing so.

Major changes are needed in what people must learn to become middle-grade teachers and in how they learn it. Primarily, prospective middle-grade teachers need to understand adolescent development so that they can communicate effectively and take advantage of the emerging strengths of these young people. This understanding should come from course work and direct, supervised experience in middle-grade schools.

Teachers must also understand cultural differences, since in the years ahead they will increasingly be teaching young adolescents of diverse backgrounds. Moreover, they need to learn to work as members of a team and to design interdisciplinary, developmentally appropriate programs of study.

Teachers will need education in principles of guidance in order to serve as advisors in a restructured middle-grade school. They will need preparation in working with all kinds of families—one-parent and two-parent families, families of various ethnic backgrounds and races, and families experiencing severe economic or other stress that may well influence their children's performance in school.

After receiving an undergraduate degree, prospective middle-grade teachers should serve a paid apprenticeship in a middle-grade school under the guidance of mentor teachers. Selection of teachers qualified to move beyond apprenticeship would be based on assessment of their classroom performance, not on pencil-and-paper tests. The next stage would include graduate course work leading to a master's degree or certification according to state requirements.

Currently, teachers are licensed or certified for elementary or secondary school, but rarely for the middle grades. Teachers licensed or certified for elementary or secondary school should, on completion of their training in middle-grade schools, at a minimum receive a supplemental endorsement to teach at that level. It would be a badge of special competence.

5. Responsibility and authority for middle schools should rest primarily with teachers and principals. A major thrust of educational reform has to do with decision making within the school. Those professionally competent and closest to the students—primarily teachers, but also those administrators directly involved in the educational process—need substantial scope and flexibility to make educational decisions.

At present, teachers and principals at all levels of elementary and secondary education, including the middle-grade schools, are severely limited in such authority. To a large extent, their hands are tied. Yet improvements in education can occur only if teachers have the opportunity to formulate individualized, responsive, and creative approaches to teaching. In this context, teachers can involve students in weighing some of their educational options and thereby give them firsthand experience in democratic decision making.

A. *Give teachers greater influence in the classroom.* Teams of teachers should have latitude in determining how best to reach curricular goals. Such teams are in the best position to allocate money and space, choose instructional methods and materials, develop interdisciplinary themes, and schedule classes. The faculty should be organized so that they have time during the school day to make these decisions, to discuss students they share, and to seek counsel from colleagues.

B. *Establish building governance committees.* Some aspects of school administration would involve all teams or houses within the school. A broadly composed building committee can have a framework large enough to help the principal make wise decisions. Teachers, parents, administrators, support staff, and representatives from community organizations should participate in establishing goals for the school. This process of shared decision making can promote trust, respect, and a shared sense of mission that fosters education even in the face of socioeconomic adversity.

C. *Designate leaders for the teaching process.* Dividing large schools into schools-within-schools or houses requires leaders for these units and new roles for principals. Each house needs a leader who can shape an environment conducive to team teaching. This lead teacher would work with teams to develop ideas, marshal resources necessary to implement the ideas, and overcome obstacles. The building principal would be responsible for the safe, efficient, and equitable functioning of the entire school and also for interacting with the surrounding community and the political environment.

6. Schools should be environments for health promotion. Health and education are intimately related. Illness interferes with learning. Conversely, the protection of near-term and long-term health is largely dependent on education. A large majority of American teachers believe—and rightly so—that poor health, including malnutrition, constitutes a real problem for their students. Because of this link between health and school success, middle-grade schools must ensure the availability of health services. As the pivotal institution in young adolescents' lives outside the family, middle-grade schools have great potential as environments for health promotion, providing information and shaping habits toward health for a lifetime.

A. *Ensure access to health services.* Every middle-grade school should have a health coordinator competent to provide limited medical assessment and treatment, someone who can refer students if necessary to health services outside the school and coordinate school health education and other health-related activities.

For those students whose health needs go beyond the resources of school personnel, school-based and school-linked clinics have emerged as a very promising approach. Evaluations of such clinics show that adolescents use them extensively and parents are usually supportive of them. The students visit them primarily for physical examinations, acute illnesses, and minor emergencies. Since mental-health problems such as depression are common among early adolescents, these clinics should also provide appropriate psychological services.

Up until now, most of these clinics have operated in high schools. Reproductive-health care accounts for less than 25 percent of the services provided there. In middle-grade schools, the percentage is even lower. Evidence suggests that counseling can delay the initiation of sexual activity from several months to one year. Nevertheless, some young people will become sexually active during the middle-grade years. Therefore it is appropriate for school-based or school-linked clinics to provide family-planning information. I'll discuss the role of these clinics more fully in the next chapter.

B. *Make school a health-promoting environment.* The middle-grade school should provide a clear example of health-promoting behavior, social reinforcement for such behavior, and the encouragement of healthy habits. Specifically:

- Schools should teach the principles of good nutrition in the classroom and serve appetizing, nutritious food in the cafeteria.
- Schools should be smoke-free and should offer programs to help students and adults quit.
- Teaching the effects of alcohol and illicit drugs on the brain and other organs should be an integral part of education.
- Physical fitness should be a matter of pride for all in the school community. Opportunities for exercise and athletic competition should not be limited to varsity competition between different schools. Physical education should not rest on a sorting process that focuses only on the most talented. Schools should join with parks and recreation departments to provide a variety of physical activities, so that every student can participate actively.
- Schools must be safe places. Surveys show that fear has become a

powerfully disruptive factor in many urban schools. Stopping violence, drug dealing, and the carrying of weapons in and around school is an urgent challenge. How can we reasonably expect our children to receive an adequate education when we can't even protect them from physical harm in school?

7. Families should be allied with school staff through mutual respect and trust. Many studies demonstrate that students' achievement and attitudes toward school benefit from the involvement of their parents. Nevertheless, parental involvement declines steadily during the elementary-school years and is minimal in the middle grades. In poor communities, this lack of connection is especially serious.

Many parents believe that adolescence marks a time of their children's emerging independence, and they do not want to intrude excessively. It is true that adolescents are moving toward greater autonomy. Yet they need continuing contact, interest, and guidance rather than a complete break with their parents and other family members. They need a gradual renegotiation of the relationship toward an adult-to-adult basis. And they certainly need their parents' ongoing interest in their education.

Middle-grade schools have not been notably active in encouraging that interest. Indeed, some schools even actively discourage parents' involvement, especially in poor communities, where the need is actually greatest. The task is not easy, but abundant evidence exists that it can be done.

Closing the gulf between parents and school staff with mutual respect and trust is crucial for middle-grade schools. Schools can reengage families by:

- Offering parents meaningful roles in school governance. The building governance committees provide a useful model.
- Keeping parents informed. They need to know the school's ground rules and expectations as they monitor their children's progress.
- Asking parents to foster the learning process at home and at school. Parents can see that children do their homework, offer consistent encouragement, and help them overcome obstacles.

Ongoing respectful contact with parents is helpful to the educational process. Teachers and advisors can be constructive links with family members.

8. Schools and communities should be linked in educating young adolescents. Schools are being asked as a practical matter to take on additional responsibilities—e.g., in coping with drug abuse. To do so, they need help from strong sectors of society. Resources from the business community, scientific institutions, community organizations, health professions, museums, colleges, and universities can add invaluable dimensions to the educational process. Finding such resources and linking them in sustained partnerships with schools will be a formidable task, yet many working models now exist that demonstrate the feasibility of this approach. There are five main ways in which communities are currently working with middle-grade schools:

A. *Placing students in community service.* Community youth service should be part of the core program in middle-grade schools. Students can volunteer to work at senior-citizen centers, soup kitchens, day-care centers, or parks. The Early Adolescent Helper Program, sponsored by the City University of New York, is a good example.

B. *Ensuring student access to health and social services.* Nearly every community has a health department, a family-planning clinic, a family-counseling agency, or a youth-service bureau. Collaboration with the school can make these agencies truly accessible to young adolescents.

C. *Supporting the middle-grade education program.* In an uneven, fragmented way, many organizations are already helping schools. Public libraries, settlement houses, churches, YMCAs and YWCAs, Girls Clubs, Boys Clubs, and other entities provide places to study, tutors, homework clinics, and homework hot lines. Community organizations also offer alternative education to students who drop out. Many professional and civic groups sponsor scholarships and other incentives to promote academic achievement.

D. *Augmenting resources for teachers and students.* An unprecedented upsurge of business interest in education is under way. In the late eighties, American business sponsored about sixty thousand school-support projects each year. Various professions contribute to local nonprofit organizations that help students. Business and professional organizations contribute funds, equipment, and skilled people in partnerships with school systems.

E. *Expanding career guidance for students.* Organizations such as Junior Achievement, Future Homemakers of America, and Future Farmers of America offer career guidance, skill building, and encouragement. Boy Scouts of America's fastest-growing program is Career Explorers. Professional organizations can help by linking members with groups of students. Some of these organizations are now searching for ways to be more helpful in poor communities.

Louis Armstrong Middle School: A Community Learning Center

Turning Points singles out this school to describe its remarkable attributes.

Learning knows few boundaries at the Louis Armstrong Middle School in the Queens borough of New York City. Through linkages to community organizations and a local college, and by setting aside traditional limits on when and where education can occur, Armstrong serves the educational needs of its students and the surrounding community.

Although no bus service is provided before regular classes begin, the Early Bird program attracts about three hundred of the 1,300 students from throughout Queens who are enrolled at Armstrong. The program provides forty minutes of sports, music (especially jazz), computers, foreign language, and crafts. In one popular Early Bird class, students develop their own radio programs for broadcast over the school's public-address system. Early Bird teachers are primarily Queens College interns, although parents and teachers also provide instruction.

After school, from 3:30 to 5:30, a community-based organization called Elmcore tutors students, in the school building, who need extra help. Young people are referred to the program by teachers, or choose to attend on their own. Elmcore also offers computer seminars, dance classes, and sports programs.

Saturday morning classes draw about two hundred students from two dozen Queens public schools and nine parochial schools. Regular teachers and Queens College interns offer two-and-a-half-hour classes in computers, pantomime, writing, and a joint child-parent art workshop.

During the summer, a program for teachers called Ways of Knowing explores how specialists such as historians, mathematicians, and scientists conduct their inquiries. Teachers conduct workshops for their colleagues on this approach to helping students learn how people discover and create knowledge.

continued on next page

continued from preceding page

Armstrong also opens its doors to individuals in the community in need of further education. About a hundred adults, mostly from the large Colombian community near the school, study English as a second language (ESL) at the school during the day. Classes for students earning high school equivalency degrees and ESL are taught at night. Often, students in ESL night courses bring their parents to learn together.

As Armstrong supports the community, the community supports Armstrong. For example, the community provides an array of youth service opportunities for Armstrong students. About forty students report for work in nonprofit service agencies, at nearby La Guardia Airport, in TV and radio repair shops, and at the local police precinct. The Lincoln Center Institute and the Museum Collaborative both offer visiting-artist programs for teachers and students.

At Louis Armstrong Middle School, the doors are always open for learning.

Turning Points has elicited extraordinary nationwide interest and helped to focus thoughtful attention as never before on the badly neglected subject of early adolescence. The approach taken in this report and its follow-up activities not only seeks basic improvement of the middle-grade school—the pivotal institution of early adolescence—but aims to facilitate the personal development of these young people in and out of school. The reformulation of middle-grade schools along the lines recommended in *Turning Points* can improve the chances of youths from many backgrounds, including those from poor communities. Experiences in several states, notably California, in the past few years show clearly that major improvements can in fact be accomplished.

12

Science and Health in Adolescent Education

The early adolescent years are so crucially formative—and now so often wasted, or worse—that they cry out for further attention. For many individuals, the fluidity of this period offers a second chance: opportunities to overcome prior adversity and move out in more promising directions. For some, early adolescence constitutes a last chance. The evidence shows clearly that this is a time when many give up and follow paths that lead nowhere—but trouble.

Among the building blocks of adolescent education, none will matter more in the next century than science and health. Given the complexity of our transforming world and its premium on technical competence, a foundation of scientific principles is crucial for economic opportunities and for intelligent participation in a democratic society. By the same token, a firm grasp of the life sciences will give our children better opportunities for a healthy life span and a greater ability to adapt to their changing world.

SCIENCE EDUCATION FOR EVERYONE

In the eighties, many national reports called for extensive reform of the educational system; high on the agenda of these reports has been the reform of science education from kindergarten through the twelfth grade.

The American Association for the Advancement of Science (AAAS) recognized some years ago that the science then taught in the nation's schools did not adequately prepare future citizens for life in a science-based, high-technology world. Indeed, recent surveys confirm that most adolescents are now scientifically illiterate. The AAAS has spearheaded national education-reform efforts including an ambitious project to recast precollegiate education in science, mathematics, and technology. Project 2061, named for the year in which Halley's comet will return, centers on a reformulation of the essential information and skills that all children should learn in order to be considered scientifically literate. The very existence of such a project signifies that the next generation will see the world transformed by science and technology. The AAAS's goal is to see to it that education in science, mathematics, and technology is likewise transformed, so that people living in 2061 will have an education appropriate to their times and to their future.

The AAAS established a National Council for Science and Technology Education to guide Project 2061. The council was composed of individuals with backgrounds in science and engineering, business and industry, government, and education. Five panels were created to undertake the daunting task of specifying the knowledge that all persons living in an age of science and technology will need: the evidence, principles, and concepts of the biological and health sciences, the physical and engineering sciences, the social and behavioral sciences, technology, and applied mathematics. Each panel consisted of people in the forefront of that science and its applications.

The five panels, clustered in different areas of the United States, met frequently, debated the issues, and formulated their conclusions in five different reports. Each panel report was interdisciplinary; for example, the one on the biological and health sciences distilled the essential knowledge from such fields as biochemistry, genetics, physiology, zoology, molecular biology, plant biology, medicine, epidemiology, agriculture, nutrition, marine biology, virology, and physical anthropology. In turn, the panel reports were integrated into a highly readable and informative overview.

The draft report underwent extensive critical review by more than two hundred members of the scientific community, including members of the National Council on Science and Technology Education. At the end of this process, the scientific credibility of the report was secure.

The report contains five major sections. *The Scientific Endeavor* focuses on the nature of science, mathematics, and technology as human enterprises. *Scientific Views of the World* recommends what people should know about the world from a scientific perspective and as it is shaped by technology. *Scientific Perspectives* deals with the use of mathematical ideas and skills to explore and understand the world, including the historical knowledge essential for understanding the development of science and the impact of technology, and thematic insights that serve as tools for thinking about how the world works. *Habits of Mind* concentrates on the values, attitudes, and skills essential for scientific literacy. *Teaching* presents some recommendations on the role of teachers in contributing to the scientific literacy of young people.

The resulting report, *Science for All Americans,* is not a national curriculum, nor is it a textbook. It is a resource document for those interested in new opportunities in science education, and it has a wide readership because of its authenticity, readable style, and comprehensive coverage. The panel reports have also been published separately.

This report makes important recommendations on the scientific knowledge, skills, and attitudes all students should acquire during the years from kindergarten through high school. It recommends emphasizing links among academic disciplines. For example, the concept of evolution is demonstrable in stars, organisms, and societies. The report also recommends emphasizing ideas and thinking skills rather than the memorization of facts. It includes several central recommendations for teachers:

- Start with questions about nature, questions that are interesting and familiar to students, rather than abstractions or phenomena outside their range of perception, understanding, or knowledge.
- Engage students actively in collecting, sorting, cataloguing, observing, taking notes, sketching, interviewing, polling, and surveying; and using hand lenses, microscopes, thermometers, cameras, and other common instruments for measuring, counting, and computing. In short, foster active participation and hands-on inquiry.
- Concentrate on the collection and use of evidence.
- Provide historical perspectives.

- Insist on clear expression.
- Use a team approach.
- Do not separate knowing from finding out—i.e., link the results of research with the process of discovery.
- Deemphasize the memorization of technical vocabulary.

Project 2061 could have far-reaching implications for the redesign of the curriculum, the organization of schooling, the creation of new kinds of educational materials, testing and assessment, and teacher education in the nation's colleges and universities. The next phase of the enterprise is under way, linking scientists with science teachers in developing specific educational activities based on this core of knowledge and fundamental approach. Evidently, the project will have a major effect in upgrading science curricula and teacher competence.

This project illustrates the considerations that will become increasingly important if science education is to fulfill its potential in the next century.

1. The scientific community will have to marshal its resources over a wide spectrum to address educational issues—not just individual disciplines, but the full range of science and technology.
2. The continuum of science education will have to be addressed in a coherent way—not just at the university level but across the board in elementary and secondary schools, and in higher education.
3. Cross-sectional approaches will not be sufficient. There will never be one time or one place to "get it right" for the ages. The content and process of science education will need periodic updates, rolling reassessments, ongoing modernization for the long term. This means that scientific organizations will have to be more deeply engaged in precollegiate education than ever before.

HUMAN BIOLOGY: TOWARD A BROADER AND MORE USEFUL VIEW OF THE LIFE SCIENCES

The life sciences offer a distinctive opportunity to stimulate students' early interest in science and to teach them how to deal more effectively with matters of deep human concern. By stimulating children's natural interest in understanding nature, life sciences can lead the way to serious study of other scientific disciplines such as chemistry and physics.

An important goal in understanding human biology is to encourage students to find better solutions—with less strife and more informed public participation—for biological aspects of social problems such as environmental hazards. Knowledge of human biology is particularly important for decisions that relate to health—decisions about using alcohol, cigarettes, or drugs; decisions about healthy diet and exercise; decisions about sexuality; and decisions on when and how to seek health care. When we teach our students the life sciences, we are also educating them for health.

Because education in early adolescence offers one of the most fruitful of all opportunities for preventing disease and promoting lifelong health—and because this opportunity is now badly neglected—I want to explore it more deeply here. There are several key points.

1. Middle-grade schools have never had an organizing principle before. Therefore the curriculum has lacked coherence and the schools have lacked pride in their ability to make a special and distinctive contribution. Why should there be a special institution for early adolescent education if it has no unique features? The life sciences can provide a valuable organizing principle.
2. The life sciences tap into the natural curiosity of early adolescents. They tend to be interested in *living* organisms generally, indeed, in life itself. They have strong reason to be particularly interested in growth and development, one of the main organizing principles for the biological sciences, since they are themselves in the midst of the early adolescent growth spurt that is one of the most striking developmental experiences in the entire life span.
3. Therefore, it makes great sense to start the life sciences with growth and development, specifically addressing adolescent development. Concomitantly, there is a strong case for emphasizing distinctively *human* biology.
4. This leads naturally to the exciting frontiers of biology that go far beyond the human case. These frontiers involve many other species and especially involve analysis at the molecular and cel-

lular level. The advances being made on these frontiers are among the most rapid and profound in all of science.

5. This approach must involve the scientific study of behavior. Behavior is one of the main attributes of living organisms, what they *do*—and is the main basis of adaptation for survival in the human species.
6. High-risk behavior bears strongly on health throughout the life span—and nowhere more so than in early adolescence.
7. Even the less visible and long-term health effects, delayed in onset, also are related to high-risk behaviors that have their genesis in early adolescence. These are the behaviors—such as smoking and other substance abuse, dietary habits and activity patterns—that bear strongly on cardiovascular disease and cancer in the long run.

A developmentally appropriate life-sciences curriculum will teach students essential concepts in biology and then relate these concepts to problems that they encounter in their daily lives. Improvement of science education at this level could capture the attention of ten- to fifteen-year-old students for the study of science, continuing their interest in the subject in high school and beyond, and encouraging healthy behaviors through the knowledge they will gain about themselves—what they can do to their own bodies and their own lives, both for better and for worse.

The Human Biology Program at Stanford University is a highly successful interdisciplinary undergraduate major that integrates the biological and behavioral sciences. It is being adapted now from the university level to the junior-high and middle-school level in an effort to engage the interest of young adolescents to study biology through learning about themselves and other people. It illustrates very well the kind of approach we need to adopt throughout the country.

The core curriculum of this program includes ecology, evolution, and genetics; cell biology; physiology; human development (cognitive, psychological, social); society and culture; and health and safety. Young adolescents also study such high-risk behaviors as pregnancy, drug and alcohol abuse, and smoking.

This program has created a detailed blueprint for a middle-grades human-biology curriculum that describes the material that should be covered and how. The outline provides essential information for professional secondary-school curriculum writers and teachers to translate the blueprint into a textbook and materials for the classroom. The Human Biology Program core lecture courses have been videotaped professionally and packaged with special written materials for the training of middle-grade teachers.

The curriculum for early adolescents stresses the relationship between science and the student's life experience. It assumes, in essence, that teachers will capture the attention of early adolescents more fully if they begin by addressing immediate questions about human life before proceeding to life on the molecular, cellular, plant, or animal level. Examination of why people resemble their parents, for example, is taken up prior to any mention of Mendel and his pea plants. Similarly, discussions of growth and puberty pave the way for study of the endocrine system.

Thus, this curriculum begins with adolescent development, focusing on the biological underpinnings of puberty and the social responses to it. During the first semester it moves directly to sexuality: the reproductive system, sexual behavior, maintaining sexual health. In the second semester the curriculum deals with the concept of culture, including marriage and the family in various cultures. The second year of the curriculum focuses on the physiology of body systems, their behavioral associations, implications for health promotion, and social consequences.

Altogether, this new curriculum highlights several basic concepts. Early adolescence provides a unique opportunity to capitalize on young people's natural curiosity about bodily changes and the transition to adulthood. An understanding of human biology and behavior can greatly strengthen the student's ability to make wise choices about drug, alcohol, and cigarette use, diet and exercise, and sexuality. Health should be an integral part of life-sciences education; and these sciences should constitute a central organizing principle for the curriculum in early adolescence.

A strong underpinning of knowledge derived in large part from the life-sciences curriculum is crucial, but by itself is not enough. Such information combined with training in social skills and decision making can help students resist pressure from peers or from the media; increase their self-control and self-esteem; and teach them ways to reduce stress and anxiety without dangerous activity. In the transformed middle-grade school, integrating a life-sciences curriculum with life-skills training would be an important part of a coordinated program to teach adolescents critical thinking, promote healthy lifestyles, develop supportive relationships with others, and foster sound decision making. We will take a closer look at this approach in the next chapter.

PREVENTION OF ADOLESCENT PREGNANCY

Adolescent pregnancy is one of the most serious health issues young students face today. Middle-grade schools provide a special opportunity to prevent adolescent pregnancies. While most births occur among older adolescents, the middle grades are not too early for preventive interventions. The average age of menarche is twelve and a half. Adolescents' rapid physical development during this period may outpace their intellectual and emotional maturity as they pass through puberty and become sexually mature. A significant number of adolescents initiate sexual activity during early adolescence.

While the rate of births to older adolescents declined in the eighties, the rate of births to young adolescents remained stable, and the consequences of early parenthood remain severe. Indeed, there was some evidence in 1990 that adolescent pregnancy rates are rising again. As I discussed in the first section of this book, adolescent mothers are likely to receive late or no prenatal care, and their infants are at high risk of low birthweight, with its associated bad outcomes. Adolescent mothers, especially young adolescent mothers, are likelier than adolescents who delay childbearing to drop out of school, seriously limiting their economic opportunities.

Poor basic academic skills appear to be a key predictor of whether a young girl will become an adolescent mother. Without basic skills and a reasonable chance for a successful future, adolescents have little reason to consciously delay motherhood. The transformed middle-grade school would substantially increase the chance that poor, socially isolated girls would have successful experiences, build self-esteem, and protect a future that they perceive to have worthwhile prospects.

The life-sciences curriculum, health education, health services, and life-skills training all bear upon adolescent pregnancy. In addition to learning about sexuality and reproduction, students should be trained in life skills such as resisting peer pressures for premature and unprotected sex. The availability of health services for all students, including family-planning information and personal counseling, would also make a difference in preventing high-risk adolescent pregnancy. More generally, early adolescence is an appropriate time for serious education on what is involved in responsible parenting, how one can become a competent parent, and the kind of profound personal investment parenting requires.

HEALTH CLINICS FOR ADOLESCENTS

Adolescent health problems are not just "growing pains." There is a serious unmet need for accessible health care. It may be located at or near a school, and in any case should be functionally linked with a school so as to be clearly visible, within reach, and "user friendly." Reproductive health is a modest but significant part of adolescent health. Important as it is to protect adolescents from sexually transmitted diseases, including AIDS, and from early pregnancy, all of this, as I mentioned in the previous chapter, amounts to no more than one-quarter of the total activity of school-related health facilities. There are many other disease problems and much other health promotion that must be addressed in this crucially formative phase of life.

Since these responsibilities go beyond the traditional functions of the school, and since they are intrinsically complex and sensitive, each school should have a specially trained health coordinator, whether it be a case manager, personal mentor, individual mediator, or youth advocate. Whatever the term may be, each young adolescent needs a clearly recognizable and competent individual who can answer the academic, personal, and social questions he or she might have and guide him or her through the maze of agencies that may be involved in providing necessary health information and care.

Susan Millstein of the Carnegie Council on Adolescent Development has recently done a careful, comprehensive review of school-linked health centers. She concludes they are a promising model for delivering services to adolescents. They are increasingly common and there appears to be a broad support for their development. Major barriers to further expansion include lack of evaluation research, of stable financing, and of health-care professionals trained to work with adolescents. Since providing contraceptives is controversial, centers differ in their handling of reproductive matters in accordance with local preferences. In any event, most centers have been well received by parents.

School-linked health centers respond to four major concerns about adolescents' health and use of health care:

- Adolescents were the only age group with rising death rates between 1960 and 1980. More recent trends show this rate leveling off, but not for all subgroups of adolescents.
- Adolescents' main health problems differ from those of children and adults, and are preventable, since they are consequences of adolescents' behavior. The principal source of adolescent death and illness are accidents, homicide, suicide, substance abuse, and the consequences of sexual activity.
- Adolescents use health services less than they need to. Solid information is scarce because this field has been neglected, but the information that exists supports this statement. For example, adolescents visit private physicians less often than any other age group, although they have more acute conditions than adults. About 12 percent of American adolescents have no regular source of medical care.
- Adolescents have special needs for confidentiality, for overcoming financial barriers to care, and for guidance in navigating the health-care system.

One hundred and twenty-five health centers for adolescents currently operate in or near schools. Over one hundred more are planned. Most serve high schools, but fifteen serve middle or junior high schools. Most provide primary health care, health education, and counseling about substance abuse, sexuality and pregnancy, and mental health. About half prescribe but do not dispense contraceptives, and about one-fifth dispense contraceptives. All existing centers maintain patient confidentiality, but most require parental consent before offering services to adolescents.

Most school-linked health centers are operated by agencies other than the school. Administrative sponsors include hospitals, medical schools, community health centers, local health departments, and local school districts. A large part of the funding for existing centers comes from the federal government's Maternal and Child Health Block Grant (Title V). Other sources of funding are very diverse, including several federal and state government programs as well as private foundations and local communities. Most of the centers are minimally funded and live a hand-to-mouth existence. This is especially true in poor communities, where they are needed most.

School-Linked Health Care for Young Adolescents: Trust Is Essential

Although most school-based clinics are located in high schools, educators and health-care professionals are increasingly recognizing the need to provide access to health services, especially preventive care and counseling, to young adolescents. Currently, fifteen of the approximately 120 school-based clinics in the United States are in middle or junior high schools.

The staff of school-based clinics develop trusting relationships that enable them to address the concerns of young adolescents about their physical and emotional changes. Further, accessibility of the clinics within schools encourages students to seek health care and advice that they might otherwise never experience. Middle-grade students are at an age when they might still depend upon parents to take them to health services. The clinics can also help teachers and administrators to understand the developmental needs of their students.

It took a long time to build up the necessary trust, but two school-based clinics sponsored by the Center for Population and Family Health at Columbia University were able to do so and thus to affirm the importance of their services in middle schools. Most of the problems faced by students in the low-income, largely minority schools where the clinics are located are psychosocial, explains Lorraine Tiezzi, director of the project. Consequently, the clinic staff often can reach out to students more effectively than can teachers. The staff is visible in the school building, talking to students in the hallways and cafeteria, and are usually perceived as genuinely interested in the well-being of the students.

An important factor in building up trust is respect for the privacy of students. The clinic staff members make it clear from the very beginning that any information shared with them will not be shared with other adults, unless it indicates a student may take an action harmful to himself or herself—and even then, the student is informed first.

continued on next page

continued from preceding page

The clinic staffs are lean: one health services provider, who performs physical examinations and screening, treats minor illnesses, and provides first aid; a health advocate, who works with families and follows through on referrals for students; and a social worker. Graduate students in social work supplement the clinic staff. Students are referred to hospital-based clinic services when needed, as for contraceptives.

Parent support for the clinics has been strong. Initially, more than 75 percent of parents signed consent forms in one school and 67 percent in the other, with the percentages increasing each of the three years the clinics have been operating.

One clinic has been accepted more by the teaching and administrative staff than the other because the principal has come to see the advantages for his students and teachers. The clinic staff in this school is now providing health education in the classrooms. This is a breakthrough, because the Columbia University programs found that educators tend to downplay the importance of adolescent physical development on classroom and personal behavior.

Experience suggests that those who want to provide school clinics must start small—Tiezzi recommends only one school at a time—and with sufficient funds to provide comprehensive services. It takes time to become established and trusted, but the rewards are great. This Columbia experience is sufficiently significant that it was singled out for description in *Turning Points*.

Several national organizations view school-linked health centers as promising. These include the American Medical Association, American Academy of Pediatrics, the Society for Adolescent Medicine, the National Education Association, the Association of School Nurses, the American College of Obstetrics and Gynecology, and the American Public Health Association. The National Conference of Catholic Bishops has issued a statement opposing provision of contraceptive services through school-linked centers. However, the bishops are not opposed to adolescent health care in general.

The experience of existing centers is encouraging. Parents are mostly supportive of the clinics and students use them. The Center for Population Options surveyed fifty-nine centers in 1987. Nearly three-quarters of parents chose to enroll their children when offered the chance. Among enrolled students, the proportion who made at least one visit to a center ranged from a third to a half. Girls were more likely to use services than boys; 64 percent of the users were female. Since many boys view such care as a sign of weakness, special attention to their involvement is needed. Many of the students served were self-referred and would probably not have received services elsewhere.

School-linked health centers appear to be both effective at delivering services and inexpensive. One study found that students missed only 5.6 percent of their scheduled return appointments at school-linked centers, compared with a rate of almost 50 percent among adolescents treated in more traditional health-care settings. Another study estimated the cost of a routine physical to be $11.25 at a school-linked health center, compared with $45 in a private physician's office. Counting the lost wages of a parent accompanying the adolescent raised the cost of the physician visit to $59.30.

However, there has been little systematic comparison of the cost or effectiveness of school-linked health centers with other models for delivering health care to adolescents, such as hospital-based services, office-based services, health maintenance organizations, and community-based centers. While school-linked health centers fulfill many of the criteria considered important for adolescent health services—confidentiality, lack of financial barriers, and accessibility—other models may do so as well.

There are several lessons for successful implementation from the experience of existing centers. The relationship between the center and the school is an important factor in the acceptance of the center by students and parents. Center staff usually participate in school activities such as classroom presentations, workshops, and parent-teacher conferences. Involvement of the school's staff, especially the school nurse, in planning for a center can prevent possible conflicts. Links with parents and with community services are also important. Most programs have parents serving on a community advisory board.

One problem with most school-linked centers is that they serve only enrolled students, excluding dropouts—a group whose needs may be greater and whose options may be more limited than those of adolescents still in school. Another problem is a shortage of health-care professionals trained to work with adolescents. There is a strong need for dissemination and replication of exemplary training programs.

A Model for School-Based Youth Services

Trouble for many young adolescents comes in multiple doses. A young person may have parents who face severe unemployment and housing problems, and a father or mother who is an alcoholic or drug abuser. The young person may be performing poorly at school and lack dental or medical care, but know no reliable adult to whom to turn for advice.

Human-service agencies that could help these youths may themselves be geographically dispersed, unattractively labeled, or socially unacceptable to young people, and not linked to one another. The agencies may rely heavily on informal referrals, with no systematic intake from the school system, and may, by failing to provide family counseling, be unable or unwilling to address problems in family relationships.

Under the leadership of former Governor Thomas H. Kean, New Jersey established school-based youth service centers that help young people to deal with complex problems they face. The centers also provide counseling to families. The system is based in or linked to schools because, state officials have found, schools offer the most effective sites for reaching and helping large numbers of adolescents on a regular basis.

Communities receiving state funds have the endorsement of the local school district and board of education. The school or organization operating the center targets services to families that have multiple problems and are at risk of becoming dependent on public assistance. Centers try to be sensitive to cultural and linguistic characteristics of the population—for example, through use of Spanish-speaking staff, special efforts to reach Hispanic students who have dropped out, and liaison with cultural groups in the community. They conduct activities such as special vocational education and recreation that attract adolescents to the site.

Centers serve young people during and after school hours and during the summer if possible, and involve them in planning and implementation of programs. An advisory board includes representatives of service organizations, the New Jersey Education Association, parents of students enrolled in the school, students enrolled in the school who are recommended by the student government, and the family-court system. The state also recommends including the school nurse and guidance counselor.

continued

Centers offer adolescents basic services (training or employment services, health screening and referrals, and mental-health or family counseling) at a single site. Beyond this core, the state encourages centers to provide child care, parenting-skills instruction, and outreach to adolescents who have left school. Although many centers offer family planning, they may not use state funds for that purpose. Others offer child care, transportation, and a twenty-four-hour hotline.

Sites include twenty-five high schools and five vocational schools. Ten of these centers send representatives to local middle-grade schools to explain the program to the students and make referrals. Coordinating agencies include schools, nonprofit agencies, mental-health agencies, a county health department, a city human-resources department, a Private Industry Council, the Urban League, and a community development organization.

The centers serve anyone from thirteen to nineteen years of age, and have served young people older than nineteen who are still in school. Between April and December 1988, the centers served 10,533 individual adolescents and provided some 35,177 services, including multiple services to the same person, repeat visits, and follow-ups. More than half of those services were provided in the core areas of the program: mental-health services (35 percent), health (26 percent), and vocational training or other employment (17 percent).

Administratively, the state requires that each host community provide at least 25 percent of program costs through direct financial contribution or in-kind services, facilities, or materials. The state pays about $200,000 to each community annually, on average. Stable funding has been a factor in convincing community organizations and schools that they should work together on the program.

The New Jersey innovation is sufficiently attractive that it is described as a model for the nation in *Turning Points.*

These centers must offer social services, since so many of adolescents' health problems are the consequences of self-damaging social behaviors. Some existing school-linked health centers do offer a range of social services in addition to more traditional health services. The program in New Jersey actually requires centers to offer employment training and mental-health and family-counseling services in addition to health screening and referrals. Since there appears to be a trend among states and school systems toward instituting school-linked health and social services, it is especially important to learn from the experience of existing integrated programs. What kinds of institutional arrangements promote utilization of services? How do different types of services affect different types of health outcomes? The current upsurge of interest in service integration—"one-stop shopping"—as reflected in the New Jersey innovation is a recognition of the practical problems of adolescents and the fact that we have been missing opportunities to help them.

A NATIONAL COMMISSION ON ADOLESCENT HEALTH

In 1990, the National Association of State Boards of Education and the American Medical Association jointly published a report of the National Commission on the Role of the School and the Community in Improving Adolescent Health. The commission's report, *Code Blue,* expressed deepest concern about adolescent health, stating that never before has one generation of American adolescents been less healthy, less cared for, or less prepared for life than their parents were at the same age. Comparing rates of various high-risk behavior patterns today with the rates twenty and thirty years ago reveals that drug use and early sexual activity have become more common; so, too, have stressful family situations such as divorce, single parenthood, and poverty. The adolescent health crisis involves every neighborhood, not just the poorest ones.

The commission made four basic recommendations.

1. *Guarantee all adolescents access to health services regardless of ability to pay.* All adolescents should have access to a triad of essential health services: medical care, family-support services, and psychosocial services. Public and private health insurance should be restructured to offer a universal benefits package to all young people.

Also, adolescent-health centers should be established in each community. These centers can be located in schools or other convenient locations. Health services in such centers or elsewhere should be accessible, confidential, comprehensive, and age-appropriate.

2. *Make communities the front line in the battle for adolescent health.* The fundamental responsibility for organizing adolescent-health services should be with local governments, school boards, and local

public-health agencies. They should establish local coordinating councils for children, youths, and families. State and federal governments should adopt policies, programs, and operations to support local collaborative efforts.

3. *Organize services around people, not people around services.* This requires interagency and interdisciplinary collaboration. Within schools, teachers, school nurses, counselors, psychologists, physical-education staff, nutritionists, and principals all must collaborate. Beyond the schools, public-health nurses, physicians, and other health professionals must collaborate with staff in service programs to prevent drug and alcohol abuse, adolescent pregnancy, and suicide. The commission also recommends that serious consideration be given to creating local neighborhood health corps, which would consist of paid nonprofessionals trained in adolescent health and education, with special skills pertinent to seriously disadvantaged communities.

4. *Urge schools to play a stronger role in improving adolescent health.* Since schools are the only institutions that touch the lives of nearly all adolescents, they have a unique opportunity. But they do not now have the resources or authority to take advantage of this opportunity. The commission urges that from kindergarten through twelfth grade, honest, relevant information be provided about disease and accident prevention, family life and sex education, drug and alcohol abuse, violence, mental health and nutrition—as well as teaching of skills and strategies to make wise decisions. It urges collaboration to enable the schools to pursue this agenda effectively.

This report is one of the results of a major adolescent-health initiative undertaken in recent years by the American Medical Association. Since this has historically been the largest and most influential medical organization, its contribution here is of special interest.

STRENGTHENING SCHOOLS

In the previous chapter I discussed the importance of linking schools with the community to enable them to cope more effectively with both educational demands and the extracurricular support they must give adolescents. This is particularly true of efforts in science and health.

We especially need to link the scientific assets of universities, colleges, corporate laboratories, and national laboratories with the elementary and secondary schools, thereby strengthening national capability for education in the physical, biological, and behavioral sciences. There are many opportunities for involving precollegiate science teachers with the science-rich sectors of our society. Strengthening their capability will have amplifying effects throughout the educational enterprise.

Of the many ingenious joint efforts, two kinds of partnerships stand out for their future potential: links of schools with colleges and universities; and links of schools with businesses and the corporate community. Both center on institutions of considerable strength that are richly distributed across the nation; many kinds of linkage with the schools are possible.

With respect to the business community, a variety of arrangements may be beneficial. There are direct contributions by business, such as the participation of corporate laboratories in science education, making skilled personnel available to work part-time with the schools, and making financial contributions. Indirect contributions may be even more important in the long run: raising the status and resources of the schools via community advocacy and political support for education and health.

If we are serious about transforming the quality of our schooling across the continuum of K–12 to graduate study, we will require a much greater degree of substantive cooperation between schools and colleges and universities than we have ever had before. Experience with such efforts in the 1980s makes clear that this is a highly promising strategy. These partnerships are good for all students and teachers, but are especially valuable for the education of disadvantaged minorities. They can strengthen schools that are highly vulnerable and increase understanding of these crucial problems in higher education.

Such partnerships are situations of mutual benefit for precollegiate and higher education, and they must be extended. We have come to a turning point: Do we make a serious national commitment to this approach? In my view, every college and university in the nation should have a strong, explicit, substantive, functional linkage with schools in its geographical area. Education is indeed a continuum from infancy to adulthood. Institutions placed at various points along this continuum need a vigorous mutual-aid ethic, an adaptable orientation to genuinely collaborative activities.

Any serious inquiry into education must recognize the centrality of teaching. If we are serious about fundamental, long-term upgrading of American education, we must find ways to strengthen the capability and effectiveness of teachers. In practice, this will mean a sustained national effort to enhance teaching as a profession—a broad, multifaceted effort, not a single flashy gimmick. Such an effort will involve:

1. Attracting very able people
2. Providing them with a substantial education in a particular subject matter as well as in the principles of human learning and their applications
3. Giving teachers means of demonstrating their competence and maintaining it in ways that manifestly help students and thereby earn public respect
4. Providing clear social and economic rewards—respect and income—appropriate to a highly valued profession
5. Providing teachers opportunities for professional development throughout the entire span of a career
6. Creating a working environment conducive to active learning and mutual respect
7. Creating a structure of opportunity that makes it possible for the profession to reflect the full diversity of our nation

A 1986 Carnegie Corporation study, *A Nation Prepared,* made the case that national success depends on achieving higher educational standards than we have ever received before, and that the key lies in a comprehensive upgrading of the teaching profession. To build such a profession, the study recommended a coordinated set of education policies that have been considerably advanced in the intervening years but still are a long way from fruition. The task is surely not beyond human ingenuity or the resources available to us in this country.

13

Teaching Life Skills and Fostering Social Support

Adolescents have to navigate through a minefield of risks to their healthy education and social development. We need to develop interventions that can help adolescents cope with several problems at once. In this chapter I will discuss programs that address some of the underlying or predisposing factors that increase the likelihood that an adolescent will engage in high-risk or problem behaviors. These factors include low self-esteem, underdeveloped interpersonal and decision-making skills, lack of interest in education, lack of information regarding health matters, weak perception of opportunities, lack of dependable attachments or enduring human relationships with mentors or role models, and limited incentives for delaying short-term gratifications—factors that bear on virtually every aspect of the adolescent experience. We have to make it possible, convenient, and attractive for adults to give *sustained, sympathetic individual attention* to adolescents to meet their needs.

INTERVENTION: LIFE-SKILLS TRAINING

Adolescents must learn how to solve problems of attachment, use social systems, develop healthy behaviors, and pursue intellectual curiosity. Normally, they acquire these skills in the family, from friends, and in school.

Early adolescents need attention from adults who can be positive role models, mentors, and sources of accurate information on important topics. They need to understand the biological changes of puberty and the immediate and long-term health consequences of lifestyle choices. They need to learn interpersonal and communication skills, self-regulation, decision-making, and problem-solving skills. Early adolescence is a prime opportunity to teach such skills. This learning needs reinforcement and supervised practice in daily life.

In earlier times, guidelines for behavior were clear. Children lived and learned in a small, cohesive social setting. Schools had a negligible influence. At the turn of the twentieth century, only 10 percent of adolescents attended school. In the latter half of the century, schools have come to occupy a predominant role in the social and academic life of adolescents. In large urban schools, adolescents associate with others from diverse backgrounds, with different perspectives and values. There are few clear guidelines available to them or even to the adults around them. Yet individual decision and choice looms larger than ever before, especially with the advent of television, with its intended and often unintended messages about sex, smoking, drinking, violence, and risky behavior. Adolescents typically consume television's messages with little supervision or guidance. So far, schools have done little to teach critical viewing skills. Radio, VCRs, magazines, and comic books are additional sources of perceptions, information, models, and values for many adolescents—a dazzling array of inputs.

Clearly, today's adolescents need life-skills training—the formal teaching of requisite skills for surviving, living with others, and succeeding in a complex society. In 1990, the Carnegie Council on Adolescent Development's Working Group on Life Skills Training, chaired by Beatrix Hamburg, published its report on life-skills training efforts. It was composed of behavioral and social scientists from a range of disciplines in basic and applied research, as well as people engaged in program development and implementation.

The early, ground-breaking research on life-skills training involved discrete, highly structured programs aimed primarily at abuse not only of illicit drugs but also of various addictive and behavior-disruptive drugs, including nicotine and alcohol. As the field has grown, different interventions have been tested. Since adolescents care so deeply about their relationship with their peers, many programs focused on peer resistance—all the way from "Just say no" to more sophisticated learning of peer-resistance skills. Broader studies went beyond peer resistance by adding some other key elements of personal and social competence. In principle, a broader interpretation makes the life-skills approach applicable to a wider variety of problems. But a broader interpretation raises the difficult question, How broad is broad enough? Some boundaries are necessary to make progress feasible.

Teaching life skills to adolescents is further complicated by questions of balance. How much specific drug information should a program emphasize? Should it be specific for smoking, for alcohol, drug by drug, or problem by problem?

A further dilemma is that most of the research on life-skills training until quite recently has been done in mainly middle-class schools. We need to focus more research on low-income communities. If we combined life-skills interventions with research on poor communities, we could learn how to adapt life-skills training methods for all poor adolescents.

To create programs that will be most useful for different social groups and different communities, we must identify the core skills that have a universal bearing on the human condition—and especially on growing up in modern societies. Two prime candidates for such focus are social skills and decision making.

Social Skills

We are such a social species that effective adaptation without social skills is almost inconceivable. One important social skill that adolescents can be taught is the ability to make connections with others. Adolescents who are vulnerable because they have been isolated and lonely, perhaps depressed, and do not have strong interpersonal skills, can learn how to form friendships. Indeed, as social-support systems have become attenuated with the deterioration of families and communities, the formation of new friendships has become more important than ever before.

Another category of social skills is assertiveness, which has several components. Adolescents have to learn how to be assertive in taking advantage of, for example, community resources such as health and social-service agencies, or job-training opportunities. Even in poor communities, there often are more community resources than young adolescents typically know how to utilize. A few states are trying to respond to that problem; for example, the New Jersey innovation described earlier (see pages 235–236) puts health, education, and social services in a single place. But whether the problem is approached from the viewpoint of teaching individuals to utilize opportunities or of changing institutions to make opportunities more easily available, it is important to help adolescents take advantage of community resources and other opportunities.

Another aspect of assertiveness is resistance to pressure or intimidation. How do you stand up to pressure without spoiling relationships or isolating yourself? Yet another aspect of assertiveness is nonviolent conflict resolution—assertiveness to achieve personal and social goals without resort to physical or verbal violence.

Altogether, social competence is a central focus for life-skills training. Early adolescence brings a heightened importance of social interactions, especially peer relationships. Adolescents must move from the more superficial. egocentric friendships of childhood to more reflective, mature, collaborative relationships. Typically, early adolescents are inept in initiating, broadening, sustaining, and deepening relationships. They are often hesitant and suffer acute embarrassment and severe disappointments. Some may lack social skills because of their temperament or prior experiences. They are at risk of becoming overly aggressive, overly compliant, or extremely withdrawn. Minority and disadvantaged youth may be socially competent within their cultural circumstances, but unprepared for school or work settings.

Life-skills training is increasingly being directed toward high-risk adolescents. Many disadvantaged youths come from disorganized social environments lacking dependable school, family, and community resources. The right interventions can give them basic skills and knowledge to succeed in the mainstream.

Winthrop Adkins has identified several elements needed to make life-skills training for disadvantaged youth successful. Programs that have structured, problem-focused sessions are more effective, because free discussion quickly becomes disorganized and group attention wanders. In Adkins's experience, such programs need strong, informed leadership and relevant program materials, since group members are generally ill-informed. Words and concepts often have different meanings for teachers and students from different backgrounds, so a common basis for interaction has to be established. The best programs take advantage of peer influence;

students who are listened to and treated with respect react very positively and learn to be organized and task-oriented.

Decision Making

Since all young adolescents—even affluent ones—are often ill-prepared to make fateful decisions with lifelong consequences and with powerful impact on others, it is valuable for them to learn how to make informed, deliberate decisions rather than ignorant and impulsive ones.

Decision making has certain basic elements: Stop and think; get information; assess information, including consequences; consider options, or formulate options; try new behavior and get feedback. These are fundamental elements of decision making that contribute to healthy adolescent development. They are more seriously needed by those who have grown up in disadvantage than by others, but they are useful for all adolescents.

Early adolescence is an important transition period in cognitive development. Adolescents develop beyond the concrete thinking of their childhood to the capability for formal operations and abstract thinking. With training, early adolescents are capable of the sophisticated information-processing needed for making more complex and responsible decisions. Recent evidence suggests that most early adolescents have greater potential for competent decision making than they actually use.

Exemplary Programs: Coping Skills

Joy Dryfoos's extensive 1990 review of research, *Adolescents at Risk: Prevalence and Prevention*, indicates that successful programs to prevent delinquency, substance abuse, teenage pregnancy, and school failure share a number of elements. They emphasize the importance of sustained individual attention to high-risk children and the necessity for developing community-wide, multi-agency, collaborative approaches. It is important to identify and reach children and their families during the early stages of the problem behaviors. Many successful programs are located in schools, including not only those aimed at school remediation but also those combating substance abuse, delinquency, and teenage pregnancy. However, successful school programs are typically administered by agencies outside of the schools and make provision for adequate staff training in the protocol or curricula they use. Many use some variant of social-skills training, and many use peers in their interventions. A number of programs have demonstrated success by directing interventions toward parents, either by home visiting or by employing parents as aides. Finally, many successful prevention programs have a link to the world of work, exposing youngsters to career planning and work experience.

Pioneering research in this field began with the development of programs offering teens constructive ways of responding to the pressure to smoke—a kind of coping skill that may have a wider utility beyond the issue of smoking itself. Learning how to say no gracefully, how to resist pressures from persons you value, even how to maintain grace and self-respect in adversity—these are useful skills both for saying no to smoking and for coping with other adolescent problems.

Research into such programs has been influenced by the social learning theory and seminal experiments of Albert Bandura, a professor of psychology at Stanford University. An important element in the interventions designed by Bandura is guided practice. At the start of each program, for example, the instructor provides a model of ways to resist smoking inducements, encourages each student to develop a distinctive way of inventing and using responses to such pressure, and gives useful feedback. The direct instruction need not be carried out by a highly trained professional; experienced peers can be valuable as instructors if they have professional supervision. Both peer-led and adult-led social pressure resistance programs can be helpful. Such programs have significantly reduced the numbers of adolescents who smoked over three years of follow-up. This basic approach has been effectively applied to many different interventions in several nations.

Gilbert Botvin, head of the Laboratory of Health Research at Cornell Medical College, explicitly puts this line of inquiry into a broader context involving training for life skills. He has conducted a variety of ground-breaking experiments and demonstration projects in this field. Botvin believes that the preparation to resist social influences is an important part of a wider variety of skills necessary for general competence. In practice, this approach involves not only teaching adolescents how to resist peer pressure but also guiding them in decision making, assertiveness, ways of handling anxiety, and fundamental social skills. Botvin's life-skills training has been provided by regular classroom teachers, older peer leaders, and outside helping professionals; groups under all three types of leadership reduced their cigarette smoking. The program is as effective as other programs based more narrowly on social pressure, though it may be adaptable to a wider variety of circumstances. There is evidence that programs based on this concept may also be useful in preventing abuse of alcohol and other drugs—in addition to reducing smoking.

Research has shown that the best way to teach adolescents how to direct their behavior toward health and education is to help them become active agents in that change and perhaps in those of other people important to them. Motivation is essential but not enough; adolescents need to acquire certain skills and perceive the steps along the way.

Any program designed to teach adolescents life skills must take into account the nature of adolescent development; attractive models of health-promoting behavior; incentives; and an effective social-support system that fosters good habits. In terms of making healthy choices, the evidence indicates that people with a strong sense of their ability to cope are more likely to adhere to preventive health practices than people who have low confidence in themselves and their ability to control their own destiny.

Exemplary Programs: Social Competence

How can intervention build adolescents' social competence? Since 1983, Roger Weissberg and his colleagues at Yale University have collaborated with New Haven schools to establish the Yale–New Haven Social Competence Promotion Program for middle-school students. This has involved many hundreds of young adolescents. The core of the program is seventeen lessons in general social competence. The students participate in role playing, see live and filmed presentations of how to handle certain situations, join small-group discussions, play competitive and cooperative games, and receive information on substance-abuse prevention. The program teaches students how to identify situations in their own lives that cause stress, and to recognize their own reactions to those situations. The young, inner-city adolescents describe the stress in their lives: physical or verbal aggression; being blamed for something they didn't do; meeting new peers; establishing more intimate relationships with same- and opposite-gender peers; and responding to teachers' and parents' expectations. The program then gives students a six-step plan to follow:

1. Stop, calm down, and think before you act.
2. Say the problem and how you feel.
3. Set a positive goal.
4. Think of lots of solutions.
5. Think ahead to the consequences.
6. Go ahead and try the best plan.

To prepare themselves to help their students, classroom teachers participate in five-day summer workshops conducted by Yale staff and experienced teachers from the New Haven school system. They also receive five two-hour follow-up training sessions and on-site coaching during the school year. Other school personnel are also trained to support the social-competence program.

Compared to students in a control group, students in the New Haven program have shown improvements in their ability to plan and to choose effective solutions to problems. The adolescents and their teachers reported that the students' involvement with peers increased, and teachers indicated that the students controlled their impulses better, were more sociable, and performed better academically. The adolescents reported less misbehavior. A version of the social-competence program is now being conducted with sixth-graders throughout the New Haven school system and is also being disseminated to other Connecticut school districts.

In summary, classroom-based social-competence programs represent a promising approach to helping adolescents adapt to a more sophisticated world and to preventing problem behaviors. Long-term programs combining general and targeted approaches seem to produce the strongest and most enduring effects. The choice of teachers, their preparation, and on-site monitoring all contribute significantly to a program's success.

Exemplary Programs: Violence Prevention

Adolescent violence is as much a public-health concern as other behavior-related health problems, and what works for the latter may be applicable to the former. Adolescents' natural experimentation with behaviors and values offers an opportunity to develop alternatives to violent responses. The Violence Prevention Project, directed by Linda Bishop Hudson in Boston, attempts to do just that. With the goal of reducing fights, assaults, and intentional injuries among adolescents, its objectives are to train providers in diverse community settings in a violence-prevention curriculum; to translate this curriculum into concrete services for adolescents; and to enlist the support of the community in preventing such violence.

First developed in 1983 by Deborah Prothrow-Stith, who in later years became Commissioner of Health for the state of Massachusetts, the project targets two poor Boston neighborhoods characterized by high violence rates. Its four principal components are curriculum development, community-based prevention education, clinical treatment services, and a media campaign. It is designed to acknowledge anger as a normal and potentially constructive emotion; to alert students to their high risk of being a perpetrator or victim of violence; to create the need in students to find alternatives to fighting by discussing potential gains and losses; to offer positive ways to deal with anger and arguments; to allow students to analyze the precursors of fighting and to practice alternative conflict resolution through role playing; and to create a nonviolent classroom climate.

During the initial stages of curriculum development, it became clear that intervention in the schools alone was insufficient. In 1986, the Violence Prevention Project extended its outreach into the community by appointing two community educators to serve these neighborhoods. These people provide violence-prevention training to youth-serving agencies and provide them with materials such as informational flyers, videotapes, rap songs, cartoon characters, church sermons, and Sunday school sessions. The aim is to reach as many community settings as possible, including multiservice centers, recreation programs, housing developments, police and courts, churches, neighborhood health centers, and schools. The community providers can offer adolescents a service-referral network for their specific problems.

The Violence Prevention Project was selected by the Advertising Club of Greater Boston for its 1987 public service campaign, which produced television and radio public-service announcements, posters, and T-shirts using the slogan "Friends for life don't let friends fight." It continues to focus on peer pressure and the responsibility friends have for helping to defuse conflict situations. Other media projects include a public-television documentary, a video, and informational print materials.

The Conflict Resolution Program in San Francisco is aimed at raising self-esteem and making students more responsible for improving the school's social environment, both of which are factors that program designers see as vital to retaining truants and potential dropouts. Students learn means of peaceful expression and conflict resolution to settle everyday disputes and to avert violence within crowded urban schools.

In fifteen middle-grade and high schools in San Francisco, disputes are resolved in a designated room. Students in conflict have the choice of going before two peer conflict managers or an adult. Student conflict managers are nominated by other students, receive sixteen hours of training from their teachers (who have in turn been trained by Conflict Resolution Program staff), and work in pairs so that they can discuss cases and arrive at a balanced and impartial position. This program was highlighted in *Turning Points*.

In these programs, the energy that might be expended in violence is channeled into creative learning experiences, and the conflicts that might have taken place give way to teamwork and responsible behavior.

Violence-prevention efforts of such a systematic and extensive sort are very recent and, unfortunately, all too rare. Evaluation of the Violence Prevention Project is under way. I include a description of the project here because of the urgency of the problem and the need to stimulate thinking about constructive approaches. This project has real promise. Still, it would be surprising if the first efforts were highly successful, because of the great complexity and difficulty of the tasks in such terribly impaired neighborhoods. One clear finding is that adolescents—and especially young black males—are urgently in need of dependable life skills and constructive social supports. We must find ways to provide solid, useful alternatives to violent behavior.

Exemplary Programs: Youth Development Agencies

Across the nation, most communities have programs that offer youngsters recreation or support or that teach them skills. Youth agencies serve about 25 million young people annually, and thus are second only to the public schools in the extent of their influence. They offer some advantages over the schools. They are free to experiment, they reach children early, and they typically work in small groups with ten to fifteen young people at a time. Only a few have carefully organized life-skills programs with clear objectives, structured curricula, teacher training, or evaluation of outcomes. A good example is Girls, Incorporated, which has well-developed programs that meet high standards and reach youngsters in great need. Three-fourths of the organization's members are from families whose income is under $15,000 per year; half are from families with an income under $10,000 per year. Half of the membership of Girls, Inc., is from single-parent families and half from minority groups. Because these programs work with young people daily (after school, all day on Saturday, and every day during the summer), they have the opportunity to make a significant impact on the adolescent. The life-skills training approach, particularly learning to use community resources, is strongly emphasized.

Girls, Inc., has a major program for adolescent-pregnancy prevention, which has four components involving hundreds of girls in multiple sites. The first, "Growing Together," focuses on parent-child communication about sexuality. It gives parents and daughters an opportunity to practice communication skills. The second, a training component called "Will Power/Won't Power," teaches young girls assertiveness training. Members are taught to analyze social influences and the media and to develop peer-resistance skills. The third component, called "Taking Care of Business," is a life-planning course. Through a series of exercises, girls learn goal setting, decision making, and how to plan for one's own future. Finally, the fourth component, "Health Bridge," links the educational services of Girls, Inc., to the clinical services in the community. For example, family-planning services are made more accessible to girls who need them.

Each resource center is full of books, ideas, tools, up-to-date equipment, and other resources for having fun, solving problems, gaining skills, improving one's academic performance, and planning for a career. High but attainable standards of achievement are set. There are many clear examples of success, of problems confronted and overcome, and of new beginnings. All accomplishments, large or small, are given recognition. The environment is supportive and conveys to every girl that she is important, interesting, and likable. Staff greet each member warmly; pictures of the girls and samples of their work are displayed on the walls; all girls are listened to attentively; and the teaching of sign language, Spanish, and other specialized courses help make everyone feel accepted and able to communicate. Diversity is valued and respect for cultural heritage is expressed regardless of socioeconomic status.

The Girls, Inc., leaders demonstrate democratic principles and offer the girls examples of how they can be effective as both leaders and followers. The leaders teach them how to make rules and how to abide by them; how to treat differing points of view with respect; and how to take on the responsibilities of membership and citizenship, including the responsibility to recommend change.

A systematic evaluation of this program is currently under way. Results to date are very encouraging. A 1991 report gives clear evidence that the adolescent-pregnancy intervention has been remarkably successful.

Exemplary Programs: Evaluation

The School Health Curriculum Project (SHCP) provides an example of an unusually thorough evaluation. Although health education comes from a somewhat different tradition than life-skills training, the two approaches can usefully be integrated, as shown clearly by SHCP, which involves many life-skills training components. I include it here because future progress can be enhanced by integrating assets for adolescent development from multiple sources and by carefully evaluating intervention results in a differentiated way—sorting out what is good for whom and when.

The United States Public Health Service has sponsored the SHCP since 1967. In 1979, the Department of Health, Education, and Welfare (now the Department of Health and Human Services) initiated a national evaluation of SHCP's efforts. The program includes a substance-use prevention curriculum for grades four through seven. Training includes fundamental knowledge of human biology and the principles of health and illness; interpersonal skills; and problem-solving strategies. The program maximizes opportunities for success in order to develop a sense of personal efficacy. It encourages cooperative learning, the development of critical-thinking skills, the involvement of family members, interactions with the community, and integration with other curriculum areas.

The curriculum focuses on the digestive system in grade four, the respiratory system in grade five, the cardiovascular system in grade six, and the central nervous system in grade seven. Methods of learning include student experiments, skits, films, audiocasettes, projects, and peer discussions. The program consists of sixty daily sessions for twelve weeks each year. Teacher training is intensive, consisting of forty to sixty hours. Other school staff in addition to classroom teachers are encouraged to participate.

A standard version of SHCP has been widely disseminated throughout the country. In 1983 Abt Associates, a well-respected private consulting firm, conducted an evaluation of SHCP and three other school health interventions. Two of these other programs were comprehensive in approach: the Health Education Curriculum Guide and Project Prevention. The evaluation revealed that students in the programs showed greater changes in attitudes and self-reported practices than students in control classrooms did. For example, based on self-reports, almost three times as many control students as experimental students began smoking in the first half of seventh grade. Programs produced greater effects after two years of instruction than after just one. The more fully and carefully they were implemented, the more effective they were. The extent of in-service training was related to fidelity of implementation. Each program had the greatest effect in the area it targeted. For example, Project Prevention had its greatest effect on decision-making skills, a major focus of its curriculum.

Fidelity of implementation is crucial for learning what works and why. Five crucial dimensions of implementation are selection of program site; entry into the system; training of teachers; presentation of the program; and evaluation. In selecting a program site, it is important to assess the social class, race, and special problems of the adolescents the program serves. Entry into a system is best designed by understanding its organizational structure and by including key decision makers in planning. For example, schools and communities may initially be hostile to an unfamiliar, innovative program, but often become constructive participants when they are respectfully included. Evaluation is important for assessing the program's effectiveness in the short run as a basis for improvements. In the long run, rigorous evaluation gives a solid basis for the expansion of the most effective programs.

WHY WE KEEP RETURNING TO SOCIAL SUPPORTS

In the profoundly transformed conditions of contemporary society, adolescents have less access to traditional social-support networks than they once did. How is it possible to restore the functions served in less complex societies by family, friends, and small communities? Constructive peer relations offer one avenue. Peers can help each other cope with the major transitions of adolescence, particularly if they have enough in common to foster communication, yet have sufficient diversity in their experience and coping strategies. But peers alone are not enough, especially for adolescents at serious disadvantage.

High-risk youth in impoverished communities urgently need social-support networks. These can be created in a wide range of existing settings, such as school sports, school-based health clinics, community organizations, mentoring programs, home-visiting programs, and church-related youth activities. To be successful, the support networks must have a dependable infrastructure and foster enduring relationships with adults as well as peers. We have already seen how this can be done in the transformed middle-grade school described in *Turning Points*.

There are special advantages of offering social support to teens through one-on-one relationships. These can be intimate, confiding, and highly personal. Small groups of peers can be friendly and sympathetic but not necessarily intimate. Adolescents can use both types of support. What is important is that they can express themselves openly, show their feelings, and handle personal problems constructively. They need the experience of dependable human attachment, of sympathetic individual concern.

A growing body of research shows that social support is effective in preventing or reducing the impact of extremely stressful experience. People of roughly comparable background and attributes undergoing similar stressful experiences react to them differently, depending on whether or not they have dependable social support available and are able to utilize such support. Unfortunately, few of these studies have focused on adolescents, but existing data indicate that adolescents are much more likely to become depressed in the face of very difficult, disappointing experiences if they do not have strong social support available.

Key Elements of Social Support

In 1978, the President's Commission on Mental Health conducted a systematic analysis of the research and experience then available on social support. This study highlighted the ability of community institutions such as schools, churches, health-care facilities, and even elements of the justice system to provide social-support functions. It called attention to three distinct aspects of social support: (1) emotional support; (2) cognitive support (information, skills and strategies); and (3) instrumental support, the provision of tangible goods and services. This framework is similar to the one put forward by the Social Supports Working Group of the Carnegie Council on Adolescent Development. Its chairman, Richard Price, professor of psychology at the University of Michigan, stated the position clearly in 1989:

> The lives of too many of our young adolescents are affected by the erosion of family and educational supports, especially among the poor or socially isolated, leaving them lonely and with a feeling of having no control over their destiny. What kind of social support is needed by adolescents? Three ingredients are needed. We call them *aid*, *affirmation*, and *affect*. Aid refers to practical services and material benefits needed for development. Affirmation refers to feedback that raises self-esteem and strengthens identity. Affect refers to the provision of affection, caring and nurturance.

This group emphasized the potential of schools and community organizations to meet these adolescent needs for social support and carefully reviewed dozens of existing adolescent-support programs. The study found considerable attention being paid to reaching alienated youth through social supports. For example, some programs put inner-city minority youth to work in community service, teaching them cooperative learning, fostering reflective behavior and altruism, and offering reliable adult supervision. Peer-mediated programs, such as peer tutoring, can also provide constructive one-on-one relationships if adequate supervision is provided.

The Carnegie working group identified several crucial ingredients that made these diverse support programs effective:

1. Like life-skills training programs, effective early-adolescent support programs tend to *respond to more than one serious problem* or risk factor. They recognize that adolescents often have not one but several problems. They try to be broad enough and flexible enough to adapt to a considerable range of needs. Thus, school-related health facilities address not only adolescents' reproductive-health problems, but a wide range of health concerns, from infectious diseases to the prevention of smoking. By the same token, programs originally aimed at providing support to encourage students to stay in school or otherwise reduce school failure soon find themselves addressing problems of drug use—and underlying factors of vulnerability that apply to both. These programs aim to help teens acquire

social skills, develop a constructive personal identity, and build dependable bases for self-esteem. Effective programs tend to provide some combination of knowledge and skill that can earn respect.

2. Effective support programs *take developmental information into account*. For instance, they take note of the point at which adolescents' sexual activity is likely to begin in offering support to lessen the risk of early pregnancy. Similarly, they determine when early adolescents start to use tobacco, alcohol, or other drugs, and plan their support interventions in ways that can make a difference before such patterns are firmly established. Interventions aimed toward effective parent-child relationships during adolescence tend to begin early enough to prevent the disintegration of such relationships during the drastic and often upsetting changes of early adolescence.

3. Effective programs tend to *create incentives* that adolescents are likely to perceive as relevant to their own lives. A number of examples are noted in school and community settings. The program pioneered by Eugene Lang, called "I Have a Dream," illustrates this approach. (I will take a look at this effort shortly.) Such interventions create a partnership between adults and adolescents, organized in such a way that it clearly communicates a sense of positive regard and identifies ways in which adolescents may earn respect.

4. Effective programs tend to *open up social roles that are respected* and provide adolescents with the opportunity to learn new skills. One of the generic problems of adolescents is the lack of enough prepared places in society, since they are neither children nor adults. How can they earn appreciation and approval? Early adolescents are typically struggling with the developmental task of forming a personal identity and a sense of worth, so a number of strategies aim at providing meaningful roles for these youngsters, including cross-age tutoring and other forms of service to younger children. Such efforts are illustrated by Schine's program for school helpers (in *Turning Points*) and Olds's for teaching parenting skills to pregnant adolescents (considered in the chapter on prenatal care). Both these programs provide an array of opportunities to acquire skills that can earn respect and build competence; both help adolescents acquire skills that can be a concrete step toward responsible participation in the modern economy.

5. Successful programs usually *have relatively clear expectations* and provide a predictable environment. At a time when so much is in flux, and uncertainty abounds, it is reassuring to have some sense

of what to expect. As adolescents move from one setting to another, e.g., from elementary to junior high school, it is helpful to convert an unfamiliar situation into a familiar one, to build a cognitive map with a predictable environment.

6. Programs that *foster active participation* by adolescents tend to be particularly effective. They provide opportunities for direct involvement, high initiative, even for leadership. For example, they may arrange for rotation of leadership in group activities. They construct opportunities for adolescents to give as well as to receive. They employ experiential learning techniques that are more successful than passive listening.

7. Programs that *foster relationships among several support elements* are likely to be effective. For example, there are programs aimed at preventing school failure that actively engage both teachers and parents, helping each to understand the adolescent better and to work together in supporting his or her efforts in school. Some programs for pregnant adolescents enlist the support both of a visiting nurse and a friend. These programs do not see their own intervention as the be-all and end-all of the adolescent's existence, but rather as a facilitating element that can mobilize support from various sources.

8. Effective programs tend to *provide considerable continuity* over time. By and large, they are set up in a way that can provide dependable relationships for one year or longer. They build trusting relationships that provide incentives and guidance for the adolescent to pursue a constructive course with respect to health and/or education.

9. Effective programs are embedded in host organizations; they *build upon organizational readiness*. Sometimes they require a good deal of cultivation of a potential host organization to enhance its receptivity. For example, school-based programs are often initiated by university research workers who spend considerable time with principals, teachers, and parents before the organization is ready to try an innovative approach. Such efforts hinge on the beliefs of critical authorities in recognizing a problem and a tangible opportunity to deal with that problem. They must commit key people and material resources to make possible a well-constructed and dependable support program.

Exemplary Social-Support Programs

Researchers at the University of Illinois carefully constructed an intervention program to address the problems of the stressful transition from elementary school to junior high school: the School Transition Environment Program (STEP). Moving away from the near-chaos that is so often the entering student's perception of junior high school, STEP constructs a predictable environment through a committed homeroom teacher and a single group of peers who stay together and tackle their academic tasks as a group. Moreover, STEP changes the homeroom teacher's role in a way that makes it possible to offer the students more dependable support on an individual basis. It provides more relevant information about the school environment. It helps teachers become familiar with each student. Follow-up measures indicate that students in this program develop a much stronger sense of belonging than do students in routine, traditional programs—and dropout rates are cut by half. Students' self-esteem shows a marked improvement, as does their school achievement.

Another illustrative program is called Project Spirit, which was undertaken by the Congress of National Black Churches. In several difficult inner-city situations, black churches participating in this project have built a small and competent staff that works cooperatively with parents and students to support education and health. For example, Project Spirit offers an after-school tutorial in which retired and active public-school teachers work as voluntary tutors to sustain adolescents' motivation and build their academic skills. There is also a six-week program aimed at strengthening parents' interest and competence. Pastoral counseling is available; in this way ministers become knowledgeable about family problems and build their own capacity to be helpful. Parents and students strengthen their motivation and build relationships through a variety of shared activities such as the production of skits and musical events, many different games, and the role-playing of interesting real-life experiences.

Such churches have the potential for reaching young people in poor communities who might otherwise be very difficult to help. Their programs can be organized to provide students sustained, sympathetic, individual attention, encourage their education, and build the skills that enhance their academic accomplishment.

Another example cited by Price's group is the "I Have a

Dream" program, which was initiated by philanthropist and businessman Eugene Lang in Harlem in the 1980s. In this program, Lang steps in as children are graduating from elementary school and promises a full college scholarship for each student who successfully completes his or her high-school education. The incentive is explicit and dependable. Equally important, Lang's program provides supportive mentoring specifically geared to help these adolescents cope with the tasks of academic achievement in high school. It is important for students to feel encouraged to move toward the tangible goal of higher education; it is also important to have the coping skills to do so. This kind of program provides these students with a new perception of opportunity and also opens up a path toward fulfillment of that opportunity.

Lang's students meet regularly in small groups and receive tutoring, advice, and encouragement throughout some of their junior-high years and all of their high-school careers. This special attention also helps to bridge the transition from junior high to high school. Five years after the first "I Have a Dream" class was initiated, the 75 percent dropout rate typical for the students in that Harlem school had changed dramatically. Indeed, fifty of the fifty-one students who were present for the original commitment were still in school five years later. About half of this initial sixth-grade class definitely planned to go to college at the time of the five-year follow-up. Stimulated by this experience, New York State passed legislation to provide "Liberty Scholarships" based on this model. Such state programs have the capacity to scale up model interventions created by private enterprise. Moreover, Lang's efforts have encouraged many wealthy people to undertake similar programs to which they pledge a great deal of personal responsibility, not only for the financial aspects of such programs but for the one-to-one relationships involved. Today there are more than 125 similar projects operating in twenty-five cities.

At this point, we connect again with prenatal care, because social support for adolescent mothers is particularly vital. Poor young mothers need to seek prenatal care early in pregnancy and stay with it so as to take advantage of the opportunities provided by comprehensive care. Some excellent programs have been developed that help not only with pregnancy but with other adolescent problems as well.

In one intriguing set of innovations, pregnant girls are connected with "resource mothers," women living in the same neighborhood as the adolescent mother who have assimilated life experience in a constructive way, have successfully raised their own children, and have learned many useful life skills most relevant for the young mother. They become counselors or mentors for a small group of ten or twelve young women. They take a serious interest in these women, try to understand their problems, try to convey what they have learned about the difficulties facing the young mother, and in general provide sympathetic, sustained attention as well as gateways to community resources. Such examples highlight the crucial value of social support for health and education during the major transitional years of adolescence.

The Prenatal/Early Infancy Project headed by Olds, which is described in the chapter on prenatal care, deserves further comment here because it exemplifies a systematic effort to mobilize social support for pregnant adolescents. It is so well designed and well evaluated—and of such widespread significance—that I want to pursue it further in the context of adolescent social support. Without such support, poor and socially isolated adolescent mothers have a strong tendency to drop out of school, to become more deeply mired in poverty, and to have a low-birthweight baby who is at risk for a variety of bad outcomes both in the perinatal period and in subsequent years. The Prenatal/Early Infancy Project teaches pregnant adolescents parenting skills designed to build their competence and self-esteem; it provides health care for mother and baby, including the capacity to self-care through health education; it recruits informal support from boyfriends and family friends; and it uses visiting nurses to link pregnant adolescents to agencies that can provide needed services in health, education, and the social environment. It is particularly interesting to note that this program builds strength partly by recruiting the informal support of various friends of the pregnant teens. The adolescent women are typically asked to name some people they know who are reliable: Whom can you count on for help? Friends and relatives so identified are encouraged by the intervention staff to enter into the world of the pregnant adolescent—especially to support her as she tries to quit smoking, to keep her weight within appropriate bounds for the pregnancy, and to avoid taking drugs.

Evaluation of the Prenatal/Early Infancy Project is highly encouraging. The women in this program experienced greater informal social support, improved their diets more, and smoked less than similar women exposed to conventional arrangements. On long-term follow-up, the mothers in this program, though poor and unmarried, were much more successful in the work force during the first four years of their children's lives than were their control counterparts. Moreover, they had substantially fewer subsequent births in that time interval, so they were better able to focus serious attention both on their babies and on employment opportunities than they would have if they followed the more familiar pattern manifested in the control group of having one baby after another with no respite. Altogether this ingenious program offers considerable hope about what can be done, not only with respect to poor, unmarried adolescent mothers, but also with a wider range of at-risk youth in the context of sound, supportive interventions.

Student Helpers

Connections between the community and the school are one important result of the Early Adolescent Helper Program (EAHP) initiated by the City University of New York. School personnel get to know the people and resources in their community as they seek placements for the Helpers. Community-agency staff gain understanding of the schools in their area through what may be their first formal agency contact with the school system. Thus, while the young adolescent Helpers are gaining a sense of belonging to the community, adults in the program are doing the same.

The EAHP trains middle-grade students as Helpers and places them in the community for after-school assignments in safe and supervised places. Helpers are sent to child-care or Head Start centers, where they read to the children, supervise the playground, assist with the snack, conduct arts and crafts or music activities, and help with math games. Other Helpers are placed in senior-citizen centers, where they join in projects with the elderly, such as interviewing one another on audio or videotape about life experiences of different generations.

An adult, usually a teacher or guidance counselor, trains Helpers in a weekly small-group seminar with hands-on activities designed to build Helpers' skills and prepare them for their role in the community. The seminars emphasize reflection and encourage Helpers to talk about themselves, think about their futures, and take responsibility for their daily lives. Helpers share experiences, ideas, and approaches and discuss their feelings about being a Helper as well as appropriate dress and behavior on their assignments.

Developing trust within the seminar enables Helpers to discuss concerns that are not usually addressed in school. As young adolescents, for example, they have had little experience in exercising authority or power, and they are able in the seminar to exchange views on this subject.

In one newsletter on the program, Helpers said they learned to listen to others, to trust and be trusted by others, to be patient and reliable, to accept responsibility, and to meet new people who became important to them. They enjoyed getting to know adults at their school outside the usual teacher-student relationships, and especially liked being treated as co-staff, feeling valued for their efforts and opinions, and feeling important to others.

Adults reported in the newsletter that the Helpers acted without exception in a professional manner, attended regularly, and assumed their work roles with complete seriousness. The adults also noted positive attitude and behavior changes. On the basis of its national survey, this program was highlighted in *Turning Points*.

PROGRAMS LED BY PEERS

A variety of reports indicate that programs led by constructive peers can be very valuable; peers can use credibility with fellow adolescents to help some young people who would otherwise be very hard to reach. Both education-oriented and health-oriented programs can function well with peer leadership—provided that these peers receive adequate supervision by teachers or other professional adults. Reviewing the evidence of peer-led programs shows that they can substantially reduce the number of early adolescents who smoke; the peer leaders serve as models who themselves have been able to resist the temptation to smoke. These models can also help adolescents discover alternatives to drug abuse. In the process, teens can make friendships and gather information on a variety of subjects, especially if the peer leader is slightly older and has successfully navigated rough waters that the younger adolescent is only now entering. With adequate supervision, peer leaders can be very effective in teaching younger adolescents social skills to resist pressures to use drugs or enter into unprotected sex; they can also help them identify and practice other healthful activities.

During early adolescence, students can participate in a variety of organized groups that contribute to the welfare of others. Such groups generally place a high premium on caring for others and help students develop skills through which they can express caring usefully in community service. Students in these groups have the opportunity to serve other adolescents, typically those slightly younger than themselves. For example, adolescents can help their peers through tutoring and counseling, provided that they have a modicum of preparation and ongoing supervision from qualified adults. They can be helpful to the elderly in nursing homes or to younger children in day-care centers—to name a few of the places where early adolescents have successfully worked.

Tutoring

Diane Hedin reviewed some peer-led programs for the Carnegie Forum on Education and the Economy in 1986 and called attention to powerful evidence of the value of one-to-one tutoring as a teaching method. Robert Slavin's recent research, described in the chapter on middle childhood, also highlights this key fact. With a trained tutor, 98 percent of students do better than those without a tutor in otherwise similar circumstances. Some researchers even found that peer tutoring is more cost-effective for student achievement in mathematics and reading than computer-assisted instruction. Despite its obvious benefits, academic tutoring is not often offered as an inherent part of the educational program of American schools. The important thrust of the new evidence is that tutoring is valuable not only when it is conducted by teachers or professional tutors, but also when it is conducted by suitably prepared students or by supervised paraprofessionals. This approach could be particularly valuable in poor communities with a high proportion of at-risk students.

There has been enough experience with these techniques to reach some dependable generalizations. Indeed, well over ten thousand American schools have had experience with tutoring in one form or another, although most of them use adults as tutors. Still, there is abundant experience over the last two decades with peer-led tutoring. What is exceedingly rare, however, is to find tutoring used as a basic instructional tool on a regular basis, available whenever the teacher judges that it will be useful. This may well provide an opportunity of great potential for the next decade.

It is particularly interesting that in elementary and secondary schools difficult subjects such as mathematics seem to respond particularly well to tutoring. In forty-five of fifty-two achievement studies that have been critically reviewed, the tutored students did better on examinations than those in a conventional class. Cross-age tutoring was more effective than same-age tutoring. Other circumstances also fostered success: structured programs using well-organized procedures; concentration on basic skills that had been fully mastered by the tutor; and the particular suitability of mathematics to this approach. All in all, there is abundant evidence that the tutees tend to benefit in academic achievement from peer teaching, especially with an older tutor.

Tutoring offers tutees two distinct benefits. The first is *individualized instruction for tutees.* Most tutoring programs try to offer individualized, systematic, well-organized learning experiences to improve students' academic performance. In dealing with a real, live person, theoretical notions are put to the test. The tutor must seek creative ways to make this particular individual interested in the material and develops a pattern of instruction tailor-made to a specific person.

The second benefit is *personal and social development of tutees.* Usually the tutor and tutee become closer as the tutoring progresses. The supervision deliberately fosters a positive climate. Thus, older adolescents may well become attractive models for younger students. The closeness in age makes for ease of communication and sharing of experience. Yet the additional experience and maturity of the older adolescent also provides guidance and stimulation. Thus, the benefits tend to be not only academic but personal. Indeed, the social skills acquired in such interactions by shy or uncommunicative tutees have much in common with the results of organized programs of life-skills training I discussed earlier in this chapter.

Although the principal focus has been either on the academic achievement or on the personal problems of the tutee, there is considerable evidence of benefits of tutoring to the tutors as well. These fall into several categories:

1. *Enhancing personal development.* With adequate preparation and a modicum of ongoing supervision, the tutor develops a sense of competence and the ability to make a social contribution, to be useful to other people. Moreover, he or she develops a growing sense of empathy for other people, as well as the ability to think analytically at a higher level of complexity in order to sort out the problems being handled.

2. *Learning or reviewing basic skills.* At every level of education, there is abundant experience to indicate that teaching is one of the best ways to master a specific body of knowledge. This is no less true for early adolescents than it is for university professors.

3. *Applying academic studies.* Students working as tutors tend to

see more meaningful uses of the knowledge they have gained in school, to understand it better, and to be stimulated to pursue the subject in greater depth in the future.

4. *Developing insight into the learning process.* The tutor's interaction with the tutee inevitably includes problems and obstacles, but also stimulating exchanges and sometimes even inspiring experiences. All this gives tutors a deeper sense of what learning is all about and often insight into their own learning processes.

Valued Youth:
Potential Dropouts Serve as Tutors

Turning Points draws attention to a remarkable Texas program that is pertinent here.

In San Antonio, 45 percent of Hispanic students drop out before graduating from high school; more than half of these youths leave before ninth grade. To stop this loss, the Intercultural Development and Research Association (IDRA), a local organization, designed the Valued Youth Partnership Program to engage potential dropouts, train them as tutors, and assign each tutor to three to five students at adjacent elementary schools.

The rationale for the program is twofold. First, IDRA research determined that teachers could spot students at risk for dropping out through a combination of declining grades, rising absenteeism, and increasing behavior problems. Second, review of numerous studies of cross-age tutoring showed that tutors made significant gains in achievement, sometimes even greater than did tutees.

The Valued Youth Program was launched with funding from a local Coca-Cola Bottling Company for pilot programs, development of models and training materials, and evaluation. Currently about 150 Valued Youth from five San Antonio middle schools (two school districts) tutor four to eight hours a week. Boys and girls participate in equal numbers.

A rise in tutors' self-esteem is the most noticeable effect of the program, according to IDRA. Remarkably, only 2 percent of all tutors have dropped out of school. This is noteworthy, since all of these students had been held back twice or more and were reading at least two grade levels below their current grade place-

continued

ment. Disciplinary problems have become less severe, grades have improved, and attendance of tutors has increased sharply.

In addition to tutoring, students learn to solve problems and the value of speaking to others respectfully. They also hear guest speakers, often successful community leaders who attended the same school or grew up in the neighborhood, describe career options. Recognition ceremonies, with T-shirts and rewards, give the tutors status at school and in their community.

Valued Youth confirms that tutors often gain even more than tutees: By teaching, one learns; by giving, one grows.

5. *Academic achievement.* In thirty-three of the forty-nine studies reviewed by Cohen's group, students who were themselves tutors did better on examinations in the same subjects than did matched comparison students. Although the results were modest, they were consistent over a wide range of tutoring programs. Again, there was some advantage to cross-age tutors as compared with same-age tutors, and some advantage for mathematics in comparison to reading. By the same token, both tutees and tutors enjoyed small but consistent positive effects on their self-esteem and attitude toward school, especially attitude toward the particular subject matter tutored.

When such programs of peer-mediated instruction are well established, there are also benefits to teachers. The classroom climate is likely to improve. Since fewer students are feeling left out and seriously alienated, a more cooperative and pleasant atmosphere tends to emerge. The teacher enjoys a more diversified set of experiences than goes beyond the typical lecture pattern. Additionally, students who are themselves working hard to become effective teachers tend to be more sympathetic to the professional teachers in the classroom. There is less boredom and more personal contact, so discipline problems tend to diminish. These techniques help to transcend the ethnic and racial barriers that exist in urban classrooms. Moreover, a well-functioning program of students as auxiliary teachers allows professional teachers to use their professional skills more fully than they could otherwise.

What does research tell us about the ingredients for successful tutoring efforts? One finding is that children and adolescents prefer to have a somewhat older student rather than a person of the same age for a tutoring or formal teaching relationship. Early adolescents perceive a gap in experience as an attractive attribute, so long as the gap is not so great as to impair communication. There is considerable evidence that students at all levels of achievement can be effective as tutors if the appropriate arrangements are made. If simple skills are being taught, an age difference of about one year works well. If complex skills are being taught, an age difference of about three years seems optimal. Students tend to prefer working with tutors of the same sex, though there is considerable variability. Programs of a few weeks' duration generally are quite successful in raising achievement scores for both tutors and tutees. If tutoring needs to continue beyond one month, as may well be the case for high-risk students, then special arrangements are needed to provide appropriate recognition of tutees' achievements as well as supervision. Not surprisingly, the best effects on the tutees' academic achievement occur when the tutoring is well organized and clearly structured.

Experienced leaders in this field generally believe that the training of tutors is vital. Many students do not have much ability at the outset to work in an empathic, well-organized way with their tutees. Indeed, in poor communities, it is particularly common to find tutors offering little more than harsh criticism to their pupils. But tutoring can be shaped in constructive ways by reasonable guidance that is not highly time-consuming. Regular contact with adults who are easily available keeps tutors on a constructive course. The training program for peer tutors involves teaching them how to give clear directions, praise and encourage the learner, confirm correct responses, correct errors in a way that is clear and not deprecating, and be patient enough to allow the tutee to become actively involved in solving problems.

Peer teachers benefit considerably from seminars designed specifically to reflect their own experiences. The evidence is that their problem-solving capacity, empathy, and ability to handle intellectual complexity can be increased when they have the opportunity to discuss their experiences as teachers, tutors, or community-service workers.

There is abundant opportunity in the years ahead to expand the use of peer tutoring in light of this encouraging evidence. More research is needed to specify the ways in which this work can be most efficient and rewarding as well as to explore new contexts of its application. But enough is known now to undertake widespread public education about the value of peer tutoring. It is very important that professional teachers be substantially involved in the formulation, planning, and implementation of such programs, which to some degree involve not only logistical considerations but new thinking about the role of the teacher. Such efforts should be seen as a way of augmenting the capacity of teachers, certainly not undermining them in any way. Teachers may well come to view themselves as managers of the educational process; their job will be not only to teach directly but also to supervise others who teach or aid in the process of educating the students. By the same token, these experiences may very well stimulate students to pursue careers in education. Altogether, peer-led programs have great potential for strengthening school experiences for all kinds of students; and they hold special promise for fulfilling the potential of the most vulnerable ones.

MENTORING

Another aspect of social support that has stimulated great interest in recent years, especially in relation to the problems in poor communities, is the relationship that has come to be called mentoring. A variety of innovative efforts have sought ways to construct dependable one-on-one relations over an extended time between an experienced, caring adult and a shaky adolescent.

In the black community of Washington, D.C., a popular radio station has organized a mentoring program. It grew out of concern about what was happening to black boys during the summer between third grade and fourth grade, when it appeared that they were turning away from school and becoming vulnerable to dropping out of education. The concern was that they did not have men in the community with whom they could identify who were doing well and felt enthusiastic about education. On-air announcements recruit volunteer mentors to serve as role models for troubled black boys. The mentors show young boys from depreciated circumstances how they can do well, just as their mentors, who come from similar backgrounds, have done. The emphasis is on personal and social skills as well as academic performance.

The boys in the program are selected by the principal of their school because they seem to be headed for serious trouble. The mentors, typically single black men in their late twenties or early thirties, take the boys, who are typically about ten years old, to a variety of enjoyable activities, e.g., movies, plays, ball games, and concerts. They try to arrange for the boys to meet black adult males who are successful in different fields. So this is an effort to prevent casualties in a very different situation by providing these youngsters with dependable social support over an extended period of time and showing them models of attractive future possibilities. This program is particularly interesting because radio stations have great potential for reaching out widely into the community in a way that is attractive and meaningful. A crucial problem is to retain mentors long enough to have a constructive impact on the mentees.

Project Literacy U.S.A. finds mentors among senior-citizen organizations and business corporations. It seeks students who are neither in deep trouble nor highly privileged, addressing a fairly wide spectrum of working and middle-class people, and providing a supplement to family experiences. Once again, mentors and students share pleasant activities such as shopping, shows, and movies. Sometimes the mentors bring students to their workplace to give them a better sense of adult responsibilities, to meet other people, and to see the mentor in action. Sometimes the mentors help the students with homework. The mentors try to encourage students' aspirations at least moderately above their original outlooks. The minimum time required from each mentor is a half hour per week. Student and mentor meet sometimes before school, more commonly after school, and sometimes at school for special activities. In some similar programs, the mentor-mentee groups meet in a free period with the guidance counselor once a week in an effort to build students' problem-solving capacity and self-esteem.

Recently, there have been systematic efforts to survey the national experience in this field. One of these, prepared especially for the MacArthur Foundation, focused on mentoring for disadvantaged youth. The findings indicate a nationwide trend to view mentoring as a powerful way to provide adult contacts for adolescents who are otherwise largely isolated from adults. These programs help adolescents prepare for social roles that can earn respect and encourage them to persist in education.

To be effective, mentors must be persistent and resourceful. They must find ways to build trust that fit the particular individual and the cultural context in which they are working. They should know how to set tangible, usually modest goals early in the relationship. Mentors should be reasonably predictable and certainly dependable. They should also be available on the telephone at any time during the week, at least under specified conditions. They should be committed to the program for at least a year. They must know how to empathize with a developing adolescent, to be reasonably sensitive to what is current and choice, what is likely to be credible, and how to make sense out of the adolescent experience.

Although the experience to date is limited, there are some widely shared impressions that need to be researched more systematically. The most successful mentors appear to be those whose experience is substantially greater than that of the mentee but whose social distance from the mentee is not enormous. The mentor does not have to be of the same race, gender, or social class; yet some similarity in social background may well ease communication and give a disadvantaged mentee a sense of authenticity in the relationship.

Mentors may have a variety of instrumental roles: teacher, advisor, inspirer, guide, advocate, coach, sponsor, gatekeeper. It is also clear that they have a psychosocial role; they offer friendship, feedback that builds a sense of personal worth, attractive modeling of roles and skills, counseling, and support in a crunch.

It is useful for the mentoring program to be integrated with other resources available in the community. Particularly for high-risk youth, who tend to have clusters of problems, the connection with education, health, and social services may be crucial. The mentor is likely to need some guidance in this respect but may also be able to draw upon resources unknown to those in the mentee's natural community. Mentors can be particularly helpful in shaping mentees' social skills, in opening doors that would otherwise be closed, and in stimulating a legitimate perception of opportunity in them.

Overall, work in this field indicates that effective mentoring can improve the social chances of poor adolescents by supporting them in their efforts to move ahead in education and in health, by encouraging new patterns of behavior appropriate to adolescent development, by providing a tangible perception of opportunity and steps toward the fulfillment of that opportunity, by sharing pleasurable experiences and stimulating curiosity around those experiences, and by providing some tangible resources as well as coping skills.

Public/Private Ventures has reviewed the experience of programs linking high-risk youth with *elder* mentors. Such efforts are predicated on the observation that many such young people grow up in circumstances that tend to be weak in caring and consistent adult relationships. Observations of longitudinal research considered earlier, such as that of Emmy Werner, indicate that a single adult relationship can offset many noxious influences. This relationship need not be provided by parents. Other relatives, neighbors, friends, or teachers may make a positive difference. Children who are resilient in the face of adversity often have this kind of support. So a sustaining relationship with even a single adult can facilitate healthy development. How can monitoring arrangements be constructed to simulate these natural relationships that serve so well to buffer the effects of stressful experience?

The Public/Private Ventures review examined five initiatives in which older people, chiefly retirees serving as volunteers, sought to help pregnant adolescents, adolescent offenders headed for incarceration, and students in jeopardy of dropping out of school prematurely. Drug abuse prominently figured in all these situations. A number of salient observations emerged. First, intergenerational relationships form despite considerable apprehension in the beginning. Indeed, strong bonds formed in most of the cases observed. Second, the relationships fall into two general categories. In one kind, there are strong attachments similar to those of a natural family with considerable intimacy and a willingness on the part of the mentor to tackle the full range of the adolescent's problems. In the other, less intense kind of relationship, the mentor acts like a friendly neighbor, offering useful reinforcement for constructive behavior on the part of the adolescent but keeping considerable emotional distance. Third, there are clear benefits for most adolescents. With very few exceptions, the adolescents involved in these relationships see an improvement in the quality of their daily lives and an enhancement of their personal skills. For those in a strong, intimate relationship, there are additional benefits, especially in their capacity to cope with highly stressful experiences. Such adolescents believe that they have become more competent, have more doors open to them, and have access to a better life than they would otherwise have had, including mainstream opportunities. Fourth, there are also benefits for the mentors. They have a sense of meeting some needs of their own, of being socially useful at a time when they had serious doubts as to whether they could ever be useful again. They also find it stimulating, getting out in the community more than they had expected to, sometimes earning money, forming satisfying relationships, and feeling challenged in a way that is reminiscent of experiences at an earlier age. Fifth, the intergenerational bonds in many cases develop a strong emotional basis. They occur when the young people are receptive, especially in need of support and guidance, ready for change, or lonely for adult relationships.

The results of the limited national experience to date make clear that older people can contribute substantially as mentors to adolescents. These interventions help two generations at once. The fact that unrelated, nonprofessional adults can usefully intervene in the lives of troubled adolescents suggests that there may well be a large, competent, low-cost pool of adults to help with the serious difficulties that now affect about one-quarter of all adolescents. Older members can stand in as an available, constructive, extended family, offering a trusting and stimulating experience that may help adolescents build other relationships in the future. This line of innovation deserves to be pursued with ingenuity and dedication in the years ahead.

FAMILIES WITH ADOLESCENTS

Another area of interest in social support is in helping families that face the specific problems of adolescents. The Carnegie Council on Adolescent Development commissioned a scholarly paper by Professor Stephen Small on this subject in 1989, following a workshop chaired by Keith Brodie, president of Duke University. These explorations showed that families with adolescents have been relatively neglected by comparison with families containing young children. Even for the affluent sector, little work has been done on strengthening support networks for families during the stresses of the great transition from childhood to adulthood. Still less attention has gone into strengthening networks for families who live in poverty or culturally difficult situations.

Although adolescents are moving toward independence, they are still intimately bound up with the family, which is typically much more important to them than meets the eye. This is especially true during early adolescence. For that reason, we need to pay substantial attention to the ways in which family relationships can be utilized to help adolescents weather the radically transformed conditions of contemporary life.

Professor Small made an informal national survey of preventive programs that support families with adolescents. He constructed a framework for understanding the tasks of families with adolescents that includes meeting children's basic needs; protecting them; monitoring them; teaching them self-protection skills; guiding and supporting their development; advocacy; and prioritizing the relative importance of various parental functions. He then examined factors that support or undermine parental competence, such as the personal and psychological resources of the parents; the characteristics of the adolescent; the contextual sources of stress and support; the marital relationship; work; and formal and informal social supports.

With this framework in mind, Small identified forty-one programs that were making a serious effort to strengthen the families' capacity to tackle the problems associated with adolescent development, especially the renegotiation of relationships within the family. Most of these programs centered around curricula developed for this purpose and made available for use by local organizations. Small identified the intellectual center of gravity of these programs in several ways: (1) general parenting; (2) sexuality; (3) substance-abuse prevention; (4) achievement; (5) multiservice family resource centers.

This enterprise is at a very early stage of development, but it does address opportunities of considerable potential. One of Small's strongest recommendations is to give parents a way to obtain social support from other parents—sharing experience and pooling information and coping strategies. A mutual-aid ethic among parents who have a common concern for the well-being of their developing adolescents and yet who bring diverse experiences to the encounter can be helpful.

Moreover, parent-education courses should probably cover developmental changes of midlife adults. In some respects, this is a difficult time for parents as well as for the growing adolescent. Parents' own marital relationship, their own coping skills, their own major transitions must be considered. There is a clear need, here as elsewhere, for such programs to be adapted to poorer communities, to reach less educated and affluent families.

If the best of current programs are utilized, and research is built in so that correction and upgrading can be made in light of growing experience, then we can reasonably expect such efforts to be implemented at low cost and put to use without great practical difficulty in diverse local communities. Since they focus on groups, they can reach a large number of people in an efficient way.

It is interesting to note that some of the promising programs identified by Small are initiated and maintained by voluntary youth-serving organizations such as the Boys Clubs of America, the 4-H Clubs, and the Parent-Teacher Association (PTA). In the academic sector, university extension services are more prominent than any other sponsoring source. These two observations suggest that it would be useful to link youth organizations with university extension services in ways analogous to the highly successful experience in agricultural communities—i.e., linking applied research with immediately useful education focused on a specific problem area. This is the essence of the valuable extension-service approach.

One of the recurrent themes in research and innovation on adolescent social supports is the need of adolescents not just to feel passively supported by others but also to be valued and useful. This also underscores the potential of work, paid or volunteer, as a situation in which to foster social support and the development of self-esteem through service and tangible accomplishment.

COOPERATIVE LEARNING

The theme of being useful, of giving service, of earning respect through adultlike roles, and of building strength through mutual aid recurs in work on adolescent development. So it is useful here to consider the research on cooperative learning in the schools. Research on cooperative learning has burgeoned since the early 1970s. These efforts stem in part from a desire to find alternatives to the usual method of teaching through lecture and to involve students actively in learning. Moreover, they are inspired by a mutual-aid ethic and appreciation for student diversity. In cooperative learning, the traditional classroom of one teacher and many students is reorganized into heterogeneous groups of four or five students who work together to learn a particular subject. Recent analyses of the research literature clearly reflect the favorable impact of cooperative learning techniques on achievement in secondary schools as well as in elementary schools.

In my view, there are several overlapping yet distinct concepts of cooperative learning that have practical importance: learning to work together; contributing in some way; learning that everyone is good at something; appreciating diversity; complementing skills and dividing labor; acquiring a mutual-aid ethic. There is good reason why cooperative learning has lately stimulated so much interest, yet it is still a very small part of formal education. It deserves far more widespread utilization than is presently the case, along with continuing research to broaden its applicability.

SCHOOL, WORK, AND SOCIAL SUPPORTS

Cooperative learning techniques and other social-support interventions point the way to some practical considerations about the nature of work in the modern economy—how educational and community experiences can better prepare young people for a constructive place in such an economy. These issues have been illuminated by the work of Professor Lauren Resnick, a distinguished cognitive psychologist at the University of Pittsburgh. Resnick clarifies the ways in which school learning now differs from other learning. For example, the schoolroom emphasizes individual performance; the outside world emphasizes the importance of sharing knowledge. Consider the necessity for cooperative effort in the highly technological work environment of the modern navy. Indeed, cooperation is necessary throughout the modern economy.

Resnick contrasts the worlds of school and work in several perspectives: the role of schools in preparing people for economic participation; the role of schools in preparing people to learn effectively over the entire course of a lifetime, especially in relation to adaptability in work situations; and the role of schools in preparing people for active participation in the life of a democracy. These are fundamental issues. School is not the place for specific job training; on-the-job training serves this purpose pretty well and is likely to do better in the years ahead. Nevertheless, schools have a great opportunity to prepare students for work in a modern economy. The foundations for lifelong learning—both cognitive and motivational—must be laid in school. Students must *want* to keep on learning through their lives, must find it interesting, even fascinating. Moreover, they must have the basic intellectual tools for adapting to new circumstances, acquiring new information, applying it flexibly in solving problems. The schools have major responsibility for these tasks—and the experience of working effectively in groups is an important component.

Resnick's own research clarifies the ingredients of success in education, especially in acquiring the higher-order thinking skills that are of increasing significance in the technologically based economies of the future. She examined closely a number of successful programs that aim to teach such skills to find out what elements they had in common. Effective programs tend to involve socially shared intellectual work organized around joint accomplishment of tasks. Also, they tend to have an element of apprenticeship through the interaction of student and experienced person. Moreover, they foster gradual development of skills from a low level, often by social sharing of tasks.

Thus, research in cognitive science converges with research in social psychology in pointing to the crucial importance of social factors in development. Not least among these are social supports in adolescence. To the extent that such supports are lacking, they must be strengthened or replaced in whatever ways are open to us. To meet the challenges of learning and human relationships that are so important for a modern economy and democratic society, it is crucial that the social-support needs of adolescents be met—and met soon. Opportunities are now emerging that will permit us to close these serious gaps and thereby enhance the long-term chances of a great many young people.

SECTION IV

TACKLING THE HARDEST PROBLEMS

14

Preventing Substance Abuse in Early Adolescence

THE CHALLENGE

Substance abuse, a widespread problem in many nations, has especially corrosive effects on youth and can lead to dire lifelong consequences. In the United States, the huge demand for drugs is backed up by vast sums of money. This demand comes not just from the poor, though it is devastating in many poor communities, but also from a broad range of middle-class and affluent sectors. Despite the pernicious and pervasive nature of this crisis, our response as a nation has been spotty and marginally effective at best.

At the root of drug, alcohol, and cigarette abuse is the problem of addiction. Addictions, once established, are hard to break. They tend to persist, recur, and shape the life of the addict—often warping it in tragic ways. It is important to emphasize that the addiction problem involves not only illicit drugs but also cigarettes and alcohol in a major way. Although addictions can be be interrupted by treatment, by mutual-aid groups, and sometimes independently, the most effective way to overcome substance abuse is to prevent people—particularly adolescents—from becoming addicted in the first place. Prevention allows adolescents to keep open many constructive options that otherwise are likely to close, e.g., doing well in school; learning how to cope; developing health-promoting habits. Being shut off from such options permanently is patently damaging. But being shut off from them for even a few years puts the adolescent in the precarious position of falling behind in knowledge and skills, losing a sense of self-esteem, alienating worthwhile friends, and losing a constructive vision of future possibilities.

Government policy over the past decade has emphasized international interdiction and internal policing as the major means of controlling the supply of illicit drugs; these measures are widely supported and receive much publicity. An analysis of this field by the RAND corporation in 1984 found that, while international and domestic policing is essential, the most serious gap is in effective programs to prevent adolescents from becoming involved in substance abuse in the first place.

The problems are complex, and research on prevention has not had a high priority. Drug-abuse education courses exist in many secondary schools and some elementary schools, at least in a modest way, and yet have failed to prevent large numbers of young people from using drugs. Young people get mixed messages about alcohol from adult attitudes, behavior, and advertising; some popular music touts the pleasures of illegal drugs. Prevention efforts must compete against the opposition of powerful industries, both legal and illegal. The economic rewards of involvement in the drug trade are a strong magnet for young people in low-income communities, especially males. Among all the pitfalls, can we hope to navigate our youth through the hazards of using dangerous substances?

In the past few years the public has begun to focus attention on education as a means of preventing drug abuse. But what exactly do we mean by education in this context? Is it enough simply to give young people straightforward information about the harmful effects of various substances? Can we be confident that such information *alone* will keep them off drugs? What else would an education program need to make it effective? In general, what can research tell us about how best to proceed on this vital matter?

There are a variety of potentially significant entry points into the problem of drug-abuse prevention. Earlier chapters have touched on several of these. For example, getting all young mothers into prenatal care early and expanding the content of that care would take advantage of a distinctive opportunity, when young mothers are particularly motivated to take care of their own health and that of their developing child. Similarly, some church-sponsored after-school education programs for children and parent-support groups incorporate a drug-abuse component. Also, middle-grades life-sciences curricula, such as the one developed at Stanford University, provide a factual basis for understanding the biological effects of drugs. Life-skills training programs often educate students about drugs. Social-support interventions are highly pertinent here, too. Many of the programs designed to help adolescents in other contexts have constructive implications for the drug-abuse problem. In this chapter, I will examine recent research that represents the most serious work ever done in preventive intervention, sampling several of the most promising lines of inquiry and innovation.

Most serious, open-minded analyses of substance abuse suggest that, so long as a vast supply of money is chasing psychoactive drugs, human ingenuity will find ways to make the drugs available, either from outside the country or by producing them internally. This poses a fundamental question. Can the demand be substantially lowered? Can social norms regarding drug use be changed? There is some reason to believe this process has already begun.

LEARNING FROM CARDIOVASCULAR DISEASE PREVENTION

In the past two decades, Americans have changed their behavior to avoid pleasurable but damaging experiences in situations that are roughly analogous to the use of illicit and other psychoactive drugs. For example, fewer people smoke cigarettes; people are drinking somewhat less alcohol; people are eating less saturated fat and cholesterol; more people exercise regularly.

These gains have been concentrated in the relatively well-educated and affluent sectors, but some progress has been made in poor communities as well.

People were motivated to make these changes in order to protect their health—to avoid heart attacks, strokes, and cancer, as well as other serious disease and disability. For such changes in behavior to occur, three factors are crucial: motivation, information, and skills. Education helps people strengthen and sustain motivation, assimilate accurate information, and develop relevant skills. Such education involves not only the schools but also, and importantly, the media. Family, churches, and community organizations can contribute as well. In very poor communities, the key to motivation is helping youngsters perceive opportunity and build hope for the future; without these ingredients, they have very little incentive to avoid the immediate pleasures of taking psychoactive drugs.

Education to prevent substance abuse must extend in at least two ways. One, it must cover *all* schools, regardless of socioeconomic status—starting in late elementary school, going on to junior high or middle school, and continuing through high school. Two, it must reach *beyond* the schools to cover the entire community. In this respect, lessons learned from adult cardiovascular-disease prevention efforts in several countries can be helpful. These efforts fundamentally combine broad *public education* with extensive *community organization* for health. They deliver their message through schools and media and community organizations in ways that suit particular cultural circumstances, so that the messages will be clear, pertinent, and fully intelligible.

Efforts to make community-wide changes in lifestyle bearing on cardiovascular disease have been most studied in the United States and Finland, although good work has been done in several other countries. About a quarter of a century has passed since the major innovative efforts were first undertaken, including a project in California communities under the impetus of scientists at Stanford University and a very broad-scale public-health enterprise in North Karelia, Finland. The focus of both projects has been on ways to decrease people's smoking and fat intake while increasing their physical activity and controlling their high blood pressure.

For example, a series of longitudinal studies conducted in Finland has demonstrated the effectiveness of using role-modeling through mass media. These studies used a television series to broadcast the efforts of a representative group of Finns in their attempts to change their behavior to improve their health. The group demonstrated ways to stop smoking, lose weight, change one's diet, drink less alcohol, and enjoy more physical activity. Viewership rates were high, with more than a quarter of the national audience following these programs and a substantial proportion responding by changing their own behavior.

A 1990 report of the ongoing Stanford research describes how participants in five cities were making lifestyle changes to decrease their risk of cardiovascular disease—the second major effort of this group since 1972. In this fourteen-year trial, entire communities try to minimize their risk through a comprehensive, integrated program of health education. After five and a third years of education, the results clearly indicate that participants have a better understanding of risk factors and have made changes to avoid heart attacks and strokes. The finding is consistent with earlier efforts suggesting that programs that influence individuals directly are effective, as are programs that influence social environment and the media.

Widespread application of these methods could have a large impact on public health. Their adaptability to problems beyond cardiovascular disease is a promising frontier of research and public-health practice. Some key elements in the success of such efforts may well be applicable to similar community-wide efforts regarding substance abuse. Indeed, some recent research makes the connection rather directly, as we shall see. What features of such programs can we apply to the problem of drug abuse?

1. We need leadership within the scientific community and medical profession to provide the public with credible, factual information, much of it derived from biomedical and epidemiological research. First of all, it is essential to get the facts straight and for the public to have reason to believe that the information is trustworthy.
2. We need continuing social reinforcement of healthful behavior. Families and friends can help each other make healthful changes; churches, voluntary organizations, professional societies, businesses, labor unions, schools, colleges, and universities can also help.
3. We need to clarify both near-term and long-term consequences of health-damaging and health-promoting behaviors in ways that are intelligible and personally meaningful.
4. We must open and maintain appropriate channels of communication, especially to vulnerable groups.
5. We need specially designed programs to give adolescents health-relevant information that is particularly meaningful to them and to give them the skills they need to cope with pressures to adopt health-damaging behaviors. In the cardiovascular-disease prevention programs, for example, adults were taught how to prepare palatable low-fat diets. Similarly, adolescents need to be taught how to resist peer and media pressures for drug use.
6. We must be sensitive to age and culture when we help teenagers prevent substance abuse.

RESEARCH ON SUBSTANCE-ABUSE PREVENTION IN EARLY ADOLESCENCE

With lessons learned from the cardiovascular-disease prevention community studies of adults as a starting point, researchers in several countries are now studying preventive programs for adolescent students taking place in several schools. These studies focus on cigarette smoking but have touched on alcohol and other drugs as well. For instance, at Stanford University, an educational program for adolescents builds directly on the earlier work in cardiovascular-disease prevention; it is based on social learning as the focus for reducing risky behaviors that can lead to disease and disability, including cigarette smoking and drug use as well as poor nutrition, low physical activity, and stress. Adolescents are provided with several helpful elements: (1) Information on the costs and benefits of different health practices so that there is a clear basis for adopting healthy patterns of behavior; (2) cognitive and behavioral skills so they can change their own behavior and get support for their actions; (3) additional specific skills for resisting peer or media influences toward health-damaging patterns of behavior; (4) specific practice with honest, supportive feedback in ways of using their newly acquired skills to strengthen competence in health-relevant matters. Such research is pertinent not only to substance abuse but to other health-damaging behaviors, such as premature or unprotected sexual activity.

Creative techniques are used to help these schoolchildren avoid starting to smoke cigarettes. Preventing smoking is important both because of the extremely damaging health consequences of long-term cigarette smoking, and also because smoking is a gateway to other substance abuse. The programs emphasize the *immediate* consequences of smoking, e.g., bad breath or inability to compete in sports. These visible consequences have a more compelling impact on young adolescents than long-term health risks, although the latter are not irrelevant. Research conducted over several years, on students from the seventh grade through the ninth grade, shows a substantial reduction in the number of individuals who take up smoking in the intervention group as compared with the matched control group. The smoking rates for control groups were quite similar to national rates. The program takes into account the natural tendency of adolescents to move toward growing independence, often with a note of rebellion; they are taught skills that foster independent decision making and the ability to resist advertising or pressure from peers. Such efforts indicate that it is possible to prevent the early onset of smoking and other substance abuse. Then, when teenagers consider these decisions at an older age, they will be able to do so in a more informed and deliberate way, and make choices that promote health.

Some of the path-breaking research in this field began in the seventies at Cornell Medical College, under the leadership of Gilbert Botvin. I noted this work briefly in the previous chapter, but it deserves fuller consideration here. The program was initially designed to prevent junior-high-school students from starting to smoke cigarettes. Previous efforts had attempted to dissuade adolescents form beginning to smoke by simply providing them with factual information concerning the adverse health consequences of smoking. Evaluation of those approaches had consistently indicated that they did not work.

Botvin concluded that the traditional smoking-education approaches failed because they were based on faulty assumptions about the factors promoting cigarette smoking and that a more comprehensive prevention approach was necessary. He set out to provide high school students with the knowledge, attitudes, and skills for resisting both internal and external influences to smoke. During the decade since its original development, increasing attention has been given to broadening the program to include prevention of alcohol and illicit-drug abuse.

The curriculum is designed to help young people develop basic personal and social skills. Because the approach was designed for junior-high-school students, it focuses on the prevention of tobacco, alcohol, and marijuana use—the gateway habits that adolescents are likely to adopt at this age.

The curriculum centers on several objectives:

- Provide students with the necessary skills to resist direct social pressures to smoke, drink excessively, or use marijuana
- Decrease students' susceptibility to indirect social pressures to use tobacco, alcohol, and other drugs by helping them to develop greater autonomy, self-esteem, and self-mastery
- Enable students to cope effectively with anxiety, particularly that induced by social situations
- Increase awareness of the negative consequences of substance abuse, particularly immediate physical and social effects
- Correct adolescents' often rosy expectations concerning substance

abuse by providing them with accurate information about the prevalence of tobacco use, alcohol misuse, and marijuana use
• Promote positive attitudes and beliefs about drug-free living

The program is administered as a fifteen-session curriculum in the seventh grade, a ten-session booster curriculum in the eighth grade, and a five-session booster curriculum in the ninth grade. It includes five major components: knowledge and information; decision making; self-directed behavior change; coping with anxiety; and social skills. Each component consists of two to six lessons taught in sequence. A detailed description of the program's content and activities is contained in a teacher's manual.

Because the pressure and opportunity to use tobacco, alcohol, and marijuana often grows during the junior-high-school years, an additional curriculum for the ninth grade has now been added to the original package. In addition to reinforcing the main points of the curriculum, the emphasis of the booster sessions is mostly on the demonstration and practice of the social and personal skills that form the foundation of this approach.

Several studies have evaluated this prevention strategy. These studies were also designed to obtain information about the effectiveness of different types of providers; the effectiveness of booster sessions; effects with different target populations, with different gateway substances, with and without a formal teacher-training workshop and ongoing consultation. Many refinements have been made over the years to strengthen the methodological rigor of the research. The studies have progressed from small-scale pilot studies involving just a few hundred students to large-scale prevention trials involving several thousand students.

Overall, the results are clear. It is feasible to diminish substantially the use of gateway substances in early adolescence. Moreover, this can be done in a way that enhances overall personal and social competence. In the nineties, more data will become available on the applicability of this approach to poor minority students. So far, the results of this and several related research efforts indicate that there are clearly beneficial effects in disadvantaged populations, underscoring the importance of social supports for education and health.

A recent experiment is one of the most extensive pieces of research so far done in this field. It deals with two major health-relevant behaviors: cigarette smoking and diet. Although it does not deal with alcohol or illicit drugs, the principles and techniques involved in this program are certainly relevant to substance abuse in general, though their ultimate applicability will have to be determined in future research. The intervention program includes more than a thousand children in fifteen schools in a suburban area of New York City. Schools were assigned to either the intervention group or a comparison group. From fourth through ninth grades, the intervention schools provided a special curriculum called "Know Your Body" that increases students' understanding of the effects of diet and cigarette smoking on health and helps them avoid health-damaging behavior.

The dietary recommendations in the "Know Your Body" program teach children to label specific foods "stop," "hold back," "go," or "best choice." It addresses three major factors that influence adolescents' decisions whether or not to smoke: health beliefs, psychological influences, and social influences. While the curriculum concentrates on the immediate effects of smoking on various bodily processes, it also teaches long-term health consequences. Special attention is given to the child's self-image, strongly held values, and stress and anxiety, all of which can relate to the decision whether to smoke. Students learn coping skills to manage stress without smoking. The curriculum also addresses parents as models, peer pressure, and media pressure. Students receive specific training on decision making, communication, and assertiveness.

The "Know Your body" curriculum is taught in the intervention schools two hours per week throughout the school year by a regular teacher who receives training and continuing contact with the research staff. Special teaching protocols have been prepared to assist the teachers. The comparison schools teach the usual curriculum without any interference from the researchers.

After six years of intervention, fewer of the students had taken up smoking than in the comparison schools, and they ate significantly less saturated fat. Current research is determining whether these beneficial differences continue through the high-school years. The program was conclusively shown to be feasible, acceptable to students as well as parents and the school system. It was effective in modifying students' behavior patterns in healthy directions. The area in which the study was done is mainly middle-class and relatively affluent. Intervention in such areas is intrinsically worthwhile, since substance abuse is common in these neighborhoods. Work of this kind will have to be adapted to diverse social and demographic settings in order to determine how widely applicable it can be. It is generally consistent with other recent studies that show promising results from paying serious attention to psychosocial factors that influence the start of smoking; such studies tend to build students' personal and social competence in ways that make it unnecessary for them to take up smoking and that help them cope with situations that ordinarily trigger the urge to start smoking.

In another major study conducted in the Kansas City (Kansas and Missouri) metropolitan area by investigators from the University of Southern California, there are encouraging indications that it is possible to reduce drug use. Indeed, every young adolescent in the fifteen communities of this metropolitan area has taken part in a community-wide program to prevent drug abuse. The study ran for five years, from 1984 to 1989, and was aimed at preventing students from using cigarettes, alcohol, and marijuana.

This intervention relied heavily on mass-media coverage, a school-based educational program for students, parent education and parent organization, and community organization. These components were introduced sequentially into communities over the course of the study. Annual assessments of adolescents' drug use were undertaken. The initial report covered the first two years, in which 22,500 sixth- and seventh-grade students received a school-based educational program with parental involvement in homework and mass-media coverage. Analysis showed that students' cigarette, alcohol, and marijuana use was significantly lower after one year in the experimental group. This result held true regardless of race, grade, socioeconomic status, and urban versus rural living conditions. Taken together, these results indicate that teens' initiation of drug use can be reduced by about half through this intervention.

The rationale for the design of the study is that in order to bring about long-term change in adolescents' drug use, they need to be influenced by many different facets of their environment. The prevention skills they learn initially in the school program must be reinforced consistently within their community. The program pays special attention to the spurt of cigarette smoking and alcohol and marijuana use that typically occurs in the middle-grade years. Interestingly enough, analysis shows that the abuse-prevention effect *increases* over time. Thus, the resistance skills and changes in the social environment induced by this program may be shifting the social norms in the adolescent population away from drug use. Overall, this study builds on the school experience of sixth- and seventh-graders but strengthens the experience by involving parents and other family members as well as community organizations, newspapers, and television.

In December 1988, the Rand Corporation published its first report on Project ALERT, a large-scale, multiyear test of a smoking and alcohol- and marijuana-use prevention program for adolescents from all different socioeconomic levels.

Project ALERT began in 1984 in thirty schools in California and Oregon. It was carefully formulated to strengthen the motivation of young adolescents to resist drug taking. Each school was randomly assigned to one of three experimental groups. The schools were statistically matched with respect to previous drug use. They covered a wide range of community environments, ethnic composition, and socioeconomic status. For example, in nine of the thirty schools, more than 50 percent of the students were from disadvantaged minority groups. Forty-one percent of the participating students came from disrupted family situations.

The intervention begins in the seventh grade. Two-thirds of the participating schools have a smoking and drug-abuse prevention curriculum. In half of these schools, an adult alone presents the curriculum; in the other half, the adult is assisted by teen leaders. The seventh-grade curriculum consists of eight lessons. These lessons deal with the motivation to resist drug use, the seriousness of drug use, personal susceptibility to harmful effects, skills to resist drug pressures, and benefits of resistance. In the eighth grade, the students have a three-session booster curriculum that reinforces their resistance skills. Thus, there is a total of only eleven sessions over two years, a minimal exposure for such a serious problem. One-third of the schools in this study are comparison schools; they receive no special training. But drug use and related characteristics are monitored in all the schools throughout the course of the study period. In addition to self-reported data, some physiological data are also collected to detect drug use.

The curriculum is built on a social-influence model that has provided the basis for many smoking-prevention programs in recent years. Major emphasis is put on resisting peer pressure. Such resistance requires both the motivation and the skill to offset pressures to use drugs. The curriculum also clarifies internal and external pressures as well as adolescents' beliefs and circumstances that affect them when they start using each targeted substance. The program gives students accurate data on drug use, clarifying the fact that most people do not get deeply involved with drugs; this helps to offset the assumption that "everyone does it." There are many opportunities for student participation—e.g., role-playing, small-group discussion, and the practice of resistance techniques. The program reinforces adolescents' desire to be accepted in a valued group and to appear grown-up.

The data collected over several years indicate that the study has been implemented as intended and engages the students in a serious way. Systematic monitoring undertaken by students' self-report as well as observations by teachers and project staff show that the classes were carried out faithfully, all of the curriculum activities were presented, both teachers and team leaders were effective, and the program worked well in the classroom. The vast majority of the students reported that the course was credible, that they were actively involved in it, and that it helped them to resist pressures to use drugs. Moreover, the school-assignment procedure produced well-matched experimental groups, so it is possible to make a rigorous assessment of Project ALERT's effectiveness among different kinds of students with respect to different kinds of drug use.

The main report of this longitudinal experiment was published in 1990. It indicates that education programs based on a social-influence model can prevent or reduce use of cigarettes and marijuana in early adolescence. The intervention had positive results for both low- and high-risk students. It was equally successful in schools with high and low minority enrollment. However, it did not help previously confirmed smokers—thus highlighting the value of avoiding the onset of smoking altogether. Also, its effects on adolescent drinking were short-lived.

Significantly, those who were hooked on smoking in early adolescence had other problems as well. Compared with two other groups, they were more likely to do poorly in school, to engage in deviant behavior, and to have disturbed family relations. To deal with these interrelated problems, we need to step into these children's lives at an earlier age, as I discussed in prior chapters. The encouraging results of Project ALERT indicate that even a minimal intervention appears to be useful. In my mind, this raises the important question of what a truly major effort in the schools could do, especially one that linked the life sciences with life-skills training and social-support networks for education and health.

Research indicates that changing social attitudes about acceptable, desirable behavior may be a key element in drug-abuse prevention efforts. All the programs described here have their greatest impact against tobacco smoking. While society has come down strongly against the dangers of smoking, it has made weaker efforts to do the same with alcohol, which is still widely used beyond moderation; and teachers often have difficulty in teaching about alcohol use. Marijuana falls in between, but recent declines in its use are believed by many to have been accelerated by declines in tobacco smoking. A hopeful feature of some current research is that we begin to see how it is possible to effect these larger social changes through the media, civic-leader training, and family outreach. Large-scale, community-based efforts, similar to those in cardiovascular-disease prevention work, may be able to modify social norms on a long-term basis. If so, there will be major savings in human life and suffering, not to mention in economic terms.

A fundamental underpinning for adequate information on drugs is provided by the life sciences, especially in the middle-grade schools, but starting somewhat before then and extending into high school as well. To make good use of this vital information, students need skills in decision making; the capacity to draw upon information carefully, to not jump to conclusions, to be deliberate in considering the meaning of information for one's own life. Thus, the decision-making component of life-skills training, which I discussed in the previous chapter, is very important. This may be considered a special branch of the movement toward critical-thinking skills that is so much a part of science education and of basic education reform at the present time.

The social-skills component of life-skills training is also important in this context: Students need to learn how to be assertive without being hyperaggressive; to negotiate in human relationships and to achieve at least a substantial part of what they want without disrupting important relationships; to resist pressure without jeopardizing crucial human relations. Such social skills have many uses, but they certainly are pertinent to the capacity to navigate the stormy waters of adolescence without becoming dependent on drugs. Social-support networks for health and education are crucially significant in the drug context as elsewhere—especially in the setting of the transformed middle-grade school.

Lessons learned from the cardiovascular-disease prevention programs show clearly that the media have an important role to play. Indeed, we have probably only scratched the surface in the constructive uses of the media as an educational system in this context and in others.

The role of health professionals in substance-abuse prevention is at an early stage of development. They can play several pertinent roles here: (1) community leadership to get the facts straight, including media activities; (2) direct care of individuals; (3) participation in the schools, both in life-sciences education and in school-related health facilities; and (4) work in the public-health system.

The capacity of community organizations to help with this problem is also at an early stage of development, especially in poor communities. For many young people, using or selling drugs seems like an attractive path to adult status. But alternate paths must be constructed, and nowhere are they more needed than in deeply impoverished communities, along the lines I'll discuss in the chapter on educating the disadvantaged.

Altogether, in school and out, we have to find ways to help adolescents build competence, earn respect, join a group of friends capable of resisting pressure to use drugs, and delineate a vision of an attractive future and prospects for a decent life. An important part of this in poorer communities has to do with economic prospects: *Early* opportunities must become visible to young people before the drug pathway becomes firmly established.

LEARNING TO COPE WITHOUT ABUSING DRUGS

Drug taking may be considered to some extent as self-medication for distress, a kind of stress management or high-risk coping behavior. More generally, drug taking may be seen as coping behavior oriented toward the transition to adulthood—a way of feeling big, strong, courageous, sophisticated, or otherwise grown-up. How can we help our adolescents make that transition more effectively and less dangerously? Research on the coping behavior of adolescents over several decades gives us some insights.

Everyone is exposed to stressful experiences in major transitions; only a small proportion of us are shattered along the way. However, a sizable and growing number of adolescents encounter serious problems that do make a grave difference in their lives: e.g., substance abuse, educational failure, early and unwanted pregnancy, violence. Presumably, these high-risk individuals can learn something from those who cope effectively. Careful observations have been made of such major transitions as puberty, the move from elementary school to junior high school, the move from high school to college, adolescent first pregnancy, and other similar situations.

Attempts have sometimes been made to place these transitions in larger contexts, such as rapid technological change and experiences of prejudice and social depreciation.

The developmental tasks of the adolescent transition include (1) growing independence from parents, siblings, and previous friends; (2) greater autonomy in making personal decisions, assuming responsibility for one's self, and regulating one's own behavior; (3) establishing new friendships; (4) moving toward greater personal intimacy and adult sexuality; (5) dealing with more complex intellectual challenges. Individuals who meet these tasks effectively tend to employ certain strategies that may be explicit or implicit in their behavior.

There are many such strategies, and no single person uses all of them. These include:

1. Reaching out for new experience
2. Initiating new activity in a purposeful way
3. Checking current situations against analogous past experiences, especially those that have been successfully mastered
4. Drawing upon competencies established earlier
5. Learning about the new situation in advance
6. Rehearsing new patterns of behavior before they are actually required
7. Identifying with a group that has successfully mastered the challenge at hand
8. Formulating a level of aspiration that is probably attainable
9. Actively searching for encouraging and supportive elements in the new situation
10. Seeking shared experience, especially with constructive peers, for support
11. Clarifying new self-definitions and career possibilities
12. Seeking intellectual stimulation through friendly, informal groups
13. Learning through pooling of information and skills with peers
14. Offering and seeking support in time of stress
15. Creating sounding boards for other points of view and different values
16. Reassessing acceptable risk in undertaking new patterns of behavior
17. Selecting slightly older peers as resource persons
18. Identifying with a teacher or other adult as mentor

19. Seeking information regarding new circumstances from multiple sources, building a cognitive map
20. Focusing on intermediate goals that are visible and probably reachable
21. Rehearsing task-specific behavior in a relatively safe situation
22. Appraising feedback on new behavior for adequacy of performance and personal satisfaction
23. Testing alternate approaches
24. Making, in due course, a commitment to a promising approach and pursuing it with vigor
25. Constructing buffers against disappointment and contingency plans for alternate outcomes

No individual carries out all of these coping strategies; different people combine them in various ways.

Overall, these strategies have been observed in many individuals coping effectively with difficult transitions between childhood and adulthood, including early adolescence. Such strategies can facilitate healthy, vigorous, constructive adolescent development. They can be taught.

Adolescents can also be taught to prepare for emotionally charged or threatening experiences. So-called anticipatory guidance can help youngsters cope with several stressful experiences that are reasonably predictable.

As we have seen, a lot of the research bearing strongly on health concerns social-support systems. Supportive relationships can help teens adopt healthy behavior and use coping skills in time of stress. In major epidemiological studies, weak or tenuous social relationships are associated with poor health outcomes, whereas strong social-support networks are associated with good health outcomes. So coping and social supports are closely linked.

The approaches discussed in this chapter generally strengthen teens' adaptive behavior and provide hopeful and realistic alternatives to the transient euphoria induced by drugs. They also illuminate pathways to healthy development that tend to overcome other serious problems arising in adolescence.

One other fundamental point: To approach the drug problem from the demand side through broadly conceived education and through public-health interventions not only addresses the problem of drug abuse but also opens the door to other basic human capabilities. That is, preventive interventions of the sort described here tend to foster education and health much more broadly. They address not only drug abuse but school failure, adolescent pregnancy, low self-esteem, and low perception of opportunity. In short, a constructive approach to the drug problem can foster all-around healthy personal development. Therefore, difficult as this problem is, it can stimulate us to understand more deeply several fundamental, interrelated problems of contemporary society that are associated with major casualties. From such analysis, innovation, and well-considered experience, it should become possible to make investments in the future that are among the most important any nation can make.

15

Educating the Disadvantaged

It is plausible that our prodigious capacities for technical innovation and social organization could be mobilized to greatly diminish human impoverishment in the decades immediately ahead, especially in technically advanced democratic societies. What would it take? Research and experience in different parts of the world suggest that several basic needs must be met if the disadvantaged are to emerge from poverty. All are technically feasible and well within human capacities, even though fulfilling these needs is an exceedingly difficult task. What is required?

1. *Adequate health.* Minimally, people need adequate health to have the vigor to carry on their daily functions. We maintain our health partly by learning to cope with the inevitable limitations and afflictions of the human organism; but mainly we can do so by science-based disease prevention from the time of conception onward. Good hygiene, adequate diet, and the formation of healthy lifestyles early in development are key elements.

2. *Education for crucial skills.* While education must be valued deeply for its own sake in every conceivable sphere of human inquiry, emphasized here are those skills most important for survival and well-being and most likely to earn income and respect—not only cognitive and technical skills, but interpersonal and organizational skills as well.

3. *Mutual support.* It is doubtful whether we can achieve good health and crucial skills, let alone a zest for living, without dependable social-support networks—family, friends, community—groups that provide a sense of secure belonging with all their immense cultural variability. Such support networks tend to provide mutual aid in the face of the inevitable stresses of living, to facilitate health and education, and to provide opportunities.

4. *A structure of opportunity.* Children have a vast diversity of aptitudes and talent—and a lot of potential. For these latent qualities to come to fulfillment, they need open paths. A child's chances can be enhanced by an intact family—up to a point. But a larger structure of opportunity is also necessary—not only a mutually supportive network in the child's community of origin, but also in the larger society—protected by law in an open economy. The child, and especially the emerging young adult, needs a social context in which he or she can bring individual capabilities to bear on real-world circumstances.

In the nineties, racial and ethnic minorities will constitute the majority of primary- and secondary-school students in twenty-three of the twenty-five largest American cities. By the year 2000, the majority of the populations of fifty-three major cities will be minorities. While the lives of many individual members of minority groups have greatly improved since the sixties, many of the millions remaining in the inner cities have been relegated to marginal status in our society. They are the poorest and least-educated Americans and are served by the least-adequate health care in the nation. As in past generations, those who can leave severely damaged environments do so, leaving behind those who have come of age on the streets, without dependable adult guidance and constructive support systems—and, often, without parents.

At the same time that the inner city and its damaging environment are becoming increasingly isolated from the rest of America, the nation itself faces a drastic transformation in its economy. As I've said, employment in the twenty-first century will require far greater technical competence than was needed in the final decades of the twentieth. Historically, minorities have been drastically underrepresented in science-based fields. For the majority of American urban schoolchildren to be excluded from the mainstream of education and worthwhile jobs in the next century would be a personal loss for the individuals themselves and a tragic waste of human resources for the country, which will weaken its economic and social foundations.

At present, minority youth are the worst-educated and disproportionately slip—or are pushed—out of the educational mainstream. Increasingly, this injustice threatens our democratic foundations—and our economic vitality as well. In the years immediately ahead, the number of young people in America will be smaller than in recent decades. By the year 2000, about one-third of the young people entering the work force will be blacks or Hispanics—the very groups now at the bottom of the educational and economic ladder. By the year 2020, nearly half of all school-age children will be nonwhite.

One upshot of the current world transformation is that the work of the future will require not only much technical competence but a great deal of flexibility; workers will need more than one set of skills acquired early and held for life; they will need to adapt to an evolving body of knowledge and new opportunities calling for greatly modified skills. Successful participation in a technically based and interdependent world economy will require a much more skillful and adaptable work force than ever before. In the United States, then, it is in the straightforward national interest that "minority" students be educated equally with white students, particularly in the science-based fields. This country can no longer endure the drainage of talent that has been the norm up to now.

Furthermore, the specter of a dual society, which is implied in the path we have taken so far, suggests great political conflict and potential social upheaval. After all, drastic economic and educational inequality in the midst of great affluence is a recipe for polarization and intense social, political, and economic conflict.

America's technologically educated work force, which has by and large been very efficient by world standards, has traditionally come from a small fraction—about 6 percent—of the white, male, college-educated population. We have skimmed the cream of a very preferred, fortunate group. Blacks, Hispanics, Native Americans, and even white women have historically been badly underrepresented in the fields that require technical competence. Now, however, the traditional white male source of scientists and engineers is inadequate. We need more technically trained people. This brings the country to a very interesting point, a point where equity intersects with economic vitality, democratic civility, and military security. Because of this intersection, there are now broader and more urgent reasons than ever before to support an unprecedented effort in the education of disadvantaged minority children. What must motivate us is not only decency, but also national interest.

In the face of daunting odds, a number of exemplary programs in individual cities across the United States have achieved remarkable results in raising inner-city students' test scores on national examinations and increasing their motivation as well as their academic and social performance. Despite the programs' different approaches, they share a single key element: They have all found ways to compensate for a damaging social environment by providing conditions that can build on the strengths and resiliency of those caught in such difficult circumstances. Many useful programs have evolved responses that amount to the equivalent of supplements to the family, or, in extreme instances, surrogates for it. In whatever form, such interventions must provide part or all of what a vigorous, cohesive, intact family would provide. In so doing, they can give steady encouragement, stimulation, and guidance to children to pursue their education and protect their health.

This chapter will focus on how education and the lives of children and adolescents can be improved in the inner cities. It will examine what is necessary for a child to reach adulthood successfully and describe the needs that are typically not being met in our poorest urban areas. It will summarize the results of various studies and programs that have achieved remarkable success in equipping poor and disadvantaged students with the skills they need for both school and the world of work. Since schools cannot meet these needs alone, the chapter will consider partnerships and networks involving the schools with a variety of strong institutions and organizations.

SERIOUS OBSTACLES

Children from very poor, marginal families often arrive at school with inadequate home preparation. They tend to lack the social skills considered appropriate at school, as well as standard language skills. Such social deficits are most frequently observed among those minority groups that have historically suffered the most traumatic experiences: Native Americans, Hispanics, and blacks. In stark contrast to the warm relationships that often develop between mainstream children and their teachers from the earliest preschool classes and continue throughout their graduate and postgraduate educations, children from marginal backgrounds frequently experience a disorienting discrepancy between home and school. Behavior that has been tolerated at home may be punished at school. This is especially true of aggressive behavior that is seen as necessary for survival or at least for manhood on the street, but considered disruptive of education in the school. All too often such discrepancies lead to a deteriorating interaction between student and teacher that culminates in low expectations, unfair labeling, and educational failure.

Schools in the United States have largely been unequipped to provide such students with the skills, encouragement, and experiences that will enable them to succeed. Parents of such children may take their children's problems at school as evidence of their own personal failure and their rejection by the mainstream. Both parents and children often react by losing confidence, even hope, and becoming defensively indifferent or downright hostile to the school and indeed to the entire American society of which the school is viewed as an agent.

In the face of such perceived or actual rejection, the children may seek self-affirmation in peer groups that, unlike teachers and most youth, do not value academic achievement. Their alienation grows as failure erodes their academic self-esteem. They are at risk for dropping out, early adolescent pregnancy, drug abuse, and crime.

Underlying all these problems is the disadvantage, the marginal status, the social depreciation—not only poverty, but demeaning attitudes and discrimination. To be poor and a member of a minority generally means attending the weakest schools, having access to the least-adequate health services, and having the fewest clear paths to opportunities for adult success. For example, rates of retention in grade—a school practice directly related to students' dropping out—are far higher among minority than nonminority youth in the middle grades. They are held back a year, fall further behind, and despair of ever catching up. For many of these young people, the decision to drop out is clearly made before they begin high school, when their perception of severely limited opportunity becomes compelling. Nearly 40 percent of Hispanic students drop out before or during the ninth grade.

Insight into current obstacles was provided a few years ago by an American Association for the Advancement of Science (AAAS) study done for the education commission of the National Science Board. That AAAS study cited specific barriers to the science and engineering education of minorities. The *generic* problems of disadvantaged minorities at the *precollege* level are the following:

- Low quality of education in the schools that minorities attend
- Failure to be offered or encouraged to take levels of science and mathematics needed to pursue science and engineering fields
- Scarcity of successful role models
- Low expectations of youth by teachers, by counselors, and sooner or later by the students themselves
- Discouraging counseling, or none, about possibilities for college work in science and engineering
- Little knowledge of career options

As information based on systematic studies and careful observations accumulates, it will become increasingly possible to tailor interventions to the actual conditions that prevail in the inner city, and to set priorities in relation to the most damaging factors that impinge on childhood and adolescent development. William Julius Wilson's ongoing research, well described in his recent book, *The Truly Disadvantaged,* delineates several major factors. These include: (1) the disappearance of living-wage jobs from the inner city as traditional manufacturing has eroded, which results in massive unemployment and underemployment for the very poor and especially for black males; (2) the exodus of relatively successful people from the inner city as opportunities have expanded, which results in the absence of constructive role models who could be helpful with knowledge and skills pertinent to jobs and key opportunities; (3) the erosion, associated with the outmigration of the emerging middle class, of local institutions; (4) the extremely high concentration of poverty in the residual areas; (5) social isolation from mainstream contacts and opportunities.

Wilson's research shows how social and economic forces beyond the control of any individual or family create an atmosphere in which child and adolescent development are likely to be impaired. Recently, the pervasive and mutually reinforcing problems of extreme poverty, addiction to such damaging substances as crack cocaine, and the crime associated with drug traffic even further demoralize and place at extreme risk all who are exposed to them daily. Each of these factors raises a particular challenge for economic, social, psychological, educational, and health-system responses. Each can stimulate the search for ways to strengthen families, schools, social services, churches, and employment opportunities.

WHY THERE IS A DISTINCTIVE OPPORTUNITY NOW

There has been a major effort in the United States, especially in the past three decades, to address the problem of disadvantaged minorities; substantial progress has been made. Despite setbacks in the eighties, there is now renewed national interest in finding ways to open the doors of opportunity. The primary impetus comes from concern about markedly heightened international competition. As demographic changes make minorities a larger part of the future work force, they must be ready to master the knowledge and skills vital to a modern technical economy.

We are a nation of immigrants; even now we are experiencing another great wave of immigration. Surely the American population is one of the most heterogeneous in the world. We need a great innovation in education to bring all groups into the mainstream of opportunities as we turn the corner into a new century. Effective action will require national leadership, a long-term vision of what we really want this country to become, and mobilization of public opinion, because only with broad public support can the problems of minority education be effectively solved.

Ending the Disadvantage of Women in Science Education

In addressing this problem, *Turning Points* described an exemplary program: Operation SMART.

Women win Nobel Prizes in physics, fly as astronauts, and fill most kinds of jobs in the contemporary high-technology workplace. Yet the myth persists, and is widely accepted by many young adolescents, that science and technology are not subjects for girls. Consequently, girls and young women, especially those from low- or middle-income families and from minority families, lack experience and self-confidence in these areas.

An out-of-school program of Girls, Inc., aims to correct that mistaken view and to direct young adolescents toward science and mathematics as rewarding subjects for study in middle-grade school and beyond. Girls, Inc., serves 250,000 girls and young women, more than two-thirds of whom are from low-income families and about half of whom are members of racial minority groups.

continued

Operation SMART (Science, Mathematics, and Relevant Technology) encourages girls to feel confident about and enjoy science and mathematics. Research shows that girls learn most quickly from hands-on experience, which is ordinarily meager during in-school instruction. Girls also learn best in groups, but schools teach individually. Finally, girls confronting science and mathematics in school may feel constrained by the rigid time periods of the daily regimen.

Operation SMART augments in-school instruction by providing the specific opportunities needed: hands-on experience, collaboration, and open-ended sessions. Girls, Inc., found that simple access to mathematics and science activities was not enough. Damaging stereotypes and socially expected behaviors had to be confronted if girls were to overcome their apprehension about science and mathematics and to make up for their lack of experience with machines, science equipment, and technology. Thus, in Operation SMART girls take apart computers, repair bicycles, design electrical circuits, and study buoyancy and gravity in a swimming pool. They learn firsthand about how large machines, such as backhoes, work, and they learn to use heavy power tools as well as screwdrivers and wrenches. They use microscopes and hand lenses, go to an observatory to use a telescope, and then build their own telescopes back at the club.

Most important, they learn to question and to become analytical, critical thinkers. Through field trips and counseling, the program ties Operation SMART activities to schoolwork by encouraging girls to take the sequential science courses and higher-level mathematics courses that are prerequisites for most college majors and careers in the sciences.

Operation SMART serves girls from six to eighteen years old, and is now focusing on the crucial middle-grade ages of nine to fourteen. With government, corporate, and private foundation support, the program has developed exercises, materials, and other resources that are used by more than two hundred Girls Clubs throughout the country.

Some Operation SMART projects meet on school sites. Girls, Inc., staff often work with school officials to plan programs. In Holyoke, Massachusetts, which has a large Puerto Rican population, Girls, Inc., and the school district jointly sponsored, planned, and conducted a bilingual Operation SMART confer-

continued on next page

continued from preceding page

ence called Expanding Your Horizons. Schools released students to attend the event, which attracted more than a hundred Puerto Rican girls to talk with Hispanic women whose careers involve science and mathematics.

Operation SMART links schools and Girls, Inc., in more than a hundred communities across the nation in the shared enterprise of educating young adolescent girls. Operation SMART does not substitute for the education that girls receive in schools. Rather, it supports that education and addresses some of the serious problems in formal education.

Women, whether or not members of minorities, have historically been neglected in science education. The AAAS study in precollegiate science education for women and minorities included a national survey of effective programs to sort out elements that have proven useful and are most likely to be applicable on a wider scale in the years to come. The study included the following important findings:

1. Unless programs in science education are oriented specifically to females and minorities, they are unlikely to be effective. (The innovations of James Comer's New Haven group, to be described shortly, illuminate this approach.)
2. Females and minorities can succeed in the educational mainstream, but will do much better if their specific needs are systematically taken into account. Indeed, some program elements for achievement of socially disadvantaged groups may usefully be incorporated into the entire educational system—e.g., early tutoring in reading skills.
3. The earlier such intervention programs are undertaken, the better the results. The national experience to date strongly suggests that specific intervention is essential at least by the third grade for disadvantaged minority students and at least by junior high school for girls.
4. Teachers are the key to these programs' success.
5. Students who are poorly equipped to do well in mathematics and science improve if their parents are involved.

The AAAS study notes a number of examples in which efforts originally undertaken especially for women and/or minorities have been adapted for wider use and built into the functioning of the whole school system. This further reinforces the prospect that thoughtful innovation with responsible assessment can help us not only upgrade opportunities for women and minorities but also improve education for all children. Later in this chapter, we shall see how one action plan for minority education develops this concept.

A first and crucial step is for minority communities to reinforce their historic priority on education, with special attention to science education, and to focus their institutions on encouraging young people to stay in school and pursue education, even in the face of formidable obstacles. Much can be accomplished by minority organizations and also by community-based youth organizations. For example, the National Urban Coalition, the National Urban League, minority fraternities and sororities, the Girl Scouts, the Girls Clubs of America, and national scientific organizations all are showing signs of growing interest in helping minority students succeed in school. One useful step is to connect minority organizations, the scientific community, and youth-serving organizations in networks that support education, particularly in its more complex and demanding aspects.

Concern over school dropouts and adolescent pregnancy figured prominently in the 1990 formation of a new coalition of black organizations—perhaps the broadest effort ever undertaken in the black community. Over one hundred groups joined to create the National Association of Black Organizations. This association plans to establish a research unit and a communication network to foster self-help initiatives and develop strategies to strengthen black institutions. However it may evolve, this exceptional development indicates the depth of concern in the black community about the social and economic conditions facing one-third of American blacks.

SOCIAL SUPPORTS IN OVERCOMING DISADVANTAGE

For the child growing up in an area of concentrated poverty, two crucial prerequisites to healthy, constructive development appear to be seriously lacking: secure attachments to dependable and successful adults; and the perception that opportunities exist in the mainstream economy. To the extent that families and communities are eroded, disintegrated, or otherwise weakened under circumstances of persistent poverty and social depreciation, it is necessary to focus on additional social support networks—by strengthening the family and/or by providing substitute experiences that meet these essential needs.

With younger children, social supports have to become a deliberate feature of effective interventions throughout development: e.g., in prenatal care, child care, preschool education, after-school and Saturday experiences during elementary years, and in reform of the middle-grade schools. At every level, in some developmentally appropriate way, it is possible to construct parent groups, parent education, outreach to families through indigenous paraprofessionals, and links with professionals as needed for more serious problems. Disadvantaged minority education crucially needs to incorporate social-support networks that sustain effort and hope.

A variety of organizations and institutions can provide surrogates for parents, older siblings, and an extended family. Across the country there are examples of such interventions. Some are based in churches (such as the initiative of the Congress of National Black Churches), some are based on community organizations (such as the Girls Clubs), others involve youth service (such as the Campus Compact based in colleges and universities), others are based in minority organizations of several kinds. The central point here is that churches, schools, community organizations, and businesses can build constructive social-support networks that attract minority youngsters in ways that foster their health, their education, and their capacity to be accepted rather than rejected by mainstream society.

PATHS OUT OF POVERTY

Several of the serious problems occurring commonly in poor communities are interrelated: educational failure and dropping out; adolescent pregnancy; and substance abuse and AIDS. As I've said, in principle, tackling any one of these problems can contribute to some solutions with respect to the others. Once again, it is clear that broad-based preventive interventions that promote both education and health can address underlying factors that heighten students' vulnerability to school failure, adolescent pregnancy, low self-esteem, and low perception of opportunities.

If we want to get a high yield on investments in our children's education, this country must transcend its demand for quick results. Educational reform takes time to evolve. Reform efforts have been under way for the better part of a decade, and the public's interest appears to be growing. Policymakers and the business community are expressing a higher level of interest than ever before. The scientific and educational communities are working together better than they have for many years. All this provides no assurance that the reform movement will grow and build, but it is certainly encouraging.

It is worth keeping in mind the remarkable accomplishments of education in the United States. There is a long history of serious efforts to widen the circle of educational participation. The G.I. Bill and Head Start are two outstanding examples. Now we as a nation are trying to be more inclusive than ever before. Embracing the needs of the educationally disenfranchised is the greatest challenge our educational system has ever faced. To have a reasonable chance of success, we must look for help beyond the schools. That is why linkages between schools and other sectors are so important.

Youth-oriented churches have offered several innovative approaches to educating the disadvantaged. The AAAS published a report in 1989 on the growing role of black churches in education. Over half of the churches belonged to four denominations: Baptist, African Methodist Episcopal, United Methodist, and Catholic. More than half of those churches offered nonreligious education programs. Most of the programs served low-income people. Almost half of the participants in nonreligious education programs were not members of the church. Many of the teachers and leaders in the churches' nonreligious education programs are certified teachers or professionals who work for reduced or no fees. Churches with nonreligious education programs reported greater parental involvement in various activities than churches without such programs.

The most common programs these churches offered were tutoring, preschool and day care, and field trips. Other programs included Scouting, career-related programs, preparation for major examinations, college-entrance workshops and counseling, health education, substance-abuse programs, programs for pregnant teenagers, black-history classes, arts and crafts, recreation, English as a second language, and music camps. Many programs aimed to enhance not only students' academic achievement but also their character and self-esteem. Examples of programs of this type include Project Pride in Chicago and Project SPIRIT of the Congress of National Black Churches. A number of churches are cooperating with local schools and universities and science-based groups. AAAS itself has a collaborative program with black churches to foster science education.

WHICH SCHOOL INITIATIVES WORK?

A window on useful educational innovations was opened by a study (supported by the Ford Foundation) of effective schools in very poor neighborhoods. Several encouraging factors emerged: (1) the principal's leadership makes a crucial difference; (2) giving teachers a modest amount of money to use at their discretion and on their own initiative to enhance classroom activities has proved to be exceedingly valuable; (3) ongoing, sustained, constructive contact between parents and teachers is vitally important to improving education.

So the challenge is to facilitate such helpful factors in and around the schools. In recent years there has been encouraging experience in cities such as Pittsburgh, San Francisco, and New York with independent school-improvement funds, established outside the formal structure of the school system but readily accessible to it—especially to thoughtful and constructive teachers. All such efforts have identified a great deal of latent talent in poor communities, often wasted. Much has been learned about ways to identify such talent and provide conditions for its fulfillment.

The Carnegie Corporation report *A Nation Prepared* is a major statement on upgrading the teaching profession. With respect to elementary and secondary education for minority children, the report recommended the following:

1. Tutoring children on schoolwork
2. Counseling them to envision wider horizons for their future
3. Introducing them to community service
4. Giving them enriching experiences during the summer, especially at work but also in ways that will help them develop distinctive talents, and special reading experiences in schools or libraries
5. Exposing them to constructive Saturday activities
6. Building bridge programs between high school and college, with similar programs to link elementary and middle-grade schools

The report recommended that these initiatives be accomplished by combinations of schools and third parties, particularly partnerships of schools with corporations and universities, though the role of state government and community organizations is also important. With respect to the federal government, the report recommended support for fellowships for minority students who commit themselves to doing graduate work to prepare for a teaching career; in return, each student would make a commitment to a specified area of service.

A 1990 study done by SRI International, a highly respected research firm, draws on recent educational research to strengthen opportunities for poor children. The conventional wisdom about academic instruction for disadvantaged elementary-school students has emphasized a remedial approach, a curriculum broken down into discrete skills, teacher-directed instruction, a uniform approach to classroom management, and the grouping of students by ability. Recent scholarship, theory, and experimentation in the classroom highlight flaws in these approaches and point to promising alternatives. Although they are an improvement over much actual instruction in schools serving poor children, the practices prescribed by conventional wisdom may unintentionally place a ceiling on students' learning.

Emerging standards of good practice for mathematics instruction would shift emphasis from computation to understanding and applications, would cover more topics in reasonable depth, and would reduce redundancy across grades. In reading and writing, emerging standards will emphasize understanding the meaning of the text over other reading skills in the early grades, give less attention to discrete skills out of context, and emphasize more exposure to different genres of writing and to material that reflects and respects the students' experiences and background.

Two crucial standards apply to curriculum and instruction in reading and writing. One is that effective language-arts curricula for disadvantaged students must emphasize the ability to communicate with and understand written language. The other is that reading and writing should be taught as meaningfully related, not as separate subjects.

Good reading and writing instruction for disadvantaged students is no mystery. We have long given good training to advantaged and gifted children. What is "new" is our awareness through research and practice that such instruction is not wasted on disadvantaged children, given the right institutional and interpersonal supports.

Reading instruction for disadvantaged students should include opportunities for extended silent reading from the earliest stages, discourse about the meaning and interpretation of material and its relevance to students' life experiences, explicit teaching of comprehension strategies, and opportunities to relate reading to other uses of language, such as written and oral expression.

Good writing curriculum for disadvantaged elementary-school students parallels that for reading in many respects: It should emphasize meaningful written communication, deemphasize learning mechanics in isolation, and draw on students' experiences and knowledge as well as on realms of experience less familiar to them.

Writing instruction should provide children with opportunities to write narratives from the earliest stages, should expose them to various genres, and should encourage them to use written language for meaningful communication.

Research on changes in instructional practices shows that disadvantaged children's improvement is gradual and requires consistent stimulation and support. Cognitive research, studies of the role of the learner's home environment, and research on instructional leadership and school organization have all aided in fine-tuning methods to reach these children. Classroom-based research has a central role because it can translate other research into terms that can guide curricula and classroom practice. Such studies document the range of practices now in place for disadvantaged students, demonstrate what is possible, and show how the school and district environment affect classroom practices.

EXEMPLARY PROGRAMS

The New Haven Project

One of the most creative and productive efforts in this field is the work under Professor James Comer's leadership, which turned around schools in very bad shape and sustained the gains over more than a decade. In 1968 Comer and his colleagues at Yale's Child Study Center began an intervention in two inner-city New Haven elementary schools. This program promoted children's development and learning by building supportive bonds among children, parents, and school staff.

Most current educational reforms deemphasize interpersonal factors, focusing on instruction and curricula. This approach assumes that all children arrive at school with adequate preparation to receive instruction and perform well. But for poor minority children from alienated, nonmainsteam families, the contrast between home and school has a profound effect on their psychosocial development, impeding their academic achievement.

Comer's program addressed that disparity directly. His intervention team consisted of a social worker, a psychologist, and a special-education teacher. Ninety-nine percent of the students in the two schools were black, and almost all were poor. Staff morale was low and turnover was high. Despite high expectations among both parents and staff, the first year of the project was difficult. Teachers and administrators could not agree on clear goals and strategies. When some new teachers tried open classrooms, the children became uncontrollable. The teachers blamed the administration for inadequate resources. Parents became angry and marched on one school to protest the innovations. These problems revealed the sociocultural misalignment between the children's homes and the school. Comer's team turned their attention to understanding and overcoming this misalignment. They established regular meetings to set goals and coordinate plans so that the schools and the project had more structure.

The intervention team decided that the key to academic achievement was to promote psychological development in students in ways that would encourage their bonding to the school. To do this, it was necessary to foster positive interaction between parents and school staff, a task for which most staff were not trained. The team set out to overcome the staff's resistance to change, instill in them a working understanding of child development, and enable them to improve relations with parents.

Comer's group created a governance team in each school, led by the principal and including about a dozen people: elected parents and teachers, a mental-health specialist, and a member of the nonprofessional support staff. The ground rules: The principal had ultimate authority, but would not push through decisions without weighing the concerns of the team members; efforts would focus on problem solving, not blaming; and decisions would be made by consensus, thus reducing the tendency to polarize the team into winners and losers.

Parents who had protested against the innovations in the first year were invited to join the team. They helped develop a program that involved parents with the school on three levels: shaping policy through participation on the governance team; participating in activities supporting the school program; and attending school events.

Social gatherings fostered good relations between parents and staff. The school climate and students' behavior improved, and more parents began to participate.

The program took a team approach to working with children having difficulties. Rather than working with each child independently, the school's psychologist, social worker, and special-education teacher met as a group to discuss each student and assign one person to meet with him or her. The team approach helped them detect students' patterns of troublesome behavior and identify harmful school practices. The mental-health group had a delegate on the governance team through whom it recommended changes in school policies. With each intervention, staff became increasingly sensitive to the concerns and needs of developing children.

By 1975, the program was clearly having an effect. Students' behavioral problems had declined, relations between staff and parents had improved, and the children's academic performance had gained significantly. At this point the team decided to implement a program of life-skills training, especially mainstream social skills. Staff and parents devised a curriculum covering politics and government, business and economics, health and nutrition, spiritual guidance, and leisure activity. Children learned how to write invitations and thank-you notes, how to serve as hosts, how the body functions, how to write checks, and how to plan concerts.

The students in the two schools had once ranked lowest in achievement among the city's thirty-three elementary schools. By 1979, without any change in the schools' socioeconomic composition, students in the fourth grade had caught up to their grade level. By 1984, students in the fourth grade ranked third- and fourth-highest in the city on the Iowa Test of Basic Skills. Attendance rates had improved and serious behavior problems had been virtually absent from both schools for a decade.

By 1980 the intervention team had left the schools. The program had been fully integrated into the practices of the staff. The program has since been implemented in several other locations, including two middle schools and one high school. Certain schools in the Prince Georges County, Maryland, and Benton Harbor, Michigan, school districts, which serve mainly low-income black students, have had successes similar to those of the two New Haven schools. The program is also being introduced in all the New Haven schools, and in Norfolk, Virginia; Lee County, Arkansas; and Leavenworth, Kansas.

Comer notes that most teachers and administrators are not trained to organize and manage schools in ways that support the overall development of students. In addition, their training does not enable them to address the social-misalignment problem of children from outside the mainstream. Therefore, he recommends that teachers' colleges and schools of education focus more on child development. Although this recommendation arises from work with disadvantaged minority children, it has considerable force for education reform in general. It would be good for *all* students to grow up in elementary and secondary schools whose teachers had a firm, practical grasp of child and adolescent development.

Mentoring

In an earlier chapter, I considered the promise of mentors for poor children. A variety of minority organizations have been providing mentors from similar backgrounds for inner-city youth. For example, minority college students have in some cases devoted three evenings a week to tutoring, joint recreation, experience in gaining access to community resources, and developing social skills. These activities are generally attractive to adolescents, and may combine entertainment with education. There is a recurring emphasis in such efforts on forming constructive human relationships, providing models of accomplishment and success, developing skills pertinent to the mainstream economy, building self-esteem, and seizing real opportunity.

Summer School

Summer school also offers disadvantaged children unique opportunities. Research suggests that the more intensive the summer-school experience, the more substantial the student's gain. Poor children tend to slip in academic performance during the summer, evidently because they get less continuing reinforcement than do middle-class students when school is not in session. Therefore, a focus on basic skills such as reading and math and an emphasis on attending school consistently can make an important difference for poor children.

It turns out that one of the most useful programs for disadvantaged children is simply to read regularly. Research focusing on sixth-graders at the end of elementary school found that summer reading can improve reading performance regardless of socioeconomic background. This suggests that relationships between schools and neighboring libraries during the summer may have much potential that can be exploited, which is particularly interesting at a time when libraries are seeking to reformulate their mission—and in some instances justify their existence and continued funding—in circumstances very different from the ones in which the libraries arose. Teachers can work out a plan for children's summer reading and connect with a library to be sure that each student is prepared with a library card, reading list, and whatever else may be necessary to facilitate summer library activity.

Cooperation in Learning Mathematics

Another interesting intervention that has potentially widespread implications is the mathematics-workshop program at the University of California, Berkeley, developed by Professor Philip Uri Treisman. Observing that black and Hispanic students tended to do badly in mathematics during their freshman year at Berkeley even when very well prepared and highly qualified, in contrast with Chinese-American students from similarly poor backgrounds, Treisman set out to investigate which factors might explain this difference. He found that the black students were generally highly capable, strongly motivated, and from homes that were very supportive of their efforts in higher education. So a good deal of conventional wisdom was negated by his direct observation.

Over eighteen months, Treisman studied the lives and study habits of a matched comparison group of black and Chinese-American students enrolled in freshman mathematics. The major difference he found was that almost all of the black students studied alone; they did not see their academic work as an occasion for social interaction or mutual aid. This was in marked contrast to the Chinese-American students, who worked in "study gangs" and provided each other with a great deal of intellectual stimulation and emotional support for mutual benefit. Moreover, black (and Hispanic) students rarely used the university's services to help them with such course work, whereas the Asian students used the services a great deal.

Treisman then set up a deliberate program of joint study, a kind of "study gang" for black students. He also became, in effect, a mentor for these students. The results were dramatic: a reversal from failure to high-level success, particularly in mathematics. He then put the program into use on a systematic and more extensive basis. The continuing results, involving hundreds of students over seven years, have been strongly positive. In analyzing the program's remarkable success, Treisman emphasizes three points:

1. Help minority students to excel, not merely to avoid failure.
2. Emphasize collaborative learning and small-group teaching methods.
3. Require faculty sponsorship.

It is interesting to note the similarities of this program to the "I Have a Dream" program introduced by Eugene Lang in the New York schools, which I described in an earlier chapter. The Lang program begins earlier—at the point of graduation from elementary school. He gives children a future monetary incentive to succeed academically and provides an enduring mentor for each student, creating an atmosphere of mutual support.

Treisman's program, like Lang's, is now having an influence throughout the country. Both offer technical assistance to schools setting up similar programs nationwide. The Charles Dana Foundation presented its award for pioneer achievement in higher education to Treisman in 1988 and is assisting him in getting the program widely adopted. The program should be adapted for minority students in high schools and perhaps even earlier.

Turning Points provides an account of a similar enterprise dealing with younger students.

Steve Parsons, an eighth-grade mathematics teacher at West Frederick (Maryland) Middle School, has used cooperative learning techniques for many years, primarily to accelerate learning among low-achieving mathematics students. Parsons is currently using a cooperative learning curriculum developed at the Johns Hopkins University called Team Accelerated Instruction (TAI).

TAI students work together to obtain individual and group rewards. Students are pretested to determine their current level of mathematics achievement, and receive a textbook based on their score. They are then grouped into teaching teams and home teams. Teaching teams consist of students who scored at about the same level on the achievement test and were assigned the same text. Home teams are made up of four students, one with a relatively high pretest achievement score, two with average scores, and one with a low score.

Students on the same teaching team are pulled out from their home teams to receive about twenty minutes of instruction on a new unit in the text focusing on several related mathematical concepts or skills. Students then return to their home teams and work on problems in the text, checking their answers with teammates. When students have trouble with problems, teammates help them to analyze the problems, thus providing immediate tutoring while the teacher continues to work with other teaching teams. Students are eventually tested for individual grades and also earn points for their home team. Teaching teams are constantly re-formed as students progress to higher levels of ability.

All students are taught the importance of encouraging others and working together to solve mathematical problems. Students are often initially uncertain that they really will be rewarded for working together, but are soon convinced and quickly come to enjoy being able to learn from each other.

Five major research studies conducted by Hopkins researchers involving more than three thousand public-school students document the effectiveness of TAI. In those studies, TAI students consistently showed a two-to-one ratio in achievement gains over control students.

Parsons, working with special-education teachers, has also had considerable success with TAI and other cooperative learning techniques in mainstreaming special education students who had been placed in an extremely low-ability mathematics track. These students, some of whom had severe emotional problems, gained the acceptance and aid of many of their peers, progressed through the series of TAI tests at mastery level, and functioned at a more mature level in the classroom.

In part on the basis of these successes, Frederick County school officials are moving toward eliminating the special education mathematics track as well as other achievement-based tracks that currently exist. This move began with several pilot efforts in the fall of 1989. Teachers involved in these trials receive extensive training in cooperative learning techniques for effectively teaching heterogeneous groups of students.

MESA

Another successful program for minorities is the MESA (Mathematics, Engineering, Science Achievement) program, based in Berkeley, which is supported by California industry and government. It has been in operation for many years and has touched the lives of thousands of students. The program takes freshmen in minority-concentrated high schools who have passed Algebra I and who voluntarily accept MESA's course requirements (biology, chemistry, physics, four years of math and English) and provides these students with special opportunities, including tutoring, attending summer programs at nearby institutions, and various interactions with nearby corporations and universities. About 95 percent of the MESA students go on to college, most of them to four-year institutions. Corporations provide volunteer tutors and counselors in the centers and summer jobs for the students as well as funds for program operation. In recent years, this program has been extended to junior high schools.

Community Service

Many believe that community service could have special value for disadvantaged minority youth by moving them beyond the constraints of the inner city, helping them make a valued social contribution, develop employable skills, and build their self-esteem through solid accomplishment.

The Campus Compact is a national program of community service intended to develop this sort of opportunity and involving many institutions of higher education across the country. It is a coalition of 230 college and university presidents committed to fostering public-service opportunities for students and to integrating service experiences with the undergraduate curriculum. The Campus Compact is administered by the Education Commission of the States and housed at Brown University. A three-year initiative called Campus Partners in Learning was launched in 1988 to encourage campus-based mentoring for at-risk youth. There are now about three hundred campus-based mentoring programs. Future rigorous evaluation will be needed to assess how much of a difference the programs can make in the lives of disadvantaged students; the indications so far are encouraging. The key element is regular, dependable, friendly contact between an older mentor and a disadvantaged student.

Urban youth corps—groups of young people engaged in rebuilding or revitalizing very poor communities—offer another promising avenue of community service. There are now more than thirty such youth corps nationwide, based largely on the famous Civilian Conservation Corps of the thirties, in which unemployed young people performed vital tasks. Quantitative research has yet to be conducted into how effective these programs are for at-risk youth, but many observations indicate that the outcomes are generally positive.

Work-Study Programs

Since lack of employment opportunities looms so large in the lives of minority families, and especially for young black males, we need to find new approaches to link education and job prospects. One option is to offer minority students part-time or summer jobs as a strong incentive to stay in school. Indeed, some educators propose paid work-study programs in which the student's pay is made contingent on performing satisfactorily in school. But perceiving job opportunities is just the first step; minority students also need help in acquiring essential, practical skills: job searches, job training, and appropriate on-the-job behavior. On-the-job training and counseling also enhance students' prospects for adapting successfully to the world of work.

PUTTING IT ALL TOGETHER: AN ACTION PLAN FOR MINORITY EDUCATION

In 1990, a broadly composed action council for minority education, based at the Massachusetts Institute of Technology and the University of Texas, produced an extraordinary report that provides the strongest basis ever formulated for progress in this difficult and crucial field.

Education That Works: An Action Plan for the Education of Minorities, the report of the Quality Education for Minorities Project, lays out a clear set of recommendations for restructuring U.S. education to better serve all American students, minorities and nonminorities alike. The report is a product of a two-and-a-half-year project funded by a grant from the Carnegie Corporation. It sets out six goals for the year 2000:

1. Ensure that minority students start school prepared to learn.
2. Ensure that the academic achievement of minority youth is at a

level that will enable them, upon graduation from high school, to enter the work force or college fully prepared to be successful and not in need of remediation.
3. Significantly increase the participation of minority students in higher education, with a special emphasis on the study of mathematics, science, and engineering.
4. Strengthen and increase the number of teachers of minority students.
5. Strengthen the school-to-work transition so that minority students who do not choose college leave high school prepared with the skills necessary to participate productively in the world of work and with the foundation required to upgrade their skills and advance their careers.
6. Provide quality out-of-school educational experiences and opportunities to supplement the schooling of minority youth and adults.

The report emphasizes the importance for minority students of school restructuring, in which student achievement is the main criterion against which teachers, principals, and administrators are judged and rewarded. In restructured schools, such as those being pioneered in Miami, Florida; Rochester, New York; New Haven, Connecticut; and other cities, teachers and principals have the flexibility, authority, and motivation to respond to the individual needs of their students. Such restructured schools involve families in the learning process; eliminate tracking and use nontraditional teaching methods; incorporate the cultures of minority children in their curricula; support students unfamiliar with English; coordinate with other social-service providers; and create closer bonds between students and educators through small learning communities and smaller classes.

The report recommends that the nation learn from successes already in place. Many interventions known to be effective, such as the federal programs of Head Start, the Special Supplemental Food Program for Women, Infants, and Children (WIC), and Chapter I (providing major federal funds for education in poor communities), as well as some excellent state and local efforts, are undersupported. Evidence shows that such interventions improve health and education for the disadvantaged. They pay for themselves by reducing malnutrition, the dropout rate, and crime, while increasing employment and productivity. They are clear instances of sound human-capital investment.

Among the comprehensive recommendations of this plan, many bear directly upon the themes of the present book. They can be briefly summarized here.

- Facilitate programs that provide postnatal training in parenting skills, such as AVANCE, to help prepare children for school.
- Ensure that all minority youngsters receive quality prenatal and postnatal nutrition and health services through funding of the WIC program and federal child-nutrition programs.
- Ensure that minority youngsters receive quality preschool and child care through full funding of Head Start and of child-care programs for low-income families.
- Establish special units within schools for children aged four to eight to help ease the transition from home to school.
- Restructure school systems on the basis of the model introduced by James Comer in the New Haven schools—including an increase in family participation in decision making and in school activities.
- As part of a larger effort to coordinate family social services around schools, prepare teachers and specialists to work with families in their homes or at schools to help improve parenting and learning skills.
- Promote small school units to give children a sense of belonging and allow them to identify closely with at least one adult.
- Support home-school partnerships in which families agree to take specific steps to encourage their children to study.
- Pay educators to work twelve months, and have them use that time to prepare adequately and provide quality education.
- Make it part of the educational program to help *parents* help their children in a variety of ways:

    1. Instill high educational expectations in children.
    2. Ensure that children get to school on time and are supervised when they leave school.
    3. Set aside a time and place every night for homework.
    4. Take children to libraries, museums, and cultural events, which are often free.
    5. Read to children and encourage them to read.
    6. Limit children's watching of television and encourage the viewing of educational shows such as *Sesame Street, Reading Rainbow*, *Square I*, and *3-2-1 Contact.*

7. Attend school meetings and become more involved in school activities.
8. Monitor student progress through frequent meetings with teachers.
9. Plan for college.
10. Enroll children in after-school, Saturday, and summer activities.

- *Teachers* can make special contributions in a variety of ways:

1. Understand the restructuring alternatives open to their schools and be advocates for such changes.
2. Have high expectations for minority students.
3. Be informed about the cultures and languages of their students and offer instruction that respects cultural differences.
4. Use effective instructional strategies such as cooperative learning, peer tutoring, and mixed-ability groups.
5. Provide mentoring opportunities for minority youngsters through churches, social clubs, and other community organizations.

- Implement a *core curriculum* that prepares all children, including those now neglected, for college or careers. All students in grades K–12 should take a core curriculum established—and revised periodically—by state and local educators, policymakers, and business leaders, to be certain students are prepared for college or meaningful careers. That curriculum should include instruction in a second language beginning by the third grade, algebra during the middle-school years, and physics, chemistry, and biology in each of the grades seven through twelve in an integrated, hands-on science program.
- Implement *year-round schooling* at least once every three years to prevent summer learning losses (which studies show are responsible for up to 80 percent of the year-to-year learning differential between advantaged and disadvantaged youngsters), and make quality after-school and Saturday learning experiences available to all youth. By increasing the length of the school day and school year as well as providing students access to quality after-school, summer, and Saturday programs, multiple benefits are attained, so schools should supplement regular schooling, provide cultural enrichment and out-of-school learning experiences, and provide constructive alternatives to unsupervised, unproductive activities.

- Move toward community schools, open after usual school hours and well into the evening, and on Saturdays, that will not only enrich the education of children, but will offer adult education, language, and other skills-development training for parents.
- Provide incentives for the best teachers to be available to the students who need them the most. Financial incentives and increased recognition should be available to those undertaking the very difficult tasks of teaching in poor urban schools or in predominantly minority schools in rural areas.
- Create a national merit teaching scholarship program offering grants to minority college students who are prepared to enter the teaching profession for at least three years after graduation.
- Increase the number of counselors in predominantly minority schools who are qualified to help students with precollege and career decisions.
- Require all students to participate in community-service programs, both in high school and in college, to help them develop skills and heighten their self-esteem as well as build a sense of responsibility.
- Provide apprenticeship opportunities for every student who does not choose to enroll immediately in college.
- Offer an optional thirteenth year of high school on selected college campuses in predominantly minority regions to equip academically unprepared high-school graduates and older students for college. Make it possible for former high-school students who wish to return to school, as well as underprepared high-school graduates, to have access to such programs.
- Establish alternative preparatory academies that would provide a supportive academic environment for minority students whose schools are grossly inadequate and for whom safe neighborhoods are not possible.

This plan draws upon the best available research evidence and the most carefully considered experience to formulate what works in minority education, even in the face of severe disadvantage. Yet inevitably, in such a complex and difficult set of interrelated problems, the evidence is still limited. No wonder. If social priorities were to move this issue much higher on the national agenda, and if science policy were to follow suit—big ifs—then within two or three decades a variety of well-designed longitudinal intervention studies could provide definitive research on what programs work best. But how much damage would be done in the meantime? Indeed, how much *preventable* damage?

Must we wait? Can we afford to? I suggest that the central question is, *Can we do better than we are doing now?* After all, the casualties in disadvantaged minority communities are now so heavy that they have a damaging effect on the entire nation. The social costs of stunted growth and development are terrible not only in the intrinsic tragedies of these shattered lives but also in how they affect our entire society, rich and poor alike—the costs of disease and disability, ignorance and incompetence, crime and violence, alienation and hatred. These are infections that know no boundaries, that cannot be effectively contained. Surely our present knowledge, evidence, and experience make clear that we can do better than we are now doing in providing conditions in which poor children can grow up healthy and vigorous, inquiring and problem-solving, decent and constructive.

We will not be able to prevent all the damage now inflicted on our children by badly warped environments. If we give adequate priority and wisdom to research on these matters, and still more to implementing what we know works or is extremely promising, we will be able to prevent a lot more damage in twenty years than we can now. And so much more in fifty years! But now is the time to draw upon the synthesis of existing knowledge and the richness of recent innovations to make a serious national effort to sustain and improve the education of the disadvantaged decade by decade.

16

Overview: The Road We Have Traveled and the Road Ahead

A baby is precious. For most adult readers, merely thinking about a baby is likely to elicit feelings of tenderness and hope, surely among our deepest, most human feelings. It is scarcely possible for us to care more or do more than we do for our own baby. And this is only the beginning of the long relationship of parent and offspring, adult and child. This is how we pass on our genes, our customs, even gain a measure of immortality. How is it possible, then, that so many casualties are occurring in childhood and adolescence, that so many lives are wasted and so many lost? Why do we encounter so many burdens of illness, ignorance, and humiliation? In a time when science and technology are advancing so brilliantly, and opportunities have opened as never before, the toll of these casualties and burdens is actually increasing markedly. How did we get into this predicament?

The human organism has flourished for a long time in a great variety of environments. Surely ours is one of the most adaptable species ever to inhabit the planet. How have we survived for such a long time, rearing our young in ways that meet whatever conditions may exist, overcome whatever obstacles we may encounter? In these pages, the reader has traveled with me over a road that emerges from truly ancient times. We have examined children's growth and development from an evolutionary perspective, trying to answer the question, What does it take to grow up well in today's world? We have looked briefly at the evolution of cognition, the evolution of attachment, the evolution of skills. We have seen how children learn adaptive behavior from other humans in their early years.

I have identified conditions that foster healthy development in childhood and adolescence:

1. An intact, cohesive, nuclear family, dependable in every crunch
2. A multifaceted parent-child relationship with at least one parent who is consistently nurturing and loving and able to enjoy child-rearing, teaching, and coping
3. Supportive extended family members who are available to lend a hand
4. A supportive community, whether it be a neighborhood, religious, ethnic, or political group: some larger helpful group, beyond the family
5. Parents' previous experience with child-rearing during their own years of growth and development, for what amounts to a kind of ongoing education for parenthood
6. A child's ability to perceive future opportunities and a tangible basis for envisioning an attractive future
7. A reasonably predictable adult environment that fosters gradual preparation for adult life

We have seen how attachment in infancy paves the way for a child's acquisition of skills, how guidance in childhood helps children pay attention to the adult models who will shape their behavior. The art and science of learning is a great human accomplishment, capable of fostering children's endless curiosity and growth.

Over the extended years of a child's growth and development, the longest period of immaturity and therefore vulnerability of all known species, a young human must acquire much, master much, try much and find much wanting, discover much and put those discoveries to use. All this takes time and care, protection and guidance, experimenting and learning from experience. For the caregivers, it is an enduring long-term, highly challenging commitment.

How can we provide a supportive environment for parents throughout the highly vulnerable period of child-rearing? In most cases, we can take action to strengthen the immediate family, and it is often possible to pull in the extended family to enrich the caretaking brew. With the recent changes in the traditional nuclear family, it has become increasingly necessary to make a deliberate, explicit organizing effort to connect children with persons who have the right attributes and skills and also the durability to promote their healthy development; we must turn to people in educational, religious, and community organizations in all their combinations and permutations.

Infants particularly need caregivers who can promote attachment and thereby form the fundamental basis for decent human relationships throughout the child's entire life. Similarly, early adolescents need to connect with people who can facilitate their momentous transition to adulthood gradually, with sensitivity and understanding. Despite the radical transformation of recent times, we can usually find such people within the child's nuclear family; if not, to some extent in the extended family. But if these caregivers cannot give a child what he or she needs to thrive, then what extrafamilial arrangements will work? I have tried to delineate such arrangements at every phase from conception to the middle of adolescence.

I deeply believe we can do substantially better than we are now doing in addressing serious problems that arise in each phase of development. I have tried to sketch a variety of promising lines of inquiry and innovation, based on the latest research, that provide a genuine basis for hope, including the toughest problems: substance abuse and the education of disadvantaged minorities. My aim is to stimulate, to facilitate, to accelerate the pace of work on these vital matters.

What will it cost to save our children, poor and rich alike? A rational and civilized sequence of developmental interventions, based on scientific facts, professional experience, and democratic, humane values cannot be implemented without substantial investment. The first and most crucial investment goes beyond economics. It is the investment in the same survival-relevant behavior that got us here, the essence of human adaptability over eons of time. During their years of growth and development, children need dependable attachment, protection, guidance, stimulation, nurturance, and ways of coping with adversity. This is the profound challenge for parents and caregivers.

The biology of our species makes necessary a huge parental investment in order to achieve fulfillment of the potential of each child. As I have emphasized, it is a continuing, relentless, recurrent demand for investment of time, energy, thought, consideration, and sensitivity. It is an investment in patience, understanding, and coping. It requires persistence, determination, commitment, and resiliency. The awareness of such a large investment, however vaguely formulated, has recently inhibited many young people from undertaking child-rearing, but others have gone ahead and started families, only to find they are unprepared for the challenge. If they cannot or will not give their children what they need, then others must do so. Other family members have historically been helpful, but they are less readily available now than ever before. Therefore, we have seen the rise of institutions that provide parent-equivalent functions. We are in mid-passage in this process; no one can say with justifiable confidence what the consequences will be for the generation of children in crisis.

We badly need to strengthen research on social change, including institutional as well as individual responses. We must learn as we go, as soon as possible. Research on parent-equivalent institutions and careful observation of leading-edge innovations can help us decide which models actually work for what purpose—and at what cost—in fostering children's healthy growth and development. Some of this knowledge is already available; much more will become available in the nineties. We must find ways to scale up the best child-development programs beyond a few communities to cover an entire population. But even as we study these changes, they often outpace our capacity to monitor and understand them. Can we build institutional capacity to catch up and stay up to date in a continuing, long-term way?

Some of the studies summarized in this book have reported responsible cost estimates, and I have briefly reflected them. But to explore these matters in the depth they deserve would require another book. In almost all cases, the expenditures required for optimal child and adolescent development are *not* simply add-ons, but can be at least partly achieved by wiser use of existing funds. Huge amounts are now spent for these purposes. Much of this current spending could be greatly improved and redirected by the measures described here. To replace inadequate interventions—e.g., poor school systems with inflated administrative structures—with much better ones would in some cases cost less and in other cases cost more than we are now spending. This sort of analysis must largely be done on a case-by-case, place-by-place basis. What is likely is that the *total* economic and social costs of present child-relevant activities could be greatly reduced.

For the atrocities now being committed on our children—however inadvertently and regretfully—we are all paying a great deal. These costs have many facets: economic inefficiency, loss of productivity, lack of skill, high health-care costs, growing prison costs, and a badly ripped social fabric. One way or another, we pay. The thrust of this book is to suggest lines of caring for our children and preventing damage to them that would lead to better results on our investment in the future that we all share.

In any event, these vital investments have to be viewed for what they are—a responsibility of the *entire* society: Not just of the federal government, but of other levels of government; not just of business, but of labor; not just of light-skinned people, but of dark-skinned as well; not just of the rich, but of the middle class and the poor. We are all in this huge leaking boat together. We will all have to pay and reason and care and work together.

Our usual short-term view will not suffice. There are many useful, constructive steps to be taken, as outlined here, but no quick fix, no magic bullet, no easy way. We will not get rich quick on the backs of our children.

Moreover, we have to move beyond the easy and pervasive recourse of passing the buck. It is *our* responsibility—each individual, each institution and organization, every business, every level of government is responsible. Specifically, it will be necessary to hammer out some broad guidelines for division of labor in each major sphere, from prenatal care to graduate education. This book is intended to stimulate serious reflections on such matters and to move us toward taking up these crucial responsibilities.

We cannot lose sight of the fact that wise investment in human capital is the most fundamental and productive investment any society can make. Constructive development of our children is more important than oil or minerals, office buildings or factories, roads or weapons. The central fact is that all of these and much more depend in the long run on the quality of human resources and the decency of human relations. If these deteriorate, all else declines.

The interventions in education, health, and social environment for children I have described in these pages have a lot to do with the kind of future we will have. Sadly, very few complete models of modern programs to meet children's needs are available, whether they embrace the enlarged vision of prenatal care or of the reformulated middle-grade school or other crucial opportunities. Major components of such programs do exist all across the country and in other nations as well. Increasingly, we will have to put these components together in ways that provide our children with the full range of developmental opportunities permitted by today's knowledge and emerging research findings.

A FINAL WORD

Most of our ancestors lived in settings of very slow technological and social change. Within a very short time on an evolutionary or even a historical time scale, there have been great changes in many dimensions of experience, mainly since the onset of the technologies of the Industrial Revolution and especially in the twentieth century. Although we live in a time of unprecedented opportunity, the recent social transformation threatens important conditions for healthy development and even the learning of survival skills.

These rapid, far-reaching changes in the conditions of child rearing constitute a powerful challenge to families and other institutions to adapt to new circumstances. If the essential requirements for child development are not met, profound damage can occur, and this is associated with great social cost. The spectrum of adverse effects has come before us in many different ways: from smashed and strained families and communities; from destroyed to disabled to distressed individuals. We have seen how risk factors can make children and adolescents vulnerable; and also how they can cope and overcome.

In contrasting today's vast, complex societies with the small, simpler societies of our ancestors—or even in contrasting 1990 with 1960—it should be clear that there is no point in nostalgic yearning for the good old days. History has plenty of dark sides—immense human vulnerability to diseases, hatred, violence, and ignorance of so many kinds. In any event, we cannot turn the clock back and there are many reasons why we would not want to do so.

What I have tried to clarify in this book is that our current difficulties in child-rearing—worldwide in nature and sharply accentuated in the United States—are not some oddity, some transient aberration, but, rather, a sea change reflecting evolutionary and historical currents of profound long-term significance.

The human organism evolved over a very long time in conditions very different from those that prevail today. In effect, the baby's machinery was built to work in circumstances that are mostly gone now. If we want children to survive and flourish, then we will have to figure out how this ancient creature can thrive in today's or foreseeable circumstances. It is even possible that this boils down to how eager we are for the human species to survive. If that is still a fundamental goal, then we will simply have to find paths of individual and institutional adaptation to the new world we have made.

A vital example of this transformation lies in the dramatic entry of most women into the paid, outside-the-home work force during recent decades. I have noted along the way that this opens up great opportunities—not only for individual women but also for the economy and society at large. This is an immense talent pool that is becoming available for the complex economic functions of modern society, not least those based on science and technology. By the same token, this talent pool is becoming available for the governance of democratic societies at every level with many foreseeable benefits for the quality of life.

From a long historical perspective—even going back to hunting and gathering societies—this should not be so surprising. Women have always had major responsibilities in activities vital for subsistence. In a very ancient era, they had the main responsibility for gathering and preparing the plant foods that were the core of survival. Later, these functions were adapted to the requirements of agriculture. Concomitantly, women had the utterly vital function—the ultimate survival function—of bearing children and taking the lead role in caring for them during the crucially formative years of growth and development. Hardly a modest set of tasks and accomplishments! The modern economic-technological transformation has rearranged these activities. In principle, the main differences are that much of women's work is now *outside* the home—indeed, typically rather far away and so not readily accessible to the children; and they are *paid* for this work in a money economy.

We have noted the multiple gains in this new arrangement. But there is no denying that it poses a great challenge to human adaptability. Who will care for the children in the new era? Some flexible configuration of mother, father, other relatives, friends—but altogether not enough in many instances to meet the extraordinary needs of human infants, children, and adolescents—needs that are in some ways heightened by the complexity of modern societies. So we are in the process of improvising extrafamilial, institutional arrangements to meet the needs. Much of this book deals with these recent, fragile efforts. After all, even public schools are a recent invention by historical standards.

What does it take now for children to grow up healthy and vigorous, inquiring and problem-solving, decent and constructive? In the years of growth and development, they need attachment, protection, guidance, stimulation, nurturance, and ways of coping with adversity. How can such experiences be provided? By an intact, cohesive family to the extent possible; by supportive, extended family and other social networks. Community resources can help if they are clearly visible and usable. Moreover, a tangible basis for hope is essential with the perception of opportunity and paths toward its fulfillment. The skills required are not only technical but also social.

Who can provide such growth-fostering experiences? If the basic, traditional sources of such strength have become weakened by massive historical changes, then how can they be strengthened? If substitutions are necessary, how can they be provided? When is it sensible to intervene? The approach taken here has been to recommend fostering early interventions that offer support similar to that of the traditional family. The pivotal institutions are schools, churches, community organizations, the media, and health-care systems. A developmental sequence of interventions starts with prenatal care and goes on to preventive pediatric care, parent education, social supports for young families, high-quality child care, preschool education, a constructive transition to elementary school, a reformulated middle school. Beyond that lies the possibility of further growth in high school, in the transition to work and to higher education, drawing on the principles elucidated here.

Much facilitation of healthy child development must occur now in schools. Research and experience have illuminated a few key concepts in fulfilling this potential from early-childhood education through the middle-grade schools: Developmentally appropriate education, in which the content and process of learning meshes with the interests and capacities of the child; schools and classes of small units, created on a human scale; sustained individual attention in the context of a supportive group; students learning to cooperate in class with an eye on future work and decent human relations; stimulation of curiosity and thinking skills; linkage of education and health—each must nourish the other.

So the essential requirements for healthy, constructive child and adolescent development can be met—if not one way, then another. Most of the book deals with a variety of serious efforts to meet these vital needs under the radically transformed conditions of the late-twentieth-century habitat. Once again, as so often before in its long history, the human species is improvising to meet unforeseen environmental conditions.

I have sketched a developmental sequence of interventions designed to meet the requirements for adaptive growth and development when they are jeopardized by family dislocations, poverty, and other risk factors. We have found that there are indeed effective responses to such jeopardy. These responses have been formulated to the extent possible on research evidence, augmented by the best professional practices and cutting-edge innovations.

I have tried to maintain high standards without making the perfect the enemy of the good. The fundamental standard of reference is whether we can do substantially better than we are now doing in addressing serious problems that arise in each phase of development. I deeply believe that we can and have described a variety of promising lines of inquiry and innovation that provide a genuine basis for hope.

The enduring significance of this approach is that it responds directly to basic needs of children as they are getting their lives under way and to adolescents as they begin to move toward adulthood. In essence, these needs center around several interrelated human aspirations: attachment; close dependable relationships; a sense of belonging in a larger group beyond the nuclear family—often the extended family, although ethnic, religious, occupational, political, or social groups can be sound substitutes; a sense of worth as a person, earned and reinforced by accomplishing tasks that are valued in relation to significant attachments and the sense of belonging in a valued group; a perception of opportunity, hope, and a constructive view of the future; and stimulation of intellectual curiosity, problem-solving ability, and lifelong learning. These needs are manifested in many different ways in different cultures, but they must be addressed in all. They are at the core of being human.

Democratic societies are now challenged as never before to give all our children, regardless of social backgrounds, a good opportunity to participate in the modern technical world, especially in preparation for modern employment opportunities; to achieve at least a decent minimum of literacy in science and technology as a part of everyone's educational heritage; to make lifelong learning a reality so that people can adjust their knowledge and skills to sociotechnical change; and to foster a scientific attitude useful both in problem solving throughout society and understanding the major issues on which an informed citizenry must decide.

In the end, I am hopeful. As a nation, we are awakening to the gravity of the problems of today's children. This should make it possible for us to utilize the experience of interventions so far undertaken and to improve them by strengthening our research capability in the biomedical and behavioral sciences that bear upon child development, health, and education. Armed with these bodies of knowledge and experience, we can construct more effective interventions for our children in the years ahead—both within the family and beyond it. We can address such great problems effectively; we can relieve terrible suffering; we can stem the grievous loss of talent and life—if we have the vision and the decency to invest responsibly in tomorrow's children and thereby in the future of all humanity.

Acknowledgments

A book like this is more than a snapshot of the author's impressions at a moment in time. It is a cumulative record of interests, values, information, and ideas developed over much of a lifetime. So this book has multiple origins and influences. Some of these I sketched in the introduction. I want to record some of the others here, even though I cannot possibly do justice to the many fine people and stimulating institutions who have contributed. I wish I could.

First—and logically so in light of this book's subject matter—I return to my family. I simply want to underscore what I have said in the introduction and the dedication about the profound and pervasive influence of my wife and children on this work. Without them, it would never have been possible. And a further sense of gratitude to both the Hamburg and Becker clans, who did so much to give me a good start—above all, my devoted parents.

In the preparation of this book, certain people have been directly helpful in many ways that have earned my deepest appreciation. Pat England has patiently seen me through innumerable drafts, visions, and revisions—all with skill, dedication, and good humor. Susan Smith not only has helped greatly with all phases of the book but also has kept my office functioning well for the better part of a decade—with unfailing judgment, sensitivity, and kindness. Irene Tsukada Germain, Annette Dyer, and Trisha Lester have also been exceedingly helpful.

I am very grateful to Naomi Goldstein for her crucial role in the preparation of this book. While pursuing her graduate education at Harvard, she helped me clarify the research evidence, linking research to policy and practice, all with fine judgment and care.

Early editorial feedback from three good friends was very helpful. Martha Angle, with characteristic generosity and acuity, read an entire initial draft and offered much useful commentary and encouragement. Ann Mandelbaum also made valuable editorial suggestions. Don Kennedy gave me substantial feedback and stimulation.

My experience with Times Books has been excellent. From the day when Peter Osnos first contacted me to the present, I have experienced nothing but encouragement, stimulation, wise counsel, and careful attention to detail. He and Betsy Rapoport and their colleagues have helped enormously. I am deeply appreciative of their skill, dedication, and integrity.

In the introduction I explained the extraordinary opportunity presented by the Carnegie Corporation to pursue the great challenge of today's children. Although this book is a personal statement rather than an institutional position, nevertheless it is profoundly influenced by my years at the helm of this remarkable foundation. Andrew Carnegie made it possible with his unprecedented philanthropy. The distinguished post–World War II leadership of John Gardner and Alan Pifer paved the way for our current efforts. Barbara Finberg has worked closely with me in all the operations of the foundation and handled her wide-ranging responsibilities with distinction. Several staff members have been deeply involved in our grant-making on the subject matter of this book, and they have been extraordinarily helpful in dealing with the substance of these issues. Vivien Stewart, as chair of the children and youth program, has had especially heavy responsibility and has taught me a great deal. So, too, has Ruby Takanishi, as executive director of the Carnegie Council on Adolescent Development. Elena Nightingale has worked effectively with me on these issues and others at the Institute of Medicine, Harvard University, and Carnegie Corporation of New York. These are remarkable people who know a lot and care a lot about today's children. In this problem area, I have also been aided over the years by Alden Dunham, Gloria Primm Brown, Anthony Jackson, Mary Kiely, Karin Egan, Bernard Charles, and more recently, Michael Levine. We are fortunate indeed to have such a staff—and that means today's children are fortunate as well.

A further word about our staff is in order. The people working on our other programs have been patient with me as I have focused a lot of attention on children and youth. I especially express my gratitude to Jean Grisi, Dee Holder, Dorothy Knapp, Fritz Mosher, Pat Rosenfield, and Avery Russell—all of whom have major responsibilities for the foundation's work.

Carnegie has been blessed with a remarkable succession of recent board chairs who have served the enterprise so well in the spirit of Andrew Carnegie's philanthropy: Bud Taylor, Helene Kaplan, and Warren Christopher. Each has given me great support and encouragement to pursue the lines of inquiry and innovation described in this book. Helene was chair during most of the period of this effort and has been extraordinary in her wisdom and generosity.

Several other members of the foundation's board have taken a keen interest in the problems under consideration here, and they have been most helpful: Tomas Arciniega, Dick Beattie, Jim Comer, Gene Cota-Robles, Dick Fisher, Jim Gibbs, Ruth Hamilton, Caryl Haskins, Fred Hechinger, Tom Kean, Josh Lederberg, Ann Leven, Ray Marshall, Pat McPherson, Newton Minow, Peggy Rosenheim, Bob Rubin, Anne Firor Scott, Larry Tisch, Tom Troyer, John Whitehead, and Sheila Widnall.

During my term at Carnegie, we established several bodies concentrating on problems of children and youth that have been simultaneously informative, stimulating, and creative. I express here my strong appreciation to the active, contributing members of these groups. The Carnegie Council on Adolescent Development, Ruby Takanishi, Executive Director. Members are:

H. Keith H. Brodie
Michael I. Cohen
Alonzo A. Crim
Michael S. Dukakis
William H. Gray III
Beatrix A. Hamburg
David E. Hayes-Bautista
Fred M. Hechinger
David W. Hornbeck
Daniel K. Inouye
James M. Jeffords
Richard Jessor
Helene L. Kaplan
Nancy L. Kassebaum
Thomas H. Kean
Ted Koppel
Hernan LaFontaine
Eleanor E. Maccoby

Ray Marshall
Julius B. Richmond
Frederick C. Robbins
Kenneth B. Smith
Wilma Tisch
P. Roy Vagelos
William J. Wilson

Tony Jackson and David Hornbeck did a superb job of bringing to fulfillment my dream of a fundamental reformulation of the middle-grade schools. They and their colleagues on the task force that prepared *Turning Points* have made a lasting contribution.

The Task Force on Education of Young Adolescents, Anthony Jackson, Executive Director. Members were:

Bill Clinton
James P. Comer
Alonzo A. Crim
Jacquelynne Eccles
Lawrence W. Green
Fred M. Hechinger
David W. Hornbeck
Renee R. Jenkins
Nancy L. Kassebaum
Hernan LaFontaine
Deborah W. Meier
Amado M. Padilla
Anne C. Petersen
Jane Quinn
Mary Budd Rowe
Roberta G. Simmons
Marshall S. Smith
James D. Watkins

The Carnegie Education Advisory Council was very helpful in shaping our programs on children and youth. The members were:

William O. Baker
Lewis M. Branscomb
Henry G. Cisneros
John W. Gardner
Fred M. Hechinger
James B. Hunt, Jr.
Donald Kennedy
Margaret L. A. MacVicar
Shirley M. Malcom
Ray Marshall
Shirley M. McBay
Michael O'Keefe
Mary Louise Petersen
Ruth E. Randall
Peter Smith
John C. Taylor III
Robert M. White
William S. Woodside

The Task Force on Teaching as a Profession made an important contribution to education reform by preparing the report *A Nation Prepared: Teachers for the 21st Century*. Marc Tucker and David Mandel played crucial roles in this effort. The members were:

Lewis M. Branscomb, Chairman
Alan K. Campbell
Mary Hatwood Futrell
John W. Gardner
Fred M. Hechinger
Bill Honig
James Baxter Hunt, Jr.
Thomas Kean
Vera Katz
Judith E. Lanier
Arturo Madrid
Shirley M. Malcom
Ruth E. Randall
Albert Shanker

The Carnegie Commission on Science, Technology and Government has been a profoundly stimulating enterprise under the wise leadership of Josh Lederberg, Bill Golden, and David Robinson. Most of its activities are beyond the scope of this book, but several of its members have been seriously involved with the problems of children and youth, and they have been exceedingly helpful: Lewis Branscomb, Jimmy Carter, and Shirley Hufstedler.

While this book was in mid-passage, I lost—and children everywhere lost—a great good friend, John Bowlby. He was an authentic pioneer in his work on attachment. He and his wife, Ursula, were an important source of encouragement for this work. So, too, was our mutual friend Robert Hinde, whose distinguished ethological work on development has been a stimulating influence on the field.

Thinking of John Bowlby takes me back to 1957 when we first met at the Center for Advanced Study in the Behavioral Sciences—under the wonderful auspices of its founding director, Ralph Tyler. And that in turn evokes many memories of people who have stimulated, guided, and encouraged me in each era of my career. A comprehensive account would probably make another book. But a sketch will at least suggest the nature of the gratitude I feel.

As an undergraduate at Indiana University, I was truly inspired by the great geneticist Tracy Sonneborn. He opened a window on science that shaped the course of my entire life. In Chicago, after medical school, I had a similar impetus from Roy Grinker. Gerhart Piers was wonderfully helpful. My professional development was greatly aided in Chicago by Therese Benedek, Joan Fleming, Thomas French, Irving Harris, Rachmiel Levine, Arno Motulsky, Mel Sabshin, and Jim and Virginia Saft.

At Yale, early stimulating encounters with Fritz Redlich and Al Solnit turned into enduring friendships of great personal as well as professional significance.

The years 1961 to 1975 at Stanford University were immensely stimulating and constructive. It was then and still is a marvelous institution—bursting with the world's whole stock of information and ideas, wide open to innovation, looking ahead to the next century. I had the privilege of building a new kind of department in a new kind of medical school. Concomitantly, I became deeply involved in the life of the university beyond the medical center. These rich and varied opportunities strongly reinforced my inclination toward interdisciplinary research and education. Though specialization certainly has its uses, the problems of the real world just do not come in packages that fit the established disciplines. Somehow, different bodies of knowledge and techniques of research have to be combined in order to penetrate the mysteries of nature, including those of human development.

So the department we built was oriented toward understanding human behavior and its disorders through multiple approaches. Among those who were especially helpful, I can mention here only a few: John Adams, Bob Alway, Jack and Pat Barchas, Keith Brodie, Bob Chase, Roland Ciaranello, Ray Clayton, Bill Dement, Hazel Eickworth, Bob Glaser, Avram Goldstein, Tom Gonda, George Gulevich, Jetty Hogan, Henry Kaplan, Herant Katchadourian, Bob Klein, Bert Kopell, Arthur Kornberg, Josh Lederberg, Herb Leiderman, Don Lunde, Dick Lyman, Jim Mark, Frank Matsumoto, Rudy Moos, Karl Pribram, Hale Shirley, George Solomon, Wally Sterling, Irv Yalom, and Alex Zaffaroni.

In shaping the developmental perspective, I was especially aided and informed by Al Bandura, Jack and Josie Hilgard, Seymour Levine, Eleanor Maccoby, Alberta Siegel—and of course my wife, Betty.

One of the most exciting ventures of the Stanford era was the creation of an interdisciplinary undergraduate program in Human Biology. It remains after more than two decades one of the most sought-after educational activities at Stanford, and it turns up in this volume, as it has been adapted for life-sciences education in early adolescence. In creating this program, I worked especially closely with Don Kennedy and Josh Lederberg; the other founding fathers were Sandy Dornbusch, Paul Ehrlich, Jim Gibbs, Al Hastorf, Norman Kretchmer, and Colin Pittendrigh. I remain indebted to all of them—and to the wonderful students with whom we worked so closely.

Some special friendships evolved during the Stanford years that have endured over the years and remain highly meaningful not only for me but for Betty and our children, Eric and Peggy, as well. No brief word can express the gratitude we feel for Sidney Akselrad; Sid, Harriet, and Dan Drell; Alex and Julie George; Bob, Nancy, Doug, and Laurie Hofstadter; Don and Jeanne Kennedy; Josh and Marguerite Lederberg; Kitty Lee; Jonas Salk; and Sherry and Henrietta Washburn. A special word of enduring appreciation goes to the residents and fellows who worked in our department during the Stanford years.

Toward the end of the Stanford era, I spent a superb academic year as a Fairchild Fellow at the California Institute of Technology and was free to develop some of the ideas that appear in this book. For that special opportunity, I express my appreciation to Louis Breger, Harold Brown, Murray Gell-Mann, Bob Huttenbach, Jim Olds, Joyce Penn, and Bob Sinsheimer.

During the first phase of my career, I spent a lot of time doing research on stress problems, partly from a biological standpoint—the response of the nervous system and the endocrine system to situations that people find difficult and distressing. In that work, I feel deeply indebted to Roy Grinker—my first mentor in psychiatry; John Mason, a boyhood friend who for many years was a valued collaborator; also David Rioch, Bob Cohen, William Bunney, Frieda Fromm-Reichman, Sheldon Korchin, Jim Maas, Harold Persky, and Ed Sachar.

In the course of that work, I stumbled onto the fact that most people cope effectively with exceedingly difficult situations beyond anything that I had imagined. I went to the research literature on these matters and found very little. In view of the ubiquity of stressful experience, I undertook a series of studies with valued collaborators on coping responses. Among these collaborators I can only single out a few; John Adams, George Coelho, Stan Friedman, Joe Handlon, Rudy Moos, Betty Murphey, Roger Shapiro, Earle Silber, Harold Visotsky, and once again, Betty.

After a while I got interested in how these responses came about. The integrated pattern of biobehavioral responses to stress add up to preparation for intensive action, as if we were going to run or fight or take some other vigorous action in the face of life-threatening situations. But most of what we do in the contemporary world is not really like that. More often, we sit and worry. In essence, mobilization for action—without action. That does not make a lot of biological sense. Perhaps such costly responses made more sense in an earlier era of human experience.

So I decided to look into the conditions under which our ancient ancestors lived that could have made that kind of preparation for intensive action adaptive. I became interested in monkeys and apes in their natural habitats. This made it possible to get some idea of how they made a living and how they coped with dangers; it led to a deep involvement in research with some remarkable collaborators. Sherwood Washburn and Jane Goodall were especially helpful in that era. Others to whom I am indebted surely include Harold Bauer, Chuck Boelkins, Irv DeVore, Charles Doering, Phyllis Jay Dolhinow, Suzanne Haber, Sally Hays, Helen Kraemer, Pat McGinnis, Anne Pusey, Barbara Smuts, Richard Wrangham, and Barbara de Zalduondo.

Much of this primate work involved growth and development, social learning, and acquiring the skills to cope with dangers and take advantage of opportunities. We had the privilege of clarifying some fundamental aspects of development in childhood and adolescence.

My evolutionary interests were greatly aided in various ways by several other remarkable people: Doug Bond, Ernst Caspari, Theodosius Dobzhansky, Gordon and Ann Getty, Walter Goldschmidt, Libby McCown, Bill McGrew, Pal Midgett, Abdul Msangi, Barbara Newsom, Lita Osmundsen, Shirley Strum, Joan Travis, and Caroline Tutin.

On the night of May 19, 1975, forty heavily armed men suddenly appeared on Lake Tanganyika and abducted four of my students and colleagues from our primate research camp in the Gombe National Park, Tanzania. They became hostages and pawns in what turned out to be a life-and-death political/military struggle involving two African governments and rebels against one of them. I went to Africa immediately and spent the next several months doing everything in my power to achieve their freedom. Luckily, very luckily indeed, the story turned out well. And we have all been close ever since, special bonds forged in the heat of adversity—yet another commentary on the deep human significance of attachment and social supports. I can never forget the courage and dedication of those held hostage: Carrie Hunter, Emilie Bergmann Riss, Steve Smith, and Barbara Smuts. So, too, the remarkable qualities of Lewis MacFarlane, Michelle Trudeau, and Beverly Carter, who helped so much in the African scene of crisis; and once again, Betty, who went beyond the call of duty on the American scene.

In the course of these events in the interior of Africa, I was deeply immersed not only in resolving a hostage crisis, but also in some of the worst problems of the world—abject poverty, disease, ignorance, hatred, and violence. I was moved by the experience to devote the rest of my career to addressing problems of this sort in terms of policies that could diminish the toll of casualties.

Later that year, I became president of the Institute of Medicine, National Academy of Sciences. During my five-year term at the Institute of Medicine, we developed a major thrust toward expanding the scope of the health sciences, exploring the biological, environmental, behavioral, and social factors affecting health. We gave emphasis to strengthening disease prevention and health promotion; improving health care; and tackling the pervasive problems of illness in developing nations. In those years, I owe so many debts I can only scratch the surface. Here are a few: Bill Baker, Bob Ball, Jerry Barondess, David and Mickey Bazelon, Caroline Boitano, Lester Breslow, Sarah Brown, Joe Califano, Bill Carey, Ted Cooper, Bill Danforth, Glen Elliott, Alain Enthoven, John Evans, Jean George, Phil Handler, Howard Hiatt, Don Kennedy, Jeanne Kennedy, Alex Leaf, Josh Lederberg, Irving London, Walsh McDermott, Margaret Mahoney, Sherman Mellinkoff, Arno Motulsky, Elena Nightingale, Delores Parron, Uwe Reinhardt, Julie Richmond, Fred Robbins, David Rogers, Walter Rosenblith, Lisbeth Schorr, Susan Smith, Fred Solomon, Mitchell Spellman, Nathan Stark, Jana Surdi, Dan Tosteson, Wally Waterfall, Bob White, and Karl Yordy.

In the early 1980s, I carried forward this work by creating a university-wide Division of Health Policy Research and Education at Harvard University, drawing especially on the faculties of the John F. Kennedy School of Government, the Medical School, and the School of Public Health—providing a broad-based approach to the examination of crucial policy issues related to disease prevention, mental health, special needs of the elderly—and a great deal of attention to the health problems of children and youth in collaboration with Julie Richmond. I am particularly grateful to Dan Tosteson, Derek Bok, and Graham Allison for their initiative in bringing this about and for their continuing friendship. Among others who were exceedingly helpful in this era were: (once again) Betty, Mary Ellen Avery, Mary Jo Bane, David Blumenthal, John Conger, Chuck Czeisler, John Dunlop, Leon Eisenberg, Glen Elliott, Sherrie Epstein, Eli Evans, Harvey Fineberg, Jerry Kagan, Gerald Klerman, Alex Leaf, Lynda McGinnis, Barbara McNeill, Martha Minow, Ann Moran, Fred Mosteller, Elena Nightingale,

Mitch Rabkin, Bud Relman, Jack Rowe, Jack Sawyer, Mark Schlesinger, George Taber, and George Walker.

To all the people I have mentioned and more besides, I express here as best I can the deep appreciation I feel for all their goodwill, encouragement, help, and friendship, which have made it possible for me to do whatever I have done. To the extent that this book may be useful to many people in different parts of the world, as I hope it will be, they have all contributed.

References

1. Families in Crisis, Children in Jeopardy

Bane, M. J. *Here to Stay*. New York: Basic Books, 1976.

Barraclough, G. *An Introduction to Contemporary History*. Harmondsworth, Middlesex, England: Penguin Books, 1967.

Bateson, P., ed. *The Development and Integration of Behaviour*. New York: Cambridge University Press, 1991.

Bogue, D. J. *The Population of the United States*. New York: Free Press, 1985.

Chase-Lansdale, L., and Hetherington, E. M. "The Impact of Divorce on Life Span Development: Short- and Long-Term Effects." In *Life Span Development and Behavior*, P. B. Bates, D. L. Featherman, and R. Lerner, eds. Hillsdale, N.J.: Lawrence Erlbaum Associates, 1989.

Cherlin, A. J., ed. *The Changing American Family and Public Policy*. Washington, D.C.: Urban Institute Press, 1988.

Clutton-Brock, T. H. *The Evolution of Parental Care*. Princeton, N.J.: Princeton University Press, 1991.

Degler, C. *Out of Our Past: The Forces That Shaped Modern America*, 3rd ed. New York: Harper & Row, 1984.

Edelman, M. W. *Families in Peril: An Agenda for Social Change*. Cambridge, Mass.: Harvard University Press, 1987.

Furstenberg, F. F. "Child Care After Divorce and Remarriage." In *Impact of Divorce, Single-Parenting, and Stepparenting on Children*, E. M. Hetherington and J. Arasteh, eds. Hillsdale, N.J.: Lawrence Erlbaum Associates, 1988.

Goldschmidt, W. *Man's Way: A Preface to the Understanding of Human Society*. New York: Holt, Rinehart and Winston, 1959.

Goodall, J. *The Chimpanzees of Gombe: Patterns of Behavior*. Cambridge, Mass.: Belknap Press of Harvard University Press, 1986.

Hamburg, D. A., and McCown, E. R. *The Great Apes.* Menlo Park, Calif.: Benjamin/Cummings, 1979.

Harlow, H. F., and Harlow, M. K. "Effects of Various Mother-Infant Relationships on Rhesus Monkey Behaviors." In *Determinants of Infant Behavior,* vol. 4, B. M. Foss, ed. London: Methuen, 1969.

Hetherington, E. M. "Parents, Children and Siblings Six Years After Divorce." In *Relationships Within Families,* R. Hinde and J. Stevenson-Hinde, eds. Cambridge, England: Cambridge University Press, 1989.

Hetherington, E. M., Stanley-Hagan, M., and Anderson, E. R. "Marital Transitions: A Child's Perspective." In *American Psychologist,* special issue, vol. 44, no. 2, February 1989.

Hinde. R. A., ed. *Primate Social Relationships: An Integrated Approach.* Oxford: Blackwell, 1983.

Hinde, R. A., "Ethology and Child Development." In *Handbook of Child Psychology,* vol. 2, P. H. Mussen, ed. New York: John Wiley & Sons, 1983.

Hochschild, A., and Machung, A. *The Second Shift: Working Parents and the Revolution at Home.* New York: Viking, 1989.

Kagan, J. *The Nature of the Child.* New York: Basic Books, 1984.

Kamerman, S. B., and Hayes, C. D., eds. *Families That Work: Children in a Changing World.* Washington, D.C.: National Academy Press, 1982.

Lee, R. B., and DeVore, I., eds. *Kalahari Hunter-Gatherers.* Cambridge, Mass.: Harvard University Press, 1976.

Lee, P. C. "Play as a Means for Developing Relationships." In *Primate Social Relationships: An Integrated Approach,* R. A. Hinde, ed. Oxford: Blackwell, 1983.

Lenski, G., and Lenski, J. *Human Societies: An Introduction to Macrosociology,* 5th ed. New York: McGraw-Hill, 1987.

Levitan. S. A., Belous, R. S., Gallow, F. *What's Happening to the American Family?* rev ed. Baltimore: Johns Hopkins University Press, 1988.

Madge, N., ed. *Families at Risk.* London: Heinemann Educational Books, 1983.

McNeill, W. H. *A World History,* 2nd ed. New York: Oxford University Press, 1971.

Mintz, S., and Kellogg, S. *Domestic Revolutions: A Social History of an American Family Life.* New York: Free Press, 1988.

Nicolson, N. A. "Infants, Mothers, and Other Females." In *Primate Societies,* B. B. Smuts et al., eds. Chicago: University of Chicago Press, 1986.

Price, T. D., and Brown, J. A., eds. *Prehistoric Hunter-Gatherers: The Emergence of Cultural Complexity.* San Diego: Academic Press, 1985.

Pusey, A. E. "Mother-Offspring Relationships in Chimpanzees After Weaning." In *Animal Behavior,* 31:363–377, 1983.

Pusey. A. E. "Behavioural Changes at Adolescence in Chimpanzees." In *Behaviour,* 115 (3–4), 1990.

Riley, G. *Divorce: An American Tradition.* New York: Oxford University Press, 1991.

Smuts, B. B., Cheney, D. L., Seyfarth, R. M., Wrangham, R. W., and Struhsaker, T. T. *Primate Societies.* Chicago: University of Chicago Press, 1986.

Suomi, S. L. "Differential Development of Various Social Relationships by Rhesus Monkey Infants." In *The Child in Its Family,* M. Lewis and A. Rosenblum, eds. New York: Plenum, 1979.

Suomi, S. L. "Biological Foundations and Developmental Psychobiology." In *The*

Healthy Children: Investing in the Future. Office of Technology Assessment. Washington, D.C.: U.S. Government Printing Office, February 1987.

Infant Mortality: Caring for Our Future. Washington, D.C.: National Commission to Prevent Infant Mortality, 1988.

Mehren, E. *Born Too Soon: The Story of Emily, Our Premature Baby.* New York: Doubleday, 1991.

Michaels, G., and Goldberg, W., eds. *The Transition to Parenthood: Current Theory and Research.* New York: Cambridge University Press, 1988.

Miller, C. A. "Prenatal Care Outreach: An International Perspective," Appendix B. In *Prenatal Care: Reaching Mothers, Reaching Infants,* S. S. Brown, ed. Committee to Study Outreach for Prenatal Care, Institute of Medicine. Washington, D.C.: National Academy Press, 1988.

Nutrition During Pregnancy. Part I: Weight Gain. Part II: Nutrient Supplements. Institute of Medicine. Washington, D.C.: National Academy Press, 1990.

Olds, D. "The Prenatal/Early Infancy Project." In *Fourteen Ounces of Prevention: A Casebook for Practitioners,* R. H. Price, E. L. Cowen, R. P. Lorion, and J. Ramos-McKay, eds. Washington, D.C.: American Psychological Association, 1988.

Preventing Low Birthweight. Institute of Medicine. Washington, D.C.: National Academy Press, 1985.

Royston, E., and Armstrong, S. *Preventing Maternal Deaths.* Geneva: World Health Organization, 1989.

Sexton, M., and Hefel, J. R. "A Clinical Trial of Change in Maternal Smoking and Its Effect on Birthweight." In *Journal of the American Medical Association,* vol. 251, 1984.

Singh, S., Forrest, J. D., and Torres, A. *Prenatal Care in the United States: A State and County Inventory,* vol. 1. Washington, D.C.: Alan Guttmacher Institute, 1989.

4. Health from the Start: Preventive Health Care in the First Few Years

Adams, B. W. "A Pediatrician's View of Prevention." In *The Ounce of Prevention Fund Quarterly,* summer 1990.

Bell, K. *Home Visits Revisited.* National Center for Children in Poverty, Columbia University School of Public Health, New York, 1991.

Boger, R. P., Blom, G. E., and Lezotte, L. E. *Child Nurturance, Vol. 4: Child Nurturing in the 1980s.* New York: Plenum Press, 1984.

Disease Prevention/Health Promotion: The Facts. Office of Disease Prevention and Health Promotion. Palo Alto, Calif.: Bull Publishing Company, 1988.

"Enhancing the Outcomes of Low-Birth-Weight, Premature Infants: A Multisite, Randomized Trial." From the Infant Health and Development Program. In *Journal of the American Medical Association,* vol. 263, no. 22, June 1990.

The Future of Child Health in New York City. A Report of the Mayor's Commission, New York City Department of Health, August 1989.

Healthy People 2000. U.S. Department of Health and Human Services Public Health Service, Superintendent of Documents, U.S. Government Printing Office, Washington (PHS) 91-50212, 1990.

Hamburg, D. A., Elliot, G. R., and Parron, D. *Health and Behavior: Frontiers of*

Research in the Biobehavioral Sciences. Washington, D.C.: National Academy Press, 1982.

Hamburg, D. A., and Sartorius, N., eds. *Health and Behaviour: Selected Perspectives.* Cambridge, England: Cambridge University Press, 1989.

Injury Prevention: Meeting the Challenge. National Committee for Injury Prevention and Control, Washington, D.C., New York: Oxford University Press, 1989.

Kempe, R. S., and Kempe, C. H. *Child Abuse.* The Developing Child series. Cambridge, Mass.: Harvard University Press, 1978.

Kinney, J., Haapala, D., and Booth, C. *Keeping Families Together: The Homebuilders Model.* New York: Aldine de Gruyter, 1991.

Klerman, L. V. "Alive and Well? A Research and Policy Review of Health Programs for Poor Young Children." National Center for Children in Poverty, Columbia University School of Public Health, New York, 1991.

Levine, M. D., Carey, W. B., Crocker, A. C., and Gross, R. T. *Developmental-Behavioral Pediatrics.* Philadelphia: W. B. Saunders Co., 1983.

Nelson, D. "Recognizing and Realizing the Potential of 'Family Preservation.' " In *Reaching High-Risk Families: Intensive Family Preservation in Human Services,* J. K. Whittaker, J. Kinney, E. M. Tracy, and C. Booth, eds. New York: Aldine de Gruyter, 1990.

New Vaccine Development: Establishing Priorities, Vol. 1: *Diseases of Importance in the United States.* Institute of Medicine, Washington, D.C.: National Academy Press, February 1985.

Pless, I. B., and Haggerty, R. J. "Child Health: Research in Action." In *Children, Youth, and Families,* R. N. Rapoport, ed. New York: Cambridge University Press, 1985.

Pope, A. M., and Tarlov, A. R., eds. *Disability in America: Toward a National Agenda for Prevention.* Washington, D.C.: National Academy Press, 1991.

Poverty and Human Development. Published for the World Bank. New York: Oxford University Press, 1980.

Richmond, J. "Low Birth-Weight Infants: Can We Enhance Their Development?" *Journal of the American Medical Association,* vol. 263, no. 22, June 1990.

Rogers, D. E., and Ginzberg, E., eds. *Improving the Life Chances of Children at Risk.* Boulder, Colo.: Westview Press, 1990.

U.S. General Accounting Office. *Home Visiting: A Promising Early Intervention Strategy for At-Risk Families.* U.S. General Accounting Office, Washington, D.C., report GAO/HRD 90-83, July 1990.

U.S. General Accounting Office. *Mental Health: Prevention of Mental Disorders and Research on Stress-Related Disorders.* Washington, D.C.: U.S. General Accounting Office, 1989.

Wallace, H. M., Ryan, G. M., and Oglesby, A. C., eds. *Maternal and Child Health Practices* 3rd ed. Oakland, Calif.: Third Party, 1988.

Whittaker, J. K., Kinney, J., Tracy, E. M., and Booth, C., eds. *Reaching High-Risk Families: Intensive Family Preservation in Human Services.* New York: Aldine de Gruyter, 1990.

5. The Family Crucible: Opportunities for and Obstacles to Healthy Child Development

Bee, H. *The Developing Child*, 4th ed. New York: Harper and Row, 1985.

Bower, T.G.R. *The Rational Infant: Learning in Infancy*. New York: W. H. Freeman and Co., 1989.

Bowlby, J. *A Secure Base: Parent-Child Attachment and Healthy Human Development*. New York: Basic Books, 1988.

Bowlby, J. *Attachment and Loss*. Vol. 1: *Attachment*. New York: Basic Books, 1969.

Bowlby, J. *Attachment and Loss*. Vol. 2: *Separation: Anxiety and Anger*. New York: Basic Books, 1973.

Bowlby, J. *Attachment and Loss*. Vol. 3: *Sadness and Depression*. New York: Basic Books, 1980.

Brazelton, T. B. "Why Is America Failing Its Children?" In *New York Times Magazine*, September 9, 1990.

Bremner, R. H. *Children and Youth in America*. Cambridge, Mass.: Harvard University Press, 1971.

Bronfenbrenner, U. *The Ecology of Human Development: Experiments by Nature and by Design*. Cambridge, Mass.: Harvard University Press, 1979.

Camara, K. A., and Resnick, G. "Interparental Conflict and Cooperation: Factors Moderating Children's Post-Divorce Adjustment." In *Impact of Divorce, Single-Parenting, and Stepparenting on Children*, E. M. Hetherington and J. D. Arasteh, eds. Hillsdale, N.J.: Lawrence Erlbaum Associates, 1988.

Clark-Stewart, A., and Koch, J. *Children: Development Through Adolescence*. New York: John Wiley & Sons, 1983.

Clausen, J. A. *The Life Course: A Sociological Perspective*. Englewood Cliffs, N.J.: Prentice-Hall, 1986.

Coelho, G. *Coping and Adaptation: An Annotated Bibliography*. Washington, D.C.: U.S. Government Printing Office, 1981.

Coelho, G., Hamburg, D. A., and Adams, J. *Coping and Adaptation*. New York: Basic Books, 1974.

Coelho, G., Hamburg, D. A., Moos, R., and Randolph, P., eds. *Coping and Adaptation: A Behavioral Sciences Bibliography*. Washington, D.C.: U.S. Government Printing Office, 1970.

Cole, M., and Cole, S. R. *The Development of Children*. New York: W. H. Freeman, 1989.

Garmezy, N., and Rutter, M., eds. *Stress, Coping, and Development in Children*. New York: McGraw-Hill, 1983.

Hartup, W. W. "Social Relationships and Their Developmental Significance." In *American Psychologist*, vol. 44, no. 2, February 1990.

Hetherington, E. M., Stanley-Hagan, M., and Anderson, E. R. "Marital Transitions: A Child's Perspective." In *American Psychologist*, special issue, vol. 44, no. 2, February 1989.

Hetherington, E. M. "Coping with Family Transitions: Winners, Losers, and Survivors." In *Child Development*, vol. 60, 1989, 1–15.

Hetherington, E. M., and Parke, R. D. *Child Psychology: A Contemporary Viewpoint*, 3rd ed. New York: McGraw-Hill, 1986.

Hinde, R. A., Perret-Clermont, A., and Stevenson-Hinde, J., eds. *Social Relationships and Cognitive Development.* Oxford: Clarendon Press, 1985.

Kopp, C., and Krakow, J. *The Child: Development in a Social Context.* Reading, Mass.: Addison-Wesley, 1982.

Levine, S., and Ursin, H., eds. *Coping and Health.* New York: Plenum Press, 1980.

Mussen, P., ed. *Handbook of Social Psychology,* 4th ed., vol. 4: *Socialization, Personality, and Social Development.* E. M. Hetherington, volume editor. New York: John Wiley & Sons, 1983.

Olweus, D., Block J., and Radke-Yarrow, M. *Development of Antisocial and Prosocial Behavior: Research, Theories, and Issues.* Orlando, Fla.: Academic Press, 1986.

Parkes, C. M., and Stevenson-Hinde, J., eds. *The Place of Attachment in Human Behavior.* New York: Basic Books, 1982.

Radke-Yarrow, M., and Sherman, T. "Interaction of Cognition and Emotions in Development." In *Social Relationships and Cognitive Development,* R. A. Hinde, A. N. Perret-Clermont, and J. Stevenson-Hinde, eds. Oxford: Clarendon Press, 1985.

Radke-Yarrow, M., and Zahn-Waxler, C. "The Role of Familial Factors in the Development of Prosocial Behavior: Research Findings and Questions." In *Development of Antisocial and Prosocial Behavior,* D. Olweus, J. Block, and M. Radke-Yarrow, Orlando, Fla.: Academic Press, 1986.

Ramey, C. T., and MacPhee, D. "Developmental Retardation: A System Theory Perspective on Risk and Preventive Intervention." In *Risk in Intellectual and Psychosocial Development,* D. C. Farran and J. D. McKinney, eds. San Diego: Academic Press, 1986.

Robins, L., and Rutter, M. *Straight and Devious Pathways from Childhood to Adulthood.* Cambridge: Cambridge University Press, 1990.

Rolf, J., Masten, A. S., Cicchetti, D., Nuechterlein, K. H., and Weintraub, S., eds. *Risk and Protective Factors in the Development of Psychopathology.* New York: Cambridge University Press, 1990.

Rosenblith, J. F., and Sims-Knight, J. E. *In the Beginning: Development from Conception to Age 2.* Newbury Park, Calif.: Sage Publishers, 1992.

Rutter, M. "Psychosocial Resilience and Protective Mechanisms." In *American Journal of Orthopsychiatry,* vol. 57, no. 3, 1987, 316–331.

Sameroff, A. J., and Emde, R. N., eds. *Relationship Disturbances in Early Childhood: A Developmental Approach.* New York: Basic Books 1989.

Sroufe, L. A. "The Role of Infant-Caregiver Attachment in Development." In *Clinical Implications of Attachment,* J. Belsky and T. Nezworski, eds. Hillsdale, N.J.: Lawrence Erlbaum Associates, 1988.

Wachs, T., and Grune, G. *Early Experience and Human Development.* New York: Plenum Press, 1982.

Waters, E., Hay, D. F., and Richters, J. E. "Infant-Parent Attachment and the Origins of Prosocial and Antisocial Behavior." In *Development of Antisocial and Prosocial Behavior,* D. Olweus, J. Block, and M. Radke-Yarrow, eds. Orlando, Fla.: Academic Press, 1986.

Werner, E. E. "A Longitudinal Study of Perinatal Risk." In *Risk in Intellectual and Psychosocial Development,* D. C. Farran, and J. D. McKinney, eds. San Diego: Academic Press, 1986.

Werner, E. E. "Vulnerability and Resiliency in Children at Risk for Delinquency:

A Longitudinal Study from Birth to Young Adulthood." In *Prevention of Delinquent Behavior*, J. D. Burchard and S. N. Burchard, eds. Newbury Park, Calif.: Sage Publications, 1987.

Werner, E. E. "Resilient Children." In *Contemporary Readings in Child Psychology*, 3rd ed., E. M. Hetherington and R. D. Parke, eds. New York: McGraw-Hill, 1987.

White, B. L. *The First Three Years of Life*, rev. ed. New York: Prentice Hall, 1990.

Williams, T., and Kornblum, W. *Growing Up Poor*. Lexington, Mass.: Lexington Books, 1985.

6. Who's Minding the Children? Confronting the Child-Care Crisis

Belsky, J. "Developmental Effects of Daycare and Conditions of Quality." In *Contemporary Readings in Child Psychology*, E. M. Hetherington and R. D. Parke, eds. 3rd ed. New York: McGraw-Hill, 1987.

Bruner, J. *Under Five in Britain*. Ypsilanti, Mich.: High/Scope Press, 1980.

Clarke-Stewart, A. *Daycare*. The Developing Child series. Cambridge, Mass.: Harvard University Press, 1982.

Clarke-Stewart, K. A. "Infant Day Care: Maligned or Malignant?" In "Children and Their Development: Knowledge, Research Base, Research Agenda, and Social Policy Application," *American Psychologist*, special issue, vol. 44, no. 2, February 1989.

Hayes, C. D., Palmer, J. L., and Zaslow, M. J., eds. *Who Cares for America's Children? Child Care Policy for the 1990s*. Panel on Child Care Policy, Committee on Child Development Research and Public Policy, Commission on Behavioral and Social Sciences and Education. Washington, D.C.: National Academy Press, 1990.

Hechinger, G., and Hechinger, F. M. "Child Care in Scandinavia: An Informal Report." In *Teachers College Record*, vol. 92, no. 1, Fall 1990.

Kahn, A. J., and Kamerman, S. B. *Child Care: Facing the Hard Choices*. Dover, Mass.: Auburn House Publishing Co., 1987.

Mitchell, A., Seligson, M., and Marx, F. *Early Childhood Programs and the Public Schools*. Dover, Mass.: Auburn House Publishing Co., 1989.

Scarr, S. *Mother Care Other Care*. New York: Warner Books, 1985.

Zigler, E. F., and Lang, M. E. *Child Care Choices: Balancing the Needs of Children, Families, and Society*. New York: The Free Press, 1991.

7. Protecting Our Children in Their First Few Years

Barnett, W. S., and Escobar, C. M. "The Economics of Early Educational Intervention: A Review." In *Review of Educational Research*, vol. 57, no. 4, Winter 1987.

Berrueta-Clement, J. R., Schweinhart, L. J., Barnett, W. S., et al. *Changed Lives: The Effects of the Perry Preschool Program on Youths Through Age 19*. Monographs of the High/Scope Educational Research Foundation, no. 8. Ypsilanti, Mich.: High/Scope Press, 1984.

Berrueta-Clement, J. R., Schweinhart, L. J., and Barnett, W.S. "The Effects of Early Educational Intervention on Crime and Delinquency in Adolescence and Early Adulthood." In *Prevention of Delinquent Behavior*, J. D. Burchard and S. N. Burchard, eds. Newbury Park, Calif.: Sage Publications, 1987.

Blank. S. "Contemporary Parenting Education and Family Support Programs: Themes and Issues in an Emerging Movement." New York: Foundation for Child Development, 1987.

Bryant, D. M. and Ramey, C. T. "An Analysis of the Effectiveness of Early Intervention Programs for Environmentally At-Risk Children." In *The Effectiveness of Early Intervention for At-Risk and Handicapped Children*, M. J. Guralnick and F. C. Bennett, eds. San Diego: Academic Press, 1987.

Clark-Stewart, K. A., and Fein, G. G. "Early Childhood Programs." In *The Handbook of Child Psychology. Vol. 2: Infancy and Developmental Psychobiology*, J. J. Campos, M. M. Haith, and P. H. Mussen, eds. New York: John Wiley & Sons, 1983.

Farran, D. C. "Effects of Intervention with Disadvantaged and Disabled Children: A Decade Review." In *Handbook of Early Childhood Intervention*, S. J. Meisels and J. P. Shonkoff, eds. New York: Cambridge University Press, 1990.

Farran, D. C., and McKinney, J. D. *Risk in Intellectual and Psychosocial Development*. Orlando, Fla.: Academic Press, 1986.

Garber, H. L. *The Milwaukee Project: Preventing Mental Retardation in Children at Risk*. Washington, D.C.: American Association on Mental Retardation, 1988.

Goldstein, R. *Everyday Parenting: The First Five Years*. New York: Viking/Penguin, 1990.

Guralnick, M., and Bennett, F. "Early Intervention for At-risk and Handicapped Children: Current and Future Perspectives." In *The Effectiveness of Early Intervention for At-Risk and Handicapped Children*, M. J. Guralnick and F. C. Bennett, eds. San Diego: Academic Press, 1987.

Halpern, R., and Weiss, H. B. "Family Support and Education Programs: Evidence from Evaluated Program Experience." In *Helping Families Grow Strong: New Directions in Public Policy*, papers from the Colloquium on Public Policy and Family Support. Washington, D.C.: Center for the Study of Social Policy, 1990.

Hammer, T. J., and Turner, P. H. *Parenting in Contemporary Society*. Englewood Cliffs, N.J.: Prentice-Hall, 1985.

Hauser-Crim, P., Pierson, D., Walker, D., and Tivnan, T. *Early Education in the Public Schools: Lessons from a Comprehensive Birth-to-Kindergarten Program*. San Francisco: Jossey-Bass, 1991.

Kagan, S. L. *Excellence in Early Childhood Education: Defining Characteristics and Next-Decade Strategies*. Office of Education Research and Improvement, U.S. Department of Education. Washington, D.C.: U.S. Government Printing Office, 1990.

Keogh, B. K., Wilcoxen, A. G., and Bernheimer, L. "Prevention Services for Risk Children: Evidence for Policy and Practice." In *Risk in Intellectual and Psychosocial Development*, D. C. Farran and J. D. McKinney, eds. San Diego: Academic Press, 1986.

McPartland, J. E., and Slavin, R. E. *Policy Perspectives: Increasing Achievement of At-Risk Students at Each Grade Level*. Office of Educational Research and Improvement, U.S. Department of Education. Washington, D.C.: U.S. Government Printing Office, 1990.

Pierson, D. E., Walker, D. K., and Tivnan, T. "A School-Based Program from Infancy to Kindergarten for Children and Their Parents." In *A Better Start: New Choices for Early Learning*, F. M. Hechinger, ed. New York: Walker and Co., 1986.

Price, R. H., Cowen, E. L., Lorion, R. P., and Ramos-McKay, J., eds. *Fourteen Ounces of Prevention: A Casebook for Practitioners.* Washington, D.C.: American Psychological Association, 1988.

Pugh, G., and De'Ath, E. *The Needs of Parents: Practice and Policy in Parent Education.* London: Macmillan Education, 1984.

Ramey, C. T., and MacPhee, D. "Developmental Retardation: A System Theory Perspective on Risk and Preventive Intervention." In *Risk in Intellectual and Psychosocial Development,* D. C. Farran and J. D. McKinney, eds. San Diego: Academic Press, 1986.

Seitz, V., and Provence, S. "Caregiver-Focused Models of Early Intervention." In *Handbook of Early Childhood Intervention,* S. J. Meisels and J. P. Shonkoff, eds. New York: Cambridge University Press, 1990.

Seitz, V., Rosenbaum, L. K., and Apfel, N. H. "Effects of Family Support Interventions: A Ten-Year Follow-up." In *Contemporary Readings in Child Psychology,* E. M. Hetherington and R. D. Parke, eds. 3rd ed. New York: McGraw-Hill, 1987.

Shonkoff, J. P., and Meisels, S. J., eds. *Handbook of Early Childhood Intervention.* New York: Cambridge University Press, 1990.

The Unfinished Agenda: A New Vision for Child Development and Education. New York: Committee for Economic Development, 1991.

8. Saving Lives in the Early Years: Putting Knowledge to Widespread Use

Blank, S. "Contemporary Parenting Education and Family Support Programs: Themes and Issues in an Emerging Movement." New York: Foundation for Child Development, 1987.

Bronfenbrenner, U., and Weiss, H. B. "Beyond Policies Without People: An Ecological Perspective on Child and Family Policy." In *Children, Families and Government: Perspectives on American Social Policy.* New York: Cambridge University Press, 1983.

Children in Need: Investment Strategies for the Educationally Disadvantaged. New York: Committee on Economic Development, 1987.

Galinsky, E., and David, J. *The Preschool Years.* New York: Times Books, 1983.

Golden, O. "Innovation in Public Sector Human Services Programs: The Implications of Innovation by 'Groping Along.' " In *Journal of Policy Analysis and Management,* vol. 9, no. 2, 1990, 219–248.

Halpern, R. "Community-Based Early Intervention: The State of the Art." In *Handbook of Early Childhood Intervention,* J. Shonkoff and S. Meisels, eds. New York: Cambridge University Press, 1989.

Harbin, G. L., and McNulty, B. A. "Policy Implementation: Perspectives on Service Coordination and Interagency Cooperation." In *Handbook of Early Childhood Intervention,* S. J. Meisels and J. P. Shonkoff, eds. New York: Cambridge University Press, 1989.

Kagan, S. L. *United We Stand: Collaboration for Child Care and Early Education Services.* New York: Teachers College Press, 1991.

Kahn, A. J., and Kamerman, S. B. *Child Care: Facing the Hard Choices.* Dover, Mass.: Auburn House, 1987.

Louv, R. *Childhood's Future.* Boston: Houghton Mifflin, 1990.

Mitchell, A., Seligson, M., and Marx, F. *Early Childhood Programs and the Public Schools: Between Promise and Practice.* Dover, Mass.: Auburn House, 1989.

Musick, J. S., and Stott, F. M. "Paraprofessionals, Parenting, and Child Development: Understanding the Problems and Seeking Solutions." In *Handbook of Early Childhood Intervention,* S. Meisels and J. Shonkoff, eds. New York: Cambridge University Press, 1989.

Schorr, L. B., and Schorr, D. *Within Our Reach: Breaking the Cycle of Disadvantage.* New York: Anchor Press/Doubleday, 1988.

Stevenson, H., and Siegel, A., eds. *Child Development: Research and Social Policy.* Chicago: University of Chicago Press, 1984.

A Vision for America's Future. Washington, D.C.: Children's Defense Fund, 1989.

Zigler, E. F., and Lang, M. E. *Child Care Choices: Balancing the Needs of Children, Families, and Society.* New York: Free Press, 1991.

Zigler, E. F., Kagan, S. L., Klugman, E., eds. *Children, Families and Government: Perspectives on American Social Policy.* New York: Cambridge University Press, 1983.

Zigler, E. F., and Weiss, H. "Family Support Systems: An Ecological Approach to Child Development." In *Children, Youth, and Families,* R. N. Rapoport, ed. New York: Cambridge University Press, 1985.

9. The Transition to Elementary School and Development in Middle Childhood

Alexander, K. L., and Entwisle, D. R. "Achievement in the First Two Years of School: Patterns and Processes." In *Monographs of the Society for Research in Child Development,* vol. 53, no. 2.

Collins, W. A., ed. *Development During Middle Childhood.* Washington, D.C.: National Academy Press, 1984.

Comer, J. P. "Home, School, and Academic Learning." In *Access to Knowledge: An Agenda for Our Nation's Schools,* J. I. Goodlad and P. Keating, eds. New York: College Entrance Examination Board, 1990.

Darling-Hammond, L., and Green, J. "Teacher Quality and Equality." In *Access to Knowledge: An Agenda for Our Nation's Schools,* J. I. Goodlad and P. Keating, eds. New York: College Entrance Examination Board, 1990.

Everybody Counts: A Report to the Nation on the Future of Mathematics Education. Washington, D.C.: National Academy Press, 1989.

Felner, R. D., Ginter, M., and Primavera, J. "Primary Prevention During School Transitions: Social Support and Environmental Structure." In *American Journal of Community Psychology,* vol. 10, no. 3, 277–290, 1982.

Goodlad, J. I., and Keating, P., eds. *Access to Knowledge: An Agenda for Our Nation's Schools.* New York: College Entrance Examination Board, 1990.

Madden, N. A., Slavin, R. E., Karweit, N. L., Dolan, L., and Wasik, B. A., "Success for All." In *Phi Delta Kappan,* April 1991, 593–599.

Maughan, B., and Rutter, M. "Education: Improving Practice Through Increasing Understanding." In *Children, Youth, and Families,* R. N. Rapoport, ed. New York: Cambridge University Press, 1985.

McPartland, J. E., and Slavin, R. E. *Policy Perspectives: Increasing Achievement of At-Risk Students at Each Grade Level.* Office of Educational Research and Improvement, U.S. Department of Education. Washington, D.C.: U.S. Government Printing Office, 1990.

A Nation Prepared: Teachers for the 21st Century. The Report of the Task Force on Teaching as a Profession. Carnegie Forum on Education and the Economy, a program of Carnegie Corporation of New York, Washington, D.C., 1986.

Resnick, L. B. "Literacy in School and Out." In *Daedalus,* Spring 1990.

Smith, P. K. *Tutoring: A National Perspective.* Washington, D.C.: Department of Education, 1983.

Steen, L. A., ed. *On the Shoulders of Giants: New Approaches to Numeracy.* National Research Council, Washington, D.C., National Academy Press, 1990.

Toch, T. *In the Name of Excellence.* New York: Oxford University Press, 1991.

What Works: Research about Teaching and Learning. Washington, D.C.: U.S. Department of Education, 1986.

10. The Nature and Scope of Adolescent Problems

Bancroft, J., and Reinisch, J. M., eds. *Adolescence and Puberty.* New York: Oxford University Press, 1990.

Brooks-Gunn, J., and Petersen, A., eds. *Girls at Puberty: Biological and Psychosocial Perspectives.* New York: Plenum Press, 1983.

Conger, J., and Petersen, A. *Adolescence and Youth: Psychological Development in a Changing World,* 3rd ed. New York: Harper & Row, 1984.

Dash, L. *When Children Want Children: The Urban Crisis of Teenage Childbearing.* New York: William Morrow, 1989.

Dryfoos, J. G. *Adolescents at Risk: Prevalence and Prevention.* New York: Oxford University Press, 1990.

Duany, L., and Pittman, K. *Latino Youths at a Crossroads.* Washington, D.C.: Children's Defense Fund, 1990.

Erickson, E. H. *Identity: Youth and Crisis.* New York: W. W. Norton, 1968.

Feldman, S. S., and Elliott, G. R. *At the Threshold: The Developing Adolescent.* Cambridge, Mass.: Harvard University Press, 1990.

Furstenberg, F. F., Jr., Brooks-Gunn, J., and Chase-Lansdale, L. "Teenaged Pregnancy and Childbearing." *American Psychologist,* vol. 44, no. 2, February 1989.

Hamburg, B. A. "Early Adolescence: A Specific and Stressful Style of the Life Cycle." In *Coping and Adaptation,* G. V. Coelho, D. A. Hamburg, and J. E. Adams, eds. New York: Basic Books, 1974.

Hamburg, B. A., and Hamburg, D. A. "Stressful Transitions of Adolescence: Endocrine and Psychosocial Aspects." In *Society, Stress, and Disease,* vol. 2, L. Levi, ed. London: Oxford University Press, 1975.

Hamburg, B. A. "Early Adolescence as a Life Stress." In *Coping and Health,* S. Levine and H. Ursin, eds. New York: Plenum Press, 1980.

Hayes, C. D., ed. *Risking the Future: Adolescent Sexuality, Pregnancy, and Childbearing,* vol. I. Washington, D.C.: National Academy Press, 1987.

Hayes-Bautista, D. E., Schink, W. O., and Chapa, J. *The Burden of Support: Young Latinos in an Aging Society.* Stanford, Calif.: Stanford University Press, 1988.

Healthy People 2000. U.S. Department of Health and Human Services Public Health Service, Superintendent of Documents, U.S. Government Printing Office, Washington (PHS) 91-50212, 1990.

Hein, K. *Issues in Adolescent Health: An Overview*. Working paper for the Carnegie Council on Adolescent Development, Washington, D.C., 1988.

Hendee, W. R., ed. *The Health of Adolescents*. San Francisco: Jossey-Bass Publishers, 1991.

Hetherington, E. M. "Coping with Family Transitions: Winners, Losers, and Survivors." In *Child Development*, vol. 60, 1–15, 1989.

Highlights of National Adolescent School Health Survey: Drug and Alcohol Use. Rockville, Md.: U.S. Department of Health and Human Services, 1988.

Hurrelmann, K., and Losel, F., eds. *Health Hazards in Adolescence*. New York: Walter de Gruyter, 1990.

Injury in America: A Continuing Public Health Problem. National Research Council, Commission on Life Sciences, Committee on Trauma Research and the Institute of Medicine. Washington, D.C.: National Academy Press, 1985.

Jessor, R. "Critical Issues in Research on Adolescent Health Promotion." In *Promoting Adolescent Health: A Dialogue on Research and Practice*, T. J. Coates, A. C. Peterson, and C. Perry, eds. New York: Academic Press, 1982.

Jessor, R., and Jessor, S. L. *Problem Behavior and Psychosocial Development: A Longitudinal Study of Youth*. New York: Academic Press, 1977.

Johnston, L. D., O'Malley, P. M., and Bachman, J. G. *Drug Use, Drinking, and Smoking: National Survey Results from High School, College, and Young Adult Populations 1975–1988*. Rockville, Md.: U.S. Department of Health and Human Services, 1989.

Lancaster, J., and Hamburg, B. A., eds. *School-Age Pregnancy and Parenthood: Biosocial Dimensions*. Hawthorn, N.Y.: Aldine de Gruyter, 1986.

Lerner, R. M., and Foch, T. T., eds. *Biological-Psychosocial Interactions in Early Adolescence*. Hillsdale, N.J.: Lawrence Erlbaum Associates, 1987.

Millstein, S. G., and Litt, I. F. "Adolescent Health and Health Behaviors." In *At the Threshold*, S. S. Feldman, and G. R. Elliott, eds. Cambridge, Mass.: Harvard University Press, 1990.

Patterson, G. R., DeBaryshe, B. D. and Ramsey, E. "A Developmental Perspective on Antisocial Behavior." In *American Psychologist*, special issue, vol. 44, no. 2, February 1989.

Petersen, A. C. "Adolescent Development," *Annual Review of Psychology*, vol. 39, 583–607, 1988.

Pusey, A. E. "Behavioural Changes at Adolescence in Chimpanzees." In *Behaviour*, 115 (3–4), 1990.

Runyan, C. W., and Gerken, E. A. "Epidemiology and Prevention of Adolescent Injury." In *Journal of the American Medical Association*, vol. 262, no. 16, October 27, 1989.

Teenage Pregnancy: An Advocate's Guide to the Numbers. Washington, D.C.: Children's Defense Fund, 1988.

Walters, J. R. "Transition to Adulthood." In *Primate Societies*, B. Smuts et al., eds. Chicago: University of Chicago Press, 1986.

Williams, T. *The Cocaine Kids*. Reading, Mass.: Addison-Wesley, 1989.

World Health Organization. *The Health of Youth*. Technical Discussions, WHO, Geneva, Switzerland, May 1989.

Youth Indicators, 1988: Trends in the Well-Being of American Youth. Washington, D.C.: U.S. Department of Education, 1988.

Zill, N. "Behavior, Achievement, and Health Problems Among Children in Stepfamilies: Findings from a National Survey of Child Health." In *Impact of Divorce, Single-Parenting, and Stepparenting on Children*, E. M. Hetherington and J. Arasteh, eds. Hillsdale, N.J.: Lawrence Erlbaum Associates, 1988.

11. Education in Early Adolescence: Turning Points

Blyth, D. A., and Simmons, R. G. "The Transition into Early Adolescence: A Longitudinal Comparison of Youth in Two Educational Contexts." In *Sociology of Education*, vol. 51, 1978.

Felner, R. D., and Adan, A. M. "The School Transitional Environment Project: An Ecological Intervention and Evaluation." In *Fourteen Ounces of Prevention: A Casebook for Practitioners*. R. H. Price, E. L. Cowen, R. P. Lorion, and J. Ramos-McKay, eds. Washington, D.C.: American Psychological Association, 1988.

Gardner, H. "The Difficulties of School: Probable Causes, Possible Cures." In *Daedalus*, Spring 1990.

Ginzberg, E., Berliner, H. S., and Ostow, M. *Young People at Risk: Is Prevention Possible?* Boulder, Colo.: Westview Press, 1988.

Hamburg, D. A., and Adams, J. E. "A Perspective on Coping Behavior: Seeking and Utilizing Information in Major Transitions." In *Archives of General Psychiatry*, vol. 17, 277–284, 1967.

Hornbeck, D. W., and Salamon, L. M., eds. *Human Capital and America's Future*. Baltimore: Johns Hopkins University Press, 1991.

Rutter, M. "Family and School Influences on Cognitive Development." In *Social Relationships and Cognitive Development*, R. A. Hinde, A. N. Perret-Clermont, and J. Stevenson-Hinde, eds. Oxford, England: Clarendon Press, 1985.

Simmons, R. G., Carlton-Ford, S. L., and Blyth, D. A. "Predicting How a Child Will Cope with the Transition to Junior High School." In *Biological and Psychosocial Interactions in Early Adolescence*, R. M. Lerner and T. T. Foch, eds. Hillsdale, N.J.: Lawrence Erlbaum Associates, 1987.

Simmons, R. G., Rosenberg, J. A., and Rosenberg, M. "Disturbance in the Self-image at Adolescence." In *American Sociological Review*, vol. 38, 1973.

Simmons, R. G., and Blyth, D. A. *Moving into Adolescence*. New York: Aldine de Gruyter, 1987.

Sizer, T. R. *Horace's Compromise: The Dilemma of the American High School*. Boston: Houghton Mifflin, 1984.

Turning Points: Preparing American Youth for the 21st Century. Task Force on Education of Young Adolescents of the Carnegie Council on Adolescent Development, Washington, D.C., 1989.

12. Science and Health in Adolescent Education

Adolescent Behavior and Health: A Conference Summary. Institute of Medicine, National Academy of Sciences, Washington, D.C., 1978.

Adolescent Health: Vol. 1: *Summary and Policy Options*. Congress of the United States, Office of Technology Assessment. Washington, D.C.: U.S. Government Printing Office, 1991.

Adolescent Health: Vol. 2: *Background and the Effectiveness of Selected Prevention and Treatment Services*. Congress of the United States, Office of Technology Assessment. Washington, D.C.: U.S. Government Printing Office, 1991.

Adolescent Health: Vol. 3: *Crosscutting Issues in the Delivery of Health and Related*

Services. Congress of the United States, Office of Technology Assessment. Washington, D.C.: U.S. Government Printing Office, 1991.

An America That Works: The Life-Cycle Approach to a Competitive Work Force. New York: Committee for Economic Development, 1990.

Atkin, J. M., Atkin, A. *Improving Science Education Through Local Alliances*. Santa Cruz, Calif.: Network Publications, 1989.

Code Blue: Uniting for Healthier Youth. National Commission on the Role of the School and the Community in Improving Adolescent Health. Chicago: American Medical Association, 1991.

Dertouzos, M. L., Lester, R. K., and Solow, R. M., eds. *Made in America: Regaining the Productive Edge*. Commission on Industrial Productivity. Cambridge, Mass.: Massachusetts Institute of Technology, 1989.

Educating Americans for the 21st Century. National Science Board, Commission on Precollege Education in Mathematics, Science and Technology, Washington, D.C., 1983.

Educating Scientists and Engineers: From Grade School to Grad School. Office of Technology Assessment. Washington, D.C.: U.S. Government Printing Office, 1988.

Fulfilling the Promise: Biology Education in the Nation's Schools. Committee on High-School Biology Education Board on Biology, Commission on Life Sciences, National Research Council. Washington, D.C.: National Academy Press, 1990.

Gomez, M. N., Bissell, J., Danziger, L., and Casselman, R. *To Advance Leaning: A Handbook on Developing K–12 Postsecondary Partnerships*. Lanham, Md.: University Press of America, 1990.

Investing in Our Children: Business and the Public Schools. New York: Committee for Economic Development, 1985.

Jessor, R. "Critical Issues in Research on Adolescent Health Promotion." In *Promoting Adolescent Health: A Dialogue on Research and Practice*, T. J. Coates, A. C. Petersen, and C. Perry, eds. New York: Academic Press, 1982.

Katchadourian, H. *The Biology of Adolescence*. San Francisco: W. H. Freeman and Company, 1977.

Millstein, S. G. *The Potential of School-Linked Centers to Promote Adolescent Health and Development*. A working paper of the Carnegie Council on Adolescent Development, Washington, D.C., August 1988.

Millstein, S., Petersen, A., and Nightingale, E. O., eds. *Adolescent Health Promotion*. New York: Oxford University Press, 1992.

A Nation Prepared: Teachers for the 21st Century. The Report of the Task Force on Teaching as a Profession. Carnegie Forum on Education and the Economy, a program of Carnegie Corporation of New York, New York, 1986.

Promoting the Health of Adolescents. Proceedings of the 1990 State Adolescent Health Coordinators Conference. National Center for Education in Maternal and Child Health, Washington, D.C., 1990.

Rosen, W. G., ed. *High-School Biology: Today and Tomorrow*. Washington, D.C.: National Academy Press, 1989.

School-Based Clinics Enter the '90s: Update, Evaluation, and Future Challenges. Washington, D.C.: Center for Population Options, 1989.

Science for All Americans. American Association for the Advancement of Science (AAAS). Washington, D.C.: AAAS, 1989.

Timpane, P. M., and McNeill, L. M. *Business Impact on Education and Child Development Reform*. New York: Committee for Economic Development, 1991.

Zabin, L., Hirsch, M., Smith, E., Street, R., and Hardy, J. "Adolescent Pregnancy-Prevention Program: A Model for Research and Evaluation." In *Journal of Adolescent Health Care*, vol. 7, 77–87, 1986.

Zabin, L., Hirsch, M., Smith, E., Street, R., and Hardy, J. "Evaluation of a Pregnancy Program for Urban Teenagers." In *Family Planning Perspectives*, vol. 18, no. 3, 119–126, 1986.

13. Teaching Life Skills and Fostering Social Support

Adkins, W. R. "Life Skills: Structured Counseling for the Disadvantaged." *Personal and Guidance Journal*, 49 (2): 108–116, 1970.

Bandura, A. *Social Learning Theory*. Englewood Cliffs, N.J.: Prentice-Hall, 1977.

Berkman, L., and Syme, S. L. "Social Networks, Host Resistance, and Mortality: A Nine-Year Follow-up Study of Alameda County Residents. In *American Journal of Epidemiology*, vol. 109, 186–204, 1979.

"Black Churches: Can They Strengthen the Black Family?" In *Carnegie Quarterly*, vol. 33, no. 1, Carnegie Corporation of New York (1987–88, Fall/Winter).

Bloom, B. S. "The Search for Methods of Group Instruction as Effective as One-to-One Tutoring." In *Educational Leadership*, 4–17, May 1984.

Botvin, G. J. *Prevention of Adolescent Substance Abuse Through the Development of Personal and Social Competence*. National Institute on Drug Abuse Research Monograph Series, vol. 47, 115–140, 1983.

Bry, B. H. "Reducing the Incidence of Adolescent Problems Through Preventive Intervention: One- and Five-Year Follow-up." In *American Journal of Community Psychology*, vol. 10, no. 3, 265–276, 1982.

Burchard, J. D., and Burchard, S. N., eds. *Prevention of Delinquent Behavior: Primary Prevention of Psychopathology*, vol. 10. Newbury Park, Calif.: Sage Publications, 1987.

Cauce, A. M., Felner, R. D., and Primavera, J. "Social Support in High-Risk Adolescents: Structural Components and Adaptive Impact." In *American Journal of Community Psychology*, vol. 10, 417–428, 1982.

Cauce, A. M. "Social Networks and Social Competence: Exploring the Effects of Service Activities on Adolescent Alienation." In *Adolescent*, vol. 21, 675–687, 1986.

Cohen, E. G. *Designing Groupwork: Strategies for the Heterogeneous Classroom*. New York: Teachers College Press, 1986.

Cohen, P. A., Kulik, J. A., and Kulik, C-L. C. "Educational Outcomes of Tutoring: A Meta-Analysis of Findings." In *American Educational Research Journal*, vol. 19, no. 2, 237–248, 1982.

Dryfoos, J. G. *Adolescents at Risk: Prevalence and Prevention*. New York: Oxford University Press, 1990.

Freedman, M. *Partners in Growth: Elder Mentors and At-Risk Youth*. Public/Private Ventures, Fall 1988.

Gartner, A., Kohler, M. C., and Riessman. F. *Children Who Teach Children: Learning by Teaching*. New York: Harper and Row, 1971.

Gottlieb, B. H., ed. *Marshaling Social Support: Formats, Processes, and Effects*. Newbury Park, Calif.: Sage Publications, 1988.

Hamburg, B. A. *Life Skills Training: Preventive Interventions for Young Adolescents*. A working paper of the Carnegie Council on Adolescent Development, Washington, D.C., April 1990.

Hamburg, B. A., and Killilea, M. "Relation of Social Support, Stress, Illness, and Use of Health Services." In *Healthy People: Background Papers* (U.S. Department of Health, Education, and Welfare). Washington, D.C.: U.S. Government Printing Office, 1979.

Hamburg, B. A., and Varenhorst, B. B. "Peer Counseling in the Secondary Schools." In *American Journal of Orthopsychiatry,* 4: 566–581, 1972.

Hamburg, D. A., Mortimer, A. M., and Nightingale, E. O. "The Role of Social Support and Social Networks in Improving the Health of Adolescents." In *The Health of Adolescents,* W. R. Hendee, ed. Chicago: American Medical Association, 1991.

Heller, K., Price, R. H., and Hogg, J. R. "The Role of Social Support in Community and Clinical Intervention." In *Social Support: An Interactional View.* B. R. Sarason and G. R. Pierce, eds. New York: John Wiley & Sons, 1990.

Hirsch, B., and Jolly, E. "Role Transitions and Social Networks: Social Support for Multiple Roles." In *Role Transitions: Explorations and Explanations,* V. Allen and E. van de Vleirt, eds. New York: Plenum Press, 1984.

House, J. S., Landis, K. R., and Umberson, D. "Social Relationships and Health." In *Science,* 156: 343–350, 1988.

Janis, I., and Mann, L. *Decision Making: A Psychological Analysis of Conflict, Choice, and Commitment.* New York: Free Press, 1977.

Kniseley, M. *Knowing You've Made a Difference: Strengthening Campus-Based Mentoring Programs Through Evaluation and Research.* Denver: Education Commission of the States, March 1990.

Lippitt, P., Lippitt, R., and Eiseman, J. *Cross-Age Helping Program.* Ann Arbor: University of Michigan Press, 1971.

Preventing Adolescent Pregnancy, Summary: Truth, Trust and Technology. New York: Girls, Inc., National Headquarters, 1991.

Preventing Adolescent Pregnancy: Vol. 1: *Effectiveness of Program Components.* New York: Girls, Inc., National Headquarters, 1991.

Preventing Adolescent Pregnancy: Vol. 2: *Narrative Description of the Preventing Adolescent Pregnancy Project.* New York: Girls, Inc., National Headquarters, 1991.

Preventing Adolescent Pregnancy: Vol. 3: *Documents Questionnaires, Forms and Instructions.* New York: Girls, Inc., National Headquarters, 1991.

Price, R. H., Cowen, E. L., Lorion, R. P., and Ramos-McKay, J., eds. *Fourteen Ounces of Prevention: A Casebook for Practitioners.* Washington, D.C.: American Psychological Association, 1988.

Price, R. H., et al. *School and Community Support Programs that Enhance Adolescent Health and Education.* A working paper of the Carnegie Council on Adolescent Development, Washington, D.C., April 1990.

Resnick, L. B. "Literacy in School and Out." In *Daedalus,* Spring 1990.

Resnick, L. B. "The 1987 Presidential Address: Learning in School and Out." In *Educational Researcher,* 16(9): 13–20, 1987.

Slavin, R. E. "When Does Cooperative Learning Increase Student Achievement?" In *Psychological Bulletin,* 94: 429–445, 1983.

Smith, P. K. *Tutoring: A National Perspective.* Washington, D.C.: U.S. Department of Education, 1983.

14. Preventing Substance Abuse in Early Adolescence

Ashley, M. J., and Rankin, J. G. "A Public Health Approach to the Prevention of Alcohol-Related Health Problems." In *Annual Review Public Health*, 9:233–71, 1988.

Best, J. A., Thomson, S. J., Santi, S. M., Smith, E. A., and Brown, S. "Preventing Cigarette Smoking Among School Children." In *Annual Review of Public Health*, 9:161–201, 1988.

Botvin, G. J., Baker, E., Dusenbury, L., Tortu, S., and Botvin, E. "Preventing Adolescent Drug Abuse Through a Multimodal Cognitive-Behavioral Approach: Results of a 3-Year Study." In *American Psychological Association*, vol. 58, no. 4, 437–446, 1990.

Botvin, G. J. "Substance Abuse Prevention Research: Recent Developments and Future Directions." In *Journal of School Health*, vol. 56, no. 9, 369–374, 1986.

Ellickson, P. L., Bell, R. M., Thomas, M. A., Robyn, A. E., and Zellman, G. L. *Designing and Implementing Project ALERT: A Smoking and Drug Prevention Experiment.* Santa Monica: Rand Corporation, December 1988.

Ellickson, P. L., and Bell, R. M. "Drug Prevention in Junior High: A Multi-Site Longitudinal Test." In *Science*, vol. 247, 1299–1305, 1990.

Falco, M. *Preventing Abuse of Drugs, Alcohol, and Tobacco by Adolescents.* Carnegie Council on Adolescent Development (a program of Carnegie Corporation of New York), Washington, D.C., June 1988.

Falco, M. *Just Say Yes: Drug Programs That Work.* New York: Times Books, 1992.

Farquhar, J. W., Fortmann, S. P., Flora, J. A., Taylor, B., Haskell, W. L., Williams, P. T., Maccoby, N., and Wood, P. D. "Effects of Communitywide Education on Cardiovascular Disease Risk Factors." In *Journal of the American Medical Association*, vol. 264, no. 3, July 1990.

Farquhar, J. W., Fortmann, S. P., Maccoby, N., et al. "The Stanford Five-City Project: An Overview." In *Behavioral Health: A Handbook for Health Enhancement and Disease Prevention*, J. D. Matarazzo et al., eds. New York: John Wiley & Sons, 1984.

Goldstein, A., and Kalant, H. "Drug Policy: Striking the Right Balance." In *Science*, vol. 249, September 28, 1990.

Hamburg, D. A., Elliot, G. R., and Parron, D. *Health and Behavior: Frontiers of Research in the Biobehavioral Sciences.* Washington, D.C.: National Academy Press, 1982.

Jessor, R. "Bridging Etiology and Prevention in Drug Abuse Research." In *Etiology of Drug Abuse: Implications for Prevention*, C. L. Jones and R. J. Battjes, eds. Washington, D.C.: U.S. Government Printing Office, 1985.

Killen, J. D., and Robinson, T. N. "School-Based Research on Health Behavior Change: The Stanford Adolescent Heart Health Program as a Model for Cardiovascular Disease Risk Reduction." In *Review of Research in Education 1988–89*, vol. 15, E. Z. Rothkopf, ed. Washington, D.C.: American Educational Research Association, 1988.

Pentz, M. A., Dwyer, J. H., MacKinnon, D. P., Flay, B. R., Hansen, W. B., Wang, E. Y. I., and Johnson, A. "A Multi-Community Trial for Primary Prevention of Adolescent Drug Abuse: Effects on Drug Use Prevalence." In *Journal of the American Medical Association*, 261 (22), 3259–3266, 1989.

Puska, P. "Community-Based Prevention of Cardiovascular Disease: The North Karelia Project." In *Behavioral Health: A Handbook for Health Enhancement and Disease Prevention*, J. D. Matarazzo et al., eds. New York: John Wiley & Sons, 1984.

Rogers, T., Howard-Pitney, B., and Bruce, B. L. *What Works? A Guide to School-Based Alcohol and Drug Abuse Prevention Curricula.* Health Promotion Resource Center, Stanford Center for Research in Disease Prevention, Palo Alto, Calif., 1989.

Schaps, E., Moskowitz, J. M., Malvin, J. H., and Schaefer, G. H. "Evaluation of Seven School-Based Prevention Programs: A Final Report on the Napa Project." In *The International Journal of the Addictions*, vol. 21, 1081–1112, 1986.

Telch, M. J., Killen, J. D., Perry, C. L., and Maccoby, N. "Long-Term Follow-up of a Pilot Project on Smoking Prevention with Adolescents." In *Journal of Behavioral Medicine*, vol. 5, 1982.

Walter, H. J., Vaughan, R. D., and Wynder, E. L. "Primary Prevention of Cancer Among Children: Changes in Cigarette Smoking and Diet After Six Years of Intervention." In *Journal of the National Cancer Institute*, vol. 81, no. 13, pp. 995–999, 1989.

15. Educating the Disadvantaged

Children in Need: Investment Strategies for the Educationally Disadvantaged. New York: Committee on Economic Development, 1987.

Comer, J. P. "Home, School, and Academic Learning." In *Access to Knowledge: An Agenda for Our Nation's Schools*, J. I. Goodlad and P. Keating, eds. New York: College Entrance Examination Board, 1990.

Comer, J. P. "Educating Poor Minority Children." In *Scientific American*, vol. 259, no. 5, November 1988.

Comer, J. P. *School Power: Implications of an Intervention Project.* New York: The Free Press, 1980.

Education That Works: An Action Plan for the Education of Minorities. Quality Education for Minorities Project, Action Council on Minority Education. Cambridge, Mass.: Massachusetts Institute of Technology, 1990.

The Explorer's Pass: A Report on Case Studies of Girls and Math, Science and Technology. New York: Girls, Inc., National Headquarters, 1991.

George, Y. S., Richardson, V., Lakes-Matyas, M., and Blake, F. *Saving Minds: Black Churches and Education.* Washington, D.C.: American Association for the Advancement of Science, 1989.

Heynes, B. *Summer Learning and the Effects of Schooling.* New York: Academic Press, 1978.

An Imperiled Generation: Saving Urban Schools. Princeton, N.J.: Carnegie Foundation for the Advancement of Teaching, 1987.

Jaynes, G. D., and Williams, R. M., Jr., eds. *A Common Destiny: Blacks and American Society.* Washington, D.C.: National Academy Press, 1989.

Knapp, M., and Turnbull, B. *Better Schooling for the Children of Poverty: Alternatives to Conventional Wisdom*, vol. 1. U.S. Department of Education, Washington, D.C., 1990.

Kotlowitz, A. *There Are No Children Here.* New York: Doubleday, 1991.

Kozol, J. *Savage Inequalities: Children in America's Schools.* New York: Crown, 1991.

Malcom, S. M. *Equity and Excellence: Compatible Goals*, Washington, D.C.: American Association for the Advancement of Science, 1984.

McPartland, J. E., and Slavin, R. E. *Policy Perspectives: Increasing Achievement of At-Risk Students at Each Grade Level.* Office of Educational Research and Improvement, U.S. Department of Education. Washington, D.C.: U.S. Government Printing Office, 1990.

A Nation Prepared: Teachers for the 21st Century. The Report of the Task Force on Teaching as a Profession. Carnegie Forum on Education and the Economy, a program of Carnegie Corporation of New York, Washington, D.C., 1986.

Poverty and Human Development. Published for the World Bank. New York: Oxford University Press, 1980.

Shonkoff, J. P., and Meisels, S. J., eds. *Handbook of Early Childhood Intervention.* New York: Cambridge University Press, 1990.

Slavin, R. E. "Team-Assisted Individuation: Cooperative Learning and Individualized Instruction in the Mainstreamed Classroom. In *Remedial and Special Education*, 5(6): 33–42, 1984.

Tomas Rivera Center. *The Changing Profile of Mexican America: A Sourcebook for Policy Making.* Claremont, Calif., 1985.

Treisman, P. U. *A Study of the Mathematics Performance of Black Students at the University of California, Berkeley.* Berkeley: University of California Press, 1985.

The Unfinished Agenda: A New Vision for Child Development and Education. New York: Committee for Economic Development, 1991.

Wilson, W. J. *The Truly Disadvantaged: The Inner City, the Underclass, and Public Policy.* Chicago: University of Chicago Press, 1987.

16. Overview: The Road We Have Traveled and the Road Ahead

America's Choice: High Skills or Low Wages! Report of the Commission on the Skills of the American Workforce. National Center on Education and the Economy, Rochester, N.Y., 1990.

An America That Works: The Life-Cycle Approach to a Competitive Work Force. New York: Committee for Economic Development, 1990.

Bellah, R. N., Madsen, R., Sullivan, W. M., Swidler, A., and Tipton, S. M. *The Good Society.* New York: Alfred A. Knopf, 1991.

Beyond Rhetoric: A New American Agenda for Children and Families. Washington, D.C.: The National Commission on Children, 1991.

Blankenhorn, D., Bayme, S., and Elshtain, J. B., eds. *Rebuilding the Nest: A New Commitment to the American Family.* Milwaukee: Family Service America, 1990.

Bowlby, J. *A Secure Base: Parent-Child Attachment and Healthy Human Development.* New York: Basic Books, 1988.

Caring for Our Future: The Content of Prenatal Care. Report of the Public Health Service Expert Panel on the Content of Prenatal Care, Public Health Service, Department of Health and Human Services, Washington, D.C., 1989.

Cicchetti, D., and Carlson, V., eds. *Child Maltreatment: Theory and Research on the Causes and Consequences of Child Abuse and Neglect.* New York: Cambridge University Press, 1989.

Cherlin, A. J., ed. *The Changing American Family and Public Policy.* Washington, D.C.: Urban Institute Press, 1988.

Cole, M., and Cole, S. R. *The Development of Children*. New York: W. H. Freeman, 1989.

Comer, J. P. "Educating Poor Minority Children." In *Scientific American*, vol. 259, no. 5, November 1988.

Conger, J., and Petersen, A. *Adolescence and Youth: Psychological Development in a Changing World*, 3rd ed. New York: Harper & Row, 1984.

Degler, C. *Out of Our Past: The Forces that Shaped Modern America*, 3rd ed. New York: Harper & Row, 1984.

Dryfoos, J. G. *Adolescents At Risk: Prevalence and Prevention*. New York: Oxford University Press, 1990.

Education That Works: An Action Plan for the Education of Minorities. Quality Education for Minorities Project, Action Council on Minority Education. Cambridge, Mass.: Massachusetts Institute of Technology, 1990.

Feldman, S. S., and Elliott, G. R. *At the Threshold: The Developing Adolescent*. Cambridge, Mass.: Harvard University Press, 1990.

Fiske, E. B. *Smart Schools, Smart Kids: Why Do Some Schools Work?* New York: Simon and Schuster, 1991.

The Forgotten Half: Pathways to Success for America's Youth and Young Families. Washington, D.C.: The William T. Grant Commission on Work, Family and Citizenship, 1988.

Fuchs, V. R., and Reklis, D. M. "America's Children: Economic Perspectives and Policy Options." In *Science*, vol. 255, no. 5040, January 1992.

Gardner, H. *The Unschooled Mind: How Children Think and How Schools Should Teach*. New York: Basic Books, 1991.

Gardner, J. *On Leadership*. New York: Free Press, 1990.

Goodlad, J. I., and Keating, P., eds. *Access to Knowledge: An Agenda for Our Nation's Schools*. New York: College Entrance Examination Board, 1990.

Graham, P. *S.O.S.: Sustain Our Schools*. New York: Hill and Wang, 1992.

Hamburg, B. A. *Life Skills Training: Preventive Interventions for Young Adolescents*. A working paper of the Carnegie Council on Adolescent Development, Washington, D.C., April 1990.

Harvard Journal on Legislation, vol. 28, no. 2. Symposium "Investing in Our Children's Future: School Finance Reform in the '90s." Summer 1991.

Hayes, C. D., Palmer, J. L., and Zaslow, M. J., eds. *Who Cares for America's Children?: Child Care Policy for the 1990s*. Panel on Child Care Policy, Committee on Child Development Research and Public Policy, Commission on Behavioral and Social Sciences and Education. Washington, D.C.: National Academy Press, 1990.

Healthy People 2000. U.S. Department of Health and Human Services Public Health Service, Superintendent of Documents, U.S. Government Printing Office, Washington, D.C., 1990.

Hechinger, F. M., ed. *A Better Start: New Choices for Early Learning*. New York: Walker and Co., 1986.

Hendee, W. R., ed. *The Health of Adolescents*. San Francisco: Jossey-Bass, 1991.

Hetherington, E. M., and Parke, R. D. *Child Psychology: A Contemporary Viewpoint*, 3rd ed. New York: McGraw-Hill, 1986.

Hewlett, S. A. *When the Bough Breaks: The Cost of Neglecting Our Children*. New York: Basic Books, 1991.

Hochschild, A., and Machung, A. *The Second Shift: Working Parents and the Revolution at Home.* New York: Viking/Penguin, 1989.

Hornbeck, D. W., and Salamon, L. M., eds. *Human Capital and America's Future.* Baltimore: Johns Hopkins University Press, 1991.

An Imperiled Generation: Saving Urban Schools. Princeton, N.J.: Carnegie Foundation for the Advancement of Teaching, 1987.

Knapp, M., and Turnbull, B. *Better Schooling for the Children of Poverty: Alternatives to Conventional Wisdom,* vol. 1. Washington, D.C.: U.S. Department of Education, 1990.

Konner, M. *Childhood.* Boston: Little, Brown, 1991.

Kutner, L. *Parent and Child: Getting Through to Each Other.* New York: William Morrow, 1991.

Lancaster, J., and Hamburg, B. A., eds. *School-Age Pregnancy and Parenthood: Biosocial Dimensions.* Hawthorn, N.Y., Aldine de Gruyter, 1986.

Lenski, G., and Lenski, J. *Human Societies: An Introduction to Macrosociology,* 5th ed. New York: McGraw-Hill, 1987.

Levitan, S. A., Belous, R. S., Gallow, F. *What's Happening to the American Family?* rev. ed. Baltimore: Johns Hopkins University Press, 1988.

Louv, R. *Childhood's Future.* Boston: Houghton Mifflin, 1990.

Marshall, R. *The State of Families.* Vol. 3: *Losing Direction: Families, Human Resource Development, and Economic Performance.* Milwaukee: Family Service America, 1991.

Mintz, S., and Kellogg, S. *Domestic Revolutions: A Social History of an American Family Life.* New York: Free Press, 1988.

A Nation Prepared: Teachers for the 21st Century. The Report of the Task Force on Teaching as a Profession. Carnegie Forum on Education and the Economy, a program of Carnegie Corporation of New York, Washington, D.C., 1986.

Oakes, J., and Lipton, M. *Making the Best of Schools: A Handbook for Parents, Teachers, and Policymakers.* New Haven: Yale University Press, 1990.

Price, R. H., Cowen, E. L., Lorion, R. P., and Ramos-McKay, J., eds. *Fourteen Ounces of Prevention: A Casebook for Practitioners.* Washington, D.C.: American Psychological Association, 1988.

Price, R. H., et al. *School and Community Support Programs That Enhance Adolescent Health and Education.* A working paper of the Carnegie Council on Adolescent Development, Washington, D.C., April 1990.

Prowthrow-Stith, D., and Weissman, M. *Deadly Consequences: How Violence Is Destroying Our Teenage Population and a Plan to Begin Solving the Problem.* New York: HarperCollins, 1991.

Research and Renewal of Education. Stanford, Calif.: National Academy of Education, 1991.

Rogers, D. E., and Ginzberg, E., eds. *Improving the Life Chances of Children at Risk.* Boulder, Colo.: Westview Press, 1990.

Rosenblith, J. F. *In the Beginning: Development from Conception to Age 2.* Newbury Park, Calif.: Sage Publications, 1992.

Schlesinger, M. J., and Eisenberg, L., eds. *Children in a Changing Health System: Assessments and Proposals for Reform.* Baltimore: Johns Hopkins University Press, 1990.

Schorr, L. B., and Schorr, D. *Within Our Reach: Breaking the Cycle of Disadvantage.* New York: Anchor Press/Doubleday, 1988.

Science for All Americans. American Association for the Advancement of Science (AAAS). Washington, D.C.: AAAS, 1989.

Shonkoff, J. P., and Meisels, S. J., eds. *Handbook of Early Childhood Intervention.* New York: Cambridge University Press, 1990.

Sizer, T. R. *Horace's Compromise: The Dilemma of the American High School.* Boston: Houghton Mifflin, 1984.

Sizer, T. R. *Horace's School: Redesigning the American High Shool.* Boston: Houghton Mifflin, 1992.

Smuts, B. B., Cheney, D. L., Seyfarth, R. M., Wrangham, R. W., and Struhsaker, T. T. *Primate Societies.* Chicago: University of Chicago Press, 1986.

Timpane, P. M., and McNeill, L. M. *Business Impact on Education and Child Development Reform.* New York: Committee for Economic Development, 1991.

Turning Points: Preparing American Youth for the 21st Century. Task Force on Education of Young Adolescents of the Carnegie Council on Adolescent Development, Washington, D.C., 1989.

The Unfinished Agenda: A New Vision for Child Development and Education. New York: Committee for Economic Development, 1991.

A Vision for America's Future. Washington, D.C.: Children's Defense Fund, 1989.

Weiss, H., et al. *Raising Our Future: Families, Schools, and Communities Joining Together.* Cambridge, Mass.: Harvard Families Research Project, 1991.

Williams, B. C., and Miller, C. A. *Preventive Health Care for Young Children: Findings from a 10-Country Study and Directions for United States Policy.* Richmond, Va.: National Center for Clinical Infant Programs, 1991.

Wilson, W. J. *The Truly Disadvantaged: The Inner City, the Underclass, and Public Policy.* Chicago: University of Chicago Press, 1987.

"World Declaration on the Survival, Protection and Development of Children and Plan of Action for Implementing the World Declaration on the Survival, Protection and Development of Children in the 1990s." Report from World Summit for Children. United Nations, New York, September 30, 1990.

Zigler, E. F., and Lang, M. E. *Child Care Choices: Balancing the Needs of Children, Families, and Society.* New York: Free Press, 1991.

Index